THE
ALPINE JOURNAL
2012

What more can be said about Everest 2012? Implicit in this photograph of the absurd, taken on Friday 18 May by Ralf Dujmovits, is all anyone needs to know about Everest climbing in the 21st century – and a good deal more than one might like to know. Dujmovits, the first German to summit all 14 of the 8000m peaks, was retreating from the South Col in the face of bad weather when he took the 'human snake' photograph, looking down the Lhotse Face from the Geneva Spur. In a probably vain plea to Nepal to control the number of tourists on Everest, Dujmovits said he had had an oppressive feeling that some of those in the queue would soon be dead. 'I was also filled with sadness for this mountain for which I have immense respect. People nowadays treat the mountain as if it was a piece of sporting apparatus, not a force of nature. It really makes my soul ache.' Four people died on Everest that weekend. *SG*

THE
ALPINE JOURNAL
2012

The Journal of the Alpine Club

A record of mountain adventure
and scientific observation

Edited by Stephen Goodwin

Production Editor: Bernard Newman
Assistant Editor: Paul Knott

Volume 116

Number 360

Supported by the
MOUNT EVEREST FOUNDATION

Published by
THE ALPINE CLUB

THE ALPINE JOURNAL 2012
Volume 116 No 360

www.alpinejournal.org.uk

Address all editorial communication to the Hon Editor:
Stephen Goodwin, 1 Ivy Cottages, Edenhall, Penrith, CA11 8SN
email: sg@stephengoodwin.demon.co.uk
Address all sales and distribution communications to:
Cordée, 11 Jacknell Rd, Dodwells Bridge Ind Est, Hinckley, LE10 3BS

Back numbers:
Apply to the Alpine Club, 55 Charlotte Rd, London, EC2A 3QF or, for
1969 to date, apply to Cordée, as above.

First published in 2012 by The Alpine Club
Typeset by Bernard Newman
Photo production by Tom Prentice
Printed and bound in India by Replika Press Pvt Ltd

A CIP catalogue record for this book is available from The British Library

ISBN 978-0-9569309-1-0

Foreword

In Eric Shipton's *Blank on the Map* he reflects on the 'real value of climbing'. The book records a glorious five months of exploration in the northern Karakoram in 1937 with Bill Tilman, Michael Spender and John Auden, the kind of mountaineering that was Shipton's first love. However, he also casts forward to Everest where he is bound the following year, and offers an opinion that those who queued at the Hillary Step this May might reflect on:

> *The ascent of Everest, like any other human endeavour, is only to be judged by the spirit in which it is attempted.*

Rereading the passage in which this quote occurs, it is no wonder there were doubts about Shipton's suitability for leading an endeavour so loaded with national prestige as an attempt on Everest. He sets out a finer vision:

> *Let us climb peaks by all means, because their beauty attracts us; not because others have failed, nor because the summits stand 28,000 feet above the sea, nor in patriotic fervour for the honour of the nation, nor for cheap publicity. Let us approach the peaks with humility, and having found the way to them for ourselves, learn to solve their problems.*

Blank on the Map was published in 1938 and each person will have their own opinion on how much of Shipton's prescription has carried through to climbing today, or chimes with their own motives. Humility may be in short supply, but appreciation of beauty and egocentricity are not of themselves incompatible. Phil Bartlett ponders these issues in this *Alpine Journal* in an essay timed for the London Olympics entitled 'Is Mountaineering Sport?' Readers can decide for themselves whether Bartlett answers or dodges his own question, but on one thing he is clear: 'If mountaineering allows itself to become entangled with the Olympic machine it will be chewed up and spat out in unrecognisable and, to my taste, ill-flavoured pieces.'

The exploratory spirit of Shipton certainly lives on in this 116th volume of the *AJ*. In the satellite age there may not be any blanks on the map in the strictest sense, but there are still plenty of gnarly expanses of rock, snow and ice where nobody has set foot or crampon points – to wit, we carry accounts of AC president Mick Fowler and Dave Turnbull on Gojung (6310m) in north-west Nepal, Bruce Normand and Kyle Dempster on the fearsome east face of Mount Edgar (6168m), Freddie Wilkinson and friends on Saser Kangri II (7518m) in the Indian Karakoram and Martin Moran leading a group over passes on the Lahaul-Zanskar-Kishtwar divides of the Indian Himalaya – very Shipton this one. And these are but a sample. It is good also to see AC members still finding new routes in the Alps: Simon

Richardson describes pioneering with Duncan Tunstall on the south-west spur of Punta Baretti (4013m) – a route made accessible by global warming – and Andy Cave and Twid Turner free the *Keusen Route* on the south-west face of the Simelistock in the Bernese Oberland.

Arts and science pertaining to mountains are once again well represented: Dr Penny Bradshaw draws on the poetry and criticism of AC member Michael Roberts (1902-48) to consider the literary treatment of mountains within the turbulent decade of the 1930s, while Paul Ramsden explains the science behind carbon monoxide poisoning from your stove. By way of an object lesson on this 'silent killer', read Dave Wynne-Jones's tale of how his ski-mountaineering expedition to the Tavn Bogd range of the Mongolian Altai nearly ended in tragedy, he and Iona Pawson being dragged unconscious from their fume-filled tent just in the nick of time.

The past 12 months have seen the passing of three former presidents of the Alpine Club, each a product of the dynamic post-war Oxbridge climbing scene who went on to make major contributions to mountaineering, both in their personal achievements and in their contributions to the mountain fraternity. The death of George Band, youngest member of the 1953 Everest team who two years later, with Joe Brown, made the first ascent of Kangchenjunga, came as a profound shock and he will be sorely missed when the 60th anniversary of the Everest climb is celebrated next year – the kind of event at which George would have been in his element. So too will be his Everest comrade and close friend Mike Westmacott who died just as this *AJ* was about to go the printers. Alan Blackshaw is similarly mourned: multi-faceted, he will be best remembered for that training 'bible' of the 1960s, *Mountaineering: From Hill Walking to Alpine Climbing,* better known simply as 'Blackshaw'; for the first British continuous ski traverse of the Alps, and for his work to secure access to the hills of Scotland.

Next year will not only be an Everest anniversary, it will also be 150 years since the first appearance of the *Alpine Journal*. A glance across the study to the editor's full set of *Journals* is a reminder what a remarkable record of mountaineering the *AJ* has become. And all those thousands of articles have been contributed without payment; for the love of the game and, let's be honest, often for the satisfaction of having one's deeds in print for posterity. As editor I am grateful to all those who words and photographs appear in this latest journal and to the team who have helped bring it to fruition: production editor Bernard Newman, assistant editor Paul Knott and his Area Notes correspondents, proof reader Margot Blyth and photo wizard Tom Prentice. A special mention should also go to Ned Kelly and John Town for their continued effort to take the *AJ* beyond print, digitising a further couple of decades so that now the *Journal* is available online right back to 1940. Many thanks to you all.

Stephen Goodwin

Contents

HIGH ASIA

Far From The Madding Crowd	*Mick Fowler*	3
Along The Corridor and Up The Stairs	*Pat Deavoll*	16
A Peak and Three Passes in Himachal	*Martin Moran*	27
The Threat	*Bruce Normand*	40
Back From The Dead	*Dave Wynne-Jones*	52
Reflecting on Gasherbrum II	*Simone Moro*	59
Spoils of War	*Freddie Wilkinson*	63

COMMENT

Is Mountaineering a Sport?	*Phil Bartlett*	77
The Tyranny of History	*Andrew Bisharat*	88

SURVEYS

Exploring The Eastern Caucasus	*Graham Dudley & Simon Richardson*	99
Zemu Gap From The South	*Anindya Mukherjee*	114
New Routes and a Mystery in West Sikkim	*Roger Payne*	124
Unclimbed Peaks in Sichuan – 2012	*Tamotsu Nakamura*	132

ALPS & NORWAY

'A Very Tempting Prize Indeed'	*Simon Richardson*	147
Ecstasy	*Andy Cave*	158
Fjord Fandango	*David Pickford*	163

AC EXPEDITION – Antarctica	*Derek Buckle & Phil Wickens*	179

SCIENCE

The Silent Killer	*Paul Ramsden*	195
The Ngozumpa Glacial Lake Imaging Project	*Ulyana Horodyskyj*	203
On The Road to a Greener Alps	*Stephen Goodwin*	209

ARTS

In Search of Nirvana	*John Fairley*	223
'Living at Our Full Compass'	*Penny Bradshaw*	229
Kindred Spirits	*Elizabeth Raikes*	238

HISTORY

L'affaire Frêney   *Eric Vola*   247
Unknown AC First in Picos *Elisa Villa, Alfredo Íñiguez & Jesús Longo*   258
One Hundred Years Ago   *C A Russell*   266

AREA NOTES   *Compiled and Edited by Paul Knott*   270

The Alps 2011   *Lindsay Griffin*   271
Scottish Winter 2010-11   *Simon Richardson*   280
Afghanistan 2011   *Lindsay Griffin*   287
Pakistan 2011   *Dick Isherwood*   289
India 2010   *Harish Kapadia*   293
Nepal 2011   *Dick Isherwood*   307
China & Tibet 2011   *John Town*   311
Bolivia 2009-2011   *Erik Monasterio*   314
Argentine Andes 2010-2011   *Marcelo Scanu*   317
New Zealand 2010-2011   *Kester Brown*   324

Mount Everest Foundation Expedition Reports
                            Summarised by Bill Ruthven   329

REVIEWS   341

IN MEMORIAM   395

Officers and Committee for 2012   428

ALPINE CLUB NOTES   429

New Honorary Members   429
Alpine Club Climbing Fund   429
Alpine Club Library Annual Report 2011   431
Letter to The Editor   432
Contributors   434

Index   440

Illustrations

Front cover: Dave Turnbull in the lower couloir of Gojung. *(Mick Fowler)*

Endpapers: Front: Kitchen porters take a break on the Saldang La (c5100m), Inner Dolpo, Nepal. Tibet in the distance. *(Stephen Goodwin)*

Back: Yak caravan approaches the Saldang La (c5100), carrying timber into treeless Inner Dolpo and probably on into Tibet. *(Stephen Goodwin)*

Frontispiece: Everest 2012. *(Ralf Dujmovits)*

1.   John Fairley, *Bhagirathi III,* oil on canvas, 590x835mm, 2009   1
2.   The west face of Gojung (6310m), Mugu western Nepal. *(Mick Fowler)*   3
3.   Gojung west face, Fowler-Turnbull line and bivouacs. *(Graham Desroy)*   4
4.   A girl in the village of Gamghadi. *(Dave Turnbull)*   5
5.   Mick Fowler at the belay after pitch four on day one. *(Dave Turnbull)*   6
6.   Dave Turnbull in the lower couloir. *(Mick Fowler)*   7
7.   Mick Fowler at first bivouac. *(Dave Turnbull)*   8
8.   Dave Turnbull on the summit slopes. *(Mick Fowler)*   9
9.   Dave Turnbull on the 6310m summit of Gojung. *(Mick Fowler)*   10
10. A place of potential: Gojung and neighbouring peaks. *(Nick Colton)*   12
11. Fowler (left) and Turnbull after eight days on the mountain. *(Fowler collection)* 15
12. Kret, Koh-e-Baba-Tangi, from across the Wakhan river. *(Pat Deavoll)*   17
13. Under the gaze of an Ishkashim local. *(Pat Deavoll)*   18
14. Upturned Russin tank in a Tajik riverbed. *(Pat Deavoll)*   19
15. Border police in Ishkashim play chess. *(Pat Deavoll)*   20
16. Pat Deavoll leading middle ice face on day one. *(Christine Byrch)*   21
17. Christine Byrch climbing above the ice gully on day two. *(Pat Deavoll)*   22
18. Christine Byrch on the summit plateau. *(Pat Deavoll)*   22
19. Qala Hurst glacier from the top camp. *(Pat Deavoll)*   23
20. On the summit of Koh-e-Baba-Tangi. *(Pat Deavoll)*   24
21. Christine Byrch approaches the summit of Koh-e-Baba-Tangi. *(Pat Deavoll)*   25
22. Porters on the return leg, Koh-e-Baba-Tangi in background. *(Pat Deavoll)*   26
23. Sukto village – roadhead of the Miyar valley. *(Martin Moran)*   27
24. Sketch map of the Lahaul-Zanskar-Kishtwar Divide. *(Martin Moran)*   28
25. North wall of Pk 5755m above the Jangpar glacier. *(Martin Moran)*   29
26. Trekking up the Miyar glacier towards the Kang La. *(Martin Moran)*   30
27. The 'snow queen' or Eva's Peak (6119m) from the Kang La. *(Martin Moran)*   31
28. Steve Birch and Mike Timar, summit arête of Eva's Peak. *(Martin Moran)*   32
29. Unnamed 5800m peaks, west of Zanskar-Kangthang glacier. *(Martin Moran)*   33
30. Steve Birch leading the ice nose on Eva's Peak. *(Martin Moran)*   34
31. Badile-like peak above the Zanskar-Kanthang glacier. *(Martin Moran)*   35
32. Virgin big walls, east side of Zanskar-Kanthang glacier. *(Martin Moran)*   37
33. On the ramp above the Sersank icefall *(Martin Moran)*   38

34.	Martin Moran on the Poat La. *(Moran collection)*	39
35.	The east face of Mount Edgar. *(Tamotsu Nakamura)*	41
36.	Kyle Dempster on crux, Mount Edgar's east face. *(Bruce Normand)*	42
37.	West face, Mount Grosvenor (Riwuqie Feng 6376m). *(Bruce Normand)*	44
38.	Kyle Dempster in central couloir, Mount Grosvenor. *(Bruce Normand)*	45
39.	Kyle Dempster, approach gully, day three, Mt Edgar. *(Bruce Normand)*	46
40.	Bruce Normand on initial ice ramp at 5600m, day four. *(Kyle Dempster)*	47
41.	Kyle Dempster leading an ice pitch at 5900m on day four. *(Bruce Normand)*	48
42.	Kyle Dempster on southern slopes of Edgar, day six. *(Bruce Normand)*	49
43.	Kyle Dempster and Bruce Normand back in Moxi. *(Bruce Normand)*	50
44.	Looking east from Mt Edgar over the foothills of Sichuan. *(Bruce Normand)*	51
45.	Hunters. *(Dave Wynne-Jones)*	52
46.	Heading up the Potanina glacier towards Khuiten. *(Dave Wynne-Jones)*	53
47.	On north ridge of Khuiten, views into Russia and China. *(Dave Wynne-Jones)*	54
48.	On the summit of Khuiten (4374m). *(Dave Wynne-Jones)*	55
49.	Skiing down the north ridge of Khuiten. *(Dave Wynne-Jones)*	56
50.	Howard Pollitt descending Peak 4152m. *(Dave Wynne-Jones)*	57
51.	The team's camel train heading back to the roadhead. *(Dave Wynne-Jones)*	58
52.	Simone Moro at 7800 metres on FWA of Gasherbrum II *(Simone Moro)*	61
53.	Gasherbrum II summit: Denis Urubko, Simone Moro, Cory Richards.	62
54.	The south-west face of Saser Kangri II, first ascent line. *(Freddie Wilkinson)*	63
55.	Mark Richey on the first ascent of Tsok Kangri (6550m). *(Freddie Wilkinson)*	64
56.	Steve Swenson and Mark Richey, Tsok Kangri. *(Freddie Wilkinson)*	65
57.	Mark Richey approaching the summit of Tsok Kangri. *(Freddie Wilkinson)*	66
58.	Janet Wilkinson on Saser Linga. *(Freddie Wilkinson)*	67
59.	Janet Wilkinson on the spire of Saser Linga. *(Freddie Wilkinson)*	68
60.	Emilie Drinkwater and Kirsten Kramer at base camp. *(Freddie Wilkinson)*	69
61.	Janet Wilkinson on the summit ridge of Stegosaur. *(Freddie Wilkinson)*	70
62.	Mark Richey and Steve Swenson, on Saser Kangri II. *(Freddie Wilkinson)*	70
63.	Mark Richey approaches the ice chimney, Saser Kangri II. *(Freddie Wilkinson)*	71
64.	Steve Swenson, summit ridge of Saser Kangri II. *(Freddie Wilkinson)*	72
65.	Richey, Swenson and Wilkinson, Saser Kangri II summit. *(Freddie Wilkinson)*	73
66.	John Fairley, *Piz Zupo & Piz Bernina,* watercolour, 590x835mm, 1995	75
67.	Cerro Torre in storm. *(Leo Dickinson)*	89
68.	John Fairley, *Trisul west face,* oil on canvas, 600x300mm, 2007	97
69.	Kazbek, viewed from Chaukhi, 30km distant. *(Simon Richardson)*	99
70.	Artwork on the walls of the meteo station hut on Kazbek. *(Graham Dudley)*	100
71.	Map: The Kazbek region of the Caucasus.	101
72.	Climbers' Cairn viewpoint at 3040m. *(Dave Coustick)*	102
73.	The party approaching the summit corridor on Kazbek. *(Dave Coustick)*	102
74.	Descending the flanks of the Ortsveri glacier. *(Dave Coustick)*	104
75.	Dawn breaking on the upper Ortsveri glacier. *(Graham Dudley)*.	105
76.	Chaukhi massif in the eastern Caucasus.	106
77.	Chaukhi North Face Topo *(Simon Richardson)*	108
78.	Javakhishvili South Face Topo *(Simon Richardson)*	108
79.	Graham Dudley, *Normal Route,* Asatiani (3820m). *(Simon Richardson)*	111

80. Graham Dudley, *Perseverance*, Javakhishvili. *(Simon Richardson)*   113
81. Map: Zemu Gap routes. *(Anindya Mukherjee)*   114
82. Base camp near Talung and Tongshyong glaciers. *(Anindya Mukherjee)*   115
83. Camp 3 on the Tongshyong glacier. *(Anindya Mukherjee)*   116
84. Final headwall below the Zemu Gap, showing line. *(Anindya Mukherjee)* 116
85. Anindya Mukherjee and Thendup Sherpa on Zemu Gap. *(Pemba Sherpa)*   119
86. Zemu Gap (5861m) in December 2011. *(Anindya Mukherjee)*   122
87. John Hunt on the Zemu Gap in November 1937.   122
88. Bahini group from Chowkidar Camp. *(Roger Payne)*   124
89. Tridesh (c. 5100m), Kinsella-Mahajan-Payne line marked. *(Roger Payne)* 125
90. Bahini group: Google Earth image showing ascents and peaks. *(Roger Payne)* 126
91. Jopuno route lines. *(Roger Payne)*   127
92. Jopuno: Julie-Ann Clyma and Hugh Sheehan, south-west face. *(Roger Payne)* 127
93. Lamalamani: the north summit seen from Jopuno. *(Roger Payne)*   128
94. Arun Mahajan on the crest of the summit ridge, Tridesh. *(Roger Payne)* 129
95. Prabha Behin, first ascent: Arun Mahajan on snow/ice crest. *(Roger Payne)* 130
96. Prabha Behin, first ascent: Arun Mahajan on crux rock moves. *(Roger Payne)* 131
97. Chola Shan North, Peak 5654m north face. *(Takao Ohe)*   133
98. Chola Shan North, Sejong II (5816m) north-west face. *(Tamotsu Nakamura)* 133
99. Gangga (5688m) north face. *(Tamotsu Nakamura)*   134
100. Kawarani I (5992m) and II (5928m) south-west face. *(Tamotsu Nakamura)* 135
101. Kawarani I (5992m) north face *(Takao Ohe)*   135
102. Jarjinjabo (5725m) south face from Zhopu Pasture. *(Tamotsu Nakamura)* 136
103. Xiangqiuqieke (5863m) south face. *(Tim Boelter)*   136
104. Yangmolong Central Peak (6033m), Dangchezhe. *(Tim Boelter)*   137
105. Below: Yangmolong massif (5850m) north-west face. *(Tim Boelter)*   137
106. Genyen massif, Cameron (5873m) east face *(T. Obtulovic)*   138
107. Genyen massif, (c. 5600m) east face. *(Katka Mandulova)*   139
108. Litang Plateau, Asa (5800m) north face. *(Tamotsu Nakamura)*   139
109. Xiannairi (6032m) north face. *(Tamotsu Nakamura)*   140
110. Xiaruduo (5958m) west face. *(Tamotsu Nakamura)*   140
111. Yangmaiyong (5958m) north-west face. *(Tamotsu Nakamura)*   140
112. Lamoshe massif, Baihaizishan (5924m) west face. *(Tamotsu Nakamura)* 141
113. Minya Konka massif, San Lian east face, summits. *(Zhang Shaohong)*   142
114. Minya Konka massif, Nyambo Konka (6114m) west face. *(Pedro Detjen)* 142
115. Qonglai Mountains, Goromity (5609m) south face. *(Tamotsu Nakamura)* 142
116. Dadu He (River) basin, Peak 5712m north face. *(Tamotsu Nakamura)*   143
117. John Fairley, *Dent du Géant*, oil on canvas, 422x593mm, 2009   145
118. Sketch map of Mont Blanc, south side   147
119. Duncan Tunstall Punta Baretti's South-West Spur Day 1. *(Simon Richardson)* 148
120. Duncan Tunstall on steep headwall, Day 2. *(Simon Richardson)*   149
121. Duncan Tunstall setting up the second bivouac. *(Simon Richardson)*   150
122. Duncan Tunstall, foot of the Red Tower, Day 3. *(Simon Richardson)*   151
123. Duncan Tunstall, to side of the Red Tower on Day 3. *(Simon Richardson)* 152
124. Tunstall and Richardson, summit of Punta Baretti. *(Duncan Tunstall)* 155
125. Andy Cave seconds pitch one of *Ecstasy*. *(Andy Cave)*   159

126. The Engelhörner south walls, Bernese Oberland. *(Andy Cave)*   160
127. Mike 'Twid' Turner approaching Simelistock. *(Andy Cave)*   161
129. Andy Cave on crux, first ascent of *Ecstasy*. *(Alistair Lee)*   162
128. 1972-style ironmongery. *(Andy Cave)*   162
130. Malin Holmberg leading *Memory Crack*. *(David Pickford)*   164
131. Malin Holmberg, pitch 3, *The Lady Of The Lake* first ascent. *(David Pickford)*   165
132. Malin Holmberg on Pitch 4 of *The Lady of The Lake*. *(David Pickford)*   166
133. Girl from the North Country: Malin Holmberg. *(David Pickford)*   167
134. A small boat heads out late in the evening. *(David Pickford)*   168
135. Looking down the last, crux pitch of *The Lady of The Lake*. *(David Pickford)*   169
136. Malin Holmberg on the crux pitch of *The Lady of The Lake*. *(David Pickford)*   171
137. Holmberg leading final pitch of *Norwegian Wood*. *(David Pickford)*   172
138. The midsummer sky at 1am, fjord at Kalle. *(David Pickford)*   174
139. *Spirit of Sydney* enters the Lemaire Channel. *(Phil Wickens)*   177
140. Starting the ascent of the Hotine glacier. *(Mike Fletcher)*   179
141. Wickens, MacIntyre, Fletcher, Mt Faraday. *(Derek Buckle)*   181
142. Buckle, MacIntyre, Fletcher, Wynne-Jones, Matin summit. *(Phil Wickens)*   182
143. AC team high on heavily corniced Mt Cloos. *(Phil Wickens)*   183
144. Derek Buckle and Phil Wickens on the east face of Cloos. *(Oliver Metherell)*   184
145. Derek and Phil on the east face of Mount Cloos. *(Oliver Metherell)*   185
146. Oliver Metherell beneath the séracs on east face of Mt Cloos. *(Phil Wickens)*   186
147. Derek Buckle kayaking amongst icebergs,Paradise Cove. *(Phil Wickens)*   188
148. Dave Wynne-Jones and Mike Fletcher, Mt Inverleith. *(Phil Wickens)*   189
149. The *Spirit of Sydney* in ice at Deloncle Bay. *(Phil Wickens)*   190
150. John Fairley, *Shivling*, acrylic on board, 310x610mm, 2008   193
151. Beware, the 'silent killer'. Mick Fowler regards the stove. *(Paul Ramsden)*   195
152. The design of the stove testing enclosure.   200
153. The grey, debris-covered Ngozumpa glacier. *(Stephen Goodwin)*   204
154. Installation of a time-lapse camera, Ngozumpa glacier, *(Ang Phula Sherpa)*   205
155. Time-lapse progression of lake fill.   206
156. Amount of lake drain. *(Ang Phula Sherpa)*   207
157. After a massive ice calving event. *(Ang Phula Sherpa)*   208
158. Meltwater cascading from the Pers glacier. *(Stephen Goodwin)*   210
159. Junction of the Pers and Morteratsch glaciers. *(Stephen Goodwin)*   211
160. Markers placed at 10 year-intervals. . . *(Stephen Goodwin)*   212
161. The author at the source of the Po river. *(Stephen Goodwin)*   212
162. The Aletsch glacier viewed from the Eggishorn. *(Stephen Goodwin)*   213
163. Zdenka Mihelic on the summit of the Breithorn. *(Stephen Goodwin)*   214
164. Ascending the Niederjochferner to the Similaun hut. *(Stephen Goodwin)*   215
165. Alois Pirpamer, one of the 'rescuers' of Ötzi. *(Stephen Goodwin)*   216
166. Memorial on the Tisenjoch to the discovery of Ötzi. *(Stephen Goodwin)*   216
167. Marker post at the Hauslabjoch. *(Stephen Goodwin)*   217
168. Ötzi the Iceman as he may have looked 5300 years ago. *(Stephen Goodwin)*   218
169. John Fairley, *NE wall of Pizzo Badile*, oil on canvas, 910x1215mm, 2012   221
170. John Fairley, *Camp at Tapovan*, watercolour, 270x180mm, 1994   225
171. John Fairley, *Satopanth*, watercolour, 270x180mm, 1994   226

172. Michael Roberts at Val d'Isère in 1935. *(Janet Adam Smith)* 230
173. Michael Roberts at Tignes. *(Janet Adam Smith)* 237
174. Edward Lear (1812-88) *Kinchinjunga from Darjeeling, Himalayas. (Christie's)* 241
175. John Fairley, *Aiguille Verte et Dru*, watercolour, 210 x 280mm, 1993 245
176. Mont Blanc showing Frêney pillars (centre). *(Chris Bonington Picture Library)* 247
177. Central Pillar of Frêney. *(Chris Bonington Picture Library)* 249
178. The French team at the téléphérique station. *(Chris Bonington Picture Library)* 250
179. Don Whillans leading on the Pillar. *(Chris Bonington Picture Library)* 253
180. Don and Chris at Chandelle bivouac. *(Chris Bonington Picture Library)* 255
181. Bonington and Whillans on summit. *(Chris Bonington Picture Library)* 256
182. Jou Tras Llambrión amphitheatre. *(Elisa Villa)* 259
183. *Western Arête* of the Tiro Tirso. *(Alfredo Íñiguez)* 260
184. Jou Tras Llambrión route lines. *(Alfredo Íñiguez)* 260
185. Alfredo Íñiguez descending the *Western Arête. (Enrique González Barbón)* 263
186. Ormsby and Eusebio's route line. *(Alfredo Íñiguez)* 264
187. The 'friction slab', crux of the 1872 ascent. *(Alfredo Íñiguez)* 265
188. Kanchenjau (6919m), Sikkim. *(Roger Payne)* 267
189. John Fairley, *Climbers on the east ridge of Lyskamm,* oil on canvas, 2008 269
190. Mont Blanc, with the line of *Chronique de la haine ordinaire. (Luca Signorelli)* 271
191. Aiguille Verte with line of Les Cascades. . . *(Lindsay Griffin)* 273
192. North-west face of the Mönch. *(Ben Dare)* 274
193. Piz Badile with line of *Sogni d'alta Quota. (Lindsay Griffin)* 277
194. Iain Small on FA of *Brave New World*, Ben Nevis. *(Simon Richardson)* 281
195. Guy Robertson on FWA *Crazy Sorrow*, Lochnagar. *(Pete Benson)* 283
196. Guy Robertson, second ascent, *Extasy*, Creag Meagaidh. *(Pete Benson)* 284
197. Malcolm Bass FA *Zapatista*, Eilde Canyon, Glen Coe. *(Simon Yearsley)* 286
198. Slawomir Kawecki, north face of Koh-e-Mandaras. *(Klaudiusz Duda)* 288
199. Russian route on the W face of Latok III. *(2011 Russian Latok III Expedition)* 290
200. North face of Latok I, showing the high point of the 2011 Korean attempt. 291
201. *Dreamers of Golden Caves* on K7 West, showing bivouac sites. *(Dick Isherwood)* 292
202. Ranglana (5554m) from the lower Obra valley. *(Harish Kapadia)* 295
203. Raldang (5499m) seen from Kalpa. *(Harish Kapadia)* 297
204. Gulmothungos Rocks, Ringdom valley. *(Harish Kapadia)* 301
205. Nyegi Kangsang (6983m). *(Harish Kapadia)* 304
206. Kangto I (7042m) and Kangto II (6953m). *(Harish Kapadia)* 306
207. Gottlieb - Kellogg route on the south face of Pangbuk Ri. *(David Gottlieb)* 308
208. Andy Houseman, west ridge of Kyashar. *(Nick Bullock)* 309
209. The Lunag peaks from the south. L-R: Lunag III, IV and V. *(Steve Holmes)* 310
210. Yan Dongdong and Bruce Normand approach Sir Duk. *(Guy McKinnon)* 312
211. Ancohuma (6430m) from Viluyo Jankohuma. *(Erik Monasterio)* 314
212. North face of Jankhopiti. *(Erik Monasterio)* 315
219. South side of Pico Ansilta 4, line of *6 Hermanos. (Gabriel Fava)* 320
220. East face of Torre La Yaya, Tierra del Fuego. *(Mariano Rodríguez)* 321
221. Tronador: *Finito Sur* and *Jeneración Descartable* marked. *(Luciano Fiorenza)* 322
222. Top pitch, Beltrame/Rodríguez route,Torre La Yaya. *(Mariano Rodríguez)* 323
223. Guy McKinnon on the summit slopes of Mt Tutoko. *(Ben Dare)* 325

224. Daniel Joll, FA *Under Pressure*, West face of The Remarkables. *(Erika Tovar)* 326
225. Elke Braun-Elwert, Hillary Ridge of Aoraki Mount Cook. *(Marty Schmidt)* 327
226. Jamie Vinton-Boot, FA west rib of Mt Walter. *(Kester Brown)* 328
234. John Fairley, *Finsteraarhorn*, watercolour, 177x253mm, 2004 339
235. George Band, Everest 1953. *(Alfred Gregory/Royal Geographical Society)* 397
236. Khumbu Icefall, Everest 1953. *(Charles Wylie/Royal Geographical Society)* 399
237. George Band, FA Kangchenjunga, 1955. *(Joe Brown/RGS)* 400
238. John Hunt and Mike Westmacott, Everest 1953. *(Alfred Gregory/RGS)* 402
239. Alan Blackshaw, Arctic ski traverse, 1979. *(Mike Esten)* 406
240. Stewart Ward load carrying up fixed ropes on Annapurna II in 1960. 426
241. Chris Bonington and Doug Scott. *(Chris Bonington Picture Library)* 429
242. John Cleare, Peter Rowland, Anna Lawford, Hywel Lloyd, Harry Melville *(ACL)* 431

Obituaries

George Christopher Band OBE 1929 - 2011 *(Bernard Newman)* 396
Michael Westmacott 1925 - 2012 *(Ian Roper)* 401
Alan Blackshaw OBE 1933 - 2011 *(Ken Wilson)* 405
Walter Bonatti 1930 - 2011 *(Bernard Newman)* 409
Alasdair Ian Andrews 1939 - 2011 *(John Monks)* 413
Alistair Gordon 1943 - 2011 414
Reverend Jim Harrison 1930 - 2011 *(Rupert Hoare)* 417
Rupert John Stephen Hoare 1956 - 2011 *(Jay Turner)* 418
Jagdish C. Nanavati 1929 - 2011 421
Tim Oliver 1956 - 2011 *(Phill Thomas)* 424
Stewart Ward 1930 - 2011 *(Chris Bonington Picture Library)* 425

High Asia

1. John Fairley, *Bhagirathi III,* oil on canvas, 590x835mm, 2009

MICK FOWLER

Far From The Madding Crowd

The First Ascent of Gojung (6310m), Western Nepal

2. The west face of Gojung (aka Mugu Chuli) (6310m) in the Mugu area of western Nepal. The *Fowler-Turnbull Route* takes a leftward diagonal line from the obvious snow diamond at the foot of the face. *(Mick Fowler)*

Agitated screaming in a native tongue was mixed with shouts of increasing concern from Jonny Ratcliffe.

'Watch out! What are you doing? The black one's in that garden. And the white one is under that house!'

I ran frantically into carefully tended vegetable gardens shouting my best Nepalese mule commands. But the more I focused on bringing one animal under control the more the others would roam off to munch carefully nurtured garden produce.

The locals were not happy and the situation was beginning to feel madly out of control. Jonny and I were trying to drive laden mules through the village of Mangri in the Mugu district of western Nepal. It wasn't as if we wanted to be doing this but the two muleteers we had employed had stopped for a drinking session and were nowhere to be seen. And we had

3

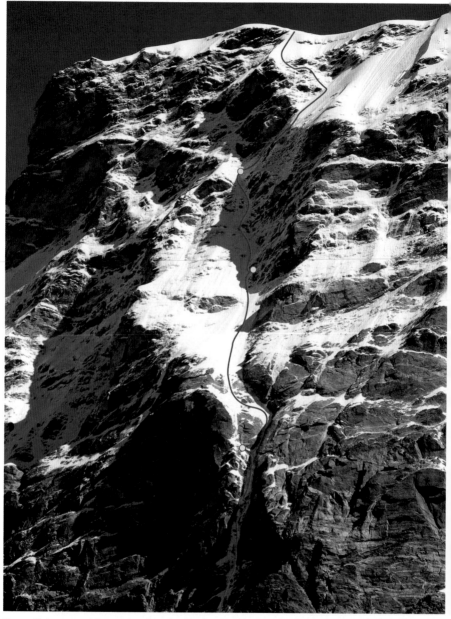

3.   Gojung west face, showing the Fowler-Turnbull line and bivouacs. *(Graham Desroy)*

already been so badly delayed by landslides that three days had passed with us being barely a tenth of the way to base camp. We only had 30 days away from Britain so unless we could somehow speed up the mule travel we wouldn't stand a chance of getting to base camp let alone climbing

4. Painting the house (and herself) for Dashain. A girl in the village of Gamghadi, near Rara lake, prepares for the longest and most auspicious festival in the Nepalese calendar. *(Dave Turnbull)*

the mountain that we had set our hearts on for the last year. And so we had taken it upon ourselves to assume mule driving. Jonny was a star at it whereas my performance was less convincing.

The mountain we were aiming for is known locally as Gojung and stands at an altitude of just over 6300m on the Nepal-Tibet border. The probable first westerners to see it were a Spanish team in 2008. They christened it Mugu Chuli, decreed it as 'outstanding' and returned for an attempt in 2009. They were not successful but the same year a British team visited the area, after which Ed Douglas kindly sent me a photograph with the caption *'came across this face which might interest you'*. And now, two years later, here I was trying to get there with climbing partner Dave Turnbull and fellow team members Graham Desroy and Jonny Ratcliffe.

Our 'trying' was not going very well. Gojung forms part of the remote Kapthang range on the border between far western Nepal and Tibet. It is not at all quick and easy to get to. To get this far we had flown to Kathmandu, endured a 16 hour bus ride to the town of Nepalganj and then flown to Rara airstrip. The precariousness of the flight leg was later emphasised to us when 'our' plane crashed and the only other plane owned by the airline broke down – fortunately without crashing. And now we were struggling to drive mules through landslide areas and counting the increasingly small number of days we might have at base camp. Agitation was beginning to run high.

The world through which we travelled gave the appearance of not having changed for generations. Subsistence farming dominated with electricity and generators in short supply and not a games console in sight. The religious environment changed from predominately Hindu in the lower reaches to prominently Buddhist as we rose into the mountains. The last settlement of Mugu, a couple of days short of the Namja La pass into Tibet, particularly charmed us with its unusual mediaeval-style buildings adorned with weighty accumulations of firewood. This accumulation had clearly gone beyond practicality and we were told it had become something of a competition which was rather obviously now challenging the structural stability of many houses. Our two muleteers livened proceedings here by having an impressive fight which resulted in one very swollen cheek,

5.   Mick Fowler at the belay after pitch four on day one. *(Dave Turnbull)*

an apparently broken thumb and yet more delays. Throughout the entire walk-in we met just one western trekker. The whole Mugu area met with my approval. It is delightfully far from the madding crowds of Khumbu.

The peaks lining the valley of the Kogichwa Khola came into view as we approached a beautiful base campsite at about 4400m. Only Kojichuwa Chuli (6439m) had been climbed here and we could not fail to notice that Gojung was not the only fine looking unclimbed 6000m peak.

It had taken seven days to walk into base camp; that left us 12 days before the mules returned. With this timescale very much in mind Dave and I set off immediately to incur some altitude headaches. Acclimatising is not exactly my favourite aspect of a Himalayan trip and normally we get as high as we sensibly can and sit there until we feel that we have suffered thin air for long enough to stand a chance of success on the main objective. Here though it was slightly different in that the terrain immediately west of Gojung was rolling hills rising to just over 5400m. This meant that from our tent at about 5100m we were able to make a couple of walking forays over hilly summits and soak up marvellous views of the whole of the Kapthang range and the Tibetan plateau beyond.

We endured three nights at our 5100m camp before decreeing ourselves acclimatised and ready to attempt to climb to the summit of Gojung. Taking into account a day sorting everything out at base camp we now had just seven climbing days until the mules arrived. With the face one day away from base camp that left just six to climb the mountain's 1100m west face and get down. And our best estimate was that it might take all

6.   Dave Turnbull in the lower couloir. *(Mick Fowler)*

six. Mmmm! Himalayan trips can pose challenging timescales for those of us on limited holidays.

The squeaky, white ice could not have been better. The heavy monsoon must have sent thousands of tonnes of spindrift cascading into the narrow lower couloir of our chosen line and compacted it to give perfect climbing conditions. Dave, enjoying his first climb in the Himalayas, expressed surprise. This was a million miles away from Himalayan soft snow plodding so often portrayed in the press. Clear skies dominated the horizon and spindrift was minimal. Desperate looking pitches succumbed with relative ease and by the end of the second day we were about half way up the face. We were going a little slower than planned but all in all it couldn't get much better.

It was at this point that I was to demonstrate that 30 years of greater range experience doesn't make one immune from the most elementary mistakes. The decision to be made was how best to bivouac when faced with a uniform 50 degree ice slope and intermittent waves of spindrift. With the lessons learned from more bivouacs than I care to remember I should have insisted that we cut a bum ledge and sit together shielded from the spindrift by the tent fabric. But the temptation of a lie-down bivouac was too much and so I suggested nose-to-tail as my preferred option.

7.   Mick Fowler at first bivouac. *(Dave Turnbull)*

As it was Dave's first Himalayan bivouac in such conditions he was happy to defer to my judgement. The bivouac sack I was using was new to me and I was wary of suffocating if I zipped myself in completely. After a night of increasing spindrift and much squirming, enough snow got into my sleeping bag to make it distinctly damp for the top 12 inches or so. Noting that this had happened when there wasn't a cloud in the sky did make me feel particularly silly. In the morning Dave, relatively snug and dry, marvelled quietly as I sheepishly packed away my bedraggled looking sleeping bag.

Our third day on the face continued with more perfect white ice and much whooping up increasingly spectacular ground to finally reach a

3. Dave Turnbull on the summit slopes. *(Mick Fowler)*

similar bivouac predicament. The slope beneath the headwall was smooth and icy and this time there was no hesitation in going for the 'cut bum ledge and sit in tent fabric' tactic.

It was only when I unpacked my sleeping bag that I fully realised the effect of the night before. That morning I had convinced myself that my bag was only a bit damp but now I could not deny that the whole thing resembled a frozen football and the upper section was heavy with blocks of ice. I unravelled it to the sound of cracking ice and tried my best to remain cheerful and get in.

I tend not to find sitting bivouacs very comfortable at the best of times but usually I am at least able to snuggle down and enjoy being warm. This time though I could not bring myself to wrap the upper section around me and was soon shivering badly. Meanwhile Dave had snuggled down, pulled his hat over his eyes, inserted enormous earplugs and was snoring gently.

I spent some time contemplating the coldness of late October night-time temperatures and wondering whether to cut the ice lumps out of my sleeping bag and throw them away. It wouldn't do my sleeping bag much good, on the other hand they must have weighed at least one kilo and there seemed little point in expending energy carrying them up with me. I dithered badly, made a midnight brew, shivered more, and was incredibly grateful that my down jacket had somehow recovered from the damp-ness incident. My shivering must have been impressive as, at one point, I

9. Dave Turnbull on the 6310m summit of Gojung. *(Mick Fowler)*

managed to vibrate Dave into a state of semi alertness and get him to agree to share his sleeping bag with me if matters should get any worse over the days ahead. Regardless of how the situation had arisen it did seem potentially silly to have one climber using up all his energy shivering while the other snored blissfully.

Ultimately I decided to leave the lumps and have the upper section of the bag hanging out of my rucksack the next day where it would hopefully dry a little in the anticipated afternoon sun.

The previous day had seen communication difficulties. Dave had been suffering from increasing throat problems which meant that he could only shout in a sort of strangulated cry. And I couldn't hear; firstly because I increasingly can't hear very well and secondly because the cold was such that I had spent most of the day with all three hoods up together. 'Pardon' had become the most used word on the mountain.

It was as we emerged from my shivering bivouac that Dave moved close and whispered in my ear. Initially I found this slightly disconcerting but it soon became clear that, much as he was in good condition in every other way, his throat problem had worsened to the extent that whispering at close quarters was now the only way he could communicate. Climbing communications would have to be in sign language from now on. At least that meant we understood the limitations and wouldn't have to say 'pardon' to each other every few minutes.

Dave continued to whisper as we enjoyed our usual Snickers bar each for breakfast, after which I started signalling manoeuvres by giving a thumbs up when it became clear that good climbing conditions continued on the next section, a potentially difficult traverse towards the summit icefields.

These traverse pitches gave fantastic climbing and were much steeper and more spectacular than we had anticipated. What we had feared might be time-consuming powder snow on rock turned out to be superb mixed ground; solid rock interspersed with soft, white ice giving delicate traversing above awe inspiring drops. Gojung lies on the main Himalayan crest and the backdrop for the traverse was a magnificent sea of unclimbed peaks stretching into the distance.

Away to the south could be seen the lush mountain valleys of western Nepal whilst to the north the skyline was dominated by the arid brown plain of the Tibetan plateau. Along the crest we could see the conical unclimbed summit that we knew Graham and Jonny would be (successfully) attempting at that very moment. I hung from the belay and couldn't stop admiring the view. It really did feel a privilege to be there.

The end of the traverse marked the end of the technical difficulties. A few pitches of easier mixed climbing, a series of lung-gasping rope lengths up the final slopes and, just before nightfall, we breached the summit crest to find a perfect wind-scoured flat area for the tent. The summit itself was just 100m or so away and could wait for the morning. It was the first time we had managed to pitch the tent since the foot of the face and we both collapsed thankfully into its protective embrace.

Dave produced a pillow and spent some time levelling his sleeping mat by wedging bits of clothing under it.

'Important to be comfortable,' he whispered before falling asleep within seconds.

The spot was wonderfully sheltered and I lay there listening to Dave's slow, heavy breathing and contemplating the fact that my efforts at sleeping bag drying had slightly improved my ice lump problem. At least I had managed to get in the bag completely and was definitely shivering less than the night before. Mind you if things had been worse the chances of being able to wake Dave looked slim and the chances of successfully sharing his sleeping bag even less so.

The weather remained absolutely perfect, not a cloud in the sky, and I looked forward to standing on the unclimbed summit of Gojung early in the morning. A slight concern was that the face had taken a day longer than planned but I wasn't going to let that interrupt the sense of elation I felt at having reached the top of the face. Anyway with a bit of luck we would be able to catch up a day and still arrive in base camp the same day as the mules.

After 20 days of near-perfect weather we were somewhat taken aback to unzip the tent in the morning and find threatening clouds scudding across

10.   A place of potential: Gojung is in the centre with Fowler-Turnbull line on its left
      side. Behind to the left is Kojichuwa Chuli (6439m), climbed by the Japanese in
      2010 via the long left-hand (west) ridge. The prominent rock pinnacle domi-
      nates the unclimbed south-east ridge which drops to the col between Kojichuwa
      Chuli and Gojung. To the right of Gojung is unclimbed Churau or Kanti Himal
      (6419m) and on the extreme right is an unclimbed 6047m peak. *(Nick Colton)*

an increasingly grey sky.

The summit was gained quickly via a pleasing snow ridge but any lingering, as I normally like to do at this point, was out of the question. A biting wind was building fast and thoughts of the descent beginning to dominate.

Possible descents had provoked much discussion during our planning in Britain. Abseiling back down the route lacked aesthetic appeal and we always knew that it might not be possible because the lower couloir would

be exposed to avalanches in bad weather. But the summit snowfields on
the Tibetan side were the key to all other options and being wild expanses
of high-level glacial terrain they required good visibility for safe progress.
The fast approaching clouds looked likely to rob us of that just when we
needed it most.

The option we chose was to traverse the Nepal-Tibet frontier for a kilometre or so over another unclimbed 6000m summit and then descend a
complex abseiling and glacier route back to the glacier at the foot of the
face. We judged that, in good weather, gaining the top of the abseiling
section should be an easy day moving together from the top of Gojung.

But by nightfall we were perhaps one third of the way along the frontier
traverse, visibility was zero and the wind was howling. The next morning
steady snowfall was adding to the challenge and by the next evening we
had managed bursts of activity between the clouds totalling perhaps two

hours. A memorably undignified crawl through deep snow had also slowed progress on one section. Along the way we used the semi-clear spells to take photographs with our digital cameras in the hope that they would aid progress in reduced visibility. They proved laughably inadequate and ultimately, in knee-deep snow and a white-out, we had to acknowledge that the only safe option was to stop, pitch the tent and wait until we could see something.

We were now two days behind schedule and the niggling concern about being late was beginning to grow. The mules ought to be leaving base camp the next morning if we were to get to Rara airstrip in time to catch the plane. So what would Graham and Jonny do? We felt guilty about causing them so much worry and inconvenience but didn't think they would leave without us. The last walkie-talkie contact had been from our bivouac on the summit ridge so they knew we were at least one day behind schedule. And, much as we had not been able to get in touch with them since, they could see the weather was bad so it seemed reasonable for them to suspect that we could have lost another day. On balance we reckoned that we had three days before they would start to get seriously concerned.

Unsettling as these thoughts were, there was nothing we could do but continue with the descent as quickly as possible as weather windows allowed. At least we had plenty of gas, a Snickers bar and a fair bit of surplus fat. I took out my book to pass the time, only to note with displeasure that it had somehow got damp and turned into a block of ice. Perhaps surprisingly we both slept well.

Dave pulled his head back in the tent and turned with a big smile on his face. It was morning again and he whispered that cloudless skies had returned. It was time to spring into action. For the first time we could properly appreciate the immensity of our surroundings. We were tiny figures, insignificant in a huge expanse of glacial whiteness. Steep ice cliffs and gaping crevasses dotted the landscape and were all too obviously a risk for the unwary. Stopping and holing up when we did had all too obviously been the right thing to do.

The atmosphere was so different from the last two days. Being able to see is amazingly useful. Suddenly we were walking easily down a gentle slope, jumping a bergschrund, feeling the warmth of the sun on our faces and then sweating uncomfortably whilst descending south-facing slopes. By evening we were on the glacier we had started from and the next morning we met a relieved Graham who had come up with Purbah, our kitchen boy, to meet us, carry our bags and deliver assorted goodies to eat. Life felt good.

As it transpired, the snowfall had stopped the mules arriving on time and base camp had only been moved down to the main valley the day before. And we had been monitored more closely than we realised. When the weather cleared Jonny had come all the way up to below our descent route and spent the day watching us through binoculars. And now, the next day, Graham and Purbah had walked all the way up from the main valley to meet us. We were incredibly grateful. It's good to have good friends.

11. Down safely. Fowler (left) and Turnbull after eight days on the mountain. *(Fowler collection)*

It turned into one of those occasions when everything worked out just right. The muleteers drove their mules through the night to make up the two days we had lost, a plane miraculously arrived to replace the crashed and broken-down ones, a vehicle somehow materialised at the sleepy airstrip we were flown to, and we were in London on the Sunday in time for Dave and I to be back in our offices on the Monday morning.

We had been away 30 days and in action every day. It is satisfying to feel that one's annual leave is being used to the full.

Summary: An account of the first ascent of Gojung (aka Mugu Chuli) (6310m) in the Mugu area of western Nepal by Mick Fowler and Dave Turnbull, 15 – 23 October 2011 (1500m of climbing, ED). Whilst Fowler and Turnbull were on Gojung Graham Desroy and Jonny Ratcliffe made the first ascent of Pt 5800m on the frontier ridge to the west of Kojichuwa Chuli.

Acknowledgements: Fowler and Turnbull would like to thank all who helped to make the climb possible: The Mount Everest Foundation, The Alpine Club, Berghaus, Black Diamond, Thermarest, MSR, Cascade, Mountain Equipment and Lyon Equipment.

PAT DEAVOLL

Along The Corridor and Up The Stairs

A New Route in The Wakhan

Forty-eight hours' supervised incarceration in a military compound in Western China leaves one with plenty of time for contemplation. It was late August 2011 and we had been granted this unwelcome period of enforced reflection while awaiting deportation to New Zealand.

My sister Christine Byrch and I were on our way home from Afghanistan after successfully summiting Koh-e-Baba-Tangi (6516m) via a new route – only the second party ever to climb the mountain and the first in 48 years.

We were on a high yet keen to get home; many days of travel and climbing had taken its toll; we were tired. But the Chinese immigration officials in Urumqui had other plans for us. 'You need a visa to transit,' we were told. 'You need to organise another flight out of China, and in the meantime you are staying here.'

Safely home a few days later we could laugh about it, though at the time we felt in a serious bind and a long way from New Zealand.

Plans for our trip to the Wakhan Corridor in north-east Afghanistan had begun to take shape in 2010. For a lifetime I'd wanted to climb there, but with one war or another the country had been out of bounds for more than 30 years. Then in the late 2000s a trickle of visitors began to return. 'Now's my chance,' I determined, and set about coercing Christine and Indian friend and renowned climber Satyabrata Dam from Delhi into coming with me. For the next 12 months we battled with embassies for visas, applied for financial grants and appealed for sponsorship. We (supposedly) organised an Afghan company named Wakhan Tourism to help with internal permits, 4WD transport and local porters. In mid-July we flew out of New Zealand bound for Dushanbe, the capital of Tajikistan, where we would meet Satya. We were finally on our way.

Arriving in Dushanbe we were surprised to find a lovely, uncongested city of elegant buildings, wide boulevards and numerous fountains; apparently it's the showpiece of Central Asia. There was not a scrap of rubbish anywhere. But the temperature was in the 40s (thank goodness for the fountains), so it was good to be on the road after a day spent organising final permits and shopping in the bazaar for the luxuries we obviously weren't going to find in Afghanistan. We'd pre-booked a 4WD vehicle via the internet with Pamir Silk Travel, and our large Nissan (or was it a Range Rover or a Hilux?) promptly arrived at our hotel at 10am on the morning of departure, driven by a cheerful Tajik named Gordo, who spoke not a word

12.   The village of Kret, with Koh-e-Baba-Tangi towering above, taken from across the Wakhan river. *(Pat Deavoll)*

of English. We roared out of town but after 10km were reduced to a top speed of 20km hour by the state of the roads, and retained this speed for the next three days as we inched slowly closer to the Afghan border.

My immediate impressions of Tajikistan were:

a) That there was not a flat piece of ground anywhere; the terrain is stupendously mountainous.

b) That the national dress for women (a baggy tunic, pantaloons and headscarf in garish colours) would leave me forever grateful I wasn't born into a culture where I'd be forced to wear anything so ugly.

c) That it was fascinating seeing upturned tanks in the riverbeds, the legacy of the Russian withdrawal from Afghanistan decades earlier.

d) That the constant allusion to drug trafficking (from Afghanistan) gave the place an exciting 'edginess' that captured my imagination.

At the end of the second day's drive we stopped in the small university town of Khorog, and next morning arrived at the Afghan border. Gordo bundled us and our bags out of the car at a large gate that fronted a bridge across the Panj river. The temperature was about 50 degrees. In the middle of the wide, dusty riverbed were two small buildings – the Tajik immigration post and the Afghan immigration post. Two smiling soldiers let us through the gate and we struggled to the first post with our entire luggage, at risk of expiring. The formalities went smoothly... but where was the representative from Wakhan Tourism who was supposed to meet us? He eventually turned up, claimed he was very ill, accompanied us up the road to the small village of Ishkashim, and then disappeared off to hospital. That was the last we saw of him.

13.   Under the gaze of an Ishkashim local. *(Pat Deavoll)*

When no replacement rep appeared, it became obvious we would have to do our own organizing. This turned out to be a blessing in disguise as we saved ourselves quite a sum of money. Wandering into the middle of Ishkashim (no more than a dirt crossroads around a rough bazaar but charming in its simplicity) Satya and I shopped successfully for the remainder of our food, purchased a pressure cooker, two 5kg gas cylinders for cooking at base camp and organised a 4WD to take us 120km up the Wakhan valley to the village of Kret from where we would start our walk to the base of the mountain. We also met the locals, a very friendly and helpful lot who were not averse to having their photos taken (unfortunately it's not de rigueur to smile for the camera in Afghanistan). There were plenty of women and girls in the colourful Wakhi dress on the street, plus the occasional burka. We were befriended by a young man named Adab who marched us round to see the regional governor and the local and border police to obtain the required bits of paper to enter the Wakhan.

(Adab is the future of tourism in this area – he speaks excellent English and is committed to introducing mountain tourism to the area. He will have a website soon – watch this space.)

Inside the border police compound, the men had laid down their AK47s and were playing chess at a large table in the sun. We spent two nights in an excellent guest house with a smattering of other western travellers and were treated to a music evening courtesy of Dua'd, another young man we'd commissioned as translator to help us locate porters in Kret. It was fun. Then it was on the road again.

Driving up the Wakhan Corridor to the village of Kret, I was reminded of the overland travel I'd done in the 80s: no internet, no mobile or satellite phone, no contact with the outside world. We were our own, incommunicado for almost a month; we had cut loose. The scenery was unworldly: sprawling, arid mountains with brief glimpses of glaciers and snow-and-ice capped peaks up the side valleys; remote villages of mud houses; all the while the vast Panj river barricading us from Tajikistan and the Pamirs on the far side. Our driver was an elderly Afghan who cheerfully dealt with a puncture and at one point backed over a huge rock. The vehicle had to be jacked up and off the rock before we could continue... but *inshallah*! These things happen. We arrived in Kret late in the afternoon and were invited to stay in the village guest house. The next day I was ill with a stomach complaint, but Satya and Christine met with the village community leader and our porters were organised. An old man tried to teach Christine to spin with a

14. Upturned tank in a Tajik riverbed, a leftover from Russia's withdrawal from Afghanistan in 1989. *(Pat Deavoll)*

spindle. Next morning we set off for base camp – the three of us, eight porters and a dog. Our adventure had really begun.

The climb up onto the glacier where we would establish our base camp was steep. On the first day we climbed 1000m, a great effort by our porters who were all lumping 25kg plus. They were a delightful team: funny, kind and generous, sharing their tea, rice and naan with us, and making sure that Christine and I especially could follow the faint trail. One porter had brought his dog. We spent the first night at the toe of the glacier after climbing a steep incline all afternoon, then next day moved on up to the place at about 4800m that an Italian team had used as base camp in 2008. This team had tried the west ridge (line of the original 1963 ascent) but given up at 6000m. It wasn't the most salubrious spot for a camp – on white ice with a smattering of moraine over top – but it was the best there was; everywhere else was too steep. After a final cup of tea and naan, the porters headed back to Kret, with a promise to return in three weeks' time. We waved them off, then set about making ourselves as comfortable as possible.

Over the next 10 days we did our best to acclimatize to the altitude before making our summit attempt. I'm never the best acclimatizer, and neither is Christine, but for Satya, who has climbed Everest without oxygen, the days were nothing more than a rest before the real climbing started. Unfortunately for Christine and I there was little suitable terrain for acclimatizing: almost everywhere involved steep and strenuous climbing bar a col at about 5200m where we spent two nights reading our books.

We also walked to the base of our chosen route – the north-west ridge – to scope the line as best we could. The route would begin with a 500m ice face of 60 to 80 degrees and then progress into a narrow ice gully. From there we weren't sure what would happen, but hoped a few days of climbing would bring us onto the summit plateau, and then the summit itself. We would either V-thread our way back down the route, or traverse over the mountain and come down the west ridge. That was the plan. In the meantime, Satya proclaimed himself camp cook, and we enjoyed some great Indian cuisine rustled up from our very limited supplies.

15. No false moves: Border police in Ishkashim put down their AK47s for a game of chess. *(Pat Deavoll)*

By early August there was little more we could do to acclimatize or prepare for the climb. Now the real work would begin. Then, to our dismay, Satya, who had been suffering an injury (from training with 5kg weights round his ankles) decided not to accompany us on the climb. It would be just Christine and I! Could we do it by ourselves? Confidence somewhat dented, we knew we had to come up with a plan for dealing with our pack-loads, should we not be able to carry them on the steep terrain. I would do the leading, we decided, while Christine would jumar the rope with the heavier 'seconds' pack. If this proved too strenuous we would haul. On 4 August we waved goodbye to Satya, who promised to raise the alarm (whatever that entailed) if we hadn't returned in 10 days, and headed up the glacier to an advanced base camp under the ice face. That night we camped under a crystal clear sky with beautiful views of Tajikistan and the Pamirs to the north.

The next day the ice face went surprisingly well. The bergschrund proved no problem and after seven pitches we were perched beneath a 'bulge' of about 80-degree ice. It was time to try out our plan. I passed my pack to Christine, who then attached hers to the end of one of our double ropes. Off I went. It didn't seem too long before I'd dispatched the pitch and

16. Pat Deavoll leading the middle reaches of the ice face on day one.
      (Christine Byrch)

Christine was seconding towards me. The pack, dangling 60m beneath us, duly followed. Another couple of pitches of lesser angle, and we reached a small col that offered a good camp for the night. I set about chopping a platform from the ice while Christine melted water. We were on a high; the day had gone well and we were on our way.

Next morning we were up at 3am in an effort to be packed and away by five. We know we had a narrow ice gully to climb but weren't sure where it would exit, and wanted to give ourselves plenty of time for hauling the packs. Things went slightly awry when I climbed the wrong way on the first pitch, but we soon had ourselves back on track and Christine led quickly out beneath a large ice cliff and into the base of the gully, where we

17.   Christine Byrch climbing above the ice gully on day two. . .
18.   . . .and (below) on the summit plateau, approaching the top camp. *(Pat Deavoll)*

9.   Christine Byrch looks out over the Qala Hurst glacier from the top camp. *(Pat Deavoll)*

discovered the ice to be rotten and fragile. Thankfully after a few moves it improved and I quickly started to enjoy myself. Here I was, climbing good steep ice, on a mountain in Afghanistan. How lucky I was! I felt confident and happy: if the weather stayed settled and if we broke the mountain down into sections and dealt with each as it presented itself... we would climb Koh-e-Baba-Tangi. After the first pitch the gully relented in angle and widened. Above, it was ringed by a cornice that even though small I could see would prove hard to climb through, so I began to lead out to the right, hoping to breach the cornice where a buttress of rock butted against the ice. But it was not such a good move: once Christine reached me and we began hauling, the pack swung into the rock and lodged there. We yanked and tugged and jiggled to no avail, and in the end Christine abseiled back down and freed it. By now the day was done and we chopped out a ledge at the apex of the ridge and settled in for another fine night.

Day three and another early start. We were hoping for the same fine weather that had graced the expedition from the start but once the sun rose could see a series of dark clouds marring the western sky. What might they bring? Now that we had exited the ice gully we were confronted with a large rock buttress; deciding to try and get around it on the right hand (northern) side, we set off trudging in deep snow. We were soon hot and bothered. Rounding the ridge, we could see another steep ice slope, fringed by a nasty looking bergschrund. I tried my hardest to climb across this but couldn't find any purchase in the rotten snow and kept falling in a heap.

22. Porters on the return leg to Kret with Koh-e-Baba-Tangi and the Deavoll-Byrch route in the background. *(Pat Deavoll)*

We'd completed what we'd come to do; now it was just a matter of making the long journey home. Two days later, during which we ate continuously, our porters returned to collect us; the next day we were driving back down the Wakhan Corridor to Ishkashim. Satya had some trouble with a recalcitrant immigration official as we crossed back into Tajikistan but managed to extricate himself; then it was the long 4WD journey back to Dushanbe. The leg across China? Well, it's something we can notch up to experience. Hopefully there's nothing in our passports that will stop us returning to what must be one of the wildest and most exciting mountain areas on earth.

Summary: An account of the first ascent of the north-west ridge of Koh-e-Baba-Tangi (6516m), Wakhan Corridor, northern Afghanistan by Pat Deavoll and Christine Byrch, 1800m of climbing, 4-11 August 2011.

Acknowledgements: Many thanks to the organisations whose support helped made this climb happen: Beattie Matheson and Berghaus, Southern Approach and Black Diamond, the Mount Everest Foundation, the New Zealand Alpine Club Expedition Fund and Icebreaker NZ.

MARTIN MORAN

A Peak and Three Passes in Himachal

23. Sukto village - roadhead of the Miyar valley. *(Martin Moran)*

How dull it is to pause, to make an end,
To rust unburnish'd, not to shine in use!
As tho' to breathe were life.

In 2012 the 'untravelled mountain world' of Eric Shipton seems a long time past. We are persuaded that all useful exploration of the Himalaya is complete and media attention is driven to the honeypot commercial peaks. My romantic soul has long wished that it were not so. Would that we could go on discovering untouched mountain kingdoms. I have visited the Indian Himalaya every year for the past 20, trying to recapture the explorer's grail. In face of every kind of bureaucratic dissuasion and despite the occasional encounter with the squalor of siege-style expeditions, I have emerged heartened and fulfilled. My teams have climbed a wealth of mountains and from their summits we have looked out over empty ranges and yet-greater peaks, never lacking an inspiration for the next year's trip.

The interior ranges between Lahaul, Zanskar and Kishtwar form one of the greatest untapped wilderness areas. In 2007 the Indian submariner Satya Dam took a group of naval colleagues and a bunch of porters into this outback and in his words 'walked off the map'. They crossed the Kang La and Poat La, glacial passes close on 5500m altitude, but baulked at a third, the formidable Sersank La. Instead, they escaped the trap of the Kishtwar valleys over the Dharlangwala Jot to regain the warmer pastures of Himachal state. Satya certainly knows how to spin romantic temptation. His article in the *Himalayan Journal* spoke of 'row upon row of adrenaline-pumping unclimbed peaks' and views of 'a brilliance that simply took the breath away'. Even allowing for a margin of descriptive hyperbole, I was quickly persuaded where to take my expedition in 2011.

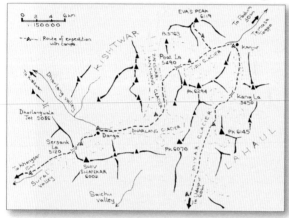

The circuit of the three passes, including Sersank, would itself be a testing adventure, involving a hundred miles of trekking with the crux at the very end. By freeing ourselves of a porter entourage we could move with speed and flexibility, cutting loose over the Kang La with a handful of high-altitude porters and 12

24.   Sketch map of peaks and passes on the Lahaul-Zanskar-Kishtwar Divide. *(Martin Moran)*

days' food. With addition of basic climbing kit we could explore some of the unnamed and unlisted peaks in the interior should time and weather allow. Soon we had a team of nine signed on, with rock-master Robin Thomas as my assistant guide.

Our arrival in Delhi on 16 September proved well-timed. The previous day a final monsoon downpour had flooded the palatial new airport terminal, but we stepped out into clear skies that were to remain unbroken for the next three weeks. We caught the Kalka Mail sleeper to Chandigarh then transferred to two Force Traveller minibuses for the onward journey to Manali. The beauty of the Kulu valley in the luxuriant weeks that follow the monsoon overwhelms the scars of India's spectacular economic growth, and there can be no finer a place to relax in the rustic charm of Old Manali than the Dragon Inn. To reach the start of our trek at Udaipur we crossed the Rohtang pass, then branched off the main road to Leh down the Chandra Bhaga valley to the north-west.

Udaipur has only been linked by road since 1978 and is in transition from a dusty one-horse town to modern a provincial centre. The valley is currently cut off throughout the winter but when the Rohtang tunnel from Manali is completed in 2015 Udaipur will have all-year access with

25. North wall of Pk 5755m above the Jangpar glacier. *(Martin Moran)*

a potential increase in traffic, trade and tourists. Up to two metres of snow can accumulate through winter, even at valley level, and in 10 years Udaipur could be a superb base for ski-touring. In the meantime accommodation facilities need drastic improvement. The charms of Hotel Amandeep extended only as deep as the layers of filth and an officious *chowkidar* who hounded us all evening waving triplicate Form Cs for completion.

By far the oldest building in Udaipur is the Marikula Mata temple, dedicated to the Pandavas and thought to have a heritage of 1400 years. We gave offerings at the shrine and took the blessing of Lord Krishna, leaving with cotton bracelets to secure our safe passage. From past experience I regard it as highly unwise to dispense with such rituals and kept my bracelet firmly tied for the next three weeks. In a delightful twist of modernity our agent Mr Pandey conducted a five-minute *puja* from his office in Delhi through my mobile phone while we were in the temple.

For the first week of the journey we followed the long curves of the Miyar Nala, from its confluence with the Chandra Bhaga at 2600m north to the Kang La at 5450m, a distance of over 90km. A road runs up the first 30km to the final village of Khanjar, but we elected to walk this section in the interests of acclimatisation. The lower valley is a happy open land of terraced cultivation, scattered villages and cedar woods. At Thingrat a young policeman came out to check our passports, and entered our details in a large ledger with undue pride. Although the Miyar valley is a fine

26.   Trekking up the Miyar glacier towards the Kang La. *(Martin Moran)*

trekking route and has a wealth of technical rock peaks we were his first foreigner entries for a month. He bemoaned the honesty of the locals. In his six-month posting not a single crime had been committed in the valley.

After a 'home-stay' in Urgos we passed Khanjar and climbed to our first camp at 3685m where I spied the white tip of a snow peak in the Uldhampu side-valley. A two-hour pursuit of this virginal vision took me to a rock plinth at 4300m where the valley finally opened to display not one but two spectacular peaks freshly clothed in the monsoon's snow. My 1:150000 Swiss map estimated their height at 5900m, and they were almost certainly unclimbed. Such revelations were to become commonplace over coming days.

For the Miyar trek we employed 16 Nepalese porters under the supervision of local sirdar Shamshir and spent two delightful days strolling up 25km of broad alluvial meadows to the Miyar glacier snout at 4100m. Here the ground changed abruptly to tortuous and exasperating surface moraine. Shamshir took us up on the left bank to avoid endless hummocks in the glacier centre, but this give scant relief. The Miyar valley is so narrow that there are no lateral moraine ridges to offer direct and speedy passage. The lower glacier is steadily sinking and the monsoon floods of 2010 had triggered countless rockslides and avalanches on the sidewalls. We spent much of the day picking our way through fresh rock debris. The sight of great rock walls, spires and arêtes up the Jangpar glacier did little to alleviate the purgatory. It was small wonder that half way up this ocean of stones we found one flamboyantly dressed porter clutching an empty bottle of Red Knight whisky.

27.   The 'snow queen' or Eva's Peak (6119m) from the Kang La. *(Martin Moran)*

The sanctuary of smooth dry glacier was reached at 4400m and here we made a chilly camp, ready to start the final push to the Kang La. Only 15 porters turned out next morning to make a last carry for us, the whisky wallah having been floored by a mysterious headache. We initially made steady progress past a succession of hanging glaciers and chiselled granite walls, but the pace flagged against a chilling breeze. The porters were cold and had to return that evening. Although we had hoped they would dump loads just under the pass, we were forced to stop 4km short at 5060m on a bleak and clouded afternoon.

Robin and I had already made major economies of food and equipment during the early days of the trek, but in the Himalaya you fight a constant battle against the natural instincts of your staff who wish to maximise comforts for their guests. A selection of kit and food was spread out far in excess of our carrying capacities. In half an hour the surplus had to be sorted, packed and sent down. If we misjudged we could be heading for slow starvation over the next two weeks or else doomed to fail under crippling loads. Our mess tent was replaced by a large nylon 'tarp' to string from boulders. Our cook Saran would not be parted from either of his two kerosene stoves, but some pans and serving dishes were prised from his grasp. Sherpa Thukpa looked crestfallen when we removed dozens of tin cans from the onward stockpile. Our Indian high-altitude porters, Govind and Mangal, fought bravely to hold on to their bags of potatoes and vegetables.

Our team were not spared the economies. 'We're all in this together', seemed the appropriate mantra. Gustavo preferred half his clothing to be

28.   Steve Birch and Mike Timar crossing the corniced summit arête of Eva's Peak.
      (Martin Moran)

removed than be parted from his zoom lenses. Others, fearful of spending two weeks in plastic boots, hid sturdy trekking shoes under their flysheets. The merits of a Kindle over paperbacks were hotly debated. The team whisky was ceremoniously decanted into Sigg bottles. When night settled we were leaner in weight and, at last, committed. I sensed the joy of freedom and slept in peace.

Glorious weather returned for the Kang La crossing. Our loads substantially exceeded 20kg. Although in summer the pass is often crossed by trekking parties, a foot of fresh snow now covered the crevasses above 5100m. Any doubts about whether we had needed to rope up were dispelled when Gustavo missed a jump and slithered three metres down a slot. I placed an ice screw anchor in the underlying ice, and rigged up a Z-pulley system. After a couple of metres hoisting Allan and I needed a rest so we relaxed our grip, expecting my 'Ropeman' back-up clamp to take the load. Alarmingly, the rope kept slipping and Gustavo screamed 'I'm going down!'. I then realised that I had put the Ropeman on the wrong way round. As Gustavo is an American passport holder I foresaw a massive legal claim if the situation was not quickly reversed. We grabbed the rope and after some frantic rearrangements established upward movement once more.

Already we were examining surrounding peaks for possible climbs.

29.   Unnamed 5800m peaks on the west side of the Zanskar-Kangthang glacier.
       (Martin Moran)

Behind us on the east side of the Miyar glacier a 'super-Alpamayo' of snow
flutes and cornices swept up to 6145m. To the north-west a gentle glacier
bay rose to the final pyramid of Pk 6294m, the cornerstone of our Kang
La-Poat La circuit. The latter was tempting but we were not sufficiently
acclimatised to stay above 5000m for another three days. Our immediate
imperative was to get over the pass and down to a lower camp in the Tidu
valley. The Kang La was a wild spot, unadorned except for the upturned
carcass of a bharal sheep. The pass lies on the watershed of the Greater
Himalayan Range and immediately to its north the terrain becomes both
arid and savage. This was the fabled land of Zanskar. Among the skeletal
rock peaks on the horizon a single 'snow queen' stood proud with an ice
boss and curving glacier shelf at her feet. She was about 10 miles away
on the north side of the Tidu valley and looked of the order of 6000m in
height. There was no way that we could walk past her.

  We made camp down at 4450m at Kanjur grazings. While our Sherpas
and porters did a second ferry of loads across the Kang La Robin and I
reconnoitred up the Tidu glacier to spy out the peak. The glacier is ringed
by ferocious ice faces, most notably the north wall of Pk 6294m. Perched
on a boulder table we opened Saran's foil-wrapped lunch offerings to find
a large slice of watermelon. How they had smuggled this into the wilder-

ness I did not know, but it was delicious. An appraisal of the approach to the 'snow queen' focused on a 300m-high barrier of near-vertical lateral moraine, which barred access to the cirque of the mountain.

A day later eight of us were back, Gustavo having been instructed to make full use of his zoom lenses at Kanjur camp. We selected the least horrifying of a series of gullies in the moraine and set to work. The strains of the Kang La were telling. All of us felt leaden and we found the gully a torment. Our doctor Chris dropped out before we made our bivouac up on gravel flats at 5000m. When the midnight alarm sounded Robin emerged from his bag in feverish state, shivering and coughing phlegm. While we dressed, he grabbed extra camp-mats and a second sleeping bag to better survive the remaining six hours of night.

Without a moon to guide us we could navigate only by intuition and vague awareness of a silhouette of rock spires against the star-filled sky. A lilac dawn found us up amongst the waves of the glacier shelf exactly where we had planned. The hanging ice boss that formed a definite crux to our route

30.   Steve Birch leading the ice nose on Eva's Peak.
       (Martin Moran)

emerged from the shadows and with great relief we spied a route directly up its crest. Gary 'hit the wall' at 5600m and returned while the snow remained firm enough to allow a safe solo retreat. I roped to Allan and David while Steve and Mike formed their own team, following our line and using our ice screws. We pitched up the 60-degree ice nose at an enjoyable grade II standard and gained an easement just as the sun built some power. The frozen crust started to give way and our rhythm was destroyed, but as the slope steepened again we found that by flexing our feet sideways we could stay afloat. The angle increased to 50 degrees and I led a long pitch on fragile fibrillations of snow to gain the summit ridge.

The panoply of peaks on the southern horizon included dozens of impressive 6000ers along the Himalayan watershed that have barely been identified still less explored. Now we could see to the north and west over rocky castellations and high white glaciers towards Kishtwar. The ridge was grossly corniced to the north and with an alternative of brick-hard ice on the south flank the finale proved more delicate than expected. We arrived at 11.20am and measured our height at 6119m. Should the peak be

31. Badile-like peak above the Zanskar-Kanthang glacier. *(Martin Moran)*

found to be unclimbed I suggested that we call it Eva's Peak, after Mike's baby daughter.

The descent featured a somewhat stressful abseil off an ice thread on the ice nose, all of us suspended from a single back-up screw, the other four dozing off while I fumbled hopelessly to thread misaligned holes. At such times the sacrifice of a Turbo ice screw is very tempting, but eventually a remarkable stack of five abseil plates was rigged and we abandoned no more than a 6mm cord. Back at the bivouac the others opted for a second night on a gravel bed while I pushed down to Kanjur into the dark for a rajma stew and tented lodgings.

Any elation at success was replaced by immediate urgency to get over the Poat La. Our schedule had dwindled to eight days. We left Kanjur to an empty hibernation that would last till next summer when shepherds would venture up for the valley's scant grasses. Halfway across the Tidu glacier we were rejoined by the summit four. Here Allan realised that at some point in a haze of fatigue he had mislaid his crampons. I had already assigned the horrors of the boulder gully to the corridors of memory, but realised that without crampons the last passes could be impossible. Better I went back up at once than shower Allan with recriminations. I spent four fruitless hours, first boulder-dodging in the gully, then combing the bivouac site and glacier snout.

Back on the Tidu glacier at 4650m I shouldered my load and bent my back to a long and weary plod to our next camp under the Poat La, pondering the coming epics of stepcutting. After an hour a lone figure emerged from the evening cloud. It was Mangal, who had come down to help me. When

I recounted my sorry tale of the missing crampons he grinned.

'Sir, I have a spare set.'

Notwithstanding the watermelon incident I was now profoundly thankful for the hoarding tendencies of our staff. Up at camp Mangal did indeed produce a battered pair of Camp strap-ons and we fitted them to Allan's boots with humble thanks.

Robin was restored to full vigour. Next day, he, Govind, Mangal and Thukpa carried loads up and over the Poat La, while the Eva's Peak team tried to recuperate. Highlight of the day was Mike and David's production of a rich and creamy cheesecake, the product of Tesco instant packets and Indian butter. Every little certainly helps up at 5000 metres. Even Allan, whose appetite had dwindled to nought over recent days, was enticed to eat a slice, but Thukpa merely giggled after one mouthful and returned to his rice and dal.

The Poat La day dawned brilliantly clear. Prayer flags on the crest at 5490m streamed horizontally in a keen east wind and we were glad to get down to the west side where a dangerously exposed rock ramp cut down through vertical cliffs. We could not imagine how or indeed why plimsoll-shod shepherds would cross with a flock, but from the discovery of droppings it was clear that they had done so in the recent past. With the passage of the Poat La we left Zanskar and entered Kishtwar region, famous for its granite peaks. The scenery of the Zanskar-Kanthang glacier had moved Satya Dam to paroxysms of joy on his trip. A series of burnished rock peaks split by tumbling glaciers and icy couloirs filled its western walls. On the east side a fabulous prow of rock opened up, apparently holdless save for a single gigantic flake at half-height. A replica Matterhorn occupied the onward view. The place ceded nothing to the Karakoram save perhaps a few hundred metres in absolute scale. This is paradise for the Alpine-style climbers of the future.

At 4500m the Z-K glacier joins with the Dharlang glacier and swings westward. Here the 2007 Indian team encountered a sea of moraines, and made an enforced bivouac. We tried to convince ourselves that we would find a clever way to avoid this trap, but come mid-afternoon we hit the stone maze, just as the efforts of a 10-hour day with 22kg loads sapped our reserves. The team was split and even Thukpa was slowing under a load of 30kg. Mutinous mutterings were voiced when I expressed a determination to push on to nightfall. Surely we could find a little meadow or a lake by which to set a camp? For two hours I forged on through the desert of rocks and dead ice before abandoning dreams of comfort. I stopped at the sound of a nearby glacier river and we set a bivouac on the boulders. The team staggered in, exhausted and demoralised. I fretted over lack of progress. Sersank la was still 15km away and if we couldn't escape the Dharlang valley within three days we would be re-booking our flights home.

The stress of the day receded when we laid out bivouac beds and a slim new moon rose. Saran cooked up soup and dal bhat under his canopy and we settled to a peaceful sleep under the stars. Robin and I left at dawn to

32. Virgin big wall territory on the east side of the Zanskar-Kanthang glacier.
(Martin Moran)

forge a route through the remaining miles of moraine. We built cairns on each moraine crest to guide the following party and after two hours found a freshwater stream in a lateral moraine that led us quickly to the Dharlang snout. By midday we reached deserted grazings at 4000m at Danga. Round the corner lay the Sersank valley and the denouement of our adventure.

Satya had described the Sersank icefall as 'totally broken with steep icefalls and huge crevasses... a near vertical maze of 800-900m of extremely treacherous ground'. Our optimism was wearing thin as we climbed on to a sharp lateral moraine and entered the jaws of the valley. The lower icefall was only 400m high but 'suicidal' seemed the appropriate adjective. However, we spotted a ramp of screes and grass running up the right side. If we could get through a rock band to gain the ramp we would have a passage. Next morning Robin and I returned with Govind, Mangal and Thukpa. Inside an hour we outwitted the rock band. Where the ramp ended we were forced on to the glacier but old patches of névé bridged crucial crevasses. Loose cliffs barred further flanking manoeuvres so we climbed direct up a second icefall, fixed a rope, and then snaked through a crevasse field to a flattening at 4800m. The pass came into view 2km away with no intervening obstacle other than a final shale wall. It had been a magnificent day of exploratory mountaineering. Wherever our way seemed barred we had discovered a slender onward passage. Exhilarated, we dropped loads

33. On the ramp above the Sersank icefall; Shiva Shankar behind. The north walls of this 6002m peak dominated the climb to Sersank La. There are two beautiful spurs in view and to their right a perfect ice and mixed face about 900m in vertical height. *(Martin Moran)*

and hastened back to Danga to report the success.

Spirits brightened at the news. Food supplies were running low, and Saran's cuisine had acquired a minimalist theme. Allan had barely eaten for a week and was absorbed in silent dreams of lamb chops and Lancashire hotpot. Gary was mid-way through a 9kg weight loss, while Gustavo needed persuasion that he was capable of the 1200m climb. Even the Indians were glad to leave some kitchenware and surplus kerosene in a shepherds' cave.

The ascent to the Sersank La commenced at funereal pace, but by 4pm the following day we were all settled in a camp under the pass. We needed just one last day of good weather. Though evening clouds threatened a change the night was bitterly cold. We packed painfully in twilight and moved towards the pass in the shadow of 6011m Shiva Shankar, which displayed a tremendous north face of linked white spiders. Robin led a diagonal line up two pitches of 60-degree rubble and at 10.15am on 6 October we reached the col. Our height was 5120m. To the south we looked out on the gentle folds of the Sural valley. A vertiginous descent of 300m of shale and a few kilometres of meandering on rognons brought us to a razor-sharp lateral moraine crest. This led for 3km to sandy flats where we spotted bear prints and a ground vegetation of willow scrub developed. Ahead, a silvery river snaked down into autumnal birchwoods.

While we camped for a final night in an oasis of tufted grasses, Govind and Thukpa pushed on to the roadhead at Khangsar village. Unwittingly, they took our last meal of soup and noodles with them, leaving us to a Spartan fare of nuts and raisins washed down by herbal tea. Thukpa made up by coming back up the valley to meet us with two Thermos flasks of sweet tea in the morning. At Tidso Adwar we passed a substantial shepherding village and gained a good path for the final miles. Despite all the doubts and obstacles of the 18-day trek we reached Khangsar one hour in advance of our planned rendezvous. We took breakfast of puris and potatoes in a village home and our jeeps arrived from Udaipur bang on time. On the same cue, milky clouds produced the first rain of the whole trip and I wore my Gore-Tex jacket for all of 10 minutes before we commenced the long drive home.

Few trips could be blessed with better weather and more fortuitous juxtaposition of events. In Delhi airport I felt sufficiently vindicated to dispense with my lucky bracelet, but the gesture was premature. During the flight back to Britain I felt the creeping onset of fever. Twenty-four hours later I was laid up in hospital in Inverness with a massively swollen leg and a severe cellulitis infection, a condition later attributed to the sanitary neglect of the Amandeep Hotel. The perfect Himalayan odyssey ended with a sharp retort from reality, but every mountain traveller must eventually make a pause.

34.   Martin Moran on the Poat La. *(Moran coll)*

Summary: A lightweight exploratory journey over passes on the Lahaul-Zanskar-Kishtwar divides of the Indian Himalaya. The team of 13 crossed the Kang La (5450m), Poat La (5490m) and Sersank La (5120m) and five members climbed a peak of 6119m on the north side of the Tidu valley (possibly unclimbed and named Eva's Peak, Alpine AD standard). Members: Martin Moran and Robin Thomas (leaders), Steve Birch, Gustavo Fierro-Carrion, Allan Isherwood, David King, Gary Motyer, Chris Sloan, Mike Timar, Govind Singh, Mangal Singh, Saran and Sherpa Thukpa. Support services were provided by Himalayan Run & Trek Pvt Ltd of Delhi.

Map: 1:150000 sheet Ladakh South by www.olizane.ch
Reference: 'Walking Off the Map' by Satyabrata Dam, *Himalayan Journal* 64, pp99-118 (2008).

BRUCE NORMAND

The Threat

Mount Edgar is no ordinary peak. Stunning and savage, beautiful and deadly, it hit the headlines hard in June 2009 when US climbers Johnny Copp, Micah Dash and Wade Johnson perished in an avalanche. In November 2010, Kyle Dempster and I used the more stable late autumn weather to attempt the mountain's infamous east face.

The Minya Konka range in south-western China's Sichuan province is barely larger than the Mont Blanc massif. Within it, however, are more than ten 6000m summits with one ascent or fewer. They form a north-south chain of satellites around Minya Konka itself, at 7556m one of the most imposing and dangerous mountains on the planet, and offer serious potential for alpine-style climbing on little known and highly committing peaks.

Mt Edgar is the highest peak not connected directly to Minya Konka. Its beautiful and imposing east face was the subject of an iconic 2008 photograph by Tamotsu Nakamura. Although the summit was reached from the south by a Korean team in 2002, it is this east face that gave the mountain instant legend status among alpinists. In May 2009, a Kyrgyz/Russian team of Mikhail Mikhailov and Alexander Ruchkin failed to climb the face because they couldn't see it. A month later, Copp, Dash and Johnson were killed in an avalanche on the approach – an event which rocked both the US climbing community and the small community of Chinese mountaineers working to develop alpine-style climbing in their home country.

The monsoon lasts from April to October in the mountains of Sichuan and because they are raked all winter by dry, north-westerly winds off the Tibetan plateau, autumn is the season to find ice. Once again denied access to eastern Tibet last autumn, Kyle and I decided to look for our alpine-style adventure in the Minya Konka range. Kyle, even more so than me, was both attracted and repelled by the east face of Edgar. Deciding, after much debate, that we'd have to try it meant making it the central focus of our expedition. Doing it in a single, fast push from the base would mean acclimatising somewhere else, such as the high valleys on the western side of the range.

We were accompanied by the independent pairs of Yan Dongdong and Gu Qizhi, both leading Chinese alpinists and our logistics experts, and French climbers Jean Annequin and Christian Trommsdorff. We bought our expedition supplies in Chengdu and Kangding, then drove to Laoyuling and trekked in two short days to a base camp at Shang Riwuqie (4300m). After a week of hiking and eating, Kyle and I decided our Edgar preparation would be aided by a little climbing. Situated directly above Shang Riwuqie, the rocky west face of Mt Grosvenor (Riwuqie Feng, 6376m)

35. The east face of Mount Edgar from the valley floor above Moxi, showing the line taken by Dempster and Norman to establish *The Rose of No-Man's Land* (WI5 M6). *(Tamotsu Nakamura)*

forms an almost perfect triangle, split in half by a single, central couloir. Tried first by Andy Cave and Mick Fowler in 2003 and later by a Korean party, this line was known to repel suitors in its spring conditions of thin ice and rotten rock. Now, however, it was October, and the ice conditions seemed solid.

We went for the single-push approach. Packing a tiny tent, one mat and a single sleeping bag for contingencies, we left BC at 3am, scrambling up moraines and our own old post-holes to reach the base of the route at 5.30. The wind was strong and a cloud front obscured the moon. We soloed up the snow cone and into the lower couloir, finding good, 45-degree ice with occasional steeper steps, and reached the crux pitches before setting the first anchor in thin ice.

Thicker ice for one rope-length at 80 degrees took us to half height. Moving back right and then up, Kyle led the crux pitch slowly and carefully. Although only WI4+, most of the pitch was rotten ice over slabby rock. At noon, I led us into four very long, calf-burning, simul-climbing 60-degree névé pitches to the very top of the gully. The clouds swirled around us for the entire afternoon while the battering wind threw blasts of spindrift from below. Kyle pulled through the steep exit step, commenting on quality ice-climbing above 6000m, and we dived under the summit cornice to enjoy

36. Kyle Dempster fully engaged with the crux pitch of Mount Edgar's east

face, on Day Four of the first ascent. *(Bruce Normand)*

37.   West face of Mount Grosvenor (Riwuqie Feng 6376m). Dempster and Normand made
      the second ascent of the mountain via the obvious central couloir, followed by an
      abseil descent of the north face, in shadow. *(Bruce Normand)*

some respite from the wind. The evening sun began to show through gaps
in the wind-torn clouds.

On the summit at 6pm, the west face of Jiazi Feng (6540m) gloomed
large beside us, ragged clouds covered Minya Konka and to the east Edgar
looked steep and menacing. Our words lost on the wind, we shook hands
and headed down the north-east ridge. Easy snow soon steepened and
turned into low-angle down-traversing beside a corniced edge. Night fell
and the wind remained strong, sucking additional warmth and strength
from us. We abandoned the ridge, descended steep snow into the north face
and then, like the first-ascent party (Roger Payne and Julie-Ann Clyma,
who climbed up by the south-west ridge in November 2003), were forced
into a long, dark abseil. Kyle is a true expert at finagling anchors in the
sketchiest terrain, and it took 15 of these to reach the upper glacier basin at
2am, where we stopped to bivouac. We awoke to a nice day, nothing like
the previous one, and were back in BC by mid-afternoon. The fine weather
lasted while we recovered, and a storm moved in when we were thinking
about more climbing, so we finished our acclimatisation with three days
spent shovelling snow. We were ready for Edgar.

Mount Edgar is a rather different story from Grosvenor. The east side
of the range resembles a subtropical cloud forest: the approaches begin in
verdant valley floors at only 1500m, and misty, rainy weather fills some-

38. Kyle Dempster following the lower section of the central couloir on the west face of Mount Grosvenor. *(Bruce Normand)*

thing like 300 days of the year. With more than 2000 vertical metres of precipitous slopes and blown-out river gorges separating the fields from the mountains, this region shrouds its peaks in a special brand of mystery.

In Moxi we met up with our Sichuan Mountaineering Association liaison officer, Li Zongli, who had also been LO for the ill-fated American expedition. A trained climber, conscientious, well qualified and genuinely passionate about the mountains, he was easily the best LO I have ever encountered in any country. In keeping with the mysterious spirit of Edgar, our first day featured unbroken low cloud and drizzle from dawn, when we'd already crossed a road-closing landslide, to dusk, by which time we'd established that the local porter we'd hired had no clue where the mountain was. Worse, we'd spent most of the day in a shockingly unstable river gully, with semi-vertical, moraine-like edges left by a recent, massive blow-out. The porter left after showing us a tiny campsite among mossy boulders in the rhododendron forests.

The next day had some brief, blue patches, but clouds and then mist prevented us from seeing even to treeline at around 4000m. Still scrambling blindly up the unstable gully, we suspected that one massive fork might be the junction of the approaches for the south-east and east faces. Occasionally we dodged bouncing rocks and thought about the video account of the American expedition, but rain in this place didn't bear thinking about. The

41. Kyle Dempster leading an ice pitch at 5900m on day four. *(Bruce Normand)*

shelf for a sitting bivouac. The night was nice, calm and clear as we brewed up while watching the stars, but towards morning the winds rose slightly and we found we were sitting in a spindrift funnel.

As the sun came up, we whipped off the sleeping bags and brushed everything down. A mouthful to eat and drink, a little thawing in the weak, early light, and we started climbing in the shadows to our left. Another steep, thin ice streak took Kyle to a long, leftward traverse across snow.

2. Kyle Dempster on the traverse into the southern slopes of Edgar, at 6300m on day six. *(Bruce Normand)*

The day turned cloudier, with wind raking the ridgeline above us. The ice turned breakable, and finally borderline useless. We could see the exit col, but two thin variants of the direct line ended up in checkmate, and our gazes turned to the terribly long and dangerous descent yawning beneath us. Failure was not an option. More rising, leftward traversing took us into another shallow groove. Kyle, leading over the tenuous, slabby rock, was forced to remove almost every vestige of white stuff to dry-tool the features beneath. Two last delicate pitches brought us into a shallow dihedral below a roof, where we pulled out onto a snowy col.

The hard climbing was over, but the alpine nature of the beast took over. In a howling gale, we threw up the tent and dived inside to rest and fuel up. In the morning the wind was unchanged, but the day was clear and sunny. Minya Konka was trailing a huge streamer of clouds, and the summit ramparts of Edgar glowed orange in the sun. Getting there required a long ice traverse, into the south-facing slopes and up through a sérac line to the rounded south ridge. The winds stayed strong and the clouds were thickening as we pulled over onto the broad shoulder of the first ascent route.

We dropped the packs and climbed the snow slopes, enough gaps in the mist showing the cornice rim to our right. I crawled over the final, steep ridge crest, ready for the summit cornice. When my axe-shafts disappeared, we were there. Kyle and I did the arm's-length summit photo, our smiles of relief only, not of any sort of triumph or success. The white-out wasn't showing any signs of another gap, so we set off down.

We launched into a fast and blind descent, aiming for a high glacier basin we'd mapped out from above. Kyle led down the firm snow slopes, heading south as the stormy winds picked up. Down-climbing steep snow, we followed a ridge and a rocky edge, passed through a col and reached another firm snowfield perfect for walking. As the wind dropped, so did the visibility. As the going flattened, the snow got much deeper. Snowfall was thickening as the light faded and we camped beneath a tiny rock overhang to avoid avalanche danger.

The morning was clear and we could look back at the summit of Edgar. Irrational exuberance made us sure we could get through the invisible glacier which fell away below us. Four hours later, we were lost in a maze of slots, hiking into crevasses, down-climbing icy fins and abseiling around corners. The morning sun turned to another white-out. We aimed for the true left and made progress in the gap between rock and ice: some down-climbing pitches, then back onto the glacier to avoid huge holes by the rock slabs, then several more abseils back

43.   Kyle Dempster and Bruce Normand back in Moxi after eight days on Mt Edgar. *(Bruce Normand)*

into the rock-ice cleft. We were abseiling steep slabs into the white-out, water freezing onto the ropes, the anchors becoming ever more flaky. Kyle explored a scree-covered ledge in fading light as I pulled our filthy, armour-plated ropes yet again. He pulled hard on a sling. Harder. The rock shifted and the sling blew. We were marooned on the stonefall-prone ledge for the night, but at least it seemed warm at 4300m.

Our eighth day dawned as white as ever, with thickly falling snow adding avalanche danger to the mix. We found an anchor, nearly failed to pull the icy ropes, and downclimbed on through endless steep, loose, snowy boulders and gullies. At 3600m things flattened out, the snow deepened, and we were thrown into a stream bed like the ones we'd climbed up a week earlier. The snow turned to rain. At 3300m the river gave suddenly onto a road. We were down. We walked for a bit, then hitched a ride out from some road workers in a classic Chinese Dongfeng truck. Low in the valley, we had to scramble over a giant landslip, where all trace of the previous road bed had been wiped out. Edgar was being characteristically hostile right to the end. Walking down the main street in Moxi, on firm ground for the first time in a week, we felt a little unsteady.

14. Looking eastward from the base of the crux pitch on Mt Edgar over the foothills of Sichuan. *(Bruce Normand)*

Our route, *The Rose of No-Man's Land* (M6, WI5), is not very direct, but it does seem to be the only safe line on the east face of Edgar. Having visited at the most stable time of year, we cannot recommend this face to any other parties. Our Edgar experience was the very definition of 'full value': a hard line on a hard mountain, climbed in the purest, ground-up alpine style (we left only our abseil slings and two dropped items on the mountain). However, the result for both of us was at best a draw – a borderline-epic adventure in a permanently threatening atmosphere. Despite the facts of our achievement, we came away with no feeling of success, or even satisfaction, just one of relief to have made it off this mountain in one piece.

Summary: An account of the first ascent of the east face of Mt Edgar (6168m), Minya Konka range, Sichuan, China, by Kyle Dempster and Bruce Normand, in an eight-day round trip from the nearest settlement, Moxi, summiting on 12 November 2010; *The Rose of No-Man's Land* (WI5, M6). The climb was nominated for the 2011 Piolets d'Or. Prior to Mt Edgar, the pair made the second ascent of Mt Grosvenor (Riwuqie Feng, 6376m), completing a new route up the central couloir on the west face.

Acknowledgements: Bruce Normand would like to thank the Mount Everest Foundation and the British Mountaineering Council for their financial support.

DAVE WYNNE-JONES

Back From The Dead

Ski-mountaineering in Mongolia

I woke with the relentless wind rattling the flysheet to see Martin looming over my sleeping bag. *I don't share a tent with Martin,* I thought. *What's he doing here?* The last thing I remembered was spooning breakfast cereal out of my mug between attempts to sort out kit for departure. *And where's Iona?*

I tried to ask but the words wouldn't come, tried to sit up but a wave of nausea slapped me back down.

'Just lie back and take it easy.' Martin's voice betrayed his anxiety.

'What happened?' I managed to slur through the barrier of rubberised lips and tongue.

'You passed out. Carbon monoxide we think.'

'Iona?'

'She's OK. Derek is looking after her. Just rest.'

45. Hunters. *(Dave Wynne-Jones)*

Over the next few hours I gradually regained coherence and co-ordination, retained the contents of my stomach, and even managed to eat and drink a little. Iona was less lucky, repeatedly vomiting, but on the other hand she'd never stopped breathing. In a sense I owed my life to her. If the team had not come to investigate the noise of her fitting they might never have dragged us from the fume-filled tent until it was too late. But it was a close thing. They went for the noisy one first, as you might with someone blue and foaming at the mouth, but consequently had no idea how long I had not been breathing when they turned their attention to me. It was a while before they had me breathing on my own.

Base camp was at 3600m in the Tavn Bogd range of the Mongolian Altai and medical help was three days away at Olgii, yet advice was literally at hand when Derek rang through to a medic on the satphone: without oxygen cylinders there was nothing more to be done beyond making sure

46.   Heading up the Potanina glacier towards Khuiten. *(Dave Wynne-Jones)*

we had plenty of fresh air, but there was every chance of recovery in 24 hours.

So how had it happened? Well I've read all the warnings about cooking in tents but frankly the conditions on many expeditions can leave you with no alternative and after a decade of experience there is a certain confidence about doing so, well-ventilated of course. The constant gusting winds of Mongolia were a case in point. The hanging stove system had been modified by the addition of a pan fitted with an integral heat exchanger but had worked perfectly well on a recent expedition to Antarctica and at 2500m at the roadhead and 3000m on the moraine of the Potanina glacier. This reinforced confidence, yet at 3600m we were at the highest altitude at which the system had been used. That difference was crucial: the cooling effect of the snow in the pot, coupled with the lack of oxygen, reinforced the tendency for the increased surface area of the heat exchanger to cool the flame to the point where carbon monoxide generated by combustion was not being burnt off. The usual ventilation was just not enough in those circumstances. It's too easy to put a headache down to altitude and we nearly died.[1]

The following morning, 7 May, we set off for Tavn Bogd Peak (4104m), Iona and I gaining confidence as the exertion took no great toll, though I caught a few searching glances from the others. Cloud gathered on the summits and we climbed into it from an icy saddle on the south ridge.

1 Carbon monoxide poisoning is considered in detail in 'The Silent Killer', by Paul Ramsden, in the Science section of this *AJ*, .p.195.

47. Climbing the north ridge of Khuiten with views into Russia and China; Friendship Peak in the background on the right. *(Dave Wynne-Jones)*

Icy enough for half the team to leave their skis but Iona and I were going well enough to join Howard in carrying ours to attempt a ski descent from the summit. The borders of Russia and China meet with that of Mongolia on this summit and we wandered about sufficiently in the snowstorm that greeted us there that we must all have put a foot into each country, with or without permits. Tricky skiing down the ridge was succeeded by much pleasanter conditions as we popped out under the cloud ceiling, with sunshine as we cruised back to camp. Once the adrenalin subsided there was a tendency for Iona and I to drop off to sleep mid-sentence and we kept a wary eye on each other whilst managing the stove but it was definitely 'game on' again.

This was confirmed when a stormy night gave way to a glorious morning and we set our sights on Khuiten, at 4374m the highest mountain in Mongolia. We skinned north towards Tavn Bogd peak then bore north-west up a crevassed ice valley under Khuiten's north-east face to cross a bergschrund and gain the broad but steep north ridge that forms the border with China. When this became too steep and icy for safe skinning, all but Martin carried skis, booting up to the summit. After taking in the alpine panorama stretching away into China and Russia, it was skis on for a traverse above ice cliffs before plunging down the ridge. Ice lurking under new snow provided a surprise or two but we still left some impres-

48. On the summit of Khuiten (4374m), highest peak in Mongolia.
(Dave Wynne-Jones)

sive tracks. A quick swing around an ice boss on the ridge and we could sneak over the bergschrund to the base of the exposed and sinuous south ridge of Nairamdal (4192m): no ski descent here, we climbed up and down on foot. The long run back to base was less demanding although Martin did manage to find a slot into which he briefly dangled a ski. Back at the tents we basked in the late sunshine, congratulating ourselves on what had been a magical day.

The next day was stormbound and we had a chance to take stock. It was clear that the winter had been very cold and windy but without as much precipitation as usual. Instead of presenting the expected steep but skiable snow faces, the mountains were often clad in hard ice with a high potential fall factor. Our objective to make ski descents of all five of the holy peaks did not look feasible in the case of Naran and Chinggis, so we decided to make the best of the situation by exploring the ski-mountaineering potential of other 4000m peaks in the area.

Over the next few days the weather held and we made very satisfying ascents of Peak 4117m (aka Russian Tent) to the north of Tavn Bogd peak, and Peak 4152 on the border ridge south of Khuiten. This last entailed crossing the south-east ridge of Khuiten quite low down where we found to our surprise that we were not alone in the range. Another party was working its way up the glacier beyond. They turned out to be largely Swiss, led by two French guides based in Chamonix, and had designs on Khuiten's summit via that south-east ridge. From the airy summit ridge of Pik 4152, we watched with some disbelief as they skinned halfway up an approach couloir then carried their skis a couple of kilometres up the ridge.

After skiing, or down-climbing according to nerve, the border ridge of our ascent and descent, they dropped in to our camp on their descent after a 12-hour day and invited us to return the visit at their camp 600m below on the moraine where we might share a beer.

We encountered fresh wolf tracks on the approach to Malchin (4051m), before cramponing up its north-west ridge. On returning to our skis we found Malchin's neighbour across the pass, Peak 3926m, too much of a temptation so we climbed that as well, four of us carrying skis. The ski descent was by a very steep south-facing couloir that provided the most exciting skiing of the expedition after an admittedly scratchy approach off the north-west ridge.

49. Skiing down the north ridge of Khuiten.
(Dave Wynne-Jones)

We then decided to explore the Alexandrov glacier from a new camp at its junction with the Potanina at 3100m, and spent Friday 13th relocating. The new camp was more sheltered and, at a lower altitude, less subject to frosting of the tent overnight. The weather too was noticeably warmer if no less windy.

On 14 May we set off to explore the right hand branch of the Alexandrov glacier, following it all the way to a high crevassed pass east of Naran from which we could see the guided party following our route on Pik 4152. We booted up a short steep ridge to the border summit of Peak 3962m with light snow falling and peered into the Chinese Altai: bags of potential there if only the permits were obtainable. On the way back we diverted from our line of ascent to take a much steeper slope direct, suddenly coming upon the bergschrund and having to make a very rapid decision on the safest line. Relaxed turns and steady schussing took us back down the glacier in fine sunshine.

Next day, fine weather was accompanied by an even stronger wind that swept clouds across the peaks like ships before a storm. The guided party passed our camp on their way to boot up a rubbly couloir on to Naran, but we were intent upon exploring the left branch of the Alexandrov. Later we

0. Howard Pollitt descending the summit ridge of Peak 4152m. *(Dave Wynne-Jones)*

saw them bunched in the rocky narrows as we passed.

The fierce wind was bodied forth in whirling dervishes of spindrift that could hurl past or hit you head on and knock you back on your heels. We dug deep and slogged on with views of the elegant snow spire of Snow Church (4073m) offering some compensation. Eventually a break in the east ridge of Chinggis turned out to be an easy pass. We took it, gaining a little more shelter on the other side. In better conditions this pass could have opened up the prospect of exploring the glaciers south of Chinggis but at that time we could not safely get across a gleaming valley of wind-polished ice. An attempt on the westerly point above the pass was aborted owing to concerns about avalanche danger on the steep snow approach; an ice-axe plunged into the slope at right angles encountered little or no resistance to the full depth of the shaft. In descent the wind ushered us all back to camp.

With time running out we lost a second day to bad weather but on the final day on the glacier Derek and Howard opted for an ascent of Naran on foot following the couloir used by the French team. Without the incentive of a ski descent, the rest of us packed up and headed across the glacier, finding our camel drivers had turned up early. When the climbers joined us the camels were rapidly loaded and we marched the 15km back to the roadhead where the mini-buses were waiting. The head camel driver's wife prepared a delicious meal, all the more welcome in that it was not dehydrated, and soon after we turned in for the night.

An early start meant that we travelled the 200km in one day to Olgi, where a call to head office confirmed that the support team had picked us up a day early or rather we had put two days into one on our exit from the range. An extra day's gentle R & R in Olgi was no problem although it was not until we reached Ulan Bataar that we found a shower that really worked. Until just over 100 years ago Ulan Bataar was little more than a *Ger* camp a few kilometres away from the present site. Now it is a small but modern city, though locals feel that independence and globalisation has sponsored an explosion of corruption. The food here was excellent.

Our agent believed that we were the first self-sufficient ski team to go into the Tavn Bogd and it certainly opened up possibilities with that level of flexibility. It is a fine remote mountain area, eminently suitable for ski-mountaineering with some challenging descents. The Mongolians we met were friendly and helpful with an integrity born of a strong sense of self-reliance. The Eagle hunters we visited by accident on our way into the range made a particularly strong impression.

Summary: An exploratory ski-mountaineering expedition to the Tavn Bogd range of the Mongolian Altai, ascents including Tavn Bogd Peak (4104m), Pik 4152 Khuiten (4374m), Malchin (4051m), Peak 3926m and Peak 3962m.

Acknowledgements: Thanks are due to the team, Derek Buckle, Martin Josten, John Kentish, Iona Pawson, and Howard Pollitt, for their excellent work in keeping us all alive, to Mongolian Expeditions for handling the logistics en route, to the Eagle Ski Club for supporting the expedition and to the Alpine Club for maps of the area.

51.   The team's camel train heading back to the roadhead. *(Dave Wynne-Jones)*

SIMONE MORO

Reflecting on Gasherbrum II

What an extraordinary expedition it was, our ascent of Gasherbrum II early in 2011. Extraordinary because once again I made a dream come true together with my good old friend Denis Urubko, because we lived an unforgettable adventure, and because on this expedition three continents were represented: America by Cory Richards, Asia by Denis, and Europe by me. This climb, and the style we did it in, belongs to the whole world climbing community; the message it sends is addressed to the next generation of climbers from all continents whose predecessors have continually pushed the boundaries in alpinism. The first winter ascent of an 8000er in the history of Karakoram was not a race, nor a competition between nations or individuals. Nor was it a race to set a record, which sooner or later would have been achieved anyway. It represents rather a stage on the progression from a classic expedition style to a different one, more adapted to modern trends, techniques and a philosophy in climbing great mountains.

In the 1970s and '80s, the Poles introduced the concept of winter expeditions in the Himalaya. It was a glorious advance and used the style of the times. However it is not surprising that after 1988 the scene changed. The era of 'competition' between Messner and Kukuczka was over and a new, more 'performance' orientated and 'sport-like' phase of climbing the 8000ers had begun: climbers and alpinism itself had changed. 'Rules' had become clearer in ice and mixed climbing and alpinism was also having to adapt to increasingly crazy weather and seasonal shifts brought about by climate change.

The year 1988 ended with Krzysztof Wielicki's incredible solo ascent of Lhotse. He reached the summit on 31 December, winter indeed, though when the expedition began it was still in autumn. Wielicki's ascent marked a generational shift. It was not the end of attempts to climb in winter, but the Polish monopoly was over and no other nation appeared as an alternative; developments were on ice. Seven of the 8000m giants still awaited winter ascents, but it was not until 17 years later that the Pole Piotr Morawski and I, on an expedition of just four climbers, managed in only 25 days to put an end to this long fast with the first winter ascent of Shishapangma. Our success was repeated in 2009 on Makalu; this time it took just 19 days in alpine style and with only with my friend and comrade Denis Urubko. The ascent brought an end to a 29-year series of winter attempts on Makalu by the world's best climbers.

On Gasherbrum II we repeated this experience for the third time, using the same approach, tactics and lightweight style. After 24 years of attempts, finally, for the first time, an 8000-metre peak in Pakistan and the Karakoram had been summited in winter. Time had again been of the essence, the expedition taking only 22 days and exploiting a very short good weather window of just 30 hours.

In all three of these winter expeditions the decisive factors were speed and tactics, and a very lightweight and small team. I believe that this is the way in which, given the changed climate of the third millennium, it is possible to increase the chances of success of a winter expedition. Alpine style, or at least a light and fast style, must now be seen as the inevitable way to climb a mountain by new routes and in new seasons. The classical way and the heavy style will always be there as alternative and proven methods of climbing, but I hope that their use will be limited to commercial expeditions and on normal routes during the traditional seasons when most expeditions take place; people do have the right to climb way they want.

So up and down Gasherbrum II in six days should be viewed more as an invitation than a simple result. There are already alpinists who regularly climb in a 'modern' and light way – I think immediately of Alberto Iñurrategi and his team, also Mick Fowler, Steve House, Ueli Steck and Marko Prezelj – and I hope that together we will be able to influence other teams to attempt similar high altitude climbs in winter and in an exploratory style.

On GII we were lucky. To survive an avalanche such as the one that caught us on descent was really a half miracle. We were swept 150 metres and partially buried. But I am not aware of great adventures that are not also kissed by a favourable star. We were simply no exception.

Quickly analysing the numbers of the expedition: we were three climbers, three high camps (5100m, 6450m, 6820m), eight-and-a half hours between the last camp and the summit and four-and-a half hours to return to the small tent. Three days of descent with snow often up to the stomach and visibility of no more than three to four metres. More than 10 falls into crevasses, an avalanche, five consecutive nights at high altitude for the summit push and return. Thirty hours of favourable weather (1 February and a half day on the 2nd). Minus 57C the coldest temperature recorded. No oxygen, no high altitude sherpas, one helicopter used for 1.5 hours in order to reach base camp instead of some 200 porters for a 15-day round trip, which would have had a greater environmental impact than the use of the helicopter (consider the physiological costs as well as a litre of kerosene burned per person per day of trekking, plus the risk of frostbite or the impossibility to walk due to snowfall).

I must of course mention Karl Gabl, our infallible meteorologist in Austria, whose forecasts proved accurate despite all the uncertainties. We trusted him 100 percent, accepted our own responsibilities and went for it – via the *Normal Route* up the south-west ridge. We climbed the first two days in horrible weather. It could have been suicide if the forecast had been wrong for 1 and 2 February. Instead, the promised 30 hours of good weather came true. Our tactic was based on that prediction, which turned into reality. Karl has advised me since 2003 and never given me a wrong

52. Simone Moro at 7800 metres on the first winter ascent of Gasherbrum II (8035m) via the *Normal Route* up the south-west ridge in January-February 2011. Gasherbrum I (8068m) in the background.

53.   On the summit of Gasherbrum II on 2 February 2011, left to right, Denis
       Urubko (Kazakh), Simone Moro (Italian), and Cory Richards (American).

forecast. The internet allowed us to communicate and also to tell of our adventure and its significance.

Denis and Cory were perfect. Denis as usual lived up to what I have come to expect of him from past expeditions, sharing fully in our efforts and decisions. Cory was able to adapt, listen to our experiences and put his personal capacities at the service of the common objective. He was amazing, working as photographer and cameraman with a reflex camera and several lenses right up to the summit. For my part, I tried to organise the logistics and the expedition as a whole based on efficiency and a good atmosphere. These two aspects are indispensable to every expedition, knowing where it is good to save energy and where, on the contrary, one should not save if one wants to return from the summit with all fingers and toes and without suffering too much from hunger or exhaustion.

As I write, two expeditions are still at base camp and fighting against bad weather and cold. I hope they can share the virtual podium of first winter ascents in the Karakoram. I wish them a window of good weather and light winds.[1] My wish for the whole world of alpinism is that our climb gives even more energy and motivation to resume great winter climbs. I have been inspired by the great Kukuczka and Wielicki. I hope, perhaps lacking some modesty, my comrades and I have added a little more incentive to this 'cold alpinism' so that it can find again the drive and enthusiasm of those glory days.

With grateful thanks to Marco Onida for translation.

1 Louis Rousseau (Canada) and Gerfried Göschl (Austria) reached 7050m on the *Standard Route* on Gasherbrum I (8068m) south face in mid-March 2011 before being turned back by 80kph winds.

FREDDIE WILKINSON

Spoils of War

The First Ascent of Saser Kangri II

54. The south-west face of Saser Kangri II, eastern Karakoram, showing line of first ascent. X marks 2009 highpoint. *(Freddie Wilkinson)*

The first time I heard of Saser Kangri II was in the summer of 2009. My friend Mark Richey was due to embark for the mountain in a few weeks time and I joined him on a training hike up our local hill, Mount Washington. It was pouring with rain but Mark was psyched. He had recruited a great team of friends – Steve Swenson, Jim Lowther, and Mark Wilford – to attempt the mountain. At 7518m, Saser Kangri II was the second highest unclimbed mountain in the world.

Things didn't go so well and Mark returned that October muttering about impenetrable ice and bivvi ledges that were all too short. It didn't take long before his enthusiasm crept back into the conversation. Mark invited me to join him and Swenson for a rematch in 2011. To further incentivize my decision and spice up the doldrums of base camp, Mark suggested that my wife, Janet, form a women's team to join us and attempt some 6000m rock peaks in the area. After that I really had no choice. Janet had recruited two

55. Mark Richey on the first ascent of Tsok Kangri (6550m) – tackled via a 600m gully with difficulties up to WI4. *(Freddie Wilkinson)*

crackerjack partners, Emilie Drinkwater and Kirsten Kramer, to join her. Over eight years of dating and climbing together, Janet and I have slowly perfected an approach that works for us on expeditions: we travel and share base camp, but prefer to climb in separate teams, usually with partners of the same sex. This relieves a lot of the pressure a major alpine expedition can put on a relationship and frees us up to genuinely enjoy each other's company along the way.

We arrived in Delhi at the beginning of July. After paying the necessary visit to the Indian Mountaineering Foundation we flew on to Leh, gateway to the eastern Karakoram. Owing to the arcane nature of IMF bureaucracy, a joint permit is required of any mountaineering team desiring to visit the Eastern Karakoram. This means that for every foreign climber, an Indian national must be listed on the paperwork. There are two solutions: join forces with a group of Indian mountaineers or *hire* your Indians. Since we didn't know any local climbers our trekking agent and logistical maverick Chewang Motup of Rimo Expeditions had arranged for six hardy Ladakhi guides to join our team.

From Leh it was a day's jeep ride over the Kardung La to reach the Nubra valley. Once an idyllic and isolated passage connecting South Asia to the Karakoram pass and the trade routes of central Asia, Nubra has been transformed by the conflict between India and Pakistan over the nearby Siachen

56.   Steve Swenson and Mark Richey follow Freddie Wilkinson's lead on the summit ridge of Tsok Kangri. *(Freddie Wilkinson)*

glacier into a bustling centre of army depots, heliports, and truck convoys. Were it not for this conflict and peculiar wrinkle of history in 1985, Saser Kangri would never have made it unclimbed into the 21st century.

***

The Saser group is the easternmost massif among the 7000-metre mountains in the Karakoram. Just to the south lies the Nubra valley, which drains the 43-mile long Siachen glacier, the largest glacier in the entire Karakoram and territory fiercely held by India as part of the larger regional conflict over Kashmir.

After Pakistan and India fought an open war in 1970, a ceasefire was negotiated in Simla in 1972. The two countries agreed to maintain a Line of Control between their hostile armies. The line was carefully surveyed and recorded from the south to north to a point northeast of Srinagar, where the survey commission deemed the mountains beyond to be impassable. From this coordinate point, designated NJ9842, the two nations agreed to an arbitrary line running 'thence north to the glaciers', presumably until it reached the Chinese frontier.

In the mid-1970s the government of Pakistan began issuing permits to mountaineering expeditions to visit the Siachen glacier. The Indian military soon caught wind and sent its own mountaineering expeditions to the

57.   Mark Richey approaching the summit of Tsok Kangri. *(Freddie Wilkinson)*

region, even going so far as to claim the first ascents of several mountains that had previously been ascended by Japanese teams who approached the Siachen over the Blifond La with Pakistani support. Tensions simmered until 1984. Then word reached the Indians that Pakistan had issued a permit to yet another Japanese expedition to attempt Rimo I, a 7300-metre mountain located *below* the Siachen glacier, 30 miles farther to the east. This, the Indian government felt, was a step too far. That April, Indian Armed Forces launched Operation Meghdoot and preemptively seized the Siachen glacier by military force.

The next year the Indo-Tibetan Border Police (ITBP) organized a joint expedition with five Japanese climbers to make the first ascent of Saser Kangri II. Fifty miles upvalley, firefights flared as the Pakistanis unsuccessfully tried to dislodge the Indian commandos holding the Bilifond La and the Sia La, two critical passes on the rim of the Siachen basin. As the conflict deepened, success on Saser Kangri II meant much more to the Indians than bragging rights – it became a vehicle to buttress their country's territorial claims. This was alpinism for political purpose, or 'oropolitics', as the mountain historian Joydeep Sircar termed it in *Himalaya Sameeksha.*

By the end of August, the ITBP had established four camps on a circuitous route up the mountain's north-west face. The line included a crux rock gully that demanded more than 1100m of fixed rope. On 30 August a group of four climbers carried loads up the rock gully to stock camp III. Returning to camp I, one member of the party, Tsering Angchuk, briefly detached from the fixed lines to retrieve a pair of goggles he had dropped earlier in the climb.

In an official report, Hukam Singh, Commandant in the ITBP and leader of the expedition, wrote: 'Tsering Angchuk had barely moved a few paces away from the fixed rope; he slipped to his death over a vertical rock face within seconds.' Angchuk's broken body was recovered and all team members retreated to advance basecamp for three days of rest. The poor weather suddenly stabilized on 3 September, catching the team off guard, and they hurried back up the mountain 'with renewed zeal', according to the report. Four days later, six climbers—five Indians and one Japanese— left camp IV for the summit. Two turned back, but the remaining four pressed on through a final rock band that consumed one of their climbing ropes and most of the afternoon.

'Precisely at 5.30pm,' Commandant Singh wrote, 'all four of them stepped on the hitherto virgin summit of Saser Kangri II (west).'

On the books, Saser Kangri II had been climbed. But had it?

Singh's qualifier— the top of SKII 'west' – cited a hitherto undoc- umented summit. A note from the editors of the *Himalayan Journal* at the end of the article explained: 'The peak is marked by a point on the eastern end of an almost one-kilometre- long summit plateau. The western end of the plateau is also reported by this expedition to be of the similar height. It is felt, after study of available photographs

58. Janet Wilkinson fits crampons at the base of a 6100m spire, climbed for the first time with husband Freddie and named by the them as Saser Linga. *(Freddie Wilkinson)*

and maps, that perhaps Saser Kangri II has two peaks, west and east.'

To cover up the fact that they had failed to reach the highest point of the summit ridge, Hukam Singh simply invented another mountain. Later, Indian military maps would denote the western end of SKII's summit ridge as being three contour lines, or 60 to 80m, lower than the east summit. Subsequent surveys of the world's highest mountains would cite 'Saser Kangri II East' as the 49th highest mountain in the world, labelling it unclimbed. Most lists don't bother to include Saser Kangri II West as an independent mountain.

***

We were grateful to leave the noise and dust behind as we set off on the three-day approach march up the Sakang Lumpa gorge. Rising 2500m in less than 15 miles, the hike was a spectacular transition into the mountains.

59. Janet Wilkinson on the spire of Saser Linga. *(Freddie Wilkinson)*

Our first night in basecamp, Mark uncorked a bottle of whisky and poured six glasses. 'I'd like to wish everyone a safe and successful expedition,' he said, raising his glass. 'And I'd like to quote a famous climber, Roger Baxter-Jones, who said, "We go to the mountains and do three things – we come back alive, we come back friends, and we go to the top. *And in that order*."'

During the 2009 expedition, Mark, Steve and crew had pioneered an approach to the South Schukpa glacier by way of a previously untravelled 6000m pass. All in all, it was about 10 miles from our basecamp to reach the foot of the south face of Saser Kangri II, and much of that terrain was snowy glacier. In 2009 the team had slogged across this route a half dozen times; in 2011 we brought skis – a decision that proved critical.

The south face of Saser Kangri II is concave and defined by a massive couloir that divides the mountain, the true summit being located on the eastern (right-hand) end of the summit ridge. Our line of ascent would follow the right margin of the couloir before breaking right through a rock-band to reach a snow ramp that slices through the steep granite walls of the upper mountain. During the 2009 attempt, locating adequate bivvi ledges had been a major problem. For 2011, Mark came prepared with several ultra-light hammocks he had designed to catch snow and debris to widen the ledges.

Our original plan was to acclimatise by climbing up the lower half of the route to test conditions and perhaps install a bivvi ledge just below the rock-band. However, the July heat foiled our plan: rockfall and avalanches flushed down the couloir incessantly and we bailed from only eight pitches up. With nothing to do until temperatures got colder, we decided to focus our attention on the myriad attractive 6000m peaks in the area. First, Mark, Steve and I bagged a 6500m peak we dubbed Tsok Kangri via a spectac-

ular 600m gully with difficulties to WI 4+. The next week, Kirsten Kramer and Emilie Drinkwater climbed a 6300m mountain they would name Pumo Kangri (WI 2). The next day, Janet and I had a wonderful outing on a rock spire reaching 6100m just above our advanced basecamp we named Saser Linga (5.9+). Lastly, Mark, Janet, Emilie, Kirsten, and I

60.   'Crackerjack climbers' Emilie Drinkwater (left) and Kirsten Kramer at base camp. *(Freddie Wilkinson)*

romped up a 6600m snow peak, dubbed the Stegasaur, which Mark and co had attempted in 2009.

By the time the dust settled from all this activity it was the second week in August, and time to get down to business. Steve had been inexplicably brought down by a sinus infection. After a week recuperating in Nubra, however, he felt ready for action.

We left our advance basecamp early on the morning of 21 August and re-climbed the eight easy pitches of snow to the 'Launch Pad', our high point from a month earlier. The next morning we set out at 2am to negotiate the couloir in the coldest temperatures of the day. By early afternoon we had arrived at the rock-band, but were having a hard time locating anything remotely resembling a suitable bivvi spot. In a moment of inspiration, I decided to continue in the hope of finding better terrain above. Two hours later we were above the rock-band, but still not finding anywhere inviting to spend the night. Mark's hour had arrived.

'No problem,' he said. 'I'll turn this place into the Taj Mahal.' In rapid succession, he deployed not one but two of his ice-hammock inventions. The main problem with constructing any bivvi site is always a lack of

61. Above: Janet Wilkinson on the summit ridge of a previously unclimbed 6600m peak named by the group as Stegosaur. *(Freddie Wilkinson)*
62. Below: Mark Richey and Steve Swenson follow Wilkinson's lead on the lower slopes of Saser Kangri II. *(Freddie Wilkinson)*

material. As Mark held each hammock open, I shovelled, chopped and occasionally clawed at every patch of snow and ice within reach and tossed it down to him. The ice hammock began to fill with the debris, forming a

63. Mark Richey approaches the ice chimney half way up the face of Saser Kangri II. *(Freddie Wilkinson)*

wall that we stomped on to pack down. Soon Mark was setting the second hammock on top of the first. Steve was oddly idle while we worked, and confessed to being a little more tired than usual. He busied himself melting water with the stove instead. By early evening we had constructed a ledge: if somewhat less than five-star accommodation it at least offered enough space for the three of us to lay down and get some rest.

The next morning I led a half dozen or so pitches up the upper ramp. It was a perfect day and as the mountain unveiled its secrets we knew we were getting close. The highlight was undoubtedly the Escape Hatch, a short but interesting mixed pitch that exited us from the dead-end couloir we had been following and gave access to snow slopes we knew would lead to the summit ridge. The one thing we weren't talking about was Steve's condition.

Next morning we left our bivvi tent anchored under a cosy rock over-hang and struck out for the summit. Mark led three pitches on insecure sugar snow weaving between rock outcroppings. The weather was perfect, yet again. At the base of the summit ridge I took over and began the long, slow grind towards the top. Each step revealed more of the Karakoram's incredible topography. I stopped about 100m short of the summit and told Mark to go first. From the beginning this had been Mark's project, his inspiration, and I knew how much these last few steps meant to him. He plodded on, and then he stopped. Then he screamed: a wild, unintelligible cry, just raw energy.

We returned to our high bivvi by late afternoon. With 30 rappels sepa-rating us from the glacier, it was important to rest, rehydrate, and prepare for the descent next morning. But Steve's condition, which had been a nagging background presence up until the summit, abruptly took centre

64. Steve Swenson on the summit ridge of Saser Kangri II. The long receding glacier is the North Shukpa Kungchang. *(Freddie Wilkinson)*

stage. Over the course of our four-day ascent his infection had returned and migrated from his upper respiratory tract down into his lungs. Now, as we huddled in our bivvi tent at 7000m, lima bean-sized snots began to clog his trachea. When he lay down he couldn't breathe. Only by sitting upright and constantly coughing could he cope.

Clouds swirled around next morning as we broke camp and prepared the first rappel. The task at hand was complicated by the fact that one of our ropes had been severely cut the day before: on every rappel we each were obliged to stop and pass a knot to continue the full 60m. Since most of the terrain we were descending was moderate ice, it should've been easy to find a stance to un-weight the rope and pass the knot. But Steve struggled. We explained to him to first tie and clip into a slackened 'Jesus knot,' *then* unclip his Reverso and re-attach it below the break. About six rappels down, I looked up to see the horrifying sight of Steve standing completely untethered as he laboriously tried to re-thread his rappel device below the knot. We chastised him for the lapse but it was obvious Steve was not his usual, thoughtful self.

Mark took over leading the rappels halfway down. Then, as we slowly made our way off the mountain that afternoon, a barrage of rockfall poured down the couloir, catching us in the open, all attached to a single ice screw.

We skied into advance basecamp late that night. It felt less like a triumphant victory than the end of a forced march. Mark and I quickly passed into deep, dreamless sleep – only to be awoken sometime after 3am by Steve, whose infection had now reached dire straits.

'I'm having trouble breathing,' Steve said. 'I'm getting scared. This feels really serious.'

Steve couldn't lie down without breaking into a coughing fit. And when he coughed the snot from his lungs clogged his trachea and he couldn't breathe. He appeared to be about to asphyxiate. Soon he stopped talking altogether. We called his doctor on the satellite phone. We handed Steve a

pen and notebook. He wrote: *If I try to hack this stuff up could I choke to death?*
'Yes,' said the doctor. 'That's a possibility.'

As the morning light seeped onto the South Schukpa glacier, Mark and I took turns caring for Steve and hitting the satellite phone, calling a string of contacts we hoped might expedite a helicopter evacuation. We knew that the Indian Army maintained a squadron of Lama high-altitude helicopters to resupply positions on the Siachen glacier. It should have been a simple matter of getting the mission approved by the right people within the military chain of command, but in India getting permission for anything is never simple. Meanwhile, with the help of several of our Ladakhi climbing-sherpas who had met us at ABC, we walked Steve around in circles, built him a recliner chair of snow and skis so that he could more comfortably rest upright, and carefully fed him mugs of lukewarm tea.

'Someone here wants to talk to you,' Chewang Motup of Rimo Expeditions told Mark when we finally got through to him in Leh. Mark's weather-worn face cracked into an unexpected smile when he heard the voice on the other end of the phone. It was his wife Teresa. After rendezvousing with Janet, Kirstin, and Emilie in Delhi, she had travelled on to Leh to meet us at the end of our expedition.

65. Mark Richey, Steve Swenson and Freddie Wilkinson on the summit of Saser Kangri II (7518m). *(Freddie Wilkinson)*

'If there's one person who can make this helicopter happen for us, it's my wife,' Mark said.

Late afternoon we heard the distant thump of a helicopter, dispatched courtesy of the Siachen Pioneers Squadron. 'Your limo is here,' Mark said, turning to Steve, his face awash with relief.

A minute later Steve Swenson was gone (to make a quick recovery in Leh) and the valley returned to stillness.

Summary: An account of the first ascent of Saser Kangri II (7518m) – and other climbs – in the Indian Karakoram by Mark Richey, Steve Swenson and Freddie Wilkinson. *The Old Breed*, SKII south-west face, 1700m, WI4, M3; 21-24 August 2011. The ascent was recognised with a Piolet d'Or at the 2012 award ceremony in Chamonix.

Acknowledgements: Heartfelt thanks to the brave pilots of the Siachen Pioneers Squadron and everyone who helped with the evacuation of Steve Swenson.

Comment

66.   John Fairley, *Piz Zupo & Piz Bernina,* watercolour, 590x835mm, 1995

PHIL BARTLETT

Is Mountaineering a Sport?

Amusement, diversion, fun. This was the definition of sport offered by the first dictionary I consulted in preparation for this lecture, and if we accept it then there is at least a sporting chance that we will all be able to agree: mountaineering is a sport. But it is not a definition that sits easily with much of what sport is currently thought to be. This talk is part of a series on Philosophy and Sport timed to mark the London Olympics, and amusement and fun are probably not the first words to spring to mind there, certainly not for the competitors. They may be a part of it, but I don't think it unreasonable to think more immediately of commerce, competition, achievement. So this evening I need to consider mountaineering within that context. I also want to make clear at the outset that I shall take mountaineering to mean not just the climbing of high snow-covered peaks, but mountain travel and exploration, and simply recreational mountain walking. There doesn't need to be anything technical involved. At the same time, I must include rock-climbing within my brief, and for at least two reasons. One is that rock-climbing and mountaineering are closely connected historically. In its early years, alpine climbing often led to rock climbing, the latter being seen as geographically convenient training for 'the real thing' – namely, the annual alpine holiday. When I was a teenager in the 1970s the influence went the other way: I began with rock-climbing in the Lake District and proceeded to alpine climbing. And secondly, rock-climbing and mountaineering are administratively and politically connected. I suspect that the former, which in Britain as often as not doesn't take place in mountains at all, now absorbs the major part of the public funds devoted to these matters. And it is predominantly on the British experience that I want to draw.

I'd like to start with some history and what one might call the traditional mountaineering outlook with which it is associated. Strictly speaking, mountaineering has no definable beginning. There must always have been farmers who found they had to climb some wretched hill, taking time they could ill afford to rescue a recalcitrant sheep; military men who were ordered to reach some strategic high point and spy out the land; Himalayan traders who found themselves delving ever deeper into mountain country to drum up business; and so on. This is not to say that these people didn't find in the mountains unexpected rewards; rewards that we would entirely understand. It is not even to say they went unwillingly. But broadly speaking we can say that they were driven by necessity whereas mountaineers in the usual sense

First delivered as a lecture on 27 January 2011 in London as one of series organised by the Royal Institute of Philosophy on the theme of 'philosophy and sport'.

of the word are not; they do not have to climb, explore, sit in snowdrifts, admire the view. They choose to do these things. Immediately, then, one has the characteristic of choice, and that means privilege. If one adds to that the fact that mountaineering is demanding of time or money – one generally needs one or the other, and both are welcome – then it is not surprising that mountaineering as we understand it today grew out of increasing affluence in the West and was for a long time dominated by a social elite.

For how long was this the case? From its beginnings in the late 18th century until well into the 20th. Alpine climbing began as the playground of an economically comfortable and culturally sophisticated group, which is part of the reason the British played a leading role despite having no alpine-sized mountains of their own. It was pushed forward by, among others, clerics and schoolmasters, because of the disposable time these groups enjoyed.

That of course leaves unexplained why they should have chosen mountains. They might have chosen basketball, or the discus, or salmon fishing, or ocean sailing. It's not hard to see the odd ones out here. Mountaineering, fishing and sailing certainly have things in common, and one very important thing: all of them are the expression of a belief in the inherent good of the outdoors, the worth of communing with an unsullied nature. And no doubt some of those who might have become mountaineers in Whymper's day did indeed take up fishing or sailing. Some did all three. All this springs from and mixes with wider movements in thought and belief: with Wordsworth and Romantic poetry, with muscular Christianity and the university reading party, not least with the requirements of an empire which throughout the 19th century needed recruits who were excited by the prospect of adventure in remote mountain country. My thesis, then, would be that we can identify a set of values and beliefs to associate with this period which are those of privilege and a degree of sophistication. We could reasonably expect that if we put the question 'Is mountaineering a sport?' to one of its protagonists, he would not merely deny it, but deny it vociferously. Mountaineering, he might say – and it probably would be a he – is more than mere 'sport'. It is more important. Not in the sense of filthy lucre, or that embarrassing tendency to gush that one's interest is not in fact merely an interest, but 'a way of life', but in the sense of subtler, deeper.

Now, quite apart from generalisation, for which I want to apologise to those who have an expert knowledge of these things, we have with all this the usual problems of historiography. It's hard to know quite how accurate this view of mountaineering history really is. But it's not a complete fiction. We have the evidence of the written word. In club journals, newsletters, and books we can trace a literary achievement whose characteristics are distinctly those of an educated and privileged class. It is often claimed – by mountaineers needless to say – that mountaineering has a more distinguished literature than any other sport or pastime. This may be correct. Certainly, the best of what is written in the major journals stands comparison with the best essay writing in the English language. Mountaineering has produced a huge library of books, and a significant number of them are of lasting importance.

In addition, I am old enough to have seen something of the 'grand old men' of traditional mountaineering at first hand. I remember meeting people like John Hunt, leader of the first ascent of Everest, David Cox, the eminence gris of Oxford mountaineering when I was a student, and Charlie Houston, the leader of the tragic and heroic 1953 American expedition to the world's second highest mountain, K2.

Figures such as these always put me in mind of the immortal remark of Maurice Herzog, leader of the French expedition that in 1950 put himself and Louis Lachenal on the summit of the first of the world's 8000 metre peaks to be climbed: 'there are other Annapurnas in the lives of men.' So much so that it is tempting to suppose that the traditional mountaineer had a civilising sense of proportion that is lost on his modern counterparts. Tempting, but perilous, I think. Less perilous, I hope, to suggest that a sense of proportion is characteristic of the best, or perhaps I should say the most admirable, mountaineers of every epoch.

So, if we grant at least some truth to this image of the 'traditional' mountaineer and 'traditional' mountaineering, is there a distinctly different, 'modern' outlook with which to compare it? Well, I'm not sure how distinct it is, but I think in contemporary approaches we can sense differences. In Britain, one way to do this might be to compare past issues of, say, the *Alpine Journal*, published continuously in London since 1863, with contemporary issues of *Summit*, the house magazine of the British Mountaineering Council. The BMC is not the governing body of British mountaineering because there is no governing body, but it is as close to one as exists, a government-sponsored bureaucracy which does valuable work representing mountaineers' and rock-climbers' interests, in particular over the ever-present problems of open access to rock climbing venues and wild country. Thirty years ago the head of the BMC was the general secretary; he or she is now called the chief executive officer, which may or may not be significant. The umbrella organisation of such national bodies is the International Mountaineering and Climbing Federation, whose website informs us that it belongs to, I quote, 'the group of International Federations who agree to be guided by the Olympic Charter and who recognise the authority of the International Olympic Committee', something which you may or may not find disturbing. Like most house magazines, the BMC's is image conscious and slick. It is full of how-to adverts; not just how to climb, but how not to kill yourself in the process, how to rescue yourself from a crevasse if you fall in, how to read clouds and come up with a weather forecast, how to make yourself as comfortable as possible during a bivouac, how to plan your activities, how to train for them, how to up your standard. All the sorts of things that my generation, or at least my social milieu, didn't know about 30 years ago, still doesn't know about, and no doubt should. Though in defence, the traditionalist might argue that there are so many things one should know that if one insisted on waiting until one knew them all, one would never actually get around to going climbing. The traditional mountaineer is an amateur and the modern a professional, and in at least two senses. As I have implied, the traditional mountaineer was assumed either to have a 'proper' job, often in education, or to have a private income; and in any event there was little market for the professional, except in exceptional cases such as Everest. That has changed. The huge increase in outdoor leisure in recent decades has created an audience, and there is now a cadre of professional mountaineers to satisfy it. But when all is said and done, only a small proportion of mountaineers, even today, earn a living from it. A more widespread aspect of professionalism is something hard to define, but perhaps connected to a greater sense that time is limited and must be used efficiently. It involves an increased focus on planning, including training, and being generally well organised. And if all this preparedness backfires and starts to blunt the excitement that all mountaineers crave, then in *Summit* magazine the modern will find further courses advertised that are likely to be of interest to today's multi-activity outdoor enthusiast – paragliding, kayaking, deep-sea diving, horse riding, sailing. Though interestingly, no salmon-fishing so far as I can see.

To caricature outrageously, we have on the one hand the slightly unworldly traditionalist, badly dressed, with a copy of Horace in the rucksack, a bumbling enthusiasm, and an unspoken assumption that finding himself here, in this previously unexplored corner of the Himalaya, with a few other chaps, some jolly keen Sherpas and a couple of months to conquer everything in sight, is really no more than the natural order of things; and on the other the 'modern', resplendent in day-glo Lycra, topo guide to hand, with a planned and steely competence and complete focus on one very particular 30 foot cliff of white limestone, where the next chapter in the history books is about to be written.

Some caveats are necessary at this point. I have talked about the 'traditional' and the 'modern', but these are convenient designations, which cannot be tied too closely to historical eras. Perhaps Bonington was one of the first of the moderns, but then what about a figure like Frank Smythe, already writing books of his adventures with a wider public in mind in the 1930s, or Captain John Noel, filming on Everest long before the modern circus arrived? And it works the other way round too – the contemporary climber who is really a throwback. What of a figure like Stephen Venables, extant in this audience and so presumably a modern in the flesh, and certainly a modern in that he earns his living from mountaineering, and yet in character and culture so reminiscent of the great presidents of the Alpine Club of London in the 19th century? Or Julian Freeman-Attwood, in all essentials an imperial explorer on the borders of British India in the days of the Great Game?

But most importantly, I am not in this lecture trying to make a judgement of whether the traditionalist or the modern is 'better'. I am interested in discussing what 'is', and perhaps what is going to be, not what ought to be. And that for the very simple reason that I am unclear what criteria one would use to decide on right and wrong, ought and ought not. It seems to me that even the incomparable Kant became unconvincing here. I hope any professional moral philosophers in the audience will forgive me, but I am not clear of the possible objective basis for these things beyond two – and two which, typically it seems, offer very different perspectives. If you believe in God, then God decrees right and wrong, ought and ought not; that is a part of his purpose. You follow his law, and there is no more to be said. Or, like me, you are a Darwinian, in which case you might be led to conflate an 'is' with an 'ought', to believe that the way things are becomes in itself their justification. This position is generally regarded as fallacious, and I shall agree. Having thereby rejected two possible sources of a moral system, I am left with sophistry, the belief that right and wrong, ought and ought not, are based, if not purely on fashion, then very largely on the everyday practicalities of a society and its convenience. What we are used to, what we have imbibed from those around us, becomes the basis of our moral system. Works like Francis Fukuyama's *The End of History* or John Rawls's *A theory of Justice* could only have been written by contemporary liberal intellectuals; in them, the values of contemporary liberal intellectuals emerge, against all statistical probability, as the objectively 'best' values by which a society can live. But that they are perilously close to being no more than statements of fashion is not the problem; the problem is that their authors would like to think otherwise. Again, the difference between naturalism and sophistry, as I understand the terms, is that the former is in the camp of those who believe that the moral truth exists in some absolute space, rather like a mathematical axiom, if only it can be found; whereas sophistry, so easily criticised as a resignation of moral courage, a degeneration into mere laissez-faire, is asserting that the very notion of an absolute moral system is intellectually incoherent; that morality must, of its nature, relate to life as we find it.

So, returning from this rather presumptuous foray into serious philosophy, it is perfectly true, and spectacularly unsurprising, that I have my own prejudices about how mountaineering should be practised, and perfectly true that these conform, as one would expect, and to a laughably high degree of accuracy, with the ideas and values of my own formative years – that is, British mountaineering circa 1970 to 1980. This much is natural I think, and not a problem. It would only become a problem if I assumed my imbibed attitudes were somehow 'right'. I hope I have made this clear. I am attracted, for a variety of reasons, to a particular way of doing things. I have no evidence, or even belief, that my own preferences are really 'better' than others.

Or have I?

Mountains deliver certain experiences to us, including some that we might find difficult to experience elsewhere. If we can show that a certain way of doing things, certain attitudes, deliver these experiences more fully or more reliably than other ways, then we might argue that this is the 'right' way. So what are these experiences?

Some of you will know that I have a theory about this, and I want now to summarise it, though I accept that any theory has disadvantages. It can be accused of being too analytical, if not reductionist. As I have indicated, mountain literature contains plenty of successful attempts to convey the experience of mountaineering, and without theorising. Amongst contemporary authors, Al Alvarez produced such an evocation in his book *Feeding the Rat*, the rat, who is male incidentally, even when inhabiting the body of a woman, being some vague amalgam of all those frustrated, craving, bored, freedom-loving aspects of the human psyche that want to throw off convention and safety and indulge in a little hair-raising adventure from time to time. The rat may have a fast or a slow metabolism – I am tempted to say it gets slower as one gets older – but sooner or later he will demand a meal. To my mind, this is an arresting and effective image. So I am not trying to suggest that in the attempt to explain mountaineering an analysis is superior to a literary approach. Rather that the two are complementary.

In any event, the theory: human beings are complex animals, with desires and sources of meaning in their lives which if not downright contradictory are sometimes very close to it. Two of these I believe form the essence of mountaineering; but more that that, mountains give us the opportunity to experience both of them simultaneously. And it is in that simultaneous as opposed to sequential experience that we can find our highest degree of contentment, satisfaction, or exhilaration.

One of them, which I will call 'the return to the primitive', flows from the arena that is mountain country. That is, we operate in places which inevitably take us back to a more archaic way of living and thinking, and this seems to satisfy a deep-seated need – not in everyone I hasten to add, but in many of us. Dr Johnston, not simply on the basis of prejudice but even after travelling to the Scottish Highlands with Boswell, seems to have been quite clear that he preferred London, and he's not alone. Nevertheless, if we believe in the influence of the past, not just culturally but genetically, then it is plausible that wild and remote country feeds into us in a profound way. We might regard much of this as a spiritual experience. In mountains we are returned to fundamental things in terms of what we do – getting comfortable, trying to stay safe, relying on each other, making camp, these things often being repeated day after day in the same way, hence attaining the flavour of ritual. But also we are reminded of philosophical truths – or simply truths. The mountains are big and don't care about us. Once, in past centuries, we might have anthropomorphised them, or filled them with dragons, as indeed was the case in the European Alps pretty much until mountaineering began, and in this sense we cannot, today, relive the mental lives of our ancestors. But so far as reminding ourselves of our insignificance is concerned, we can. There is a change in perspective, a change in the value of things, which soaks into us in wild country. By just being there and undertaking the tasks which need to be done, we engage in what the darling of British mountaineering in the 1970s, Pete Boardman, called 'serious play' – a good phrase, because mountaineering is serious, that is profound, in a way which a theme park is not. But it is also, for us, all play. We visit a more archaic world on a temporary basis, with the knowledge that we can return to our western lifestyle at any time we wish. What we are doing is drawing the benefits of a more natural way of living, but in general without paying the price that the true primitive pays. So there is nothing in the philosophy I am propounding that requires us to idealise or sentimentalise the rural poor, or the primitive, or to rail against western materialism. We are not required to follow Rousseau and arrive at the flawed concept of the noble savage, or even more disastrously to sail with Margaret Mead to the South Seas and fantasise over Samoa. We can remain with our feet on the ground and admit that this is all fantasy, yet still claim that wild country, and being forced to operate in it, satisfies us. And even those who do not want to claim that much can at least agree that it's all one hell of a contrast. There are so many fewer people out there than in Oxford Street. The sounds of man are less, even if the sound of the wind is greater. There is less to do, but more time to do it properly. In fact there is altogether less confusion – assuming a refusal to countenance satellite phones, laptops and other such impertinent paraphernalia. There is suffering, but arguably less anguish. There is in some senses less freedom, but thereby less stress. You do not decide what to do – you do what has to be done. You decided days or months ago what you were going to do – climb this peak, cross that pass. All you have to do now is get on with it. And most of that is already defined – put on your boots, get moving, put up the tent, make supper. And in the unlikely event there is any time left, you can always read all those dauntingly long Russian novels you've always intended to get around to.

All of this amounts in large degree to a lesson in humility, an encouragement to downgrade the importance of one's own ego. But shadowing it in mountaineering is the complete reverse – the celebration of the ego, the explicit goal of giving it free rein. Mountaineering is an egocentric pursuit, an opportunity for the individual to assert him or herself not only against nature, but against other people. The image of the mountain climber, ice axe raised, standing in triumph on top of some conquered snowy summit, is accurate. He has proved he can 'do', that determination leads to results, that he has climbed higher and further than the competition. If the humility of the Taoist ideal leads to peace, it is equally true that exercising the muscles of the ego, the sense of being a big cheese, leads to exhilaration.

It is an obvious thought to connect return to the primitive to what I have called the 'traditional' approach, and the egocentricity of individual achievement with the 'modern'. But the merest consideration of history shows us that this is false. The great climbers and explorers of the golden age – these people were as egocentric as Messner, or Bonington, or any of the teenage superstars of today. And I know of no evidence to support the notion that today's climbers are any less appreciative of wild country and of a return to the primitive in general than their predecessors were. In fact, as you listen to this lecture you may be beginning to feel, as I do, that a historical division into traditional and modern is looking distinctly tenuous. A neat division into categories is always a pitfall for intellectuals, and perhaps that's the case here. Furthermore, I think there is something in the role of commentator, as opposed to participant, that encourages one to overstate change. If as a commentator one considers, say, the number of people involved in climbing, if one looks at the statistics, then yes, the numbers have gone up dramatically. It's true that if you go to Stanage you will find more people there on an average weekday than there used to be on a Bank Holiday Sunday. But as a participant, it feels less dramatic. Many of the mountain crags in the Lake District have fewer visits today than they did in the 1970s. In any case, when you are climbing your world contracts to a few feet; there is you, your companion, and the immediate surroundings. What is happening globally is not part of the experience.

So if an historical progression from traditional to modern is to be rejected, is there nevertheless a change in focus within the experience of each individual? I have argued that a return to the primitive and an expression of egocentricity are both essential to the fullest satisfaction mountains can deliver, and furthermore that our most treasured moments occur when we experience them together. But that does not mean they need be equally important throughout our lives. And in general, I don't think they are. When we are young the satisfaction of ego is more likely to take centre stage. This is the time when we are ambitious, not in that private sense that endures, that sense in which throughout life we take pleasure in our achievements, however modest, but in the public sense, the sense that we want to be recognised. It is this desire for recognition perhaps that weakens with time, though it can be difficult to know if the weakening is really due to age or rather to assuaged hunger. I remember looking up in the searing cold of an Arctic dawn at the first unclimbed mountain I had ever confronted. I was young, and exceedingly motivated to succeed. But was I motivated because I was young, or because this game was new? These days I still like to bag unclimbed peaks when I get the chance, but I am beginning to wonder about the likelihood of ever quite recapturing the excitement, the exhilaration, the sheer joy, of that first time. Is that because I am older, or because I have been there? How would I feel had I never climbed anything new? Well, the mountaineering world is full of experienced people who have never climbed anything new, and I don't get the impression they are all full of angst at the fact. They are older, and if not necessarily wiser then at least more knowing. In youth, things are seen too much in black and white. So and so climbs some untrodden peak, explores some undiscovered country, and is thereby a few rungs further up the ladder. The more experienced realise it was probably largely a matter of luck anyway. When I read *Summit*, I sometimes catch myself becoming irritated at yet another enviable adventure gleefully recounted by the same person as last month. How do they manage to get so much done, these people? Then I recall that the person in question was in the education business, and that their age has made them one of the blessed generation; public servants who were able to retire years early on a full pension. Luck, you see. Something similar applies to most, if not all, achievement. Did the early Everest climbers really represent the best that Britain could produce – out of several tens of millions of people? Of course not. But when the social, educational and financial criteria that I have alluded to were taken into account, organisations like the Royal Geographical Society and the Alpine Club, organisations that determined who should go on these jollies, really had a remarkably limited pool of people to draw on.

Bearing all this in mind, it is not hard to see why there is a sense in which mountaineers believe that mountaineering should not be taken too seriously, just as there is a different sense in which they insist that it should. It should be taken seriously to the extent that it has the power to satisfy profound human needs. And also because it is dangerous. And yet part of that danger is statistical and unavoidable, a servant of fate, and what might be required here is not so much seriousness as acceptance. Hemingway famously remarked that there were only three sports: bullfighting, motor racing and mountaineering, all the rest being mere games. Part of what he meant I think was that in all three the individual, without having anything like the complete information one would like, must make decisions and then accept the consequences. Consequences which may not be to one's liking, of course. A premature appointment with death, for instance. Jumping the queue, as it were. Well, bad luck! As in history generally, 'stuff happens'. Of course mankind can 'do', of course our effort, courage, expertise, matters; but none of this is in itself decisive. Luck, or the lack of it, remains forever at the heart of events. Mountaineering is profound in what it promises, and at times delivers, and yet we should not take our own part in it too seriously. A certain lightness of touch is appropriate. If the process itself is valuable, the level of achievement to which it leads is empty.

It's hard not to feel that the Olympic outlook on sport is pretty much the complete reverse of this. I find it hard to see that beach volleyball, say, satisfies any profound human needs – unless we include the voyeuristic desires of men – yet how seriously they all take it. Look down on these ants from windswept heights; some running round and round, others throwing things as far as they can, yet others batting balls backwards and forwards. The less important it is, the more seriously it is taken. As Einstein once enquired of Charlie Chaplin when he was a new boy to the absurdity of public adulation, 'What does it all mean?' and as Chaplin replied, 'Nothing'. And yet, if sport is a surrogate for war, whether people generally realise it or not, then we should be grateful. The more sport the better. And in Olympic sport to a greater extent than in war, it is generally clear enough who has won. Mountaineering doesn't so readily oblige. It is not, for example, self-evident that he who has climbed the most mountains deserves the most medals. Perhaps it should be the person who has survived the longest. Or enjoyed it the most. Or most successfully combined their egocentricity with an acknowledgement of the wider perspective.

Consider two iconic figures of the last century – the Manchester plumber Don Whillans and the Edinburgh intellectual Dougal Haston, who famously climbed together on the south-west face of Everest, once the last great problem of world mountaineering. Whillans said that if you die in the mountains that wipes out the standing of all your previous achievements. Haston claimed that the experienced – and by implication expert – mountaineer is the one who has been in a lot of dicey situations and been lucky enough to survive them all. Whillans and Haston both, you notice, chose a philosophy to suit their life and character – as most of us do. Perhaps only the saint and the madman ever really does otherwise. Whillans died in his sleep, arguably of overweight. Haston died in an avalanche, ski-ing an alpine couloir he knew to be in risky condition. Both moved mountaineering forward with new climbs at home, in the European Alps, and in the greater ranges. So who was the better mountaineer? Well, this is silly. One might as well ask, who was the better philosopher? They were both figures of international standing. Why say more? Mountaineering achievement simply cannot be quantified in the way an Olympic outlook would require.

This is intuitively understood I think by all mountaineers, though not necessarily by those in the media, sports administration and so on who have their own interests. I suspect it will come as a surprise to many mountaineers to learn that the intention to give medals for mountaineering goes back to the Olympic congress of 1894 and that medals have indeed been given, if sporadically and with no very clear rationale, ever since. It is perhaps worth mentioning a couple of examples, to indicate the bizarre, the mistaken, or just the plain unfortunate position that this relentless attempt to quantify leads to. The members of the Everest expedition of 1922, the archetypal old school trip if ever there was one, were all awarded medals. The leader of the expedition, Charles Granville Bruce, was a Ghurka officer, a great bull of a man, and apparently worshipped by his men. He went on to become a general, so I suppose he was used to medals. George Mallory, too, one can imagine, might have been pleased. But personally, I would like to know the reaction of Howard Theodore Somervell, doctor and after Everest dedicated medical missionary, also a mountain painter of originality. I would imagine he felt both amusement and bemusement. And then more recently, Reinhold Messner, the first man to climb all 14 of the world's 8000-metre peaks, and much else besides, was awarded a medal at the 1988 Calgary Winter Olympics. But only a silver. Who made that decision I wonder? As Doug Scott has commented, it does rather beg the question as to what a climber has to do to go for gold. Perhaps climb Olympus Mons, without bottled oxygen. Olympus Mons, as you doubtless know, is 82,000ft high and situated on Mars.

So much for quantification. But in addition, Olympic sport requires the mirror that is other people to make it meaningful. It is not just that winning the 100 metres is egocentric, but that it's a public form of egocentricity. It needs an audience, and preferably some other athletes. Would you run round an Olympic stadium or throw the discus if you were the only person in the world? I can't envisage it. Might you climb a mountain? Certainly. The Olympics today is inconceivable without public accolade, and without TV coverage, whereas mountaineering is still – in 2012 – uneasy about such things. Bill Tilman wrote to the effect that every true mountaineer would be dismayed to see anything about mountaineering in the newspapers; how many latter-day enthusiasts have been secretly relieved when some live outdoor climbing spectacular has had to be cancelled because of bad weather? Though admittedly, this may be no more than an instance of the old Chinese proverb: happy is he who sees his friend fall off a roof.

Contemporary rock climbing throws up a lot of bright young things who shoot to stardom before puberty, only to give up the whole game before they've left school because they are no longer getting any better at it. This is perhaps most true of indoor climbing and that, I think, is telling. There used to be a wicked joke that Boardman climbed Everest whilst still a virgin; but even if he had – and probably someone has by now – one could never imagine him giving up. He had too profound an awareness of what mountaineering gave him for that. Whereas one can easily imagine a well-heeled client on a contemporary commercial expedition to the mountain getting to the summit and thereafter not giving the game another thought, particularly if they had just achieved some unrepeatable 'first' of the sort I have just alluded to.

So I would suggest that the answer to our question is something along the following lines: There have been changes to what mountaineering is over the last 200 years or so. It has become bigger, more socially diverse, and standards of performance have progressed astonishingly. But philosophically, in terms of values, the changes have been less than headline news might suggest. The real change takes place within the mind and experience of each individual. And it is there, in private experience, rather than outwardly in public achievement, that the value of mountaineering ultimately lies. I hope I have now said enough to demonstrate that there is very little ground on which mountaineering as currently understood sits easily with the Olympic movement. There are styles of rock-climbing, specifically indoor-climbing, that may soon be taken into the Olympic fold, and why not? These are aspects of gymnastics after all, and are only really connected to the mountaineering debate by default. Otherwise, much depends on whether one wishes to remain true to historical precedent. I have made my own view clear, I assume. But that's all it is: a view, formed of habit as much as rationale. Others must decide for themselves. Nor, incidentally, should anything I have said be construed as an attack on awards per se. The Piolets d'Or for example, world mountaineering's premier award for outstanding achievement, seems recently to have refound its sense of direction. My impression is that this is largely due to its being controlled by practising, or at least recently retired, mountaineers. The same is true, up to now, of the BMC. So far, it has been controlled and run by committed practitioners, some of them operating at the highest level, rather than by – well, anyone else. It would be hopelessly narrow-minded to predict that all such initiatives, all such organisations, will prove detrimental to mountaineering, even mountaineering in the traditional sense. But one prediction I am confident of is this: that if mountaineering allows itself to become entangled with the Olympic machine it will be chewed up and spat out in unrecognisable and, to my taste, ill-flavoured pieces. Mountaineering is a sport, yes, but of a different hue to the Olympic variety. As the dictionary wisely suggests: amusement, diversion – fun.

ANDREW BISHARAT

The Tyranny of History

Though the most famous question in climbing is 'Why?', the answer is actually quite boring. The infinitely more interesting question is 'How?' You don't even need to be a climber to understand why you'd want to climb Cerro Torre. She is the Queen. At 3128 metres, Cerro Torre is an enormous granite turret whose slender majesty is a paragon of mountain architecture. More than any other, this fearsome, beautiful mountain has challenged climbers to define the rules of our game. Cerro Torre has brought out our best and worst, and dared us to face one question: How do you climb the impossible?

***

When Hayden whooped after pioneering his way up new, brilliant terrain at the top of the Cerro Torre headwall, Jason, down at the belay, knew they had done it. It was 16 January 2012. Hayden Kennedy, 21, and Jason Kruk, 24, had become the first people ever to climb the elegant spine of rock and ice that is Cerro Torre's striking south-east ridge without using the infamous bolt ladders placed there by Cesare Maestri in 1970.

Their 'fair means' ascent of the *Compressor Route* was the apotheosis of an idea that has been a work in progress. (More on this later.)

Hayden and Jason sat for 45 minutes atop the wind-sculpted snow of Cerro Torre's summit, fuelling-up and debating what to do next. They hadn't exactly expected to reach the top so quickly, just 13 hours after leaving the Col of Patience 900m below. Chopping Maestri's bolt ladders had not been their original intention, even though that idea had been stirring for years within the climbing community.

On Cerro Torre's headwall, Maestri's bolt ladders lead you onto completely blank rock. To the right and left of the bolt ladders, however, are perfectly climbable features.

Hayden and Jason had just shown that the bolt ladders were unnecessary and that the route could be climbed via its natural features at the relatively attainable grade of 5.11 A2. On their ascent, they had clipped five bolts that were not originally placed by Maestri and used two of Maestri's belays (which double as rap anchors). Hayden did most of the leading, and free climbed well over 90 percent of the route onsight, mostly standing in aiders for speed and efficiency: for example, while cleaning ice out of cracks to place cams. His leads were extremely bold, as he short-fixed off anchors and free climbed out on lead with 35-metre loops of slack.

The two sat on the summit and weighed their options. They could go

This article was first published in *Rock and Ice* magazine, April 2012 issue. Andrew Bisharat is the magazine's senior editor.

Cerro Torre in storm. *(Leo Dickinson)*

down, leave the bolt ladders in place, and return to El Chalten with a pretty proud tick. Or they could chop the superfluous bolts, and deal with the inevitable fallout. The summit of Cerro Torre was an audacious but somehow perfect place to make such a momentous decision.

Their ideals and emotions churned within them. Would chopping the bolts be the best way to pay respect to the mountain that had just given them one of the greatest climbing experiences of their lives? Swept up in their exuberance – a sense of being on top of the world and having a rare opportunity to change it for the better – Hayden and Jason descended Cerro Torre and removed the bolt ladders Maestri had placed on the headwall.

They placed their ice tools into the eyelets of the 'bolts' – which, in fact, are more like soft-iron pitons banged into drilled holes – and pried them out. The bolts popped relatively easily, but the toil added some three hours to the descent. All in all, they removed about 120 of Maestri's 450 bolts – the majority from the headwall ladders.

Five days later, almost unbelievably, the south-east ridge received its second 'fair means' ascent, this time with the 21-year-old Austrian climber David Lama making the first free ascent of this striking line, redpointing the now very runout route at 5.13b.

Twice in one week, this next generation of alpinists proved that the relics of an intractable egomaniac from four decades ago were not needed to climb Cerro Torre. In fact, in 2007 – when the debate about the bolt ladders came to a head as various climbers in El Chalten caught wind of Josh Wharton and Zack Smith's intentions to climb Cerro Torre by fair means and, if successful, chop the bolts on the descent – Cerro Torre had been climbed only seven times by other routes without using Maestri's bolt ladders.

That year Wharton and Smith came close but ultimately failed either to climb Cerro Torre by fair means or to chop a single bolt. However, their intentions brought the issue to the table and it created a stormy public debate that had an interesting and little-known consequence. By 2008, climbers' attitudes in Patagonia seemed to have changed, and fewer people aspired to climb the *Compressor Route*. That year the number of non *Compressor Route* ascents doubled, and seven parties summited Cerro Torre via the west face – the route used on the mountain's first true ascent, by an Italian team of six led by Casimiro Ferrari in 1974. By 2011 the number of non *Compressor Route* ascents was up to 15; at the time of writing it's 17.

The reaction to the recent bolt removal has been mixed, muddled and heated. Cerro Torre, once again, has become a catalyst for a seething debate. The tyranny of history that has prevented these actions from occurring for so long and the nuanced ethical complexity of the whole situation, seem to have challenged the climbing community to re-evaluate what it thought it knew and to decide what it now believes.

***

Cerro Torre is climbing's greatest theatre, and the recent drama upon the vertical world's most savage stage is nothing short of Shakespearean. A close but not quite perfect rendition would be Hamlet, with Cesare Maestri as the treacherous uncle Claudius, who 'murdered the impossible', if you will, as Reinhold Messner famously put it in his polemic, only to have, 42 years later, this 'death' avenged by a couple of Hamlets (albeit Hamlets who act) in the forms of Hayden Kennedy and Jason Kruk. With 120 of Maestri's evil bolts now removed, in an unforeseen plot twist, the one-time Patagonian villain David Lama nabs the route's first free ascent, setting him up for what ought to be redemption in the eyes of the blunt and blood-thirsty climbing community.

This story has been one twist and turn after another. And now we are left with, exactly, what?

To fully understand the events of this past season one must go back to 1959 when the 29-year-old Italian climber Cesare Maestri and the Austrian ice ace Toni Egger – supported by a third partner, Cesarino Fava – claimed the first ascent, via the east face, of Cerro Torre in a lightning-fast, four-day alpine-style push.

Considering that Cerro Torre was the most technically difficult summit on earth, and that the two were using 12mm hemp ropes and slow prusik ascenders, theirs would have been the greatest climbing achievement of all time… had they actually done it. All evidence points to the conclusion that Maestri and Egger climbed little more than 300m – essentially reaching no higher than the shinbone of this granite giant. The only certainty is that at some point during those four days Egger was somehow killed by the mountain. Blatantly wrong route descriptions, the unsupported nature of their unbelievable claims and a total lack of evidence of their passage up high indicates that Maestri and Fava conspired to perpetrate one of climbing history's greatest hoaxes.

Definitively proving a lie, however, turns out to be quite difficult – especially considering that Maestri, now 81 years old and still living in Italy, has always maintained that he did in fact make the first ascent of Cerro Torre in 1959, despite having refused to speak to anyone about the details of their expedition for the last four decades. Argentine climber and Patagonia expert Rolo Garibotti, however, did a bang-up job of disproving Maestri and Fava in his exhaustively researched article, 'A Mountain Unveiled', in the *American Alpine Journal* of 2004.

A year after publishing the article, Garibotti, then 34, confirmed his research when he climbed – with Ermanno Salvaterra, 51, and Alessandro Beltrami, 24 – Maestri's purported line. They called their route El Arca de los Vientos, and found no evidence of the anchors Maestri claimed to have left up high.

Though Maestri and Fava returned as heroes to Italy in 1959, by 1970 doubts had grown in the public sphere, eventually driving Maestri so mad that, as he wrote in *2000 Metri della Nostra Vita*, he returned that year to Cerro Torre, to 'attack [his detractors'] routes, the routes they were not able to climb. I will humiliate them, and they will have to feel ashamed of having doubted me and having insulted the memory of my fallen partner'.

In a complete and curious reversal to the alpine-style he had claimed in 1959, Maestri and his team (which again included Fava) fixed ropes and hauled a 200-pound gas-powered compressor up the south-east ridge and indiscriminately bolted his way straight up blank rock, disregarding many naturally climbable features on either side. In fact, the south-east ridge had received an attempt in 1968 by an Anglo-Argentine team – Martin Boysen, Mick Burke, Pete Crew, Jose Luis Fonrouge and Dougal Haston – that, without placing bolts, reached a point higher than the one where Maestri first broke out the drill.

Motivated by vengeance, Maestri was literally gunning for the summit. He would stand on top regardless of how he got there.

Ironically, he failed once again. Drilling up the headwall, he reached a point 35m below the rime-covered summit and decided that that was close enough. Strangely, he dubbed his ascent a success, reasoning that he didn't need to go any higher. 'It's just a lump of ice,' he said of the summit. 'Not really part of the mountain; it will blow away one of these days.'

After calling it good, Maestri then began chopping his own bolts on his descent. He later wrote: 'A devilish plan comes into my mind: I'll take out all the bolts and leave the climb as clean as we found it. I'll break them all, so that whoever tries to repeat our route won't even be able to benefit from the holes we've drilled.' However, he only managed to take out about 20 of his own bolts and also to break, so it wouldn't work for others, the compressor, which he abandoned at the belay at the headwall's base.

Again Maestri had failed, only this time he had left Cerro Torre severely altered. In his wake over 450 bolts remained, creating what Jim Donini has called 'the world's hardest via ferrata'.

I'd call it really, really bad style.

***

One thing many climbers misunderstand is that not all bolts are equal. It's one of our sport's great ironies that a piece of metal smaller than a human finger can incite such vehement, emotional responses spanning a very large spectrum of opinion. How, where and why bolts are placed, and even who places them, are all important pieces of information, but can carry extreme biases that rival the selective blindness of religious beliefs.

It would be easier to be of the opinion that all bolts are categorically good or bad, but climbing is far from being black and white. The result is that the most outspoken zealots either don't climb or, if they do, inevitably become hypocrites. Meanwhile most climbers are just too confused to really understand why one bolt is OK, and the other isn't.

To me one of the most interesting aspects of 2012's Cerro Torre drama is the degree to which the events have challenged our understanding of climbing ethics. It seems like many of the same people who were upset about David Lama's crew adding new bolts to existing fixed anchors in 2010 are now upset that the headwall bolt ladders are gone.

Many climbers have argued that chopping the bolts has somehow robbed us of an important piece of history – even though the 'first ascentionist' himself intended to remove his own bolts and leave the mountain clean. (Further, there are still 300-plus pieces of history, including the compressor, still on the mountain.) Some people, who probably will never climb Cerro Torre in their lives, are upset about the bolts' removal – but can they honestly condone what Maestri did in 1970?

With so many multifarious egos adding to the fray, this already fraught situation becomes even more problematic due to how difficult it is to separate sentiments driven by ego from those that may be justified.

Those who believe Maestri, or who have climbed the *Compressor Route* and feel that their ascents of this route on Cerro Torre were crowning achievements of their careers, have a lot to lose with the recent events. Why? Because any ascent that needed to use Maestri's bolts to get to the top of this difficult mountain is now a diminished achievement.

My own impression is that most people don't really know how to feel about Cerro Torre being chopped. Most people will never set foot on the Col of Patience, let alone blitz up the 900m south-east ridge. Most climbers' understanding and subsequent espousal of climbing ethics is derived more from principles than direct experience. Most of our ethical foundations are derived from key manifestos that we've read over the years and then pieced together into some kind of semi-coherent Frankenstein of a viewpoint.

One reason that this story is so engaging and widely discussed is that we feel like we are being tested on our climbing ethics. And I would say that we are realising how little we actually understood about them in the first place.

***

Creation and destruction are two sides of the same coin, and maybe in some ways history has to be destroyed – which does NOT mean forgotten or rewritten – in order to be created again. I believe that that is what has happened on Cerro Torre this year. The tyranny of one history has ended, allowing a new one to begin.

I'm astounded by the sweeping scope of characters who have played a part in shaping the plot of this mountain's uncontainable story. Even the climbing community as the audience, with its newfound and extremely powerful voice on the Internet, has been prominent in helping to decide Cerro Torre's fate.

Everyone is talking about the bolt removal, but the real story of 2012 is that David Lama free climbed the entire *Compressor Route* – without the bolts. This incredible individual achievement, however, is actually the capstone to a pyramid of many other climbers' efforts that directly run back to 1999, and before that even to Maestri himself.

In 1999 Ermanno Salvaterra and Mauro Mabboni pioneered three new pitches, adding a total of five bolts, and avoiding 200 Maestri bolts. This variation took an arête that would turn out to be the crux (5.13b) free pitch for Lama.

In 2007 Josh Wharton and Zack Smith made the first explicit effort to avoid using Maestri's bolts. They followed the 1999 variation down low, and then discovered a completely rad chimney of perfect, steep water ice that allowed them to skip the next bolt ladder. All those years, when people had just been following Maestri's path, there was really good climbing to the side. Cold, windy conditions that prohibited free climbing high on the route, however, forced Smith back onto the bolt ladder and ended this endeavour.

Wharton tried removing one of Maestri's bolts, just to see how difficult it would be. When climbers in El Chalten caught wind, some were outraged. Tempers flared. Blows were exchanged. Steve Schneider was so pissed at Wharton for intending to chop the route, which Schneider has tried over multiple years, that he dismantled Wharton's tent and left his gear strewn about.

'That whole episode really made me lose faith in the climbing community,' says Wharton, who abandoned his goal of chopping the *Compressor Route*. Wharton, however, is happy that the deed is now done. His sentiments are also shared by such prominent climbers as Reinhold Messner and the Argentine legend Carlos Comesaña, who did the first ascent of the *Supercanaleta* on FitzRoy for the mountain's second ascent, in 1965.

After Wharton and Smith's attempt, a town-hall style meeting took place in El Chalten, and attendees voted on whether they wanted to see the *Compressor Route* stay or go – 30 voted for it to stay, 10 for it to be chopped. Wharton wasn't there, however. 'The meeting took place in a good weather window,' he says. 'I was out climbing. In fact, most of the climbers in El Chalten weren't there for the meeting.'

Cerro Torre returned to the spotlight in 2010 when Lama – who has a background in sport and competition climbing, but in recent years has put in time repeating hard big-wall trad climbs in the Dolomites – came to Patagonia to free the *Compressor Route* and film the whole process with the Red Bull Media House production team. The producers added bolts to the route for rigging, and when bad weather moved in, the team abandoned two haulbags and 300m of rope on the route. Team Red Bull peaced out of Argentina and discreetly paid other climbers in El Chalten to take down their gear for them.

Adding bolts to what was already considered the most over-bolted route in the world created yet another outrage, with this one taking place almost entirely on the Internet – mostly because word only got out months after the fact. Nearly all of the public ire was directed at Lama, who didn't place any bolts himself. Internet forums were afire. One poster suggested that climbers: 'Beat this a-hole to a pulp. Knock out his front teeth next time you get within arm's reach. This douchebag is screwing up the future of the whole sport so he can spray to his sponsors. Yeah, go to the Valley, and add 60 bolts to the Nose. I hope you get beaten till your bowels unload in your pants. I hope Red Bull tastes good in your hospital bed.'

Much misinformation revolved around the number of bolts Lama's team placed, with estimates jumping from 30 to 60. In 2011 when Rolo Garibotti went up on the *Compressor Route* to see what kind of damage had been done, he found the actual number of Red Bull bolts placed to be 37: 20 above the Col of Patience, and 17 below. Garibotti and Doerte Pietron removed 17 of the 20 bolts above the col, and Pietron and Colin Haley removed 12 of the 17 below.

Lama deserves a lot of credit even for returning to Patagonia after he was so thoroughly condemned and maligned. Certainly part of the criticism he received was justified, but part of it was excessive. Regardless, one can't help but believe that the heavy criticism in some way pushed Lama into climbing Cerro Torre in a better style, even though it was sheer circumstance that the headwall had been chopped right before his successful redpoint. Still, he persevered and realized his goal in a bold style.

Lama used Wharton's ice chimney to approach the headwall. In freeing the headwall, he took a variation to the right of Maestri's bolts, instead of climbing left as Kennedy and Kruk did. Many people believe that Lama's line will become the preferred path for future ascents. Lama styled many 40-plus-foot runouts on 5.10 to 5.12 terrain. However, he did have a camera crew hanging on fixed ropes directly above him, which may create a footnote to his 'onsight' of this section. The impressive camera team – which included the onetime Yosemite climbing ranger Lincoln Else – had climbed the west face and rapped down from the summit to capture the action.

***

In the end, I think that Kennedy-Kruk's and Lama's ascents complement each other. Had the bolts not been removed, Lama's first free ascent would not have been as impressive and his redemption not as absolute. In the same vein, Lama's ascent helps justify Kennedy and Kruk's actions by emphasising that the next generation of alpinists is here, and stepping up to the true challenge of the mountain.

As one young, local up-and-coming Argentine climber, Jorge Ackerman, put it: 'Maestri's bolts would have eventually come out, especially with the level of climbing that is around these days, and I respect [Kennedy and Kruk's] decision to do so... The Red Bull fiasco was deplorable... but one thing that [Lama's] free ascent does show is that the bolts are not necessary. For those of us who aren't as strong as Lama, Kruk and Kennedy, a lot of training lies on the road ahead to climb Cerro Torre for real.'

History has not ended with the removal of these unnecessary bolts. In fact, it's just beginning. Yet amid the enduring debates remains one sad irony.

Says Kennedy: 'The ironic thing is that no one will ever care about the actual amazing climbing that's on this mountain. No one will ever care about the climbing because this controversy runs so deep.'

Surveys

68.   John Fairley, *Trisul west face*, oil on canvas, 600x300mm, 2007

GRAHAM DUDLEY & SIMON RICHARDSON

Exploring The Eastern Caucasus

69.   Kazbek, viewed from Chaukhi, 30km distant. *(Simon Richardson)*

An overview by Graham Dudley

The Caucasus have always had an air of mystery: rich in culture and history, full of tragedy and adventure and wreathed in stories of the Silk Road and Genghis Khan. Political tensions across the borders of Georgia and Azerbaijan with the Russian Republic territories of Dagestan and Chechnya have made the region difficult to access in the last 10 years, and sometimes very dangerous. Today it is still not possible to cross the border into the Russian territories, and it is advisable to seek the latest Foreign Office advice and world news on these regions. However, access to the Georgian and Azerbaijan parts of the Caucasus is relatively straight-forward and safe, and while living and working in Baku I had the fortunate opportunity to explore the mountains in both countries.

The Azerbaijan Caucasus consists of 19 peaks exceeding 3500m. They can be accessed by a four to six hour drive from the city of Baku, and many of the peaks can be easily climbed within a long weekend of three to five days. Most of my ascents in Azerbaijan were done in the summer months, as road access in winter was not always reliable. It is very easy to fly from Baku to Tbilisi for a weekend however, and often in mid-winter a team of us would head to the Gudauri ski resort in Georgia and make the most of the quiet ski area and large snowfall. During these trips I discovered the potential of Mount Kazbek and its suitability for ski-mountaineering.

It was during my last year in Azerbaijan that I suggested to my regular ski-mountaineering friends, Ewan Clarke, Dave Howard and Dave Coustick, that we should have a crack at something different to our usual Alpine destinations. With the knowledge I had gained from visiting Gudauri, and a better understanding of how to get things done in Georgia, I felt confident that we would have a good trip exploring a new area.

Extending 1500km from the Black Sea in the north-west to the Caspian Sea in the south-east, the Caucasus are 24 to 28 million years old and made up

70.   The splendid artwork on the walls of the meteo station hut at 3652m on Kazbek. *(Graham Dudley)*

of folded and faulted mudstones, silts and sandstones, interspersed with occasional limestone and volcanic rocks. The highest point within Georgia is Mount Shkhara (5068m) in the Svaneti region. Azerbaijan's highest point is Shahdag (4243m). The highest point of the range as a whole is the well-known Mount Elbrus (5633m) in neighbouring Russia.

The topography of the Eastern Caucasus is characterised by deeply incised rivers that have created long valleys. The highest summits have permanent snowfields, however due to the southerly latitude major glaciers are limited in extent and only really present on Kazbek. The mountain slopes are covered in short highland grass, wild flowers and shrub, interspersed with scree and rocks with the tree line at around 2000 metres. Trees are sparse and mainly feature on southern slopes or in deep river valleys. The grassland provides excellent pasture for sheep and cattle and in the summer months it is not uncommon to encounter sheep grazing above 3500m.

The rock scenery can be very impressive, but it is not always reliable and can be fragile, loose and vegetated, hence it does not make for good rock climbing. Some areas have better quality rock, such as the Chaukhi area, but care is still required. Anyone with an adventurous attitude, and a willingness to explore, will no doubt find some good rock climbing; and in particular the upper cliffs on Shahdag look stunning.

The seasons are a blend of Alpine, continental Tundra and a semi-arid climate. Summers can be a mix of rain and sun, and on occasions similar to Scotland. Generally the climate is drier further east and more settled with

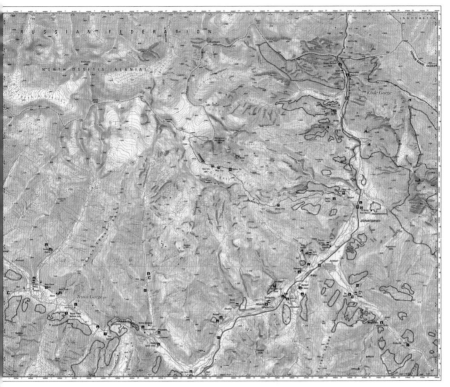

71. The Kazbek region of the Caucasus. From *Geoland Maps 4: Khevi, Mt. Kazbeki, Gudauri, Truso. (Kind permission of Geoland)*

prevalent high-pressure systems. At the height of summer it can be very hot in the valleys. The weather is most stable around July to September, but it can also be very changeable, as with any mountain area. Winters are cold and snowy; the first snow can arrive as early as October although November is the norm. Further west into Georgia the snow can stay on the high meadows and peaks well into May. Overall the weather is not much different to that of the European Alps, both in winter and summer.

The Caucasus offer the full range of mountain activities from ice climbing, alpine climbing, skiing, and rock climbing to mountain biking, horse riding and hill walking, often in remote and relatively unexplored terrain. Today, there are a number of small guiding companies and tourist organisations that operate adventure trips in both Azerbaijan and Georgia.

Mount Kazbek on Ski
by Graham Dudley

Mount Kazbek (5034m) is a prominent volcanic mountain located close to the Georgian and Russian border. It lies alongside the Georgian military highway, which runs from Tbilisi to Vladikavkaz in Russia, across the spectacular Jvari pass (2379m). The name Kazbek stems from Mongol

72.   Climbers' Cairn viewpoint at 3040m looking directly up Ortsveri glacier and south
flank of Kazbek (Mkinvartsveri). The approach to the meteo station follows the
lefthand flank of the glacier before crossing directly over to beneath the southern spur
of the mountain. *(Dave Coustick)*

73.   The party approaching the summit corridor on Kazbek. *(Dave Coustick)*

roots back in the period of invasions in the 12th century, although Georgians have their own name, Mkinvartsveri meaning 'ice-top' or 'top of the glacier'. It is the easternmost 5000m peak in the Caucasus and was first climbed by Douglas Freshfield in 1868.

Kazbek is well suited to ski expeditions and is commonly regarded as one of best ski mountains in the range. It is not known when the summit was first skied, but regular ascents of the normal *North Face* route are recorded every year and graded at around SAM S2-3 on the Blanchere scale. The impressive south-east face, which lies directly above the meteorological station, is the most direct route to the top, and finishes a few metres below the summit. The face begins at about 4100m with a short, gently inclined narrow funnel, and then broadens to 40 to 45 degree slopes that finally steepen to 50 degrees for the last 200m. The first full descent of the southeast face (via a variation around the rock gendarme) was by Simon Schels (snowboard), and Dominik Bartenschlager and Michi Stacheder (ski) in 2007, and the first full descent of the *South-East Face Direct* was by Peter Schön and Andi Riesner in 2008. Be aware that the prevailing wind and storm direction in this region is from the west, and that these winds can heavily load the face with snow.

The best place to prepare for a ski ascent of Kazbek is Gudauri, a small ski village at about 2000m above sea level and 2.5 hours' drive from Tbilisi. Kazbek is another 1.5 hours' drive over the Jvari pass. Gudauri offers chalet and hotel accommodation and easy access to several 3200m peaks. The typical ski season is long and ski lifts only start to close around the end of April, depending on the snow conditions and demand. We stayed at the Gudauri Hut Hotel, a small, family-run hotel located close to the piste with ski-in and ski-out access to the slopes. I have used the hotel on three separate trips and found the management and staff to be friendly and well organised. After a few visits I have managed to pick up a few words of Georgian, and I've always felt if you can greet someone (*gamarjoba*), and say thank you (*madloba*) in the local language, you are showing you are trying to engage with the local culture.

In late April 2010, I took the short flight from Baku and met Ewan and the two Daves at Tbilisi International Airport late at night. We were promptly picked up by a minibus and driven directly to the hotel along the route of the Georgian military highway. It was all very efficient and well organised. On arrival we were greeted by Nana Bekauri, the hotel manageress, and shown our rooms. The hotel was comfortable and warm, with plenty of space to chill out. The food was good and there was plenty of opportunity to try classic Georgian dishes such as *khachapuri* and *khinkali* washed down with the fruity red wines. A sauna provided welcome relaxation in the evening and the ice-cold water in the plunge pool a powerful tonic.

Day one was spent getting organised and checking equipment. After a late start we ascended one of the 3000m peaks just off the piste. Although the lower slopes were still open, the upper mountain was closed due to

74.   Descending on perfect spring snow on the flanks of the Ortsveri glacier.
       (Dave Coustick)

poor visibility. Later that afternoon we met our local guide Gia Apakidze, who is also the owner of the hotel. We were introduced to four Austrians who were also aiming to ski Kazbek during the same week. Although the mountains are not technically demanding, a guide is a big advantage in terms of organising transport, supplies and getting help quickly in an emergency. Also, being close to the Dagestan border it is useful having someone in the group with local knowledge and who can speak the language.

Day two we ascended Mount Sadzele (3307m) via the south-east ridge and descended the west ridge and south face which held heavy powder snow (SAM S3). Throughout the day we were accompanied by two large and very strong Caucasus mountain dogs (*dzarli*), that were amazingly friendly, especially when it came to any spare food. Generally the Caucasus sheep dogs should be treated with great respect as they can be aggressive. Often it is worth carrying a solid stick or having rocks to throw if they come too close for comfort. Sadzele can be accessed directly from the village and involves a 12km round trip. Though not a long day, it is important to start at first light to ensure the best quality snow. By mid-morning, the hard-packed surface layer at lower elevations would start to give way to unconsolidated mush. Higher, the snow was a mix of wind pack and soft snow on the sheltered slopes. In springtime this area is prone to high avalanche risk late in the afternoon. During our visit, the Jvari pass was closed for several days due to an avalanche that wiped out a jeep and killed all its passengers.

Day three we ascended to the Gobi pass and then on to the summit of Mount Bidara (3174m) via its east ridge (SAM S3). Though visibility was very poor on the summit, we made a steep, icy descent down the

75.   Dawn breaking on the upper Ortsveri glacier, looking south towards the inspirational
      Chaukhi massif. *(Graham Dudley).*

south-east face. Day four we made a short ascent from the Jvari pass up
the west slopes of Peak 3174 and Peak 3011 and descended south back to
Gudauri (SAM S2). It was noted that in higher snowfall years, or earlier
in the season, other excursions would be possible on the north side of the
Gudauri mountains towards the village of Gobi in the Tergi valley. Also it
is possible to ascend Mount Lomisa (2452m) from the village of Mleta in
the Argavi valley.

Kazbek was our next objective. While we relaxed, sorted out gear and
made last minute preparations, our guide and his assistant went into Tbilisi
to load up with food supplies for the three-day trip. The plan for the ascent
was to start from the village of Gergeti at 1900m, and walk and ski to the
meteo station (3652m) via the lower Ortsveri glacier. On the second day,
we would climb the upper Ortsveri glacier to the saddle and Maili plateau
at 4478m, and then ascend the north slopes to the summit of Kazbek at
5034m. We would return to the meteo station for a second night, and
descend back to Gergeti on the third day.

The next day dawned superb with magnificent views of the mountain.
It was one of those days when you wished you were already high on the
mountain and ready to go. Our intended early start was delayed, and we
were not dropped off above Gergeti until after 9am, when the sun was
already feeling warm. Gia managed to drive his 4WD trucks up on to the

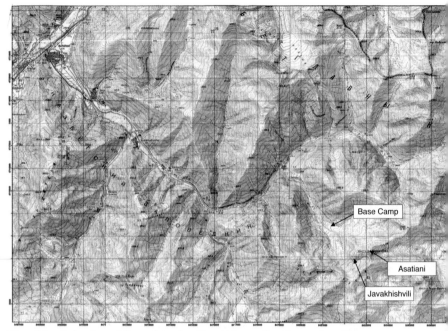

Base Camp

Asatiani

Javakhishvili

76.　'The Dolomites of Georgia' – the Chaukhi massif in the eastern Caucasus.

ridge near Sameba church very close to the snowline. It was an enchanting starting point, though we did not visit the 14th century church as time was already getting on.

The route ascends the flank of the Bashi drainage along the line of a broad spur, which terminates at around 3040m at Satertse and the Climbers' Cairn. The skinning was easy and the snow pack still firm, but already the mid-morning warmth made the exercise thirsty work. At the cairn we had a great panoramic view of Kazbek and the Ortsveri glacier. The next 2km traversed across north-east to east facing slopes to a final spur of lateral moraine that rose to meet the glacier at around 3480m. The initial section of traverse was steep in places and we needed to control our edges. Once on the glacier the meteo station looked close, but it was still more than a kilometre away. There was no need to rope up and the last skin up to the hut on the north side was straightforward. We arrived around mid-afternoon and the sun was still warm enough to dry the skins.

From the outside the hut looks well decorated, but inside the setting is less colourful and very basic. It was constructed during the Stalin era and like many ex-Soviet buildings has suffered neglect and disrepair. There are several four-person bedrooms, a communal kitchen/dining area and other rooms full of junk and rubbish that people could not be bothered to take back down the mountain. Gia and his assistants did a good job of tidying up the main rubbish and we were able to pack out some of the excess on our descent.

The hut's basic interior meant that most of the time everyone gathered in the kitchen to keep warm. Various Georgian dishes were served both hot and cold, but mostly cold with the obligatory toast of vodka. The hut is cold and a good sleeping bag is essential. The situation with the hut is now improving and it has been renamed the Bethlemi hut (http://bethlemihut.ge/maps.php?lang=eng)

The sunset was glorious with the distant southern ranges of the Chaukhi massif draped in orange mist and shadows. The weather looked encouraging with few clouds and the prospect of a good day to follow. Everyone rested well that night even though we were above 3600m; our acclimatisation in Gudauri seemed to be working well.

Dawn broke clear and cold, with the summit visible and no cloud. The night had been very cold and it proved difficult to stick the skins on to the skis first thing, causing a few false starts with skins coming off on the ascent. The 12km trip involved around 1300m of ascent. We followed the north-east moraine flank of the glacier, and once on the glacier stayed on the right-hand side passing under the Khmaura Rock at around 4150m. The route continued at a gentle angle all the way to the saddle at 4478m on the edge of the Maili plateau. The glacier was very straightforward and there was no requirement to rope up.

From the saddle we had great views of Mount Maili (4598m) to the north on the Dagestan border – a good option for another visit. At the saddle the route changes direction and starts to traverse the north slopes of Kazbek. At first we made good progress on skis, but around 4700m the slope steepened and became extremely irregular due to sastrugi. It was somewhat disappointing, as the slope, at 25 to 30 degrees, potentially offered some great skiing, but it made sense at this point to dump the skis and continue on foot with crampons and ice-axes. The next 200m ascended easily up a wide snow slope to a small col at around 4900m, which lies between the top of the north-west ridge, called Serabeki, and the main summit. The remaining ascent to the top followed a steepening snow corridor (40 to 45 degrees) with occasional rock outcrops. Here the snow was soft and less wind-packed, and proved to be deep and slow going. The best means of ascent was to scramble up the small rock outcrops.

Once at the top of the rocks, the angle dropped away to a gentle snow slope to the final summit of 'Mkinvartsveri'. The panorama was spectacular: north-west, the eye followed the snowy chain of the Caucasus along the Russian border towards Elbrus, though in the early afternoon the misty haze prevented perfectly clear views; in contrast, looking east and south, the snow slopes quickly faded into deep grey valleys of the Tergi river and then onwards to the Chaukhi mountains.

The descent route followed our line of ascent, with the added excitement and pleasure of skiing downhill. While on foot and on the upper slopes we had one near miss when one of our Austrian colleagues broke through a small crevasse and strained his leg joints. It was nothing serious, but it was a timely reminder to keep a watch on what appeared to be a very benign

77.   Chaukhi North Face Topo *(Simon Richardson)*

78.   Javakhishvili South Face Topo *(Simon Richardson)*

snow slope of the glacier.

Soon we were back at our skis. The initial section of sastrugi proved to be quite difficult to ski as the relief on some of the scours was in excess of 40cm. Once back on the main glacier we enjoyed easy unroped skiing in the wide basin towards the hut. Below 4300m the snow was starting to soften and had become wet from the warmth from the sun; in places it was crusty and unpredictable to turn on. As we descended further, thick mist made route-finding a little more complex and slowed our pace. The route took us directly to slopes above the hut, which provided the final set of turns back to the meteo station.

By the time we were back at the hut it was late afternoon and the snow pack had changed to wet mushy porridge. Even though we had sufficient daylight to ski back to the roadhead, the snow conditions would have made it very unpleasant and dangerous. So the rest of the day was spent relaxing and making the most of our isolated location. The mist hung around the hut into the night and it was not certain what the weather would bring next day. Once again our evening meal was spent huddled in the small kitchen dining area, toasting our success with local vodka. We were surprised to learn that one of our assistant guides had decided to descend all the way, late in the afternoon and on his own, as he had been feeling sick due to altitude. The ski conditions must have been awful.

Next morning was perfect with cold, clear blue skies. The snow pack had frozen and the mush from the afternoon before was rock solid. We were all now looking forward to the 9km and 1800m of descent. The early upper sections of the Ortsveri glacier were still untouched by the sun and were icy, but as we dropped height below 3000m the top layer of snow softened to give outstanding spring ski conditions. We managed to ski within 200m of the roadhead by mid-afternoon and were greeted by two Mitsubishi 4WD trucks and Gia offering cold cans of beer. What a great way to finish the descent. Our way out was now back to Gudauri to clean up, then into Tbilisi to enjoy some of the cultural delights of the Georgian capital before heading home to Scotland.

Climbing in the Chaukhi Mountains
by Simon Richardson

When Graham Dudley and I were talking about a quick climbing trip for September 2010, Chamonix was the obvious destination. Stay low and grab some sunny rock routes above the Argentière glacier was the plan. Then, out of the blue, Graham suggested an alternative.

'We could always go to the Caucasus.'

Now the Caucasus have been on my hit list ever since the early 1980s when the great Czech climber Miroslav Smid showed me his slides of climbing on Ushba, so Graham had hit a real hot button here.

'But surely a week is too short for the Caucasus?' I suggested. 'They're far too high and it will be cold in September.'

'I'm not talking about Ushba,' Graham grinned. 'Let's go to Chaukhi.

The locals call it the Dolomites of Georgia.'

'Tell me more...'

That spring, Graham had skied Kazbek (5034m), the great peak at the eastern end of the main Caucasus chain. Graham had spent three years working in Baku in neighbouring Azerbaijan and had climbed many of the local peaks in weekend trips. Kazbek was the next step, but it was to be his swansong, for soon after, Graham left Baku and moved to Aberdeen. From the upper slopes of Kazbek, he had seen an attractive jagged rock peak framed in the valley beyond, about 30km away. The mountain was called Chaukhi and had a reputation for good alpine rock climbing; Graham resolved to climb it.

Chaukhi sounded perfect for a short trip. Graham knew how to access the area, the mountain was less than 4000m high so altitude was not going to be a problem, and the peak looked to be covered in tempting rock routes. The only problem was that we could find very little information about the actual climbing; although we'd heard that there were a dozen routes up to Grade VI in difficulty, there was no guidebook. We were advised to have someone look after our base camp whilst we were away climbing, so it was suggested that we employ a local guide for a couple of days to show us the routes. It was all very simple. All we had to do was arrive at Tbilisi and we would be picked up and driven into the mountains ready to start the approach next day.

Travelling to Chaukhi was surprisingly easy. An early Aberdeen flight connected with the London-Baku flight, which continued on to Tbilisi. We arrived a little early but were picked up by a small minibus that took us to Gia Apakidze's hotel in Gudauri. After a leisurely breakfast we were met by our guide, Tato Nadiratze, and Lasha, our base camp guard. They were well prepared with two kitbags full of food, a large gas cooker and an assortment of pots and pans. A further 30km in the minibus took us to the village of Kazbegi with its eponymous mountain towering above; we turned up a side valley and drove to its end at a little village called Juta. Here we were met by a couple of horsemen with five horses that took all our belongings on an easy two-hour walk along the Roshka Pass Trail and up to base camp. It was stunningly beautiful. The hills were green and rolling, like a larger version of the Cairngorms, but the showpiece was Chaukhi itself. The massif consists of a ridge of unusual (slightly crumbly) volcanic rock, with four separate summits, surrounded by grassy hills rising to 3500m. The highest point is Asatiani (3820m), but all summits have 600m-high rock walls sweeping down to steep grass slopes below. Our stay caused a frisson of local excitement, because although the area is becoming popular with trekkers, we were apparently the first foreign visitors to attempt technical routes. However, it soon became clear that we could not have been the first overseas party, as Tato told us that the mountain was first climbed in the 1930s by an American woman. Russians must have climbed here also, and there was mention of a Czechoslovak team in the 1980s.

We spent our first day climbing with Tato on the *Normal Route* on

79. Graham Dudley climbing the variation to the *Normal Route* (4a) on Asatiani (3820m). *(Simon Richardson)*

Javakhishvili (3650m), Chaukhi's second highest summit. Graded 3a, the route was about Alpine PD, and started up an easy snow/scree couloir, followed by V. Diff rock to the summit. Rather conveniently there was mobile reception on the top so we texted home, feeling rather surprised to have climbed one of Chaukhi's summits within 36 hours of arriving in Georgia. Next day Graham and I went it alone and climbed a variation to the *Normal Route* (4a) on Asatiani. Initially this took a long couloir and finished with four, long, protectionless Hard Severe pitches up skyline slabs. We descended the upper section of the *Normal Route*, which followed a series of loose corners and chimneys, before down-climbing the couloir. Overall, the route felt quite serious, and equated to about Alpine D-.

We said goodbye to Tato that evening and packed our sacks for our next objective – a sustained 5a rock route on the north face of Javakhishvili. Unfortunately the weather had other ideas and after an eight-week dry spell it became wet and unsettled for the rest of the trip. We made two attempts on the north face but despite twice waking to a star-filled sky it soon clouded over and each time we were greeted by rain and howling winds at the foot of the route.

On the morning of the third attempt we were a little wiser and rather than rush up the approach slopes in the dark decided to wait a little longer in base camp. As dawn broke it was raining as usual on the north face, but it seemed a little brighter on the more sheltered south side of the mountain. We decided to take a chance and follow the better weather, and perhaps snatch a pitch or two on a low-lying nunatak at the foot of the glacier. As we gained height, the clouds covering the impressive south face of Javakhishvili began to break and the occasional patch of sun lit up the 400m-high wall.

'Are you thinking what I'm thinking, Graham?'

'I think so... let's have a look at Javakhishvili.'

'Why not, there's nothing to lose. We could try that new line right of Tato's route.'

Earlier in the week, Tato had shown us a succession of unclimbed ramps and corners that led diagonally up the face to the right of an impending steep corner system that Tato had climbed with fellow Georgian guide Gujabidze. We were a little apprehensive as we uncoiled our ropes in the swirling cloud at the foot of the initial steep wall. We were concerned about weather, but we had also developed a healthy respect for the volcanic Chaukhi rock and did not always trust how well it was attached to the mountain. As it turned out the climbing was no more than VS, the rock quality was within acceptable limits, and we were on the summit by late afternoon. Our gamble had paid off, and *Perseverance* (4a) seemed an appropriate name.

It rained even harder on our final day, but despite the weather, we would go hill walking in the rain, and reached the tops of almost all the surrounding 3500m tops during our visit. Although the unsettled weather was a surprise (it certainly felt very Scottish), we returned to Aberdeen after a short but satisfying week-long trip.

The story should have ended there, but a few months later I was talking to Robin Campbell about the Caucasus at the SMC dinner in Fort William. Robin was intrigued by the suggestion that Chaukhi was first climbed by an American woman, and suggested that it may have been Una Cameron who made the first ascent. Robin kindly sent me a photocopy of Cameron's book (*A Good Line*, 1932, published privately), and sure enough she visited the Eastern Caucasus with two Courmayeur guides in 1932.

Their experience was far tougher than ours; just reaching the mountains was a journey of epic proportions. After travelling south across Europe, they took a steamer along the Mediterranean and the Black Sea to reach Batum on the western border of Georgia where the Russians treated them with the utmost suspicion. Their journey to the mountains was hampered by uncooperative horsemen and infestations of lice. Eventually they reached Chaukhi (phonetically spelled 'Tschauchee' by Cameron), but frustratingly only a handful of pages in *A Good Line* (which reads more like a travel diary than a mountaineering account), are devoted to details of their climbing. Over four consecutive days they made first ascents of all the four major Chaukhi summits, and they climbed Asatiani by almost the same route that we followed, in the remarkably fast time of four hours.

So the Georgians were incorrect. Graham and I were not the first non-Georgians to climb technical routes on Chaukhi, although in hindsight the peak name Kameruni, the third highest summit in the range, should have given us a clue! The redoubtable Una Cameron had been there nearly 80 years before, and as is so often the case in the mountaineering world, a British climber had been there first.

0.   Graham Dudley on first ascent of *Perseverance* (4a), Javakhishvili.
     (Simon Richardson)

ANINDYA MUKHERJEE

Zemu Gap From The South

The First Documented Ascent

The history of exploration around Kangchenjunga, especially around its south, south-east and east flanks, has always fascinated me. The classic journeys and adventures of pioneers like W.W. Graham, John Claude White, Douglas Freshfield, Alexander Kellas, Harold Raeburn, N.A.Tombazi, John Hunt and Paul Bauer ignited my imagination. The height of inspiration of course came from reading my hero Bill Tilman's account in the *Himalayan Journal* (Vol. IX) of his attempt on Zemu Gap from the south in 1936.

The primary challenge of climbing Zemu Gap from the south has always been its remote and complicated approach. Many failed just to reach the foot of this col, beyond which its apparently impregnable defences took Zemu Gap to a new level of exploratory climbing. In 1925, Greek photog-

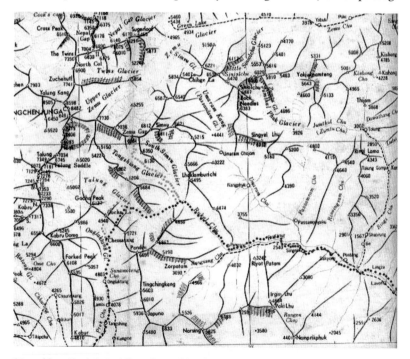

81.   Map: Red dotted line shows March 2011 route. Blue dotted line shows November 2011 attempt on Zemu Gap. Green dotted line is December 2011 route to Zemu Gap. *(Anindya Mukherjee)*

82. Base camp near the junction of streams from the Talung and Tongshyong glaciers. Sunrise on Pandim in the background. *(Anindya Mukherjee)*

rapher N.A.Tombazi is said to have made its first ascent from the south; but he did not take any photographs. To me, and to my long time expedition partner Thendup Sherpa, all the above factors seemed highly intriguing and certainly worth investigating.

From the south summit of Kangchenjunga (8476m) a high ridge extends east separating the Zemu glacier valley on the north from Tongshyong and Talung glaciers to the south. On this ridge, between Zemu Peak (7730m), Unnamed Peak (7038m) and Simvu Twins (6812m and 6811m) there is a sudden drop in altitude to form a col. At 5861m this col is more popularly known as the Zemu Gap[1]. To its north is the Zemu glacier and to its south the Tongshyong glacier. Its coordinates are 27° 40' 9" N, 88° 12' 53" E.

From the Zemu Gap a small, steep glacier flows down to Tongshyong as a tributary glacier. To climb the Zemu Gap from Tongshyong, one would have to negotiate two icefalls on this tributary glacier first and then find a route on the head wall. But first comes the approach problem. Approaching Zemu Gap from the north is straightforward. From the south, however, one has to cross the Guicha La from the Prek Chu valley, cross the Talung glacier, climb onto the Tongshyong glacier by Timan's 'snow col' and then arrive at the foot of the tributary glacier. Another way of reaching Tong-shyong could be to reach its snout (either from Guicha La-Talung route

1 Also referred to as 'Zemu La' and 'Cloud Gap' in some journals

83. Above: Camp 3 on the Tongshyong glacier showing the second icefall below the Zemu Gap, with part of the route marked. *(Anindya Mukherjee)*

84. Below: Final headwall below the Zemu Gap, showing line. *(Anindya Mukherjee)*

or through the Rukel-Rongyoung gorge route) and then traverse towards its head to reach the base of the tributary glacier that descends from the Zemu Gap. In 1975, an Indian team (A.J.S. Grewal) found the first option exhausting. They did at least reach Tongshyong and the base of Zemu Gap's glacier. In 2008 and 2010 respectively, a British team and another Indian team failed even to reach Tongshyong by the first option. I somehow preferred the second alternative. Since I had survived what Tilman called 'the trackless vale of tears', the Rukel-Rongyoung gorge route, in March 2011, I had planned for a direct approach to Tongshyong from Mangan via the gorge route.

Though Sikkim is reasonably accessible, only some half-dozen of its countless lofty peaks have been conquered, and many of its fascinating valleys and uplands have scarcely been trodden by Europeans. There is therefore plenty of scope for explorers and naturalists as well as for climbers. ... Nevertheless he is a bold man who, reading of these determined assaults, sometimes successful, sometimes splendid failures, will pronounce the summit of any peak in the Sikkim Himalaya to be definitely inaccessible.
Exploration and Climbing in the Sikkim Himalaya, Lt Col H. W. Tobin, 1930, *Himalayan Journal vol.II*

Albeit more than 80 years have passed since Tobin wrote the above lines, some part of Sikkim Himalaya has managed to retain its original flavour. While the factor of inaccessibility has reasonably abated over the past decades, a whole new hurdle has entered the equation – bureaucracy! The Talung Basin[2] (which falls partly within the Kangchenjunga National Park and partly in the north Sikkim Lepcha sanctuary called 'Dzongu') is a classic example. Even though this valley system has no proximity or direct access to the Indo-Tibetan borders it remains curtained behind restrictions and a mountain of paperwork.

In 2008 a British team got permission to cross Zemu Gap from the south and traverse the Zemu glacier valley down to Lachen. This was particularly encouraging news for me and Thendup Sherpa. With the support of my friend O.T.Lepcha (Tholung Ecotourism Cooperative Society) we too succeeded in procuring the necessary permits, resulting in the series of expeditions I would undertake in 2011.

To begin our exploration we reversed Claude White's route of July 1890, forcing up the Rongyoung-Rukel Chu gorges to connect Mangan, north Sikkim with Yoksum, west Sikkim in March 2011. This success reinforced our confidence that we were ready to attempt the Zemu Gap from the south. In November 2011 we crossed the Guicha La and went down the Talung glacier to set up a high camp on Tongshyong. But a five-day snowstorm halted our progress and we returned down the Rukel-Rongyoung gorges to Mangan. Finally, in December 2011 we were successful in climbing Zemu Gap from Tongshyong glacier – that is, the south.

2 Mostly referred to as Rukel - Rongyoung Chu gorges in this report.

Zemu Gap and the Talung Basin: Exploration, Attempts and Ascents

1890: John Claude White crossed the Guicha La, went down to Talung glacier (which he referred to as the 'Kangchen' glacier) and then followed the 'Talung/Ronggyaong' Chu ('Rungnu'- as per White) eastwards to Sakyong and finally to Ringen (present day location of the North Sikkim government offices above Mangan).
In his book, *Sikhim and Bhutan- Twenty One Years on the North–East Frontier 1887-1908*, White writes:

In 1890 I made one of my first expeditions to the snows, crossing the Giucha-la pass and from there making my way to Ringen, following a route the latter part of which had certainly never been traversed by a European, and I doubt by anyone, except possibly a very occasional Lepcha.

Tilman later called this gorge route 'the trackless vale of tears' (*When Men and Mountains Meet* p.321). Lepchas of the Dzongu valley referred to the Talung Chu as 'Ronggyaong' or simply 'Rongyoung' chu. In this report I have used 'Rongyoung'.
1899: Douglas Freshfield, accompanied by Professor Garwood attempted to determine the practicability of an ascent to the Zemu Gap by its northern approaches (Zemu glacier). Bad weather prevented them from making much progress beyond 'Green Lake'. Rinzin Namgyal and the Sella brothers were also part of this 'high level tour' (Freshfield, *Round Kangchenjunga*).
1910: Alexander Kellas with three coolies camped at 18,200 ft, just below Zemu Gap and went to the col on the morning of 12 May. 'The slope fell away steeply in front, and a few yards down there was a crevasse that stretched right across the gully.' ('The Mountains of Northern India and Sikkim', *AJ* 26, 113-142). This is probably the first documented ascent of the Zemu Gap from the north, i.e. Zemu glacier.
1920: First attempt on Zemu Gap from the south. Tobin and Harold Raeburn explored the Talung and Tongshyong glaciers. Tobin describes the approach to the Zemu Gap from the Tongshyong glacier: 'the narrow entrance and the mountain sides raked with such a continuous hail of rocks and debris that an approach by this route would have been little short of suicidal...' On their way out of Talung Basin they took Claude White's route of 1890 following the gorges of the Rukel and Rongyoung rivers. ('Exploration and Climbing in the Sikkim Himalaya', *HJ* II, 1-12).
1925: Tombazi made a tour of the locality and claimed to have made the first ascent to the Zemu Gap from the south. However he provided no photographic evidence. (*AJ* 38, 150; *Geographical Journal* 67)
1926: Captain Boustead declared he reached the Zemu Gap from the south (*GJ* 69, 344-350). His description raised the suspicions of Tilman who, after his own attempt from the south in 1936, suggested Boustead may have mistaken a col located at the head of Tongshyong glacier as the Zemu Gap.

Anindya Mukherjee (left) and Thendup Sherpa on the Zemu Gap. Looking north and north-east, upper Zemu glacier below, Twins glacier in the distance. *(Pemba Sherpa)*

Tilman wrote: 'The Zemu Gap differed so widely from the account I had read that I half believed a mistake had been made and that the genuine gap lay concealed behind some corner near the head of the Tongshyong. There was, however, no other break in the mighty south-east ridge of Kangchenjunga, and the low, easy col at the head of the glacier obviously led over into the wide bay at the head of the Talung. Is it possible that, in the thick weather prevailing when Captain Boustead was here, this had been mistaken for the Zemu Gap?' ('The Zemu Gap', *HJ* IX)

1929: Karl von Kraus and Joachim Leupold of Paul Bauer's German Expedition to Kangchenjunga climbed to the Zemu Gap in July-August 1929 from the Zemu glacier – the second ascent from north.

1936: Tilman's first attempt on the Zemu Gap from the south. He and Pasang Kikuli reached the Tongshyong by crossing a 'snow col' on the ridge running west to east that separates the Talung and Tongshyong glaciers. Tilman wrote: 'Although we were loath to give in, defeat seemed imminent, for beyond these obstacles lay the final ice-wall which from below appeared impregnable.' He was thwarted where the pair 'had a good view of the final wall .It was fully as high as we had feared, all iced, and appeared to overhang in places.' On his way out he followed the White (1890) and Raeburn (1920) route down the Ruykel-Rongyong Chu gorges to Sanklan Sampo below Mangan (*When Men and Mountains Meet*).

86. Above: Zemu Gap (5861m) in December 2011. *(Anindya Mukherjee)*

87. Left, John Hunt on the Zemu Gap in November 1937, having climbed from the north (Zemu glacier) side, cf. above.

Day 10: Poor visibility and worsening weather conditions made orientation difficult and forced an early halt after three hours. Camp 2 was at 4968m on the left lateral moraines.

Day 11: The sky finally cleared revealing that we were still far away from the small tributary glacier that descends from the Zemu Gap to meet the Tongshyong near its head. We did a recce and ferried loads to the intended site of camp 3.

Our observations revealed that there are two icefalls and a final head wall guarding Zemu Gap from any approach from the Tongshyong glacier. While the first icefall could be avoided by taking a scree gully on its true right, the second icefall has to be tackled head on. Not much could be seen of the final head wall. With mixed feelings of hope and despair we returned to Camp 2.

Day 12: We moved up to camp 3 established at 5250m on a moraine shelf above the first icefall. From here we had good views of the second icefall. Thendup Sherpa did a further recce that afternoon and came back to camp with optimism. The weather seemed to be stable at last and we had a great view all around. We felt privileged to be in a place that very few had reached.

Day 13: The three of us left camp III at 5.15am. It took six hours to climb the second icefall, which has a vertical height of about 250m, and the 200m head wall. The latter was climbed by a rock line that avoids the overhanging blue ice that dominates the centre of the Gap.

Standing on the Zemu Gap we felt very satisfied. North we could see the upper Zemu glacier, the junction of the Twins and Zemu glaciers, Sugarloaf (6459m) and surrounding mountains; east and ENE was the Simvu massif; west lay a steep slope with threatening séracs rising towards Peak 7038m; SSE we saw Peak 6350m, at the head of South Simvu glacier; and south were Pandim (6691m), Tilman's 'snow col' between the Talung and Tongshyong glaciers, the Guicha La (4940m), and Peak 5962m.

After taking lots of photographs we began retracing our steps. Many short pitches of down-climbing and five abseils on rock and ice brought us to relative safety at the foot of the second icefall. The Zemu Gap had been climbed from the south and this time we had come back with photographs.

Day 14: Descended to base camp.

Days 15 to 17: Over three days we retraced our route through the Rongyoung-Rukel gorges to 6th Mile village and Mangan.

Acknowledgements: This expedition would not have been possible without the support of my friend Kevin Hynes. I am also grateful to TECS, George Rodway, Priyadarshi Gupta of the Himalayan Club, Kolkata section and Colin Knowles of the British Zemu Gap Expedition 2008.

ROGER PAYNE

New Routes and a Mystery in West Sikkim

Between 16 October and 3 November 2011 David Kinsella (Aus), Arun Mahajan (Ind/USA) and I explored mountains on the east side of the Thangsing valley in West Sikkim, and climbed three summits as alpine-style day routes. This report corrects some information published in the 2009 *Alpine Journal* and mentions other climbs on nearby peaks, which help to answer questions that have surrounded the earliest ascents in this area by WW Graham in 1883.

88.   Bahini group from Chowkidar Camp (A Col, B unnamed, C Prabha Behin, D unnamed, E Kali Behin, F Soneri Behin, G Churi, H Kanchi Behin). *(Roger Payne)*

The Thangsing valley is the route of the popular trek to the Gocha La, which enjoys magnificent views of Kangchenjunga. The area explored in 2011 is just to the south of Lamalamani (c5650m), and above the Arralang valley. Julie-Ann Clyma and I had made an initial reconnaissance of this area on a trekking trip in October 2004 with Loreto and Ian McNaught-Davis. Having seen the potential and made some local contacts, we

On 12 July 2012, as this *AJ* went to press, Roger Payne was among nine climbers killed in an avalanche on Mont Maudit. A full tribute will appear in the next *Journal*. The *AJ* salutes a fine mountaineer and good friend.

89.　Tridesh (c. 5100m) showing the Kinsella-Mahajan-Payne line up the
north-east flank (II-III, PD+). *(Roger Payne)*

returned in March 2005 to make the first ascent of the lower north summit
of Lamalamani (with Kunzang Bhutia and Saga Rai of the Sikkim Amateur
Mountaineering Association – SAMA) and the first alpine-style ascent of
Tinchenkang (6010m), which we understood to be the third ascent of that
mountain.

We saw some peaks to the east of Lamalamani, which later I mistook
for Narsing in one of my photos that was published in the 2009 *AJ*
(vol.114,155). The peak shown is not Narsing, but an unnamed peak given
5526m on the 1:150,000 Sikkim Himalaya map (published by the Swiss
Foundation for Alpine Research 2006).

Bahini group

We called the group of peaks explored in 2011 the Bahini group, and
named individual summits to reflect the character of each peak. These
peaks are not shown on the Swiss map and as far as we could ascertain,
none of them had names or had been previously climbed. We hope the
nomenclature we have used (see below) is acceptable locally, regionally
and to any interested organizations.

With our base camp at Thangsing, we established a very simple but
comfortable advanced camp at around 4800m below a prominent rock
tower we called Chowkidar. On 23 October we made an acclimatisation
reconnaissance to the col between Lamalamani and Prabha Behin (an area
I first explored in 2005, but did not discover much then because of cloudy
conditions).

Tridesh (c5100m) was our first peak, which is just west of the Bahini
group, and was climbed on 27 October by Kinsella, Mahajan, and Payne.

Initially we descended from our camp to reach the peak, which we climbed via its north-east flank on snowed up rock (II-III, PD+). From the summit we could see that the east and south side of the mountain had extensive rock faces, and we had good views of the lakes below at Lam Pokri.

Soneri Behin (c5250m) was our second peak, which was climbed on 28 October by Kinsella, Mahajan, and Payne (also PD+). We initially retraced our route of the previous day, then headed up to a hanging valley with a very small glacier which we ascended to reach the east ridge via some very unstable rock. The ridge itself was more stable with enjoyable rock steps (II). From the summit we retraced our route down the ridge, then

90. Bahini group: Google Earth image showing ascents and peaks. *(Roger Payne)*

descended the snow couloir (II) on the north side to make a circular route back to Chowkidar camp. The northwest ridge of Soneri Behin includes another lower summit we called Kanchi Behin, and some remarkable rock towers we called Churi.

Prabha Behin (c5500m) was the third peak and was climbed on 29 October by Mahajan and Payne. It is the highest in the group, and is probably the summit on the Swiss map marked as 5480m (but felt somewhat higher). The ascent was via a snow and ice crest (III) in the broad northwest couloir, with a traverse at its top to the left to reach the crest of the north ridge. The crest of the ridge is mixed and exposed with some technical rock climbing (IV, AD+/D-). The summit block is small, and required an athletic single tool pull-up and heel hook to reach (and which turned out to be completely unnecessary as an easy ramp comes up from the south side). The connecting ridge to the lower summits to the west looked loose initially, but the lower summits look attractive, in particular Kali Behin,

91. Jopuno: (**A** direction of 2001 ascent, **B** presumed line of 2008 route, **C** false summit, **D** likely highest point of Jopuno, **E** line of 2009 ascent). *(Roger Payne)*

which seen from the west is a very impressive black tower.

Lamalamani and Jopuno

Just north of the Bahini group, in spring 2010 a UK/USA team led by Geoff Cohen climbed a new route on the north summit of Lamalamani (Cohen came to the conclusion, as we did in 2005, that the unclimbed south summit is higher). Cohen's team also visited the cols on both the south and north sides of Lamalamani, and made an ascent of the prominent rock summit in the north col. The team also planned a new route on Jopuno (5936m), but instead repeated the elegant and technical west ridge to the top of the granite (which was

92. Jopuno: Julie-Ann Clyma and Hugh Sheehan on the south-west face. *(Roger Payne)*

93. Lamalamani: the north summit seen from Jopuno. The right-hand skyline was taken during the first ascent in 2005. The face on the left was attempted by Payne and James Astill in 2009. *(Roger Payne)*

first climbed in challenging weather in March 2008 by an American team led by Jason Halladay).

Also on Jopuno, Julie-Ann Clyma, Hugh Sheehan and I climbed a new route on the south-west face on 7 November 2009, which provided very enjoyable mixed climbing at around D. We reached the crest of the west ridge at the top of the golden granite and followed the ridge on loose black rock and snow crests. We climbed towards a high point, which from photos of the 2008 ascent I had understood to be the summit. However, on getting close it seemed that the highest point was much further on. It was too late to continue along the ridge, so we reversed our route back along the ridge with darkness arriving just as we started a sequence of abseils down the face.

In 2001 Deepak Kumar Chettri, Kunzang Bhutia, and Sagar Raj climbed on the right side of the south-west face and along the south ridge of Jopuno (which was a very notable effort undertaken with minimal equipment). Having recently checked with them, it seems they reached a summit on the south ridge that may not be the highest point of Jopuno.

Hence, as for Jopuno, until someone makes a traverse of the summit ridge, or reaches the summit on a clear day to verify the highest point,

4.   Tridesh: Arun Mahajan enjoying the crest of the summit ridge. *(Roger Payne)*

the ascent by Halladay and Josh Smith in 2008 could be the first time the highest point of the mountain had been reached.

Meanwhile, what is certain is that there are many peaks and summits in Sikkim that can be explored and climbed in alpine style, and that access can be arranged through the local tourism organisations and Sikkim state authorities in Gangtok. In eight trips since 2004 to peaks in West and North Sikkim, I have enjoyed valuable assistance and great help from friends in SAMA, and Barap Bhutia and the staff of Sikkim Holidays in Gangtok. Also, the Travel Agents Association of Sikkim (TAAS) has undertaken impressive work to increase capacity and skills of service providers, and recently initiated actions to develop a structure for mountain rescue working with SAMA and the state authorities. So, you can approach organisations in Sikkim with confidence and know that they can make the necessary arrangements for exploratory treks and expeditions.

Nomenclature for Bahini group

Bahini - sisters,
Behin - sister,
Chowkidar - sentry/protector,
Churi - knife
Kali - black

Kanchi - small
Prabha - radiance/shine/glow
Soneri - golden
Tridesh - three lands

95. Prabha Behin: Arun Mahajan on the snow/ice crest during the first ascent. Koktang, Rathong and Kabru peaks in the background. *(Roger Payne)*

W.W. Graham in 1883
by Geoff Cohen, Roger Payne and Glyn Hughes

The first claimed ascent of Jopuno was by WW Graham who described his climb in 1883 as 'incomparably the hardest ascent we had in the Himalaya, owing to the great steepness of the glacier work' (*AJ* 12 [August 1884] 25-52). However in the opinion of several parties who have recently been to the area it is impossible to make any sense of his description of his climb. For example Graham wrote 'the glacier was crowned with steep rocks, which formed the edge of a noble amphitheatre formed by Jubonu and Nursingh'. The panorama sketch of the Kangchenjunga range published in 1882 (reproduced in *AJ* 114, p220), which was presumably available to Graham, indicates a topography somewhat like such an amphitheatre. But in fact there is an intervening ridge and those who have been high on Jopuno cannot understand what Graham means by this glacier, particularly since it is quite evident that if he climbed Jopuno he must have done so from the west, whereas Narsing is well east of Jopuno.

Graham also claimed to have climbed to within 40ft of the top of Kabru (7338m). This would have been by far the highest summit reached at that time, and for many decades after. However although Graham seems to have been a strong climber and explorer, and had two very experienced and fit Swiss companions, one of them the guide Emil Boss, at the time of Graham's reports some questioned the accuracy of his claims. A reappraisal by Willy Blaser and Glyn Hughes of the mountaineering world's reception of Graham's climb of Kabru was published in *AJ* 114 (2009) 219-228. Unfortunately that article was written without the benefit of Ian Mitchell and George Rodway's biography of Alexander Kellas *Prelude to Everest* (Luath Press, 2011 – *reviewed on page 352 of this journal*). Kellas, whose pioneering Himalayan explorations and scientific research on high altitude physiology have been somewhat ignored, had explored the Kabru area intimately and was of the firm opinion that Graham had been mistaken in his identification of Kabru (Mitchell and Rodway p.182). Kellas could make no sense of Graham's topographical description of Kabru's eastern flank.

96.   Prabha Behin: Arun Mahajan on the crux rock moves during the first ascent. *(Roger Payne)*

Kellas also devoted a great deal of thought to human performance at altitude; he was one of the first to make a scientific study of factors affecting acclimatisation and, together with the eminent biologist J.S. Haldane, conducted experiments in a hypobaric chamber to assess the possibility of climbing Everest without oxygen. He correctly predicted that an oxygen-free ascent of Everest might be made, with the summit slopes being climbed at a rate of about 300 feet per hour, exactly the speed achieved by Messner and Habeler in their first oxygen-free ascent of Everest in 1978. Graham had claimed an ascent from 18,500 feet to the 23,700-foot summit of 'Kabru' in just under eight hours, an average rate of about 670 feet per hour. This was not so different from the average rate of 600 feet per hour recorded by Longstaff's party on Trisul in 1907. What appears to have raised Kellas's doubts was Graham's assertion that he was not in the least affected by the altitude, though nobody seems to have doubted Carl Rubensen's report of suffering no 'real physical inconveniences' on the Norwegian near-ascent of Kabru in 1907. As Mitchell says, 'Victorian gentlemen did not stoop to accusing one another of lying' and indeed Kellas wrote 'while not attacking Graham's veracity, which is quite unimpeachable, he was almost certainly mistaken in the mountain he ascended'. In a letter to Norman Collie dated 9 April 1921, Kellas said: 'I will write to you again more fully with regard to this matter.' Presumably this second letter was never written. Two months later Collie died en route to Everest, and took any more detailed doubts about Graham and Kabru to his grave at Kampa Dzong.

TAMOTSU NAKAMURA

Unclimbed Peaks in Sichuan - 2012

In October 2011 one of the last 6000m-plus 'problems' in Sichuan was finally solved when an American-Chinese team reached the long-coveted main summit of Yangmolong (6060m). However that is by no means the end of Sichuan's story. Though, as shown on the map below, only a few unclimbed 6000 m peaks remain in the West Sichuan Highlands of China there are many alluring peaks not exceeding this magic number which should inspire and attract ambitious climbers. In this article I have updated, area-by-area, information on Sichuan's notable unclimbed peaks, giving an overview from north-west to south-east current to January 2012.

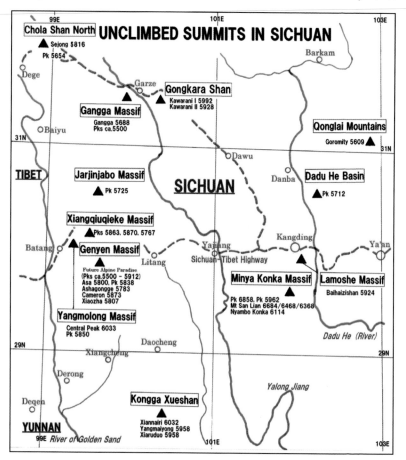

97. Above: Chola Shan North, Peak 5654m north face. (Takao Ohe)

98. Left: Chola Shan North, Sejong II (5816m) north-west face. (Tamotsu Nakamura)

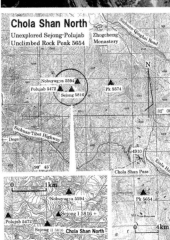

Chola Shan North

The Chola Shan is divided into North and South at the Chola Shan pass (4910m). The northern part is a massif comprising Sejong I and II (5816m), Nobuyugya (5594m) and Polujabu (5472m). It lies not far south of the ancient Zhogcheng Gompa. The highest peak Chola Shan I (6168m) (climbed) is south of the Lake Xinlujhai in the southern part of the range where several expeditions have already made ascents.

The area north of the Chola Shan

pass has been reconnoitred only by Tom Nakamura, in the fall of 2000, and by a party from the Hengduan Mountains Club (Japan) in summer 2011. However no one has attempted any ascents yet and therefore all the peaks remain untrodden. In addition an outstanding rock peak (5654m) just south of the Chola Shan pass is regarded as a worthy objective.

99. Gangga (5688m) north face. *(Tamotsu Nakamura)*

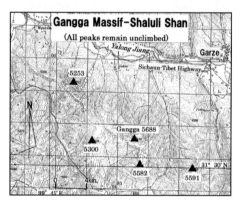

Gangga Massif – Shaluli Shan

This massif stretches southeastwards from the Chola Shan to Garze town south of the Yalong Jiang, a large tributary of the River of Golden Sand (the upper Yangtze). The highest peak, Gangga (5688m), has been attempted by a Japanese party from Nagano Prefecture. Several attractive rock peaks of some 5500m are clustered in the vicinity of Gangga; all remain unclimbed. The diplomat and orientalist Eric Teichman admired the grandeur of Gangga massif in his travels in 1918.

(Note: A Chinese map shows that the Shaluli Shan range covers a vast area up to the Genyen massif and beyond to Kongga Xueshan, crossing the Litang Plateau.)

Gongkara Shan – Kawarani

The two principal peaks, Kawarani I (5992m) and II (5928m), are located 30km east of Ganzi town and the Yalong Jiang river. Two Japanese parties and a British party have tried to set up a base camp for reconnaissance and climbing, but hostile monks of a lamasery in the vicinity have hindered

100. Kawarani I (5992m) (right) and II (5928m) south-west face. *(Tamotsu Nakamura)*

101. Kawarani I (5992m) north face *(Takao Ohe)*

their approach. The monks believe the Kawarani peaks to be sacred and have not allowed foreigners to climb them. This situation did not change through 2011 and the Ganzi Mountaineering Association did not issue any climbing permit to foreign expeditions.

Jarjinjabo Massif – Unclimbed Peak 5725

To the best of my knowledge almost all the prominent peaks in this group have been climbed, except for the second highest peak – one of 5725m. A Japanese party was first in the field, in 2001, climbing a rock tower that soars north of the Zhopu Pasture in 2001, and since then adjacent rock peaks west of Lake Zhopu have been climbed by American parties. The highest peak, Garrapunsum (5812m), was scaled by an Anglo-American party in October 2007. They had originally planned to attempt Kawarani in the Gongkara Shan but were denied access to the mountain.

Xiangqiuqieke Massif

This largely unknown massif is located south of the Sichuan-Tibet Highway and northeast of the Yangmolong massif. It stretches west to east for about 20km and includes peaks of 5863m (called Xiangqiuqieke), 5870m, 5767m, 5702m, 5595m and 5562m.

102. Jarjinjabo (5725m) (right snow peak) south face seen from Zhopu Pasture. *(Tamotsu Nakamura)*

103. Xiangqiuqieke (5863m) south face. *(Tim Boelter)*

In October 2005 a Japanese party from Yamanashi Prefecture approached the northern side on a reconnaissance. In July 2010 Tom Nakamura tried to gain access, also from north, i.e. from the Sichuan-Tibet Highway. In September 2011 Tim Church and Yvonne Pfluger of the New Zealand Alpine Club made an attempt on Xiangqiuqieke from the south

104. Above: Yangmolong Central Peak (6033m) (right), Dangchezhe.
(*Tim Boelter*)
105. Below: Yangmolong massif (5850m) north-west face. (*Tim Boelter*)

side. Unfortunately they were forced to abandon their ascent after setting up base camp because villagers refused to support the pair. All the peaks in the area therefore remain unclimbed.

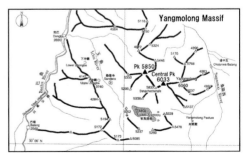

Yangmolong Massif

Situated some 16km east of Batang town, this massif has three principal peaks: Dang-chechengla (5833m) climbed by a Japanese party in 2002, Yangmolong Central or Makara (6033m) and Yangmolong Main (6060m), the highest peak. The main summit was scaled in October 2011 by an American-Chinese party led by Jon Otto and filmed by Tim Boelter after repeated attempts by Japanese, British and American-Chinese parties. Yangmolong Main is reckoned one of the toughest peaks in Sichuan.

There was a report that Yangmolong Central was climbed by a Korean party in 2002, but no detail or evidence has been forthcoming and climbers who have been to Yangmolong question the Korean ascent. For the purposes of this article, therefore, the Central Peak is treated as unclimbed. Another outstanding peak of 5850m also remains unclimbed.

106. Genyen massif, Cameron (5873m) east face
(T. Obtulovic)

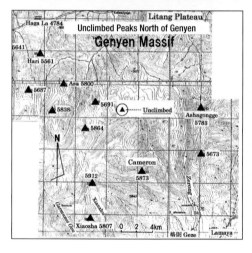

Genyen Massif – Future Alpine Paradise

The Genyen massif covers a wide area on the Litang Plateau south of the Sichuan-Tibet Highway and in near future is likely to become an 'alpine paradise'. It is already beginning to draw climbers' attention.

The main summit, Genyen (6204m), was first climbed by a Japanese party in 1988; an Italian party made the second ascent via a new route on the east face. The second highest peak (5964m) and Sachun (5716m, seen from an ancient lamasery, Rengo Gompa, were scaled by American parties. Americans Charlie Fowler and Christine Boskoff perished on Genyen in December 2006.

Many challenging rock peaks of 5500 to 5900m north and north-east of Genyen remain untouched: These include:

1. Asa (5800m) and Ashagongge (5783m) seen from the Sichuan-Tibet Highway passing through the Litang Plateau.

2. Fantastic granite peaks Cameron (5873m) Xiaozha (5807m) and other challenges viewed from a high pass, Three Smith Brothers (4800m) between Litang and Lamaya.

3. Rock peaks clustered just north of the Genyen and further north

107. Genyen massif, (c. 5600m) east face. *(Katka Mandulova)*

including attractive peaks of 5838m and 5784m and several others between 5700 and 5900m.

Kongga Xueshan (Kongkaling) Massif

The Kongga Xueshan massif lies in Daocheng County and has three famous snowy peaks, all still unclimbed:

1. Xiannairi (6032m), the highest peak, was attempted by a Japanese party in 1989.

108. Litang Plateau, Asa (5800m) north face. *(Tamotsu Nakamura)*

2. The stunningly beautiful pyramid Yangmaiyong (5958m) – circumambulated in 1928 by the botanist-explorer Joseph Rock who called the mountain Jambeyang. Fowler and Boskoff reached to within 500m of the summit.

3. Xiaruduo (5958m) – once attempted by an American party.

At present the local government of Daocheng County does not permit climbing on any of these peaks, regarded as sacred

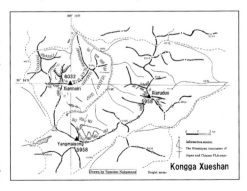

by the local Tibetan inhabitants. The area is developing as a tourist destination and attracting hundreds of trekkers.

109.
Kongga Xueshan,
Xiannairi (6032m)
north face.
(Tamotsu Nakamura)

110.
Kongga Xueshan,
Xiaruduo (5958m)
west face.
(Tamotsu Nakamura)

111.
Kongga Xueshan,
Yangmaiyong
(5958m) north-west
face.
(Tamotsu Nakamura)

Lamoshe Massif – Daxue Shan

Early explorers referred to Lamoshe as the 'Mountains of Tatsienlu', the massif being situated just east of the town of Kangding, the Tibetan name of which is 'Tatsienlu'. The highest peak is Lamoshe (6070m), first climbed by an American party in 1993; a Czech climber made the second ascent, solo, in 2010. Other peaks of around 5800m have been climbed by New Zealand, American, Canadian and Chinese parties, but the second highest peak, Baihaizishan (5924m) remains unclimbed.

12. Lamoshe massif, Baihaizishan (5924m) west face. *(Tamotsu Nakamura)*

Minya Konka Massif – Daxue Shan

Daxue Shan is the largest range in Sichuan. Only a few of its 6000m peaks remain unclimbed, the most outstanding, from south to north, are as follows:

1. Nyambo Konka (6114m): an NZ-American party attempted the east face in 2009.

2. San Lian (called Long-shan) comprising summits of 6684m, 6468m and 6368m. All three look hard propositions.

3. Peak 6858m, highest unclimbed peak in the massif, just south-west of Minya Konka (7556m)

4. Peak 5962m between Donogomba (5960m) and Daddomain (6380m).

5. Unattractive peak of 6209m on the ridge between Mts Edgar (E-Kongga) (6618m) and Grosvenor (6376m).

113. Minya Konka massif: San Lian east face. Summits from right: 6684m, 6468m, 6368m. *(Zhang Shaohong)*

114. Minya Konka massif: Nyambo Konka (6114m) west face. *(Pedro Detjen)*

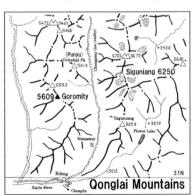

115. Qonglai Mountains: Goromity (5609m) south face. *(Tamotsu Nakamura)*

Qonglai Mountains

Climbers have flocked to the Qonglai mountains in the last decade. In consequence, almost all its notable peaks, including Siguniang (6250m) and surrounding 5200 – 5900m peaks have been ascended and new routes have been opened on difficult rock peaks. According to Kenzo Okawa, a Japanese photographer, who works in the Siguniang National Park, the only unclimbed peak is Goromity (5609m) which was attempted

6. Dadu He (River) basin, Peak 5712m north face. *(Tamotsu Nakamura)*

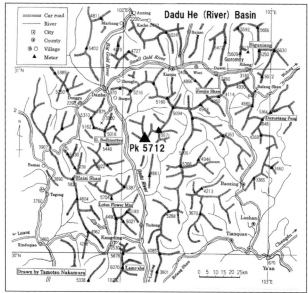

by a Chinese party about 2009 and by a Japanese party in the summer of 2011.

Dadu He (River) Basin

Many 5300m to 5700m peaks range along both sides of Dadu He (River) between Danba and Luding. The highest peak is 5712m on the left bank of the river however there is very little information on the mountains in this area and no climbing recorded.

Alps & Norway

117. John Fairley, *Dent du Géant*, oil on canvas, 422x593mm, 2009

SIMON RICHARDSON

'A Very Tempting Prize Indeed'

Punta Baretti's South-west Spur

My fascination with the Italian side of the Mont Blanc range began
way back in July 1980. It was my second alpine season and, with
fellow student Mike Harrop, I made an ascent of the *Contamine Route* on
the west face of the Petites Jorasses. It was my first *grande course*, and we
climbed the route in big boots and carried bivouac gear, as was the custom
of the time. I can remember balancing on the tips of my boots, and finding
the slabby climbing a little run out and scary, but it is the descent into
Italy that remains firmly imprinted on my mind. We just made the upper
reaches of the Frebouze glacier by nightfall, bivouacked on a little rocky
rognon, and next morning made a glorious walk down past the Gervasutti
hut to the valley.

The sunny ambiance of
Val Ferret with a backdrop
of high and mysterious
alpine walls contrasted
sharply with the more
austere, but better-known,
Chamonix valley. The
satisfaction of starting in
one country and finishing
in another added a sense of
journey, only to be emphasised by the hitchhike back
to France via the Mont
Blanc tunnel. Thirty years
on, it is a little sad that
modern alpinists rarely
enjoy the same pleasure

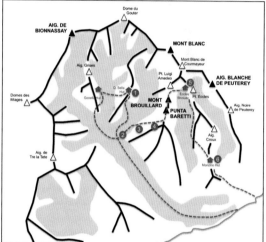

118. Sketch map of Mont Blanc, south side

of traversing the range after climbing this classic route. The chains and
bolts on *Anouk* now lead straight back down to the glacier. Going down
into Italy would be extremely perverse with such a straightforward abseil
descent, and as a result, this classic mountain route has been transformed
into a straightforward rock climb.

Val Ferret and the Italian side of the range made a big impression. I was
back in 1982 with Nick Kekus to climb the *Gervasutti Route* on the east face
of the Grandes Jorasses and the following summer, Roger Everett and I
made the third ascent of the east face of the Petites Jorasses via the *Bonatti*

147

119. Duncan Tunstall climbing the west wall of the First Tower on Day 1 (Pitch 11) of the first ascent of Punta Baretti's South-West Spur. *(Simon Richardson)*

Route. The granite was so good that I returned to climb on the east faces of the Gruetta (twice) and Leschaux, and then back to the Petites Jorasses again. All these routes were climbed on perfect rock, away from the crowds and encompassed a genuine sense of adventure – all very different from the hustle and bustle of the Chamonix Aiguilles. Meanwhile the Italian side of

Mont Blanc beckoned. Ascents of the Central Pillar of Frêney and the Red Pillar of Brouillard were rites of passage, but a new route on the South Pillar of Frêney in 1995 (the first time it had been climbed in its entirety) with Chris Cartwright brought the most satisfaction.

During the spring of 2009, the urge to return to the south side of Mont Blanc returned. Rather than adopt the standard alpine approach of lightweight raids into the mountains to snatch routes, the idea was to treat the trip more like a mini-expedition. The plan was to spend the majority of our nine-day visit in the mountains, as you may do in the greater ranges, and hopefully travel some new ground too.

Luckily, Duncan Tunstall was keen on the idea, even though I was rather vague about what our objective might actually be. By chance, that June I came across a reference from Luca Signorelli on the internet

120. Duncan Tunstall moving up to the foot of the steep headwall on Day 2 (Pitch 25). *(Simon Richardson)*

about a recent ascent of Punta Baretti from the Miage glacier. Three Italian climbers had repeated *Au Bout de la Monde*, (a 1200m long couloir that had been first climbed then skied by Pierre Tardivel and friends in 2006), descended to Col Emile Rey and then made the long descent to the Quintino Sella hut in a very long day. Punta Baretti (4013m), and the neighbouring Mont Brouillard (4069m), are situated on the lower Brouillard Ridge of Mont Blanc. They are rarely climbed, except by collectors of 4000m peaks, but their remote position gives them a certain cachet. 'For inaccessibility and solitude, the pair are unsurpassed anywhere in the Alps,' says Martin Moran in his AC guidebook *The 4000m Peaks of the Alps*.

I wasn't aware of the existence of the Tardivel couloir, but news of the Italian's ascent sent a tingle down my spine. I knew there was a huge unclimbed rock spur on the south-west side of Baretti. I'd seen a small picture of it in *Vertical* magazine in the early 1990s, but it appeared completely inaccessible, dropping into the steep and chaotic Mont Blanc glacier, which was full of tottering séracs and impossible crevasses.

Intrigued, I read the Italian's trip report and was astonished to see that the lower part of the glacier had receded so much that instead of being an impenetrable icefall, it was now a steep smooth ice snout that led all the way to the foot of the spur. Global warming does not often help mountaineers, but in this case it had given Duncan and I a compelling objective. A new 1200m-high feature leading directly to the summit of a 4000m peak was a very tempting prize indeed.

121. Duncan Tunstall setting up the second bivouac at the end of Pitch 29. *(Simon Richardson)*

Summer 2009 was warm and dry and the Alps looked rather tired when I arrived in Chamonix at the end of August. Duncan had already been in town for a week climbing with Francoise Call. The weather was poor as we drove through the tunnel and walked up to the Petit Mont Blanc bivouac hut, and next day we scoped the upper two-thirds of the route from near the summit of Petit Mont Blanc. Through the blowing clouds our spur looked steeper and more complex than I imagined, and rather worryingly, it appeared to be defended by a series of steep towers near its base. (We would find out later how big a barrier they really were). The weather remained poor, so we spent another night in the hut before descending back to Courmayeur to pack our sacks for the route.

The descent from the summit of Punta Baretti was preying on my mind. It is most commonly climbed from Col Emile Rey reached from the Eccles bivouac huts, but the summer had been so dry that the small hanging glacier below the Brouillard Pillars was said to be impassable, and a fixed rope had even been installed to allow access to the rognon containing the Eccles huts themselves. Our alternative descent was to go down the west side of Col Emile Rey and cross the upper Mont Blanc glacier to the Quintino Sella hut as the Italians had in June. So we agreed on a rather bizarre sports plan. On day one we would climb up to the Quintino Sella hut – a mini alpine route in its own right – and leave a cache of food. On day two we would descend back to the Miage glacier and bivouac below the route

122. Duncan Tunstall moving along the ridge to the foot of the Red Tower on
       Day 3 (Pitch 32). *(Simon Richardson)*

ready to start climbing on day three.

We rose before dawn on 5 September and set off from the end of the
road in Val Veny just after daybreak. Stormy weather had cleared to leave a
magically clear morning. As we gained height, Mont Tondu and the Aiguille des Glaciers came into view, covered in a dusting of fresh snow and
tempting us to return for a future visit. Progress on the moraine-covered
Miage glacier was frustratingly slow with our heavy loads packed with six
night's food. After a couple of hours we made a cache for the technical

123. Duncan Tunstall making the delicate traverse to reach the bottomless chimney on t
right hand side of the Red Tower on Day 3 (Pitch 33). *(Simon Richardson)*

gear on the glacier and continued up to the hut. Our spur on Punta Baretti
was grossly foreshortened from below and the glacier snout of hard grey
ice looked alarmingly steep. More concerning was that the easiest line
followed a central scoop that was a natural funnel for anything that fell
down it. And sure enough there was a pile of ice blocks, the size of foot-
balls, scattered around its foot.

The climb up to the Quintino Sella hut was long and tiring. The initial
glacier section had stretches of steep ice and the scramble up to the hut itself
was rather exposed in parts. With hindsight, I suspect we went the wrong
way, but Duncan is in his element on ground like this, and led the way
up little vegetated grooves and airy traverses until we eventually gained
the final steep path leading to the tiny wooden hut perched on an eyrie
overlooking the Mont Blanc glacier and the spectacular Miage basin. Next
morning we took the alternative descent down the Y Couloir to the Miage
glacier. The couloir is renowned for stonefall, but we were early enough to
avoid it although we had a testing time finding our way through the maze
of crevasses to cross the glacier to reach the Gonella hut, which was in the
process of being rebuilt.

We arrived back at our cache of gear below Baretti's south-west spur
on the lower glacier later that afternoon. The prospect of a bivouac on

the crumbling moraine was not very inviting, but then Duncan, with a gleam in his eye, announced he had found the perfect solution. I was a little perplexed, until he pointed to a sheet of eight by four plywood lying on the top of an adjacent moraine. It had presumably been dropped from a helicopter ferrying supplies for the Gonella hut rebuild, so we carried it to the foot of the spur and set up our bivouac in relative luxury. We had been on the move for two long days. The weather was good, but travel on the dry and depleted glaciers was desperately slow.

We slept fitfully and woke at 2 am. The plan was to climb the glacier snout before dawn. It looked easy enough to solo – no more than Scottish Grade III – but the ice was hard and brittle and I was concerned about the consequences of being hit by falling ice. We decided the safest approach was to pitch the route, leapfrogging our two ice screws from belay to belay, so we were always protected. I can't pretend I enjoyed those 13 rope-lengths. It took a long time but at least we were relatively safe. The route followed an icy runnel of softer ice – easier climbing but in the line of fire – until it eventually veered right through a series of triple bergschrunds to enter the mouth of the Couloir au Bout de la Monde. We climbed this for another three rope-lengths to gain a steep gully cutting the right side of the south-west spur.

Now was the moment of truth. What would the rock be like? It is easy to think of Mont Blanc being comprised of perfect granite, but the Miage lies on the junction between granite and schist. Duncan took the lead, and the rock was truly awful. Fortunately we had practised our loose rock climbing skills earlier that summer whilst climbing on a previously unclimbed 200m-high crag in the Southern Cairngorms. We climbed five pitches of IV until the gully steepened and the rock became too shattered. Duncan took to the right wall and led a difficult pitch of VI before returning to the gully and continued up the west side of the spur. Above loomed the First Tower. We climbed its west wall in the afternoon sun for another four pitches to reach a notch below the dramatic Second Tower. Duncan was in a sombre mood when I arrived.

'We're going to have to go down. It's impossible to go on from here.'

It certainly looked difficult above. The Second Tower was a vertical 30m-high blade of schist, no more than two or three metres thick and narrowing to a smooth wafer-thin blade of rock on its leading edge. It was like an upturned knife with its cutting edge facing towards us.

'How about crossing the ridge and looking down the other side?' I suggested.

'I've had a look – it's miles down the other side, and there's no way of regaining the crest.'

I peered into the depths and it appeared that Duncan was correct. But the east side of the spur was now in deep shadow and I was hopeful that the morning light would reveal another solution. The weather was good and there was no point in going down right now. We had nearly 30 pitches of rock and ice below us and we were tired. So whilst Duncan put his garden improvement skills to good use excavating us a bed for the night, I cooked our dinner of soup and noodles using the remnants of old snow lying on the sloping ledge.

What a difference a good night's sleep makes! When the rising sun illuminated the other side of the ridge next morning, it looked like we would be able to outflank the Second Tower by making two diagonal abseils across the steep east wall to gain a ledge system on the right. Before we left Courmayeur we had debated what kind of abseil tat to take. Duncan had bought 5mm perlon cord because it was light (and cheap) whilst I insisted we need at least 7mm to be safe. Unfortunately we could only find 7mm Kevlar cord on sale in Courmayeur, so we reluctantly bought a 20m length at great expense. When Duncan put his weight on the 5mm cord for the first abseil, the sharp crest cut through it like a knife (he was backed up). Second time around, with the Kevlar in place, we made it safely down. Diagonal abseils can be nasty affairs, but eventually we gained solid ground on the east side of the spur, and two pitches later we had outflanked the evil Second Tower.

Another two rope-lengths saw us past the Third Tower and we continued along a whaleback ridge for three pitches. It felt as if we were really gaining height now with ever-increasing exposure on both sides. Two steep pitches up the Grey Tower led to a huge gap in the ridge, which was fortuitously bridged by a huge jammed boulder the size of a small car.

The terrain above was steep, and Duncan led a fine pitch of VI up a grooved arête to gain easier ledges and the transition from schist to granite. We continued for another four pitches below the steep headwall trending left towards a prominent notch in the skyline, before moving up an open chimney system that led to a cosy ledge on the west side of the spur and our second bivouac. Our progress had slowed considerably from Day One and we had only climbed 13 pitches, but the terrain had been steeper and we were in an upbeat mood, confident that we would finish the route the next day.

We woke to another glorious morning and high on Mont Blanc we could see the Bosses Ridge on the skyline, with dozens of climbers moving along it like tiny ants. It was cold on the west side of the spur and we were keen to start moving. The rock was a little snowy from the bad weather earlier in the week, and we climbed steep ground to the foot of the steep Red Tower that we assumed would be the last obstacle on the spur.

But the route kept us guessing. Above was a steep shattered tower with a narrow shattered crest. To reach it we followed a narrow tightrope, and I hand traversed a wafer thin ridge, to reach the Red Tower. Duncan led across a delicate traverse and then climbed an awkward bottomless chimney that led to a notch and the west side of the spur. We could smell success now; and all that was left were three pitches up icy grooves to easier ground. The way to the top was clear and an hour's scrambling took us up the final 200m to the summit.

We shook hands, slapped each other on the back, took the obligatory summit photos, and generally felt pretty pleased with ourselves. But our

124. Duncan Tunstall and Simon Richardson on the summit of Punta Baretti
on Day 3. *(Duncan Tunstall)*

elation was tempered by thoughts about the descent. We traversed broken
rock across Mont Brouillard and descended to Col Emile Rey. We had
already written off the stonefall-ridden descent to the Miage glacier; our
way back was now via the Eccles huts. The east slope of the col comprised
wet snow and loose blocks and we made nine long abseils to the little
pocket glacier below the Brouillard Pillars. We should have made our third
bivouac here as it was now dark, but I blindly led through the maze of late
season crevasses to reach the foot of the rognon supporting the bivouac
huts. We were completely off route, but three pitches of icy rock guided
by ancient debris that had been dropped from above finally led to the sanctuary of the tiny Eccles Bivouac huts.

It was nearly midnight. As we entered the lower hut we woke a couple of
young Swiss climbers who were intent on climbing the Red Pillar of Brouillard the next day. They couldn't understand where we had come from.

'But there are no rock climbs from the Miage glacier up Punta Baretti.
You climb it from the Eccles, no?'

We were too tired to try and explain, so we smiled dumbly and pretended
that we were just a pair of incompetent British climbers, and quietly went
to sleep.

Next day we slowly descended through the detritus of a long hot summer.
The snow slopes had been transformed into stone-raked slabs of black ice,
and the only way to cross the glaciers was to follow underground mazes
of ice. We arrived at the Monzino hut in time for dinner and decided to
stay the night – we were on holiday after all. Next morning we wandered
down to Val Veny and walked back up to the car. Our plan had worked.
We had climbed Punta Baretti by its south-west spur, but more importantly

we had enjoyed a memorable adventure in the mountains. We had been on the move for seven days, made three bivouacs, and climbed 42 new rock pitches and 13 pitches of ice.

Once we arrived home, we were surprised to find our ascent reported on various climbing news websites across the world. At first there was incredulity that such a prominent feature could remain unclimbed in the heart of the Mont Blanc massif, but soon enough our outing was recognised for what it truly stood for – with a little imagination it is still possible to have a wild and remote experience and seek out new ground, even in a mountain range as well-known as Mont Blanc. Without doubt, throughout the Alps, many more exploratory adventures remain.

Summary: An account of the first ascent of the South-West Spur of Punta Baretti (4013m) by Simon Richardson and Duncan Tunstall, 7 to 9 September 2009. The 1200m-long ED1 route was climbed in 42 pitches and was part of a seven-day journey crossing the divide between the Miage and Brouillard glaciers on the south side of the Mont Blanc range.

South-West Spur Punta Baretti (4013m), 1200m ED1
Simon Richardson and Duncan Tunstall, 7-9 September 2009

A sustained mountaineering route up the prominent spur left of the Couloir au Bout de la Monde (*Tardivel-Janody-De Sainte Marie 2006*). 60m ropes used. Approach from the Miage glacier by climbing the glacier snout of the right branch of Glacier du Mont Blanc (ice up to 45 deg.) bearing right to reach the foot of the Couloir au Bout de la Monde.

1-3 Cross the bergschrund on the right and continue up the couloir for 3 ropelengths to the foot of a steep gully cutting the left wall.
4-10 Climb the gully for 5 ropelengths (IV). When the gully steepens avoid loose rock by climbing the steep chimney on the right wall (VI) for another pitch. From the top of the chimney traverse back left into the gully and continue up it for another ropelength to reach ledges on the west side of the spur.
11-14 Climb the steep west wall of the First Tower for 4 ropelengths up a series of cracks and grooves, trending left where possible to reach a small ledge just below the top of the First Tower (V+). First bivouac.
15 The continuation to the Second Tower is a knife-edge holdless ridge that completely bars upward progress. Instead, make 2 diagonal abseils on the east side of the spur, then climb up and right for 15m to gain a crescent-shaped ledge below a prominent fault-line cutting the east side of the spur.
16-17 Climb the fault-line for 2 pitches (V+) to the top of the Second Tower.
18-19 Continue up easier ground for two pitches turning the Third Tower on the right.

South-West Spur Punta Baretti
1200m, ED1
Simon Richardson and Duncan Tunstall
7-9th Sept 2009

Second bivouac

Tardivel Couloir

Approximate line

Punta Baretti 4013m

Red Tower

Prominent Notch

Steep Headwall

Grey Tower

Whaleback Ridge

Third Tower

Couloir au Bout de la Monde
Tardivel-Janody-De Sainte Marie 2006

Second Tower

First Tower

Mont Blanc Glacier

20-21 Continue easily along the horizontal Whaleback Ridge for 100m to the foot of the steep Grey Tower.

22-23 Move right onto a giant chockstone (V) to gain the right side of the tower and then turn it on the right for two ropelengths before descending into a deep notch floored by a large flat chockstone.

24 Exit the notch by climbing the grooved arête above with a steep exit (VI) to gain easier ledges. This marks the transition to granite.

25-27 Move up and left for three pitches below the Steep Headwall above to gain the Prominent Notch on the left skyline (IV).

28 Move up and right on the west side of the spur to gain a ledge just left of a slabby corner (IV). Second bivouac.

29-30 Climb the slabby corner (V) and continue up easier ground to foot of the Red Tower.

31 Climb the tower on the right and climb cracks on the east wall (V).

32 Continue up and right up cracks on the right flank of the spur to below a steep shattered tower (V+).

33 Turn the tower on the right to gain a steep chimney (V+) and climb this to a notch.

34 Continue up easy ground on the west flank of the ridge.

35-36 Climb icy grooves (past an initial chockstone) to the crest of the spur and easier ground.

37-42 Continue up scree and snow slopes for 200m to reach the summit.

ANDY CAVE

Ecstasy

Simon Nadin and I abseiled through thick, cascading mist down the south face of the Simelistock. It was summer 2002 and we had just climbed *Agony*, a Kaspar Ochsner masterpiece on impeccable rock. The final abseil was free hanging and out to the left a line of ancient cord fixed to withered bolts fidgeted in the wind. I vowed to track down the route and return, but I never made time for it; there were so many big trips to do and whenever I was in the Alps I was always working as a mountain guide. As the years passed I began questioning whether the route even existed. Maybe I had imagined it. After all, I couldn't find any information about it.

I assumed that if it was an existing climb it must be an aid route and that to free it we might need to place bolts. I had only ever placed one bolt before, on an unclimbed wall in the Karakoram to hang a tent from. It's the only time I have ever carried a bolt kit, a hand drilling set-up borrowed from Paul Nunn. I had clipped plenty of bolts mind and I had respect for some of the long committing routes established in Switzerland that mixed the use of traditional gear with bolts and kept the climbing engaging. Whilst climbing such routes on the walls of the Rätikon and the Wenden, you probably weren't going to die if you fell, though at times it might feel like it.

Over the years, my memory of the line on the Simelistock dimmed, but the flame was never quite extinguished. Perhaps I realized that even to attempt it I would need to be in great shape. *Agony* had felt hard and this climb looked steeper. More recently I had been doing a lot of rock climbing, I was doing F8a's quickly and then fired an F8b. Life in the old dog yet, I thought. I have never been one for writing lists of objectives, but recently I've scribbled a few. I kept writing 'Swiss Thing' right at the top. Eventually, I emailed Twid Turner, one of the keenest and most accomplished wall climbers anywhere. He is strong, addicted to adventure, loves to see things through and has a sense of humour. We would need all of those qualities.

It is only when you arrive at the Engelhörner hut in the Bernese Oberland that the potential of these peaks is revealed.

'Locals call it little Patagonia,' Twid said.

'Such a wild place,' I said, staring at the tight cirque of spires and walls.

The solemn guardian, Bruno, didn't seem interested in our probing, but eventually passed us an old guidebook.

'That must be it,' I said. 'The *Keusen and Burkli Route*, 1972, A2/3.'

'Bruno, do you know of this climb?' Twid asked.

'Argghh you should not go there, very bad equipment. Nicht gut.'

I felt the hunger growing. We filled up our water bottles then continued,

25. Andy Cave seconds pitch one of *Ecstasy*. *(Andy Cave)*

126. The Engelhörner south walls from the Engelhörner hut, Bernese Oberland.
(Andy Cave)

weaving our way up a damp gully and across a sweep of slabs until beneath the base of the bulging wall. We decided the best plan would be to climb it as an aid route first. Twid led off, veering left of the original route over two big overhangs, placing some new bolts along the way before joining the aid line at the first belay. It was late now. Abseiling off, Twid landed 10 metres out from the base; and the next pitch looked savagely overhanging too.

For the next few days the air was cold and damp and to add to our trials the original fixed protection was mainly marginal golo-bolts interspersed with the occasional better looking specimen. We had to place more bolts than originally planned and our already blunt drill bit stopped working. We retreated to the valley to relax and to visit a DIY store – not an experience I had previously tasted on an alpine holiday. Returning to the mountain, we made it to the terrace a couple of pitches beneath the summit. The next day started cold and dreary, but we had no choice but to try and free climb it; I had to fly home from Geneva that evening.

After a couple of false starts and with freezing fingers, Twid valiantly freeclimbed pitch one. This pitch itself was world class, tiny fingerholds to start and technical before two tiring bulges and a final sting in the tail to gain the belay.

'Right, are you feeling strong?' Twid joked as I arrived.

We craned up at the bulging wall.

'I'm going to crush it,' I said. Inside I felt stressed and rushed.

I tightened my boots and then powered up to clip a Leeper peg that hung upside down from a hollow flake. I bounced to an edge, clipped an old bolt and then moved swiftly to a decent hold. Forearms swelling rapidly, I began the first crux sequence reaching for a one-finger layaway and then jumped rightwards. Suddenly I was off, arcing backwards down the wall. I hung on the rope, pulled back up and placed small dabs of chalk where I thought I needed to place my feet next time. I went back down to the ledge and pulled the ropes.

We both felt this pitch would be the key to unlocking the climb. Just one move that is too difficult could mean failure. I had to put this fear of failure out of sight and stay focused. An hour later I made it through the first hard section and pounced from two tiny pockets to a razor sharp ramp. My shoulders were tiring, the skin was thin and we had two more steep pitches. I caught the very edge

127. Mike 'Twid' Turner approaching the south face of the Simelistock, left, Vorderspitze to the right. *(Andy Cave)*

of the ramp. Somewhere on a wall to the right a couple of Swiss climbers shouted encouragement. I felt my fingers uncurling. Off!

'Argghh!' I hung on the rope dejected.

'Let's go to the top and maybe try it again on the way down,' Twid suggested.

The next two pitches were superb but intricate and it was late by the time we reached the terrace. We descended and dashed to the airport making a promise to return at the end of the summer.

The forecast was variable for our second visit, but we felt this was it; we simply had to do it. It had not been easy to stay fit through the summer: Twid had been guiding a lot and I had been nursing a shoulder injury. Alistair Lee joined our team, hoping to get some images and film footage. Al is a great guy, but undoubtedly the camera brought extra pressure.

'So how are you feeling right now?' Al held the camera just a couple of metres away as I tightened my boot before the fierce second pitch.

Twid had climbed the first pitch well. Now the sun beat down on the sea of tiny holds that disappeared up above.

'I feel stressed,' I replied.

But something inside of me wanted to do this. The first glimpse of it all those years before, the attempt earlier in the summer and now this. I was ready for it. After one or two attempts, I would be exhausted. It would be ideal to climb it straightaway. From the one finger layaway I jumped right and grabbed a small horn of rock, yelling with relief. From the two tiny pockets I had to wait for Al to move out of the way and then slapped the ramp. I rested and then attacked the next section, even managing to find an unplanned rest. With each move the thought of falling became more unpalatable. Then I started to traverse back right past the old bolts, feet pasted on smears, hands straining on faint undercuts, heart beating wildly.

129. Andy Cave at the crux on the first ascent of *Ecstasy* (F7c+, 250m) on 13 September 2011. *(Alistair Lee)*

'Come on Andy!' willed Twid.

Trying to control movement when you are at your limit is not easy, but without control all is lost. Twice I started to fall but pulled back in. The sweat ran across my cheeks as I chalked fingers.

'Keep going!' urged Al, as the lens flew from his camera, narrowly missing my head. As if I didn't have enough to deal with for goodness sake. I clawed and fought, blowing until I reached the belay. Sheer elation.

Twid took a while to climb the next pitch and was frustrated at having to make a very difficult move above old rotten bolts, only being able to clip the new one afterwards. But his tenacity was impressive. I congratulated him at the belay. Our finger tips were sore and numb from pulling on so many small sharp holds, but there was no way of stopping us now.

'We've done it!' I shouted down the wall.

An airy arête and ridge led to the summit where we scrawled our names in the book and then paused to admire the magnificent views; Meiringen behind us, the giant Kingspitze north face straight ahead. Finally, the 'Swiss Thing' had come alive.

Summary: *Ecstasy* (F7c+, 250m) , first free ascent of the *Keusen Route* on the south-west face of the Simelistock (2482m), Engelhörner, Bernese Oberland, 13 September 2011 by Andy Cave and Mike 'Twid' Turner.

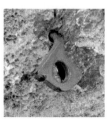

128. 1972-style ironmongery. *(Andy Cave)*

DAVID PICKFORD

Fjord Fandango

North

Waking in the dawn light at quarter to five, last night's traffic silenced and gone, I smell the midsummer air coming off the streets and the harbour and the dirty wild flowers that grow along the edges of the tramlines. I open my eyes and birdsong drifts through the open window of our tiny flat in downtown Gothenburg. In a swish of bright red hair she's already up and the smell of fresh coffee fills the room as the day breaks outside. Here, I wake to a different life.

The solstice just past, we're drawn north towards Norway's magic islands and the land of the midnight sun. Our road north is long. Bags are quickly checked and packed again with last minute thoughts – an extra chalkbag, an extra set of cams, another roll of tape – and in a flurry we're out the door and jumping in the van, hands full of kit and coffee and maps.

Uddevalla. Trollhättan. Fredrickstad. Oslo. The names on the signboards make bold signals as we pass beneath them, music loud, all sense of being at home already gone. Running north from Sweden's south-west coast for almost a thousand miles, the E45 is one of Europe's longest roads, connecting Scandinavia's fertile south with the barren tundra of Arctic Norway. We reach Östersund at noon and by evening we're leaving the shuttered windows of Storuman hunkering down behind us, as if the town itself were already preparing for the long isolated months of winter. Shutting out the forest's gloom, those bolted windows also protect the townsfolk from its vicious mosquitoes, the rank smell of endless bogs and an impossible vastness.

Midnight. The sun's rolling along the horizon by the time we reach the unmistakable marker of the southern edge of northern Scandinavia, and the point at which forest dramatically gives way to tundra. Huddles of reindeer have long replaced passing cars as our travelling companions; small groups break as we pass, the animals trying to shake off mosquitoes with our slipstream.

3am. Malin's driving the graveyard shift as we climb the slow hill before Kiruna. I open my eyes just as we crest the bluff and the sun hits the central extraction tower of the world's largest iron mine, which looms over the town like a monstrous UFO, the Arctic summer light sparking off the quartz shards that litter its humped slagheaps. As we turn across the sun, the reflected light from the mirror of mine debris covering the mountain fills the windscreen, blinding us for a moment, then melting across the dashboard into pools of quicksilver and burnt gold. It is a moment of such

130. Malin Holmberg leading *Memory Crack* (9- / E7 6c). This fierce Robert Caspersen single pitch crack climb was used as a warm up by Holmberg and Pickford before their new routing campaign on Djupfjord Wall in July 2011. *(David Pickford)*

extreme, sudden beauty we both remain very quiet as we turn again and descend towards the town, passing sidings of rusting ore trucks and the snowmobile salvage yard locked in the bright, sleepless silence of the morning. Winter grips Kiruna for most of the year and summer is a stranger, a traveller from the south country, like me. But Malin grew up here: her Dad worked in the mine for 40 years, and as we turn into the drive of her family home, she says with a smile, 'I know this place.'

Only a native can know the true nature of Kiruna's isolation at the very top of the European continent, of what it's like to spend a winter holed up in one of its insulated, narrow-windowed Soviet-style apartment blocks, or to comprehend the reticent, hardworking folk whose will is famously as strong as the iron they hack from the guts of the mountains. Scandinavians have a word for those who live in these Arctic regions: Nordlenska.

After a few hours' sleep, we leave Kiruna. Driving west out of town beside the railway that freights out thousands of tonnes of iron ore every week, the tundra shines in the morning sun. We hug the southern shore of the lake of Tometrask, passing deserted ski lifts, and cross the Norwegian border at the pass of Riksgransen.

Among The Islands

Stendhal wrote that beauty is the promise of happiness. If this is true, the first glimpse of Norway's north-west coast after the long drive north through the endless forests of Sweden might be its physical expression.

31. Malin Holmberg seconding the flying ramp on pitch 3 of *The Lady Of The Lake* during
     the first ascent. *(David Pickford)*

To the west, south, and north, a concatenation of mountains and islands stretches into the far distance, sharp outlines that cut the sky and sketch patterns in the blue ocean. We find a stopping place late in the evening by the shore beyond Eggum. Wild grass blows in the wind beyond the dunes and the sound of the sea picks up between the gusts. Gulls dart and turn overhead, filling the air with wheeling cries. Tonight, for the first time in a long time, we two are free.

For the first few days we climb a bunch of Lofoten classics from mild to wild. On the final pitches of Presten's elegant, thousand-foot line *Heaven Can Wait*, a white-tailed eagle soars behind us on the final pitches, leading us to the sunlit summit. On the shady dihedral of *Odin's Bow*, the sun swings around the corner of the wall as we prepare to descend, washing the introductory slabs with golden light 200 metres below. Then, intent on sterner stuff, we tape up for the unrelentingly steep single pitch of the Robert Caspersen testpiece *Memory Crack*, Lofoten's hardest trad route at the time. Late in the evening we emerge with bloodied hands, flushed with success after consecutive leads.

Djupfjord Days

Driving around the coast road to Henningsvaer, I spy the elegant north-facing wall that looms steeply up from the calm waters of Djupfjord, noticing what appears to be a thin crack splitting the centre of its upper headwall.

'Look at that!' I exclaim to Malin as I pull over. 'Just imagine if we could climb it directly, finishing up there.'

She contemplates the wall as I run along the shore of the fjord with

132. Malin Holmberg leading the technical, thin crack on Pitch 4 of *The Lady of The Lake. (David Pickford)*

binoculars to try and get the best view. Tracing the line of weakness from the base, I link features through the strange perspective of 300% magnification: a deep chimney leads to a bottomless flake, a flying ramp, a steep wall seamed with incipient cracks, then a devious traverse across the slab capping the headwall before the base of that one-in-a-million seam. Even through the binoculars, it was impossible to tell how thin or deep it was. It could be a straightforward locker finger-crack, an impossibly blind and gearless seam, or a just-climbable, just-protectable jewel. I secretly hoped it was either the former or the latter, because either way it would make a stunning finale to one of the best unclimbed granite lines I had ever seen.

After a rest day, we set off for Djupfjord Wall with a light rack and hopeful hearts. We picked a route through the boulders along the shore, up around a rocky bluff, through dewy moss and cloudberries, to find the fixed rope that leads down the other side. Suddenly cut off by the bluff's natural impasse, making an easy retreat impossible, Djupfjord Wall rises above us in all its shady glory, countless mysteries beckoning from the gigantic jigsaw of its architecture.

I set off up the huge water-worn chimney that bisects the lower cliff, providing a natural drainage line for the entire central section of the wall. I bridge and contort up the dripping, slime-filled slot with a mixture of trepidation and excitement. 'Wow! We're actually here', I think as I reach the belay and see the flying ramp rising into the heart of the wall up to my left.

Malin's quickly at the belay and soon setting off up the wild suspended flake that forms the second pitch. As she pauses to wonder whether to layback or offwidth the jutting tooth, the sun hits the water of the fjord below and light fills the cool air. She belays at the base of the ramp and I follow the booming flake, reaching her with damp, numb feet from the wet chimney. I take off my shoes and try to work some blood back into my toes as Malin swaps over the rack, both of us peering up at the ramp.

It's one of the most beautiful and unusual features I've ever seen on a big wall, this perfect gangway of smooth granite leading up into the sky. With my feet still numb and the fresh, thick lichen skidding under them, I set off and fiddle micro-wires and the smallest TC3s into the corner-seam. None are good, but there are plenty of placements, and after I've stuffed the seam with gear I try to forget my frozen feet and pull into the thin layback. Shuf-

fling my fingertips up the seam, my feet follow on the ramp below, edging up on slippery, lichenous smears.

Seven metres out from my cluster of tiny placements, and just at the point where I don't want to run it out any further, I spy a widening in the seam and a better cam placement three metres above. Forgetting about the run-out for a moment, I sprint for it, and breathe deeply as I reach my hoped-for goal and my fingers sink into the first perfect jam on the entire pitch. Here, the ramp narrows to the left and vanishes into an ocean of blankness. My only hope is the ledge five metres above. But how to reach it? Searching for clues, I

133. Girl from the North Country: Malin Holmberg, Scandinavia's best woman rock climber. *(David Pickford)*

glimpse a shallow depression up to the right, and span out from undercuts at the top of the ramp to reach another perfect finger-jam. I can hardly believe this gift of nature as I cross through, step up, and rock over on to the made-to-measure belay ledge, just wide enough for two people to stand comfortably side-by-side. Without that one-off finger-lock in the middle of nowhere, there is no way the ledge could be reached without an aid move. Things like that in climbing often make me wonder if there's a creative force in the universe far beyond our human capacity to understand.

At the ledge, we rehydrate and try to warm our feet. After a while, Malin's re-racked and ready to set off up the imposing wall above. Steep and seamed with tiny cracks, it leads up into an atrium where the angle of the wall eases, and I know that final seam in the headwall will be in sight. She has to fight the bouldery moves that lead into the main crack system, her fingers slipping in precarious fingertip jams and her feet skittering on tiny crystal footholds, but soon she's established and moving up towards the golden light that's now flooding across the upper section of the wall. I check the time: it's 5pm. The wall will now be in the sun until just before midnight, when the sun dips for just two hours below the ridge to the north of the fjord before rising again.

As I follow Malin's lead, warmer now at last, clouds blow in and blot out the sun; by the time I reach her belayed in a tiny niche she's shivering with cold. I give her my balaclava and windproof before leading straight through into pitch five, a beautiful leftward-trending crack system that allows access to the seam in the headwall. We can see it now, 70 metres above us, and it looks more perfect now than ever. The cracks are sometimes running with drainage water from the summit slopes and they lead me up a twisting path towards the head-wall as the mist thickens below us.

After a while, I pause to take my bearings and see that the only way to gain the ledge below the seam is a wild traverse across the very apex of the capping slab. Again I search for clues and again the wall gives just

134. A small boat heads out late in the evening from Kalle for some midsummer night-fishing. *(David Pickford)*

enough – a tiny smear for the right foot, a crimp, a layaway, another, better crimp – and suddenly I'm there, landing on the sloping ledge below the incredible seam.

The cloud has come down around us and the wind picked up to a near-gale. With chattering teeth Malin sets boldly off up the seam. Reaching the first moves and placing a micro-cam as the first drops of rain come down, I suggest we take the easier finish up the wide crack to the right, and return for the final pitch the next day. She flashes a smile between her shivers and readily agrees, scampering up the straightforward dihedral to the summit as the storm picks up. We top out and descend the steep gully to the left of the wall knowing we have opened of the finest lines either of us has ever climbed.

By the time we've reached the base of the wall, the weather's cleared and the wind-rippled fjord has settled to translucent calm, reflecting the serrated shadow of Budalstinden high to the east. We pack our gear and pick a way through the jumble of huge boulders to the beach. I check my watch: 1.30am. I show Malin the time and her green eyes blur with tiredness. Then we look back up to Djupfjord Wall, at the line we've just climbed, and smile. We don't need to say anything, because it's all there in front of

135. Looking down the last, crux pitch of *The Lady of The Lake* in the late evening, with Holmberg in the shadows below working the final pitch prior to her successful ascent.
(David Pickford)

us: 220 metres of the best granite climbing imaginable. We turn the point of Djupfjord Buttress as it dips into the water, and I see that the midnight sun's hidden below the bulk of Vestvagoya that blocks the horizon to the north. Silence fills the fjord in the brief Arctic summer twilight, only broken by the occasional crunch of small stones under our feet and the call of a lone night bird that echoes among the rocks and is carried over the surface of the water.

The next day we rest, swim in the crystal sea, and read in the afternoon sun on the huge flat boulders under Presten, repairing our tired bodies and preparing our minds for the challenge ahead. Late that night, dark clouds blow in over the sea and rain hammers the roof of the van, increasing in intensity until we can't hear anything else. The short but ferocious storm blows out by midnight, leaving bright lines of surface runoff cascading from the highest slabs.

We wake to another perfect Lofoten morning, the air so clear that simply drawing breath feels like gulping an overdose of magic. The sun's already drying off the upper section of Djupfjord Wall as we organise gear and prepare for that final, beautiful, desperately difficult pitch. An hour and a half after leaving the van, we're at the top of the wall again and uncoiling ropes on the cosy square-cut ledge that sits at the top of the route and neatly under the huge boilerplate slabs that cap the upper right-hand section of the wall. Malin goes down first. I lower her slowly, strapped securely to bomber natural anchors on the ledge. 'Ok, ok, ok... STOP!' She climbs a few moves, then lowers down, then climbs again – a pattern repeated for almost an hour. 'Ok, ok, all the way this time!' she shouts up. I lower her almost to the end of our 60m static line, which just reaches the last belay on the sloping ledge under the headwall seam, and feel the rope slacken as she sets off. She climbs quickly on top rope, and I feel she's almost through the hard climbing when my optimism is curtailed with a frustrated 'NE!' carried on the wind and I feel her weight drop on the rope. After a while, she climbs on and eventually appears, bounding up the summit slabs in a whirl of excitement.

'It's amazing!' she bursts out, a huge smile spreading across her face. 'Just amazing... one of the most beautiful pitches I've ever tried. But it's super-hard. I don't know if I can do it, I really don't know.'

I go down next, and am astonished at what I see: the seam is nowhere more than two centimetres deep, and takes only the smallest offset wires and the two smallest sizes of TC3 cams. And there are absolutely no foot-holds anywhere on the face, meaning the only way to climb it is by some of the most tenuous and complex laybacking I've ever tried anywhere. First I must face left, then make the desperate crux transition moves to face right, before sprinting up the seam towards a respite and better gear after 25 metres. What a pitch! Yet I struggle with the crux, my fingers never able to quite fit the deeper, more solid jams in the back of the seam I know Malin managed to get with her tiny fingers. I've climbed long enough to know when something's quickly achievable or not, and now I realise there's only one solution to this extraordinary final pitch of our route – it's her lead, not mine.

We rest for half an hour on the summit, quietly taking in the panorama of mountains and islands that stretches north beyond the horizon's limit. Then I back-coil our ropes into a lightweight pack to make belaying easier and disappear down the ab' rope, setting up a sophisticated anchor on the sloping ledge that means I can give Malin the most dynamic belay possible should she fall on the marginal micro-gear that protects the pitch. She comes down quickly, ties on, cleans her boots, and looks up at the seam then across at me. We both take a deep breath, and clasp our hands into fists before touching them together, as has become our habit before a hard lead.

'Ok. Go for it.' I say as she sets off. 'Full attack!'

'Yeah, I'm going.' she replies as she steps quickly up into the first moves. With pro from a side runner in the wide dihedral crack to the right to safe-guard her on the first moves, she steps up into the seam. Fighting from the very first move, she arranges the first gear and cranks out the initial hard layback sequence before placing the TC3 and micro offset that protect the crux. I see her hesitate for a moment before she pulls hard on her right jam and steps into the ferocious transitional layback that guards the upper part of the seam. Her left foot skids on some lichen and her right jam slips slightly, and for a moment I think she's blown it. But with amazing tenacity she holds the slip and steps up strongly into the seam's upper section.

Resting for a while at the first proper foothold since the belay, she places

136. Malin Holmberg leading the amazing thin seam on the crux final pitch of *The Lady of The Lake* (9- / E8 6c). *(David Pickford)*

137. Holmberg leading the spectacularly positioned final pitch of *Norwegian Wood* (7-/E4 6a, 220m) on the first ascent in July 2011. *(David Pickford)*

the first gear for many metres with audible relief, and we both relax for the first time since yesterday. She powers strongly up the final difficult section, her feet dancing across the slab as she makes the long reaches between poor finger-locks, and eventually a scream of joy breaks the sound of the wind ruffling the hood of my smock: she's made it. And what an incredible effort it was, I realised as I seconded the pitch to remove the gear. The climbing was probably at least French 8a in physical difficulty, and with long run-outs above marginal gear, this was truly a pitch for master technicians with nerves of steel.

We celebrate our success with a can of candy-sweet Swedish cider at the top, then quickly coil our ropes and pack the gear as I've got another new line in mind down on the lower section of the wall close to the fjord. We half-scramble, half-run down the descent gully and half an hour later I'm setting off up a steep finger-crack in the very toe of Djupfjord Wall that leads into a wild face-climbing sequence on marginal holds. A pair of old bolts out right are clear evidence of an early aided ascent hereabouts, but my goal was to link the beautiful lower splitter into the upper wall via that improbable rising leftwards traverse across the smooth face. After cleaning the crack, I return to the ground to rest for a few minutes. As I set off, a sudden wind picks up off the fjord, displacing the humid, leafy air at the base of the cliff, and I know I'm in luck. The lower crack flows perfectly, and I reach the crux fresh and prepared. Grateful again for my tall frame, I make an immense span off an undercut to a tiny crimp, then crucifix out left and plug my left forefinger into a sharp mono at full stretch. Running my feet up, all my weight on the mono now, I make a wild crossover and

catch the first of a rail of slopers in the horizontal break that leads out left
to the base of the wider upper crack. Feet skittering across the holdless wall
below, I make a series of wild slaps until eventually throwing my left heel
in the break. With more gear now, I can relax and enjoy the easier upper
crack, although I must clean it as I go this time. My hands slipping from
flared jams in the lichenous crack, and with soil and decomposing crud
pouring down my T-shirt, I grope over the top and land on a flat terrace
about a metre wide. As I take in the ropes and belay Malin as she follows
my lead, I can hardly believe it: in one afternoon, we've made two first
ascents of two of the best granite pitches I've ever seen anywhere in the
world, and the former completing our first ascent of the hardest trad route
in Lofoten.

Long swatches of evening mist swirl over the fjord as Malin leads on
up the slabby crack system that forms the second pitch. The sun's just
dipped below the ridge opposite and I feel a sadness washing over me as I
realise that sunset will come earlier every day from now until the sun disap-

138. The midsummer sky at 1am reflected in the fjord at Kalle. A derelict fishing wharf on the shore here provided Holmberg and Pickford with a base camp during their campaign on Djupfjord Wall. *(David Pickford)*

pears completely from the north Norwegian sky sometime in late November. But we've had one of the best afternoons I can remember in 20 years of messing about on rocks, so I should be grateful. Soon we're at the top, and after a quick, warm, forgetful kiss we're heading down through the near-vertical beech forest that fringes Djupfjord Buttress. I break trail; dead wood snaps around me, and fresh branches slap everywhere, as if the forest were closing up behind us as we move.

As we contour the steep slope near the toe of the wall back to our packs, Malin lets out a cry of joy and I run over to find her stooped on a ledge covered in bright orange cloudberries. Like a last gift from the fjord, we devour this welcome feast from nature, the sweet berries quelling our rapacious hunger. In the deepening twilight, we pick our way again along the beach and back to the road. A few men and women are fishing on the seaward side of the breakwater, casting with long rods in the hope of catching a giant cod or bass entering the fjord on the midnight tide.

I strip off and dive into the cold sea, swimming out as far as I dare into the bay before my head burns and my limbs start to slow as the warm blood drains away into my core. Djupfjord Wall looms on the skyline to the east,

'The evening is forever'
Lito Tejada-Flores, *Crooked Road To The Far North*

shrouded in darkness and mystery. As I swim, I stare back at the wall and think of the harder climbs it still holds, and of how lucky we have been to craft these creations on one of Norway's most beautiful cliffs. And as I turn for the shore I am reminded, too, of that far greater gift than climbing – simply being here at all.

Summary: An account of two first ascents on Djupfjord Wall, Lofoten Islands, Norway, made by Malin Holmberg and David Pickford in mid-July 2011:
The Lady of The Lake (E8 6c / Norwegian 9-, 220m) and *Trapezium Wall* (E7 6c, 90m). No bolts or pegs were placed on either route, and all the pitches were climbed onsight except for the crux final pitch of *The Lady of The Lake*, which was headpointed by Holmberg. As of early summer 2012, *The Lady of The Lake* awaits a continuous ascent. During the same trip, Holmberg and Pickford also made another first ascent on the central section of Djupfjord Wall, *Norwegian Wood* (E4 6a, 7-, 220m).

AC Expedition

139. The view from the mast: *Spirit of Sydney* enters the majestic Lemaire
Channel on the AC expedition to Antarctica. *(Phil Wickens)*

DEREK BUCKLE & PHIL WICKENS

2010 AC Expedition to Antarctica

140. Starting the ascent of the Hotine glacier after leaving the yacht at Deloncle Bay. *(Mike Fletcher)*

Many people imagine Antarctica as a frozen land where none but the most hardy of animals can survive. In winter this belief is undoubtedly true, but summer brings remarkable changes. Fracturing sea ice permits access by boat and daytime temperatures can be almost balmy. For all but the most enterprising, this then is the time for exploratory mountaineering. Even so, visiting Antarctica by anything other than a plane or cruise ship rarely crosses the mind of the average tourist, let alone climber. Our plan on the other hand, hatched by Phil Wickens during one of his regular lecture tours to the continent, involved sailing from the tip of Argentina to the Antarctic Peninsula in a 60ft yacht by way of the Drake Passage; probably the roughest and least forgiving stretch of water on the planet.

Everyone thought that we were insane, and to some extent this view was understandable, but the potential rewards were great. Few explorers, let alone mountaineers, had delved deeply into the heart of the Antarctic Peninsula, where numerous unclimbed peaks remain.

Although the Antarctic Peninsula was first sighted by sealers in 1820, further exploration did not occur until 1898 when the Belgian explorer Adrien de Gerlache charted many of its coves and bays aboard his ship the *Belgica*.

This expedition, whose members included Roald Amundsen and Frederick Cook, made many landings along the Antarctic Peninsula, as well as the first ski and sled journeys away from the coast, and became the first to spend a winter trapped in the Antarctic ice. The names of many features along the Peninsula were given by members of this expedition.

Five years later the French explorer Jean-Baptiste Charcot further explored the west coast of the Peninsula. The expedition wintered on Booth Island and, on 28 November 1903, Charcot and four others climbed Cape Tuxen (884m), which marked the first ascent of a significant Antarctic mountain. During the winter and following spring Charcot's team charted the surrounding coastline and calculated the heights of the major summits. One of these, which they measured to be 1360m high, they named Mt Matin after the newspaper *Le Matin* which contributed generously to the cost of their expedition.

Many areas of the Antarctic Peninsula were subsequently explored by the Falkland Island Dependencies Survey (now the British Antarctic Survey) teams, who also summited a number of peaks both during the course of their work and as recreation close to the bases.

In 1984-5 the British Joint Services Expedition climbed the major summits on Brabant Island, and in recent years an increasing number of private yachts have brought climbing teams to these areas. However, although a few of these have climbed some major peaks and committing lines, most engage in one-day ascents of smaller peaks from boat-based camps. As a result, many of the higher, more committing mountains remain unclimbed.

Climbing in the Antarctic has several unique characteristics; access and extremes of weather being just two. Safely manoeuvring a yacht through seas heavy with sea ice and bergs – especially the more insidious growlers – is one obvious hazard; locating suitable landing sites free of unstable ice-cliffs and calving glaciers is another major challenge. Clear weather, essential for safe route finding on highly crevassed glaciers and mountains, is rarely continuous and is often accompanied by cold winds and significant drops in temperature.

Ushuaia to the Antarctic Peninsula

After assembling in Ushuaia in the south of Argentina, the party joined Cath Hew and Darryl Day on the yacht *Spirit of Sydney* for the voyage to Antarctica. With food and other provisions already stowed aboard all that we needed was clearance from the harbour prefecture before sailing. Failure to follow strict procedure in Argentina could be inconvenient, and very costly, so we followed the rules to the letter. It was therefore not until 4am on 25 November that we were eventually cleared to sail down the Beagle Channel to the Chilean frontier town of Puerto Williams; the most southerly permanent habitation in South America. Later that afternoon we received clearance to continue along the Beagle Channel towards the Drake

141. Phil Wickens (top), Richmond MacIntyre and Mike Fletcher descending the north face of Mount Faraday. *(Derek Buckle)*

Passage and Antarctica. In the calm waters of the Channel we had regular visits from penguins, cormorants, petrels, albatrosses, seals and dolphins, but we would lose all bar the petrels and albatrosses as we entered the rougher seas of the Drake. Unfortunately, for some of us that was not all that we would lose.

It was reputedly calm when we entered the Drake Passage proper on the 26 November, but this information seems not to have been relayed to the stomachs of the less hardy seafarers on board. Gradually the team began to suffer, for some the nausea persisting for several days. Operating watches of three hours on and six off broke the discomfort somewhat, but two of us at least – the Chuck-up team – were less than effective deckhands. Relief came to all a little after crossing the Antarctic Convergence, where the cold waters of the Southern Ocean subduct under the relatively warmer waters of those to the north.

On 29 November, after sailing some 620 nautical miles, we spotted the first land since leaving South America as Wiencke Island and the Fief mountain range came into view. The first growlers and icebergs were also encountered as we neared land. Navigating through the Neumayer Channel we passed to the south of Anvers Island before mooring, around 11am, near the historical British wartime base of Port Lockroy on Goudier Island. Forgetting all formalities, gear was rapidly assembled in order to make an ascent of the prominent nearby peak. Due to easy access Jabet Peak (552m) receives numerous ascents each year, but for us it served both to exercise weary legs after four days at sea and as an introduction to Antarctic mountaineering on skis. This 'baptism of fire' also served to convince Richmond that life would be easier for him on snowshoes.

An incoming storm the following day provided an opportunity to visit the staff and museum at Port Lockroy and to see its resident population of gentoo penguins; possibly one of the most abundant species of penguin worldwide. At the time, Goudier Island was also home to a lone elephant seal, various gulls and the odd chinstrap penguin.

With the storm behind us we left Port Lockroy on 1 December to motor south through the majestic Lemaire Channel. Fortunately, the timely emergence of the *Polar Explorer*, one of many Antarctic cruise ships, had forged a path through the thick ice blocking the northern entrance to the Channel, allowing our more fragile vessel to progress to the relatively ice-free waters beyond. Entering the sheltered Deloncle Bay a little later we were

142. On the summit of Mt Matin (2400m). Left to right: Derek Buckle, Richmond MacIntyre, Mike Fletcher and Dave Wynne-Jones. *(Phil Wickens)*

dropped by Zodiac onto a rocky outcrop from which we could start a nine-day exploration of the Hotine glacier and its surrounds.

Exploration of the Hotine glacier

The area to the south was explored during two sorties by members of Charcot's second expedition in September 1909, who travelled 16 miles from their the ship to a spectacular place they named the 'Cul de Sac des Avalanches', which lies below the north-west side of what is now known as Mt Peary. The area to the north, whose glaciers flow into Deloncle and Girard bays, had never been visited, and would potentially give access to Charcot's Mt Matin and several other notable peaks.

From the drop-off, a steep rising traverse round the base of Mt Cloos led to relatively level ground on the Hotine glacier proper; severely testing our embryonic haul-bag dragging skills from the outset. Surprisingly, these strong, cylindrical plastic bags behaved remarkably well; largely due to the incorporation of a rotor designed to prevent the haul line tying itself in knots as the bags somersaulted on the slopes. Keeping well clear of major crevasse zones – clearly visible on satellite images – we passed to the north of Mt Nygren before establishing an interim camp on the glacier at 550m. Having taken five hours to reach this camp it was late by the time that we were settled, but in the perpetual daylight of the Antarctic summer it was

3. AC team high on heavily corniced Mt Cloos. *(Phil Wickens)*

only the drop in temperature that enforced a sense of urgency to climb into our sleeping bags.

Skinning for 2hrs 30mins next day led to a base camp at 850m, within striking distance of our main objective, the imposing and unclimbed Mt Matin. This camp was also well-positioned for attempts on Mt Nygren, which was also unclimbed, and what we called False Mt Shackleton (since it is incorrectly marked as Mt Shackleton on the 1:250,000 British Antarctic Survey map; the true peak of this name actually lies immediately to the south-west), which we later found had been climbed from the south side on 22 January 2010 by Ludovic Challeat. All of these mountains looked like attractive propositions. Later in the day an attempt on Mt Matin was made via its broad south-west ridge but this was eventually defeated by increasingly poor visibility. Intriguingly we turned around at over 1400m, higher than the designated height of the mountain (1360m), yet it was clear that we were still a long way from the summit, both in height and in distance.

On the morning of 3 December the weather seemed good enough for most of the team to make an attempt on Mt Nygren. Only Olly decided not to join us as we skinned/snow-shoed up the broad east ridge until it noticeably narrowed and steepened at about 1000m. From here we followed a fine corniced ridge that snaked upwards into the mist, allowing us to make the first ascent of the 1454m summit a little under three hours after leaving camp. We graded the route Alpine PD+. Heavy cloud denied what should have been a superb summit view, but we were able to make radio contact with *Spirit of Sydney* before returning the same way; arriving back at camp just as it began to snow.

High cloud still surrounded us the following day but on the promise of a good weather forecast we decided to attempt False Mt Shackleton. After crossing the Leay glacier, Dave, Olly and Stu decided to return, leaving just

144. Derek Buckle and Phil Wickens on the east face of Cloos. *(Oliver Metherell)*

four of us to deposit skis at the foot of the north face before continuing on foot. Post-holing up the 50-degree slope led first to two wide bergschrunds, which were eventually taken direct, before we weaved upwards through a maze of séracs and crevasses. Towards the top the face steepened sharply to 60 degrees before joining the west ridge. Turning right we followed the corniced ridge past a false top before becoming the second party to reach the main summit, and the first by the north face, at 1475m, a little under six hours after leaving camp. We graded this route Alpine AD. Our proposed name of Mt Faraday, to commemorate the former British Base of the same name that lies immediately to the west and from where the ozone hole was discovered, has been officially accepted for this mountain. In contrast to the ascent of Mt Nygren, we were now bathed in brilliant sunshine and had stupendous views in all directions. The south faces of Nygren and Cloos dominated the view north and Mt Matin rose to lofty heights towards the east. From this viewpoint it was obvious that Mt Matin was substantially higher than its recorded elevation and that the true summit lay at some considerable distance east of the south-west ridge. Towards the south lay the true Mt Shackleton and the broad massif of Mount Peary, both of which had been climbed previously. Mount Scott, another peak that has received several ascents, rose on the coast to the west. Descending to our skis we arrived back at camp almost 12 hours after leaving.

45. Derek and Phil on the east face of Mount Cloos. *(Oliver Metherell)*

Early in the morning of 5 December it was perfectly clear, but a moderate southerly wind reduced temperatures to well below freezing. Fortunately the 3m-deep ice *lapa* (from the South African open air enclosures surrounded by mud walls that are used as meeting places) that Richmond had constructed during a period of restlessness afforded respite so that we could gear up in relative comfort. With Olly still feeling uncomfortable with the conditions, and Stu suffering from painful sciatica, it was a reduced party of five that left at 7am to re-attempt Mt Matin. Skiing back up the south-west ridge we essentially followed our earlier tracks to reach a broad shoulder which led over several kilometres to the broad summit plateau. Only a short section, which with hindsight could have been climbed on skis, was tackled on foot. Facing a strong, cold wind we traversed the icy dome until at 1.30pm we successfully made the first ascent of the 2415m summit. While the views were extensive, the cold was not conducive to a long stay and only Phil enthusiastically continued his photo record of our surroundings. At over 2400m – more than 1000m above its recorded height – Mt Matin was the highest remaining unclimbed peak on the Antarctic Peninsula north of the Antarctic Circle and despite its relatively easy grading (Alpine PD) it was undoubtedly a worthy prize. Certainly the effort involved made it feel like a major achievement, and skiing back on spring-like névé was a delightful reward. We eventually returned to camp 9hrs 30mins after setting off; well

146. Oliver Metherell beneath the séracs on the east face of Mt Cloos.
(Phil Wickens)

before increasing wind, precipitation and snowdrifts started to create mild
chaos during the late evening and night.

Having now climbed all of the peaks readily accessible from this base
camp we decided to move closer to the coast. Initially we had considered
the possibility of crossing the Leay glacier and returning to the yacht via
the Wiggins glacier, however since this involved bag hauling over the steep
ridge of Mt Faraday we now realised that this was not a viable option. The
next day we therefore relocated lower down the Hotine glacier to camp
at 307m, beneath the south-east face of Mt Cloos. This attractive mountain forms the dramatic and steep east side of the Lemaire Channel. It
was discovered in 1898 by the Belgian Antarctic Expedition and named 10

years later by Charcot's expedition. Although many people pass right below it as they cruise through the Lemaire Channel, the mountain remained unclimbed, and so it became the focus of our next ascent.

After a day camp-bound due to heavy cloud the whole party was keen to attempt Mt Cloos on 8 December. Thus, following a cold, clear and windy night, five of us left early with Dave and Stu deciding to follow later. Skinning beneath the south face we reached the foot of the small, but prominent, South Peak, the last few metres of which were climbed on foot to the airy summit at 935m. A traverse along the corniced ridge between the low and high summits then led past a high point at 940m that culminated in a massive projecting cornice overlooking the Lemaire Channel and Deloncle Bay. It was an impressive photogenic place to be, but we did not linger as we still had thoughts on the main summit, providing we could find an objectively safe route to it. Following in our tracks, Dave and Stu also climbed the south summit before traversing the ridge, but chose to return rather than attempt the higher north summit. We, in the meantime, crossed under the impending east face to climb below a series of large, but seemingly stable, séracs to the left of an obvious rock face. Ascending steep, icy slopes we skirted around the lower large overhanging ice cliffs until a drafty wind scoop and awkward ice chimney led through to the upper slopes. From here it was a relative walk to the 1200m summit and its superlative 360-degree views. It had taken us 7hrs 30mins to reach this previously virgin summit by a route that we graded Alpine D+. It was now 5.30pm. Moreover, it had been extremely cold all day and was now getting appreciably colder; we needed to get down. Reversing the route was the only option, although we knew that this would not be quick and the chimney would provide a major challenge. Bomber ice-screws protected the descent from below, but there was no easy way to protect the last man from above. It all took time but eventually, after a single long abseil, we were on relatively easy ground and looking forward to a late supper. A concerned radio call from Stu at around 8.30pm made us realise how late it was, but by then the major difficulties were behind us and we could make reassuring noises that all was OK. Two hours later we were back at camp after one of the most memorable days that any of us had experienced in the mountains.

Exploration of Paradise Harbour and Andvord Bay

With the completion of all that we could reasonably do on the Hotine glacier, and having arranged for a midday rendezvous with the *Spirit of Sydney*, we decamped and descended to the drop-off point the next morning. Fortunately, the state of the sea ice was sympathetic to our plan and we were duly collected on schedule to be sumptuously dined by Cath before sailing south to anchor at Pleneau Bay. The Bay provided an ideal opportunity to relax after the previous days' exertions and we could at last take advantage of the kayaks we had on board. For most of us it was a novel experience just to be paddling among icebergs and sea ice, but to watch penguins surfing and darting underwater in their natural environment was truly magical. Later that day a southerly wind pushed extensive pack ice into the bay and enshrouded the mountains in mist. We had been lucky during our climbs but would not be moving anywhere until conditions improved.

Sun returned on 11 December but we were still enclosed in extensive 10/10 (virtually continuous) ice. In such conditions we would normally stay put, but with a storm forecast for tomorrow we needed to find a secure harbour. Having posted Mike high in the mast as a lookout, and with everyone else scanning the water for the more major hazards, we edged slowly past the entrance to Deloncle Bay (which was now completely impassable) and into the clearer waters of the Lemaire Channel. It was a harrowing time for Cath and Darrel as they had never motored under such extreme conditions, but to the more naïve amongst us it was an exciting

147. Derek Buckle kayaking amongst the icebergs of Paradise Cove. *(Phil Wickens)*

few hours amid spectacular and majestic scenery simply watching the pack ice drift slowly by. Continuing past the Seven Sisters of the Fief Range, the gargantuan bulk of Mt Matin, and other by now characteristic landmarks, we encountered minke whales, seals and penguins as we motored towards the safety of the aptly named Paradise Harbour to ride out the approaching storm.

As bad weather was not expected until later on 12 December we chose to make a rapid ascent of one of the peaks bordering the Harbour. With so many options to choose from we eventually selected a mountain subsequently identified as Mt Banck. At the time we thought that this peak was unclimbed, but it later transpired that three separate teams had summited previously; the first being an Antipodean team early in 2000. After being dropped off at Sturma Point all except Olly climbed the easy north face (Alpine PD) on skis or snow shoes until finishing on foot up a short, steep couloir which led directly to the 710m summit. It took less than two hours to reach the top and it was even quicker descending with skis on near perfect snow. By now the weather was deteriorating rapidly so we took the opportunity to visit the Gabriel Gonzales Videla Chilean Base near which we had moored for the night.

This put us within easy reach of several more significant but unclimbed mountains. The largest of these is Mt Inverleith, marked at 2000m on the BAS maps. Named and charted by the Scottish geologist David Ferguson in 1913-14, this mountain dominates both Paradise Harbour and Andvord Bay. The Paradise Harbour side is guarded by chaotic sérac

48. Dave Wynne-Jones and Mike Fletcher ascending Mt Inverleith. *(Phil Wickens)*

bands and unstable ice cliffs and so we motored north to Andvord Bay on 13 December. A suitable landing site was found at Steinheil Point and, after being dropped off in very difficult conditions, we skied steeply up the icy Grubb glacier in the face of a strong, cold wind. A leftwards traverse through an impressive icefall led onto a further steep, icy slope before we eventually made camp below the impressive east face of Dallmeyer Peak in a large windy snow bowl at 600m. Unfortunately, due to persisting sciatica Stu did not join us and remained on the yacht with Olly.

With the wind diminishing overnight we set off the next day to climb Mount Inverleith in glorious weather. Leaving the skis on the col between Mts Dallmeyer and Inverleith, we meandered up the steep, broken North Face (Alpine AD+) between seracs and open crevasses before emerging onto a broad snow shoulder at around 1700m. We then climbed more easily south-westwards up an unrelenting glacial slope to make the first ascent of the 2038m summit around 7 hours 30mins after leaving camp. Like that of Mt Matin, the summit plateau of Mt Inverleith was vast, broad and rounded, but it did afford extensive views over a range of unclimbed peaks. In developing mist we returned to camp some 11 hours after leaving.

With time now running out and a storm due later on the next day we hurriedly decamped on 15 December in order to be back on the yacht and in a safe berth before the bad weather arrived. Anchoring at Port Lockroy that afternoon essentially completed the mountaineering aspect of the expedition but we were due some unexpected excitement before landing in South America for the flights home. The Drake Passage was again relatively benign on the return crossing but a close encounter with two hump back whales, one passing uncomfortably close to one side of the yacht and the other diving just in time to clear the keel, was a stark reminder of the ever present dangers in these Antarctic waters.

Summary: During November to December 2010 seven Alpine Club members under the leadership of Phil Wickens sailed to the Antarctic Peninsula on the yacht Spirit of Sydney. From several inland camps various members of the team made first ascents of Mts Nygren (1454m), Matin (2415m), Cloos South (935m), Cloos Main (1200m), and Inverleith (2038m). Members of the party also made the second ascent of False Shackleton (aka Mt Faraday,1475m) by a new route from the north, and the fourth ascent of Mt Banck (710m). Team: Derek Buckle, Mike Fletcher, Stuart Gallagher, Richmond MacIntyre, Oliver Metherell, Phil Wickens and Dave Wynne-Jones.

Acknowledgements: The expedition gratefully acknowledges the support of the AC Climbing Fund, the Gino Watkins Memorial Fund, the Mountaineering Council of Scotland, Lyon Equipment, Primus and First Ascent. This expedition would not have been possible without the skill and commitment of Darryl Day and Cath Hew, who piloted the *Spirit of Sydney* through some of the most challenging waters on earth.

149. The *Spirit of Sydney* in ice at Deloncle Bay. *(Phil Wickens)*

Science

150. John Fairley, *Shivling*, acrylic on board,
310x610mm, 2008

PAUL RAMSDEN

The Silent Killer

Carbon Monoxide: a Mountaineer's Perspective

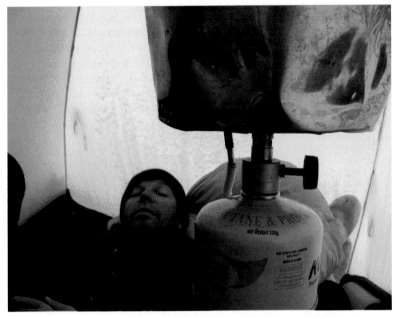

151. Beware, the 'silent killer'. Mick Fowler regards the stove while on
Manamcho, Nyenchen Tanglha East, Tibet, April 2007. *(Paul Ramsden)*

There are two facts to remember about carbon monoxide (CO). Firstly all stoves can produce CO and secondly the CO levels that will produce a headache at sea level could be fatal at high altitude.

While CO is one of the most common source of poisoning in the 'civilised' world, its dangers in extreme polar and mountain environments has never been fully understood.

My own experiences of CO poisoning have in retrospect been many and varied. A particularly memorable episode of headache, dizziness, nausea and partial unconsciousness while at the Bivouac des Dames Anglaises, halfway along the *Peuterey Integral*, won't be forgotten in a hurry. Equally a period of depression and manic behaviour after spending two weeks tent-bound in Alaska now starts to make sense.

People who have read about my climbs are often surprised to hear that I am actually a health and safety consultant during office hours. Recently I completed an MSc in Occupational Health. My dissertation involved experimental work on CO poisoning in tented accommodation, in conjunc-tion with the British Antarctica Survey. While my research was based on Antarctica I realised that much of the information was of relevance to anyone using stoves in cold locations, especially at higher altitudes.

Where does the CO come from?

All camping stoves require the burning of hydrocarbon fuels such as propane and paraffin. Upon heating the hydrocarbons' molecular bonds break down or disassociate. At 800-900°C, carbon bonds are cleaved by the heat to form carbon radicals. At 1150°C, carbon radicals are stripped of hydrogen atoms forming acetylene. This in turn is decomposed creating free hydrogen molecules and carbon atoms.[1] The hydrogen molecules are broken down into hydrogen atoms by thermal dissociation before reacting with oxygen to form water, which in turn releases energy, thereby heating up the surrounding carbon atoms. The heated free carbon bonds with free oxygen atoms (similarly caused by the heating of O_2), forming CO.

$$C + O = CO + energy$$

The release of energy makes the flame hotter. With sufficient heat (1000°C) and the presence of oxygen, the CO will link up with more free oxygen to form CO_2. Therefore in the presence of oxygen, CO burns with a blue flame forming CO_2.

$$CO + O = CO_2 + energy$$

In simplistic terms, hydrogen burns rapidly at the base of the flame maintaining the combustion process. A little further up the flame carbon and oxygen combine to form CO. If the flame is hot enough, CO_2 will be formed further up the flame. However, if the flame does not reach the required temperature CO is released.

The flame can be inhibited from reaching high temperatures due to oxygen depletion or by coming into contact with a cooler object such as a pan. This process is known as quenching. Any object in the flame acts as a heat sink, draining energy from the flame reaction process. The surface will also act as a means of breaking the chain of flame propagation. Flame quenching will increase as the surface to volume ratio of the combustion area increases.

In most cases, the less contact the flame has with any surface the more complete the combustion process will be and the less potential for CO release will exist. However, in reality the situation is more complex than this, as a pan in contact with a quenched flame will heat quicker than one positioned well above a more efficiently combusting flame.

In addition, there are associated direct factors such as the way a pan may cause more flame turbulence resulting in new areas of flame propagation resulting in faster heating. There are also indirect factors, such as concerns over pan stability in an elevated position and the flame's resistance to wind dispersal.

The fact that CO is formed first and at cooler temperatures in a quenched flame is a critical factor in flame chemistry and the unwanted generation of CO.

The first scientific reference to flame quenching in camping stoves was in a paper by Henderson and Turner published in 1940 in *Nature*. 'That part of the flame which impinges upon the kettle or other vessel is cooled below the temperature requisite for complete combustion and CO is formed.'[2] This subject was again touched upon in a publication from 1942 entitled 'Carbon Monoxide from Melting Snow' by Davis from the University of Alaska, Fairbanks.[3]

Interestingly, there is no further scientific reference to this phenomenon in camping stoves from that date forward. For information on quenching in camping stoves today, it is necessary to review specialist online camping discussion groups such as www.backpackinglight.com that contains some very useful and interesting, though unpublished, work by Roger Caffin.[4]

Very little, if any, work has been carried out on the effects of high altitude and its associated reduced oxygen levels in the flame combustion processes. However, it is probably safe to presume that its effects will be detrimental to efficient combustion and that the potential for CO production will be increased.

What are the health effects of CO poisoning?

Carbon monoxide (CO) is a colourless, odourless gas known as 'the silent killer'. About 50 people die and 200 are severely injured as a result of CO poisoning in the UK every year.[5]

The main symptoms of CO poisoning develop in those organ systems most dependent on oxygen such as the central nervous system and the heart.[6] The initial symptoms of acute CO poisoning include headache, nausea, malaise and fatigue.[7] Headaches are the most common symptom of acute CO poisoning; it is often described as dull, frontal and continuous. [8] Increasing CO exposure produces cardiac abnormalities such as fast heart rate, low blood pressure and cardiac arrhythmia. Central nervous system symptoms include delirium, hallucinations, dizziness, unsteady gait, confusion, seizures, central nervous system depression, unconsciousness and respiratory arrest.[9]

One of the significant concerns following acute CO poisoning is the severe delayed neurological manifestations that may occur. Problems may include difficulty with higher intellectual functions, short-term memory loss, dementia, amnesia, psychosis, irritability, a strange gait, speech disturbances, Parkinson's disease-like syndromes and a depressed mood. Depression may even occur in those who did not have pre-existing depression.[8]

Delayed neurological conditions may occur in up to 50% of poisoned patients after 2 to 40 days.[10] It is however difficult to predict who will

Table 1. Summary of symptoms and their relationship to carbon monoxide exposure (13)(14)(15)		
CO concentration (ppm or ppm/exposure time when expressed)	Symptoms	COHb Concentration %
35	Headache and dizziness within 6 - 8 hours of constant exposure	0-20
100/8hr to 200/4hr	Mild frontal headache within 2 hours	10-20
200	Loss of judgement	-
400	Frontal headache within 1 - 2 hours of constant exposure	-
500/2hr	Headache ± tachycardia	20-30
200-1200	Steady symptom progression	-
300	Collapse	30-40
-	Coma	50-60
>1000	Chemical asphyxiate actions	-
650-1000	Dizziness, nausea, and convulsions within 45 minutes, insensible within 2 hours	60-70
1600	Headache, tachycardia, dizziness, and nausea within 20 min, death in less than 2 hours	-
2000	Death in less than 1 hour	80-90
3200	Death in less than 30 minutes	90-100
6400	Headache and dizziness in one to two minutes. Convulsions, respiratory arrest, and death in less than 20 minutes	-
8000	Death in less than 10 minutes	-
10000	No symptoms before collapse and death	-

develop delayed symptoms, though old age, unconsciousness while poisoned and initial neurological abnormalities may increase the chance of developing delayed symptoms.[11]

Carbon monoxide binds very strongly to haemoglobin with an affinity 210 times greater than oxygen. This leads to elevated carboxyhaemoglobin (COHb) levels and subsequently a diminished oxygen carrying capacity of the blood. For a normal non-smoker, the average COHb concentration is <1% rising up to 15% in heavy smokers.[12] Symptoms usually begin when the COHb concentration rises above 10%, with coma and death associated with levels above 40%.

While opinions vary on the exact relationship between CO exposure, COHb levels in the blood and the onset of symptoms there is, however, a broad consensus that headaches may begin with exposures to CO of as low as 35ppm, but will consistently develop with exposures in the range of 100-200ppm. Loss of judgment is expected with exposures as low as 200ppm with collapse occurring at concentrations as low as 300ppm. In most cases this refers to long-term eight-hour exposures, with short-term exposures requiring higher concentrations to have an effect. At

650-1000ppm, convulsions may start in 45 minutes and unconsciousness within two hours. At 1600ppm, death will occur in less than two hours.

The CO tolerance level for an individual is altered by many factors, including activity level, rate of ventilation, the presence of a pre-existing cerebral or cardiovascular disease, cardiac output, barometric pressure and metabolic rate.[7]

The effects of higher altitudes

The human lung works based on the gradient pressure difference between blood and air. Therefore, a decrease in inhaled oxygen pressure will have an adverse effect on how much oxygen can enter the blood. While moderately elevated COHb levels at sea levels might go unnoticed or result in moderate symptoms, at high altitudes these effects may be much more significant. Work done by Forbes et al published in 1945 showed that four out of 17 health subjects, at a simulated altitude of 4725 metres collapsed when their COHb levels reached between 9 and 19%. At sea level this would normally occur between 30 and 40%.[16]

Altitude contributes to the danger of CO exposure, firstly by decreasing the oxygen uptake into the body and secondly through the effect that the reduced pressure effect of altitude will have on increasing the time it takes for CO to be cleared from the body. In addition, at higher altitudes faster respiration rates allow inhalation of more CO, if present.[17] Higher altitudes are always colder and windier, therefore increasing the likelihood that tent ventilators will be closed, with the resultant increased potential for elevated CO levels, often sustained for long periods.

Research on CO exposures in tents

Research in this area has been very sparse. Leigh-Smith's review 'Carbon Monoxide Poisoning in Tents' details most of the previous work investigating CO production from stoves in tents up to 2003.[13] In all of this work CO production was found to be lowest with a freely burning flame and was found to increase by the addition of a pan in contact with the stove.

Irving et al were the first to mention the prevention of CO accumulation through improved tent ventilation and increased tent fabric permeability.[18] Pugh noted that this might be inhibited by snow and ice accumulation and condensation.[19] Turner et al noted the decreased ventilation rates from tents in zero wind conditions.[20] Keyes et al found elevated COHb concentrations when a stove was used for cooking as compared to simply heating the tent.[21]

Leigh-Smith et al found that the while a blue flame is present, pan temperature had no effect on CO concentrations, with elevated CO levels only occurring when the flame was dispersed by another object.[22] Pugh's studies showed that CO production did not reduce as the pans contents got hotter.

Leigh-Smith et al did find that as pan size increased there was a significant increase in the levels of CO generated.[23] This is likely to be due to the increased flame quenching effect of the larger pan's surface area. They also found that in conditions of poor ventilation, stoves failed to maintain a blue flame, but continued to burn at lower temperatures producing increased CO levels. Schwartz et al demonstrated significant differences in the CO produced by different fuel types, with paraffin generating more CO than any other liquid fuel. [24]

My work in this area (as yet unpublished) focused on the use of the venerable Primus stove, still the stove of choice for the British Antarctic Survey. While this stove is unlikely to appear on your next alpine bivvi ledge, I believe that the lessons learnt in my research are directly applicable

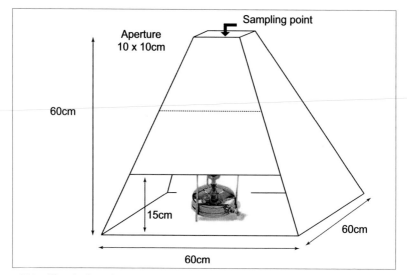

Sampling point

Aperture
10 x 10cm

60cm

15cm

60cm

60cm

152. The design of the stove testing enclosure.

to the modern setting.

In order to replicate stove tests under standard conditions I constructed an enclosure. This was based on a 60cm high pyramid funnel design with a base measurement of 60cm x 60cm tapering to a vent aperture of 10cm x 10cm. The enclosure was sealed on three sides with ventilation on one side via a 15cm high and 60cm wide vent. The CO monitoring point was located in the centre of the exhaust aperture, 1cm below the top edge.

Stove trials were carried out both at room temperature and at -20C in a cold room provided courtesy of the British Geological Survey.

I was able to show that ambient air temperature, pan temperature and pan size had no significant effect on CO generating. However the presence of any object directly in the combustion zone of the flame could have a very significant effect on the levels of CO generated. In the case of the Primus stove the pan and pan support plate resulted in a x100 increase in the CO generated as compared to a flame burning without obstruction.

While carrying out this research on the Primus I was able to carry out a variety of trials on my own more high tech cooking systems with some quite startling results. It appeared that the current range of more fuel-efficient pans and stoves had the potential to generate significantly more CO than a standard camping stove and pan arrangement.

Many of the cooking set-ups likely to be used by the modern mountaineer enhance their fuel efficiency through maximising the pan's contact with the flame through an arrangement of metal fins welded to the base of the pan. Examples of this include the MSR Reactor and Jetboil stoves. In addition a variety of pans are available for standard stoves with fins in place on the base to maximise the surface area such as the Optimus Heat Exchanger Pan.

While this equipment clearly works in terms of fuel efficiency, their increased quenching effect on the flame has a corresponding increased potential for CO generation.

What can the mountaineer do about CO?

Before I give the impression that I think the new style of energy efficient cooking arrangements are excessively hazardous, I should state that on all my recent expeditions I have used an MSR Reactor (modified to hang but that's another story) and I will continue to use this stove until something better becomes available, as its incredible fuel efficiency has halved the weight of gas cylinders I have to carry and increased the amount of time I can comfortably stay on the mountain.

What I am saying, however, is that using this equipment requires a higher level of vigilance than you would normally devote to your stove. Cook outside if you can; if cooking in the tent, keep it well ventilated and be extra careful of nodding off while cooking. Remember that frost or a covering of snow can render highly breathable bivvi tents completely impervious, so yes that vent does need to be open!

The second point to make is that when we think of CO poisoning we tend to think of death as the health effect to be concerned about. However I believe that the low level exposure to CO and its associated effects on brain function are of much more concern. Symptoms such as hallucinations, dizziness, unsteady gait and confusion could easily be missed and simply put down to the altitude, when in fact they could be easily avoidable.

I am convinced that many of the well-known incidents at high altitude involving peculiar decision making, poor route choice and incorrect use of equipment or individuals making unexplained mistakes are potentially caused, or at the very least contributed to, by CO poisoning and not necessarily just due to the altitude as we often say.

References

1. Bilgera RW, Stårnera SH. A simple model for carbon monoxide in laminar and turbulent hydrocarbon diffusion flames. *Combustion and Flame* 1983, 51: 155-176

2. Henderson Y, Turner J. Carbon monoxide as a hazard in polar exploration, *Nature* 1940,145: 92-95.

3. Neil Davis T. Carbon monoxide from melting snow, Article 336, University of Alaska, Fairbanks (1942).

4. www.backpackinglight.com (Accessed 2011).

5. Walker E, Hay A. Carbon monoxide poisoning is still an under recognised problem, *BMJ* 1999, 319:1082-1083.

6. Kao LW. Nanagas KA. Toxicology associated with carbon monoxide, *Journal of Clinical and Laboratory Medicine* 2006, 26(1): 99-125.

7. Hardy KR, Thom SR. Pathophysiology and treatment of carbon monoxide poisoning, *Journal of Toxicology - Clinical Toxicology* 1994, 32(6): 613–629.

8. Choi IS. Carbon monoxide poisoning: systemic manifestations and complications, *Journal of Korean Medical Science* 2001 June 16(3): 253–261.

9. Weaver LK. Clinical practice. Carbon monoxide poisoning, *New England Journal of Medicine* 2009 March 360 (12): 1217–1225.

10. Nelson LH. Carbon Monoxide. *Goldfrank's Toxicological Emergencies* (7th ed.) New York, McGraw-Hill (2002): 1689–1704.

11. Myers RA, Snyder SK, Emhoff TA. Sub-acute sequelae of carbon monoxide poisoning, *Annals of Emergency Medicine* 1985 Dec 14(12): 1163–1167.

12. Raub JA, Mathieu-Nolf M, Hampson NB, Thom SR. Carbon monoxide poisoning — a public health perspective, *Toxicology* 2000,145: 1-14.

13. Leigh-Smith S. Carbon monoxide poisoning in tents – a review, *Wilderness and Environmental Medicine* 2004,15: 157-163.

14. Struttmann T, Scheerer A, Prince TS, Goldstein LA. Unintentional carbon monoxide poisoning from an unlikely source, *Journal of Family Practice* 1998,11(6): 481–484.

15. Goldstein M. Carbon monoxide poisoning, *Journal of Emergency Nursing* 2007, 34(6): 538–542.

16. Forbes WH, Sargent F, Houghton FJW. The rate of carbon monoxide uptake by normal men, *American Journal of Physiology* 1945,143: 594-608.

17. Tannheimer M, Thomas A, Gerngross H. Oxygen saturation course and altitude symptomatology during an expedition to Broad Peak (8047m), *International Journal of Sports Medicine* 2002 July, 23(5): 329-335.

18. Irving L, Scholander P, Edwards G. Experiments on carbon monoxide poisoning in tents and snow houses, *Journal of Industrial Hygiene and Toxicology* 1942, 24: 213.

19. Pugh LGCE. Carbon monoxide hazard in Antarctica, *BMJ* 1959, 34(5116): 192-196.

20. Turner WA, Cohen MA, Moore S, et al. Carbon monoxide exposure in mountaineers on Denali, *Alaska Med* 1988, 30: 85-90.

21. Keyes LE, Hamilton RS, Rose JS. Carbon monoxide exposures from cooking in snow caves at high altitude, *Wilderness Environmental Medicine* 2001,12: 208-212.

22. Leigh-Smith S, Stevenson R, Watt M, et al. Comparison of carbon monoxide levels during heating of water to boiling point with a camping stove using different diameter pans, *Wilderness and Environmental Medicine* 2004,15: 165-170.

23. Leigh-Smith S, Watt I, McFadyen A, et al. Comparison of carbon monoxide levels during heating of ice and water to boiling point with a camping stove, *Wilderness and Environmental Medicine* 2004,15: 164-170.

24. Schwartz RB, Ledrick DJ, Lindman AL. A comparison of carbon monoxide levels during the use of a multi fuel stove, *Wilderness and Environmental Medicine* 2001, 12: 236-238.

ULYANA NADIA HORODYSKYJ

The Ngozumpa Glacial Lake Imaging Project

The Ngozumpa is one of the giant glaciers of the Nepal Himalaya, snaking southwards from Cho Oyu. Its debris-covered surface is a familiar sight for climbers and trekkers heading up the Gokyo valley in the Khumbu – and on each visit there seems to be less of it. Some 20km from Cho Oyu, towards the snout of the glacier, an enormous lake is growing behind a wall of rock debris; called 'Spillway' the lake has the potential to be about 6km long, 1km wide and 100m deep. The threat of downstream flooding may not be immediate but the dynamics of the surface lakes need to be better understood. In this preliminary report researcher Ulyana Horodyskyj from the Cooperative Institute for Research in Environmental Sciences (CIRES) at the University of Colorado, Boulder, details attempts to monitor the lakes of the Ngozumpa.

The formation and evolution of supraglacial (surface) lakes constitutes a major catalyst for removing ice stored in debris-covered valley glaciers. Hitherto their contribution to ice loss has been conjectural and largely qualitative. The lakes contribute to the demise of debris-covered glaciers that would otherwise be insulated from solar melt processes (due to the thickness of the debris) through the development of bare ice vertical walls that migrate, typically northward, from melting, backwasting and collapse (eg, Benn et al, 2001; Sakai et al, 2002; Sakai et al, 2000). The ponded lakes, once formed, can lead to catastrophic mobilization (flooding) at the vulnerable villages downstream. They also contribute to major loss of water (volume) from the glacier. It is important that we not only use satellite and aerial imagery in our analyses of these glacial lakes, but 'boots on the ground' tactics, as well as oblique angle, real-time imagery of lake processes, to better understand the causes of on-going events and to develop models which can forecast future changes.

Our pilot study (June 2011) on the Ngozumpa glacier revealed that multiple fill/drain events occur in lakes during the melt season (Horodyskyj et al, 2011). Time-lapse imagery focused at an oblique view and taking one photo per hour (Fig 1), allowed us to quantify water inputs and outputs in realtime during the course of the melt season. This reveals that satellite imagery may alias the net loss from the system by at least a factor of two, and perhaps by an order of magnitude, especially given that they consist of 'snapshots' spaced months or years apart.

Ngozumpa is one of Nepal's largest and longest glaciers, flowing 25 kilometres from Cho Oyu (8201m) and Gyachung Kang (7952m). Its lower

153. The grey, debris-covered Ngozumpa glacier dwarfs the trekker lodges of Gokyo. Everest, Nuptse and Lhotse loom in the background. *(Stephen Goodwin)*

154. Figure 1: Installation of a time-lapse camera off the lateral moraine of Ngozumpa glacier, Nepalese Himalaya. *(Ang Phula Sherpa, Peak Promotion)*

6 kilometres are considered 'stagnant', moving at <10 m/yr (Quincey et al, 2009). This is where most of the supraglacial lakes are concentrated, including 'Spillway' lake, the growth and expansion of which has been documented by Thompson et al, 2012. This lake has the potential of growing into one of the largest glacial lakes in the Khumbu Himal region.

Three cameras were installed along the mid-ablation (melting) zone of the glacier in order to target different lake expansion and growth processes. Rcam was installed near the terminus (end of the glacier) in order to observe lake changes due to monsoonal (precipitation) inputs. The lake was seen to double in surface area in only two weeks' time and change in

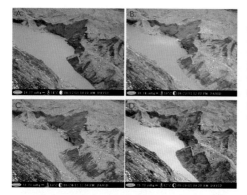

155. Figure 2: Four photos selected from the more than 400 images obtained during the field season show a time-lapse progression of lake fill (A. 6/22), drain (B. 6/23), continued drain (C. 6/24) and refill (D. 6/29). Arrows in B and C point to top of ice-water line.

colour from milky blue to brown, due to the mobilization of sediment on the glacier's surface. Future imagery, in the form of time-lapse and satellite imagery will reveal if the lake remains the same size, shrinks, or grows significantly larger.

A second camera, Dcam, was installed to observe a supraglacial lake that historically (through ASTER satellite imagery and field studies) has fluctuated significantly in area (Benn et al, 2000; 2001). During the melt season, the camera captured oblique-view imagery of a fill, drain and refill event during the course of a single week (Fig 2). For the first week water levels remained relatively constant. On 22 June the lake level began to rise significantly (~3 m, preceded by a ~1 m rise on June 21). We consider it probable that this rapid increase in water volume resulted from downhill flow via an englacial conduit. By the morning of 23 June, this water level had not only drained to its earlier level (Fig 3) but continued to fall the following day, resulting in an eventual loss of former lake volume by ~55,000 m³, and a total loss of 105,000 m³ to the downstream fluvial system. Five days later, by 29 June, the day of our departure from the glacier, the lake regained half of the volume it had lost (water level rose to where it had been on June 23). It is unknown whether this was an isolated event, or the start of a sequence that recurred throughout the summer season. We are awaiting a mid-February download that will provide a photographic record of the entire melt season.

Finally, a third time-lapse camera (Ucam) monitored a lake with vertical walls that primarily fills from calving inputs (Fig 4). To quantify the timing and frequency of calving and the resulting changes in lake water level we used a pressure transducer immersed in the lake with millimetre measurement precision and a 5-minute sample interval. We discovered that large calving events tended to occur preferentially in late morning. This lake is known to have completely drained in 2000 (Benn et al, 2001) but has been gaining volume steadily since then.

The project is currently in need of funding. Hopefully by the time this report is published we will have been able to return to the field in May 2012. The visit is important for project continuity. We intend to check on

156. Figure 3: Amount of lake drain is clearly seen from the water 'high mark'
just a day earlier. 23 June 2011. *(Ang Phula Sherpa, Peak Promotion)*

157.   Figure 4: After a massive ice calving event on a supraglacial lake.
       (Ang Phula Sherpa, Peak Promotion)

current cameras, install a few more at higher elevation, to get an 'overview' look of the glacial lakes, and to conduct a field survey of 'Spillway' lake to determine how much it has expanded and deepened in recent years. If we can quantify this then we can gain a better understanding of its future growth and flooding potential.

References
Benn. D.I., Wiseman, S., and C.R. Warren, 2000, Rapid growth of a supraglacial lake, Ngozumpa Glacier, Khumbu Himal, Nepal, IAHS Publ. 264, 177-185.
Benn, D.I., Wiseman, S., and K.A. Hands, 2001, Growth and drainage of supraglacial lakes on the debris-mantled Ngozumpa Glacier, Khumbu Himal, Nepal, Journal of Glaciology, 47, 626-638.
Horodyskyj, U.N., Breashears, D. and R. Bilham, 2011, Feeling the Heat: Supraglacial Lake Changes as Observed at Ngozumpa glacier, Nepal, AGU Fall Meeting, abstract C53D- 0705.
Quincey, D.J., Luckman, A., and D. Benn, 2009, Quantification of Everest-region glacier velocities between 1992 and 2002, using satellite radar interferometry and feature tracking, Journal of Glaciology, 55, 596-606.
Sakai, A., Nakawo, M., and Fujita, K., 2002, Distribution characteristics and energy balance of ice cliffs on debris-covered glaciers, Nepal Himalaya, Arct. Antarct. Alp. Res., 34, 12–19.
Sakai, A., Takeuchi, N., Fujita, K., and Nakawo, M., 2000, Role of supraglacial ponds in the ablation process of a debris-covered glacier in the Nepal Himalayas., IAHS Publ., 264, 119–130.
Thompson, S., Benn, D.I., Dennis, K., and A. Luckman, 2012, A rapidly growing moraine dammed glacial lake on Ngozumpa Glacier, Nepal, Geomorphology, 145, 1-11.

STEPHEN GOODWIN

On The Road to a Greener Alps

Glacier retreat may be old news but it still has the capacity to shock. Hiking off the Morteratsch glacier in June last year I came to the point where the snout of this leviathan would have rested at the time of my birth in 1949. Where then there would have been an ice cliff and a silty stream issuing from beneath it to run through bare stones there were, instead, mature larches, thickets of alder, grasses and alpine flowers.

I had stepped off the ice nearly half an hour earlier, a full 1.5km up the valley. It's a sobering business measuring one's years by glacier retreat, almost like seeing your life in geological time. And there's little comfort in the knowledge that in this instance what is so extraordinary is not one's age but the speed at which the Morteratsch is disappearing.

Many of you will know the Morteratsch glacier. It grinds northwards to the Swiss Engadine from between Piz Bernina, the most easterly 4000-metre peak in the Alps, and Piz Zupo (3966m) on the border with Italy. Climbers on the Biancograt, the classic snow arête to Bernina's 4049-metre summit, can look down on the infamous 'Labyrinth'; for ski-mountaineers, the name of this contorted icefall says it all. The crevasse jumping there can be heart stopping.

But to return to those measurements: a special feature of the Morteratsch valley is that since 1900 signs have been erected at 10-year intervals at the foot of the glacier snout, or tongue in direct translation of *gletscherzunge*. The latest sign went up in 2010, recording a retreat of 2185 metres since 1900. Even with my slender grasp of arithmetic it was obvious that the pace is literally hotting up, more than 300 metres less glacier than at the turn of the millennium compared to die backs of only around 100m in each of the early decades of the 20th century.

Calculating the loss of mass of the Morteratsch is beyond me, suffice to say that the moraine walls to either side of the glacier appeared vastly higher than on my last visit some 20 years previously and the Boval hut is now so far above the ice that the detour was just not worth the effort, welcome though a beer would have been on that scorching day. Where the Pers glacier flows in from beneath Piz Palü, a junction once of ice has crumbled to grey cliffs and cascades of melt water.

None of this should have surprised me; even if I hadn't observed particular instances over many years – notably all those extra ladders to climb to the Concordia hut – glacier retreat in the Alps is a phenomenon well recorded and extensively publicised. Seeing it so 'in your face' – chunks of the Pers collapsing before one's eyes and willow herb and alder where

158. Meltwater cascading from the Pers glacier, a tributary of the Morteratsch
      glacier in the Bernina Alps, Switzerland. *(Stephen Goodwin)*

I remember walking on seemingly permanent ice – is another, brutally confirmatory, matter.

As we stood at Morteratsch station waiting for the train to Pontresina, Marco Onida, secretary general of the Alpine Convention, must have felt of glow of satisfaction at 'mission accomplished'. He had wanted to show a group of international journalists the reality of climate change in the Alps and the melting Morteratsch had driven the message home as if with a sledgehammer. A blunt instrument is often necessary to convince sceptical hacks, though in this case the group included a handful of mountaineer-journalists familiar enough with the evidence of glacier retreat, if not in such dramatic form.

Except that it wasn't really 'mission accomplished', just a very small step along a road that has no ending. Marco's mission, and that of Alpine Convention, is, to put it at its broadest, a sustainable Alps. What would that be like? Man and nature occupying this 1000km long arc of mountains and valleys in harmony; the landscape undefiled yet able to provide a living to the 14 million who live among the Alps and space for the 120 million people who take their holidays there each year; mountain ecosystems kept intact while their waters are exploited for hydropower and agriculture to serve the cities of the plains. Surely that's a pipe dream?

Better, though, to set out on the road than give up on the journey altogether. In 1991 the eight Alpine states and the European Union signed a treaty – the Alpine Convention – 'with the objective of furthering sustain-

159. Junction of the Pers and Morteratsch glaciers, bare rock and water where once was continuous ice. *(Stephen Goodwin)*

able development in the Alps while safeguarding community interests and the region's natural beauty and abundance'. The eight states are, Austria, France, Germany, Italy, Liechtenstein, Monaco, Slovenia and Switzerland. Operated by a small secretariat based in Innsbruck and Bolzano, the treaty provides a framework for these countries to develop and implement common policies for a 'greener' Alps. And as habitués of these mountains, climbers, hikers and ski-tourers should have a keen interest in their success.

Fortune favoured the Convention in the choice of the Italian lawyer Marco Onida to head its secretariat. A specialist in European and environmental law, Onida is also an experienced mountaineer with family ties to the Aosta valley. He thus combines elements of a Brussels bureaucrat (which in a sense, on secondment, he is) with Italian flair and a deep-rooted love of the mountains. This last, the psychological affinity with the mountains, is important for it is something Onida shares with many of the people – regional politicians, councillors, rural business folk and local conservation activists – who he has to keep on side. There's a common bond with Alps as 'home' even though they may have different ideas on its preservation or exploitation. As in UK national parks, nothing antagonises a farmer or local entrepreneur more than being told what to do by 'an outsider' from an environmental agency.

Each of the last three summers I've spent 10 days with Onida and one or two of his colleagues, criss-crossing the Alps by bus, train, bike and on foot; seeing the consequences of ill-considered development, greed, regional rivalries and climate change, and then the myriad of initiatives by communities, scientific bodies, enterprising individuals and public authorities to restore some harmony in the relationship with their alpine environment. Often it is really enlightened self-interest. For example, summers are getting drier in the southern Alps, winters wetter, the apple growers of Trentino will have to adapt to this; ski resorts below 1500m need to develop alternative incomes, snow cannons, besides scarring the hillsides, just will not produce the white stuff as temperatures rise; Alpine clubs like the CAF and the SAC are having to dig deep in their coffers to rebuild

160. Markers placed at 10 year-intervals at the snout of Morter-atsch glacier chart the retreat of the ice. *(Stephen Goodwin)*

161. The author at the source of the Po river. Drinking from the spring is said to restore a full head of hair. It doesn't! *(Stephen Goodwin)*

popular refuges, like the Goûter, Albert Premier and the Monte Rosa, according to sustainable principles.

In 2009 on my first of these Alpine Convention roadshows – SuperAlp is the banner – the theme was water.[1] We began by rafting on the crystal waters of the Soca in Slovenia, but the abiding memory of the trip is of rows of identical headstones at two cemeteries in northern Italy, memorials to the victims of inundations by water and mud at Longarone (1963) and Stava (1985) when warnings were ignored and dams overwhelmed. In both cases corporate greed and arrogance had over-ridden respect for water and the mountains it flowed from. Hundreds perished. Part of the Convention's unglamorous remit is to persuade states and authorities in the Alps to adopt best practice in river and water management, covering everything from hydro power, to fish ladders and keeping pristine the glacial headwaters of at least some alpine rivers.

Then in 2010 the mood lightened as SuperAlp focused on food – slow food to be more specific – and the mountain farms that produce it. Priming the market for speciality cheeses, cured meats and honey from alpine flowers helps keep alive alpine communities and counter the drift of populations to cities and service jobs in big resorts. I wouldn't want to blunt your appetite for the peaks, but with the occasional diversion to sample say, *Bleu de Queyras*, a blue cow's cheese from the Tarine and Abondance breeds in the Hautes-Alpes, *Banale Ciuighe*, a type of salami in the Brenta

1 'Who Cares About the Playground of Europe', *AJ 114*, 129-142 (2009).

162. The Aletsch glacier viewed from the Eggishorn with the Mönch rising at its northern end. Approximately 23km long, the Aletsch is the largest glacier in the Alps, but it too is shrinking. *(Stephen Goodwin)*

Dolomites, Mercantour olives from the Alpes-Maritimes, dried Calizzano and Murialdo chestnuts in the Bormida valley of Savona, or *Mustardela*, a blood sausage from the valleys above Turin, your taste buds would get to share in the pleasure of being in the mountains and you would, as the saying goes, 'be putting something back'.

From the Monviso hut we had ascended in pouring rain towards the ridge that runs north from the eponymous peak and then, at nearly 2900m, 'slipped' into Italy through Europe's oldest cross-border tunnel – an 80m shaft, partially blocked by old snow, cut beneath the jagged crest in the 15th century for the salt trade. Below, on the Pian de Re, is the source of

165. Mountain guide Alois Pirpamer, one of the 'rescuers' of Ötzi, on the spot where the mummified corpse was found. *(Stephen Goodwin)*

166. Memorial (in four languages) on the Tisenjoch to the nearby discovery of Ötzi the Iceman, or Similaun Man. *(Stephen Goodwin)*

Midi top station and walked across the Glacier du Géant to Pointe Helbronner – currently a construction site at 3462m with work in progress on the world's most expensive cableway. When the €110m project is completed it will carry up 300,000 people a year from Entrêves, four times the current number and a worrying (for environmentalists) increase in people pressure on the Mont Blanc range. There also seemed an irony in listening, as we did, to scientists telling of delicate measuring of rock temperatures and melting permafrost, while up above an 80m hole is to be bored through the granite of Pointe Helbronner to stabilise the new lift station and provide an escalator to the Torino hut. The two may not be technically incompatible, but the contrast in scale makes one wonder about relative priorities.

Next day, again assailed by glaciologists and geographers, we left Cervinia by cable car, hiked over the Theodulpass and on to the summit of the Breithorn (4159m) before descending to Zermatt and a different sort of glacier – the Glacier Express. With a two-night stopover to visit Altesch glacier, we travelled in comfort over the Oberalppass and on to Pontresina, ready to tread the Morteratsch. All the glaciers we surveyed are diminishing. It's incredible that when the Boval hut was built in 1870 it was only just above the level of the Morteratsch and now it is 200 metres above; but while this makes for a dramatic illustration of global warming, it is not glacier shrinkage per se that most concerns the boffins. Over the Alps as a whole, glaciers account for only five percent of the water coming from the mountains. Much more important for farmers and water consumers generally is the decrease in snow cover. Instead of being stored in the snow pack and released gradually, it melts or falls as rain too early in the spring to be of much use for agriculture or hydropower, and is in short supply during the needy summer months. This is a simplification, and drought is likely be more prevalent on the south side the Alps than the

167. Marker post at the Hauslabjoch with Similaun (3606m) beyond. *(Stephen Goodwin)*

north, but whatever, some old assumptions about the mountains as inexhaustible water towers will have to change.

Our last glacier was in the Ötztaler Alps in the Austrian Tirol. It is sometimes referred to as the 'Similaun', simply because that is name of the popular ski-mountain from which the glacier forms the usual descent line. On the maps it is the Niederjochferner, a name of such length that in print on my ÖAV (Austrian Alpine Association) sheet it extends beyond where, in reality, the snout of glacier now rests. Though I'd skied the 3606m-peak, I'd never been here in summer or stayed at the rebuilt Similaun hut. It would be an interesting visit on several counts.

Vent, at 1900m, is the roadhead village for several routes into the Ötztaler, including the Wildspitze (3774m) via the Breslauer hut. It is also a classic example of a *Bergsteigerdorf*, one of a family of mountain villages across Austria brought together under an initiative started by the ÖAV and supported by the federal government. Espousing low impact tourism while safeguarding landscape, nature and local culture, the *Bergsteigerdorfer* project exemplifies Alpine Convention principles in action. The community of less than 200 inhabitants has also seen off, at least temporarily, a major dam project for the Rofen valley above the village.

A pleasurable day's walk up the Niedertal, grazed by lop-eared sheep, and on to the dirty, melting ice of the glacier leads eventually to the scene of one of the most important archaeological discoveries of recent decades – a flattish patch of snow-covered ice near the Hauslabjoch on the Austrian-Italian border, where on 19 September 1991 Helmut and Erika Simon discovered the head and shoulders of a body protruding from the ice. The corpse would soon become known as 'Ötzi the Iceman' who now holds court from his own specially designed fridge at the South Tyrol Museum of Archaeology in Bolzano.

In 2004, some 5,300 years after Ötzi died on the Hauslabjoch of an arrow wound in the back, Helmut Simon also died alone on a snowy mountain in the eastern Alps, and I wrote his obituary for *The Independent*. Another actor in the Ötzi story was Alois Pirpamer, a former president of the UIAGM, Vent hotelier and head of the volunteer rescue service. Aged 74 and seeming sprightlier than most half his age, Alois escorted us from Vent to the spot at 3210m where the body was found. Sadly, two months after our visit, Alois passed away – 20 years to the day after Ötzi emerged from the disputed patch of ice. The exact location was important, for Ötzi was going to be a Copper Age celebrity and very big box office. While all the discovery action was on the Austrian side and Ötzi lay refrigerated in Innsbruck until 1998, he resides in Bolzano today because of a false stroke of a surveyor's pencil.

168. Ötzi the Iceman as he may have looked 5300 years ago. A reconstruction in the South Tyrol Museum of Archaeology, Bolzano. *(Stephen Goodwin)*

Following the bitter fighting between Austria and Italy in the First World War, the 1919 Treaty of Saint-Germain decreed the border to be the watershed of the Inn and the Adige rivers. However mapping out the watershed on glaciated terrain did not prove easy and in the area of the Hauslabjoch the surveyors adopted the expedient of drawing a straight line between identifiable watershed points. Much of that ice has since gone. Standing with Alois on the Ötzi spot, while cartographically we were 100m within Italy, we were, simultaneously, about 70 metres on the Inn (Austrian) side of the now clearly visible watershed. 'Without any doubt Ötzi should have been Austrian,' complained Alois. 'The government didn't fight for Ötzi because Austria was just getting into the EU and it didn't want to upset Italy.'

Next day we descended from the Similaun hut into Val di Senales and on to Bolzano to pay our respects to Ötzi in person. Director Albert Zink cheerfully admitted the border had been drawn incorrectly but added that it 'wasn't right to argue about it. It has to be respected as it has been drawn.' Ötzi had provided an instructive end to the 2011 SuperAlp: glacier retreat had exposed both the true watershed of the Austria-Italy border and the Iceman himself, a herald of a warmer world if ever there was one. The tussle over his 'nationality' had also demonstrated a regard for self-interest that is probably the biggest obstacle for the Alpine Convention and all those seeking a common endeavour on behalf of the Alps.

Arts

169. John Fairley, *NE wall of Pizzo Badile*, oil on canvas, 910x1215mm, 2012

JOHN FAIRLEY

In Search of Nirvana

As I write, facing me is Bhagirathi III. Seated none too comfortably, my computer balanced on my knees, I gaze at the pillar of the *Scottish Route*, the Fyffe and Barton route up the south-west pillar climbed in 1982. It is the end of winter. And two of my companions ski to the end of Tapovan meadow. Here, it is winter also and frost lies melting in the sun. But all is not quite what it seems from these few words. For I am sitting now, 18 years later and 7000km distant from the real Tapovan: I am looking at a painting.

When in late 1982 as the new Hon Ed of the *AJ* I received Bob Barton's article about the ascent of the ENE pillar of Bhagirathi III I knew that his photo would be the cover photo for my first volume. Little, then, did I think that I would see it for myself 12 years later; I was on an expedition led by John Cleare to climb Kedar Dome on ski and this would lead to me painting the self-same view, but in winter.

In the picture (*reproduced on page 1*), the figures on the snow in the distance were heading east along the moraine of Tapovan to gain our first view of Kedar Dome. Now, they never reach the corner and disappear from sight as they then did, and I will never climb that beautiful ridge to the summit of Bhagirathi III as I then wished. Yet in painting it I experienced once more the awe and wonder that I felt on first gazing across the Gangotri glacier and again, I feel at one with the mountain as I gaze anew at that vast scoop of the north-west face.

Why do we climb? Why do I paint? The book I am reading, Frank Kingdon Ward's *The Riddle of the Tsang Po Gorges* (a massive tome and hardly one that I would carry on expedition) in some way starts to answer the question. Most races, it says, have their promised land, a land that is always inaccessible; a paradise. To many, paradise is external, a place, far off, that you reach by dint of a difficult journey, but for Buddhists, paradise is already present, yet veiled by habits of perception. It is how you live that reveals paradise; that you reach nirvana.

For mountaineers, the perfect line, the exertion and the exhilaration of overcoming difficulties, the rush of adrenaline on the crux, the euphoria of success, all are reason enough to climb. But all too soon, paradise slips away. The slog back to the road-head, the drive to the airport, the long flight home, quickly destroy what turns out to have been a fleeting illusion.

We take our photographs and think to have captured the moment. But you cannot capture paradise. After the initial airings of our pictures to friends and perhaps for a lecture or two, our hundred slides return in their

Camp at Tapovan

boxes. Our thousand digital photographs remain in our archives waiting to be processed or enhanced some day. When, by chance or design, we look at them again, we find we have forgotten most of the wonder of the moment that we had hoped to remember. Daily life takes over and paradise slips away once more, elusive as ever, so we return again to seek yet again lest we forget. A mountaineer's paradise is in the doing. It is not a place. Shangri-la is always beyond the next hill.

Many of us keep diaries. Some write and a few of us paint. Writing diaries, especially, captures our emotions as far as we are prepared to reveal them on paper, for diaries contain much that we might prefer to keep private, our innermost thoughts. Re-reading some of my own brings back happy memories of days in the hills with the best of companions but something is missing: the hills themselves, the mountains soaring into the sky, the glaciers far below in the valleys, the moon rising over the distant summit.

So why do I paint when I could use a camera? Well, one reason is that my sketchbook is also my diary, a diary that for me contains far more than

170. John Fairley, *Camp at Tapovan*, watercolour, 270x180mm, 1994

mere words can convey.

Art was for me at school, my favourite subject, but pressure to study for a profession and a 'proper job' pushed this to one side and it was not until I was 30 that I rediscovered my enthusiasm and started to paint once more. In 1973 on honeymoon with Lizbet we went to the Bregaglia and with me I carried a tiny sketchbook and an even smaller box of paints. Those were the days of carrying quite heavy gear by today's standards and we carried a tent up to camp below the Sciora hut. The amount that I could carry did rather limit the amount of blank paper I was prepared to carry. But sitting in the sun, surrounded by impressively jagged mountains that I was seeing for the first time, it was the perfect place to restart painting.

From the start I resolved to draw with the brush rather than block in colour on a preliminary pencil drawing. Either approach is perfectly valid for there are no rules. It was just that that was how I felt I wanted to paint and I found that I could achieve a fantastic spontaneity in my pictures. The drawback soon became apparent, to my intense frustration, for more than one of those early watercolours quickly ran out of paper long before the painting was complete. What I learnt from that holiday has stayed with me ever since, for whilst a photograph will record the fleeting moment, it is only in painting that you learn really to look at the mountains. The longer you look (and you must look when you are painting) the more you discover that you have not seen. There is no better way to fill the time at a hut between returning from a climb in the afternoon and supper than painting the surrounding mountains, so painting became the norm and now I always carry a sketchbook, paints and brush. The problem now is deciding what to leave behind in the tent.

Having more or less overcome the problem of transferring mountain landscapes onto paper, I came upon another problem: what to do in the evening or when the weather was too bad to go outside. My long-suffering companions soon started to discover that I was secretly drawing them – not always particularly accurately or sympathetically. This is an altogether

Satopanth   *chaukhamba*

171. John Fairley, *Satopanth*, watercolour, 270x180mm, 1994

different activity for, unlike mountains, the subject is never still for more than a few seconds and the shape or gesture that attracted my attention immediately vanishes. There is no choice but to stalk my quarry, waiting for the moment when the pose returns again and grab it with a few more strokes of the pen or brush before it vanishes once more, usually in the moment of a downward glance. It's surprising just how often this technique can be successful.

Whereas the camera records exactly what is before it, its field of view

Kharchakund

is severely limited. Even a wide angle lens limits the view and it can be difficult to convey the extraordinary impression that an extraordinary view makes on you at the time by seeing it through the lens of the camera. All too frequently the photographer's complaint is that 'it didn't come out'.

It is a frustration that inflicts the painter too. How do you squeeze all the scene onto a sheet of A3 paper (the largest that will fit without too much damage into a rucksack, though more likely the paper size is A5 or even A6) and convey the feeling, the impression, that made you want to paint in the first place? What you can see extends from the sky to the depths below, from the east to the west but it has to be portrayed within a view of at most 10 degrees. The laws of perspective don't seem to work any more. It is a struggle and a struggle that confronts every artist who attempts to paint a mountain 'close up' as I do. Try as I will, a sheet of A3 is far too small. Yet it is too big as well, for cloud gathers and vanishes, and the light constantly changes before you are even started, let alone halfway finished. Even on the stillest of days, the mountain scene is not still for the sun never ceases to march across the sky, lighting what was in shadow and drawing new lines across the rock face as every newly lit spire casts its shadow below. Speed is of the essence. Inevitably you paint a picture of something that nobody has ever seen, of something that did not exist. Filling the paper with what you see is impossible. The trick is to paint what you want to see.

In the studio I am attempting to overcome another problem. It is a problem not just of physical perspective. There is a psychological aspect that has to be addressed as well. No mountaineer looks at a mountain without looking at all of it in its entirety, from the glaciers and rocks that cover its feet to its soaring ridges and sparkling summits. No mountaineer looks at a mountain without considering how it can be climbed. The longer you look, the more you see and the more you feel, especially when close up where no camera can capture the scene. Perhaps a painter who has never climbed might not recognize this problem, but to a climber who paints, the mountain must be believable.

It is here in my studio that I am painting now. On my easel is a view of the ENE wall of Pizzo Badile. It dominates the room but (at 900mm x 1200mm portrait format) it feels too small already and I wish that I were working at twice that size.

But once more I can feel the warmth of that summer day when Lizbet and I, climbing from the Cappano Gianetti, stepped from the confines of the crack that leads to the Colle del Cengalo. Suddenly the vast expanse of the ENE wall towered over us. Some 400m below the ice of the Vadrec dal Cengal butts against the foot of the north face. In the far distance, the peaks of the Val Bregaglia close the view to the north. Nearly 40 years ago we had climbed the north ridge and from its lower sections, gazing across the face to the East, our present standpoint could be seen before it disappeared behind the bulge of the eastern edge of the north face. Here, the tumble of rocks rise to the Punta Sertori and on the ENE wall you see a group of climbs not that frequented by British climbers, including the *English Route* first climbed by Isherwood and Kosterlitz in 1972.

Yet I know that no one else will view my painting the way in which I do. Inevitably it will be hung at the wrong height. Inevitably it will be viewed from too far away. I wish that I could insist, 'To look at this painting you must stand there! Your eye must be exactly here!' Only then would the viewer be in just the correct position for the physical perspective to be correct and the psychological perspective to work. It has always been so.

Will I see paradise? I doubt it but maybe, I hope, I might achieve nirvana whilst I am painting.

PENNY BRADSHAW

'Living at Our Full Compass'

Michael Roberts and The Poetry of Mountaineering

In a paper delivered to the Alpine Club in 1939 the poet, editor, and mountaineer, Michael Roberts points to the enduring symbol of the mountain in the human imagination, commenting that 'From the earliest times the loneliness, immensity and permanence of mountains have made men think of a power beyond themselves' (Roberts 1940, p.28). Within the paper he goes on to celebrate important Romantic literary responses to mountains but crucially he also distinguishes between his own poetic response and that of his Romantic predecessors, and begins to establish a new mountain-inspired poetics appropriate to the period in which he was writing. In so doing Roberts reminds us that cultural responses to natural phenomena such as mountains are variable rather than constant and are subject to historically specific economic, political and aesthetic pressures. In this essay I draw on Roberts's poetry and criticism to consider the literary treatment of mountains within the turbulent decade of the 1930s.

In his 1955 book, *The Lakers: The Adventures of the First Tourists,* Norman Nicholson argues that the Industrial Revolution brought about a fundamental rupture in man's relationship with the natural world and he suggests that in one way or another we have been trying to get back to nature ever since. Nicholson describes three post-industrial 'cults of nature – the Picturesque, the Romantic and the Athletic' which are all symptoms of our society's problematic separation from the natural environment (Nicholson 1955, p.207). Of these 'cults,' the Romantic, which obviously lends itself to a contemplative and imaginative response to nature, continues to be prioritised in our understanding of poetic responses to certain key privileged natural landscapes such as the Lakes and the Alps. The later Athletic cult, which is predominantly a phenomenon of the inter-war period, has received comparatively little attention in these terms, since it is defined by a primarily physical rather than imaginative engagement with the natural world. Nicholson depicts the Athletic response to nature through a range of physical pursuits such as swimming, climbing, cycling and hiking which allow the city-dweller to experience 'at least for the week-end, a more heroic and adventurous relation with the world about him' (Nicholson 1955, p.207). However, as Michael Roberts suggests in his 1939 paper and in his own poems, a post-Romantic and more athletic approach to the natural world can also engender new imaginative and creative directions for poetry.

The predominant poets publishing during the interwar period, or the

'Auden generation,' as they became widely known, are often seen to prioritise industrial and urban imagery above the pastoral and are defined in terms of their anti-Romantic aesthetics. However, during the period in which they were writing there is, as Nicholson indicates, a widespread cultural resurgence of interest in our human relationship with the natural world, an interest which can be traced in the fashionable rise of camping, hiking, and other fresh-air leisure activities during the inter-war period; four major British Everest expeditions took place during the 1930s and this decade also witnessed the formation of the Youth Hostels Association and the Ramblers Association, as well as a rapid growth in the Scouting movement. Not surprisingly, and despite an apparent intellectual prioritisation of the civic and the industrial over the natural, this cultural influence filters through to the poetry and other literature of the period.

172. Michael Roberts at Val d'Isère in 1935.
      (Janet Adam Smith)

Roberts is a much underestimated poet and writer who is little read or studied now even within literary circles but he is an important figure within the thirties context. While W. H. Auden is often viewed as the unofficial leader of the thirties generation, Michael Roberts is in some sense its spokesman. He is remembered primarily in terms of the role he played in his editorial work in defining and shaping the poetic terrain of the 1930s; as an editor and reviewer Roberts put together a number of landmark anthologies including *New Country* (1933) and *The Faber Book of Modern Verse* (1936), which were largely responsible for establishing this new literary territory of the Auden generation by bringing together for the first time some of the most significant emergent poetic voices such as Cecil Day Lewis, Stephen Spender and Louis MacNeice. His analysis of the contemporary poetry scene in his 1932 preface to the anthology, *New Signatures,* is widely regarded as a founding document of the 1930s movement and has been described as a 'manifesto' for the thirties generation (Woolf cited in Hynes 1976, p.75). If critics have tended to emphasise the urban to the exclusion of the natural in thirties poetry then this is partly a result of Roberts's own apparent prioritisation of urban industrial imagery in the *New Signatures* preface. But later critics have tended to isolate such elements from Roberts's wider argument which, when considered as a whole, reveals far less hostility to nature-poetry than has been assumed. In the preface Roberts certainly does point to the importance of seeking new poetic forms and images to express new experiences. He writes:

> ...we may appreciate the elegance of poetry written by men whose whole experience was different to ours; but we cannot accept it as a resolution of our own problems. It is not only that our response to certain words and rhythms has changed; new knowledge and new circumstances have compelled us to think and feel in ways not expressible in the old language at all... We have become too analytical, too conscious of our own motives, to react in the old way to the old symbols. (Roberts 1932, pp.7-9)

He also claims at one point that 'Rural poetry in recent years has been, in general, a cowardly escape into the past' but he goes on to suggest that it is possible to produce a different kind of nature poetry, which does address the values, concerns, rhythms and experiences of modern life, and he praises Julian Bell – whose poems are included in the anthology – for producing poems which engage with natural landscapes in a non-sentimental way:

> Julian Bell... write[s] of the English countryside in rhythms which show that for him it means no weekend cottage or funkhole from the town: his clear-cut delineations of landscape express neither jingoism nor sentimental affection but a feeling for the land itself; a sentiment which, though local in origins, leads to sympathy with that same feeling in others, and to a love of the earth irrespective of place. (Roberts 1932, p.17)

Here and elsewhere in his work Roberts looks to nature to provide symbols of something permanent and enduring to set against his vision of a decaying and corrupt industrial society. In this he reiterates a fundamentally Wordsworthian position and shows the relevance of certain Romantic ideals for his own generation. In later work he would more explicitly relate man's destruction of his own moral and psychological health to his mistreatment of the natural world; in his final unfinished book *The Estate of Man*, published posthumously in 1951, he presents what is essentially an ecological perspective, arguing that 'man has to live in harmony' with nature 'if he is to find harmony at all' (Roberts in Grubb 1980, p.176). In his poetry Roberts turns again and again to the natural world, not as a retreat from the political but as the only means of achieving a certain kind of clarity and understanding within a society riven by ideological divisions and hovering on the brink of war.

For Roberts the most powerful symbol offered by nature is the mountain and his ideas about poetry, politics, and mountains are closely intertwined. A keen mountaineer himself, Roberts met the critic, editor and biographer Janet Adam Smith, who shared his passion for mountaineering, in the early 1930s and they married in 1935. Their exhilarating pre-war climbs around the mountain ranges of Europe are recorded in Adam Smith's classic 1946 book *Mountain Holidays*. In Roberts's poetry it is apparent that the Alps and the Lakes, those key Romantic locations, take on a renewed significance in the twenties and thirties. Roberts visited the Lakes several times on climbing holidays before and after their marriage, and for a brief period following the outbreak of war moved with his wife to Penrith as a result of the relocation of Newcastle Grammar School at which he was then working. The young poet Kathleen Raine joined Roberts and his wife and their children at a house in Wordsworth Street at the start of the war and Raine's autobiography, *The Unknown Country*, offers a fascinating record of their domestic and intellectual life together. She describes also her occasional and rather reluctant outings with them on bleak excursions up Fairfield and Blencathra, where she says they would eat frozen sardines under the summit while the 'wind... cut like a knife and rattled the wedges of ice which adhered to the underside of every blade of grass' (Raine 1975, p.113). On these excursions Roberts is figured in terms of his energy, his leadership, and his insistence on facing personal danger and hardship in order to reach a summit. In one account of an expedition up Helvellyn, Raine says that he:

> enjoyed the effort and the victory... Michael was essentially a conqueror of summits. Whenever I see the constellation of Orion, I think of Michael tirelessly striding ahead of whatever party of us lagged behind. (Raine 1975, 113-4)

The language used by Raine here is echoed in Adam Smith's descriptions of her husband in *Mountain Holidays* and relates to the ideological context of the thirties in which mountaineering became what critics have described as a prominent 'myth-making activity'; Roberts with his physical rigour and determination to reach new places comes to represent the archetypal 'climber-hero' of the period, a figure which recurs again and again in poetry by Auden, Spender and others of the period (Hynes 1976, pp. 236-7). Adam Smith develops this persona in the introductory memoir she wrote for Roberts's posthumous *Collected Poems,* in which she characterises him as one of life's 'explorers', those figures who are 'always heading for the limits' and 'willing to risk breaking the accepted patterns of thought, knowledge, faith, action' (Roberts 1958, p.29). Roberts himself explores and celebrates such constructions of modern male identity and in a 1934 review of a work by Cecil Day Lewis, which he titled 'The Return of the Hero,' presents this ideal type as the defining man of his times:

> These figures represent something essential in humanity magnified to heroic proportions. They represent the answer to doubt, uncertainty and indecision, and the reintegration of divided personalities. The returning hero, the man who knows his own mind and is certain of his own desires is the antithesis of Eliot's Prufrock. (Roberts 1934, p.72)

In Roberts's poetry Prufrock's counterpart comes to be defined as the semi-autobiographical climber-poet and this figure strives to find answers to the questions raised by the turbulent early decades of the 20th century. In 'La Meije 1937,' Roberts describes the pleasure of cutting steps in the ice and finding 'a new alternative' to the more problematic established routes, but in the poem this becomes a metaphor for the new pathways his generation had to take intellectually and he connects here the physical rigour of the climb with the intellectual, political and creative challenges which they faced:

A man should use every nerve and muscle,
A man should puzzle out the hardest questions,
A man should find words, for the thoughts that no one knows.
(Roberts 1958, p.135)

Roberts's real and metaphorical mountains are dangerous and physically demanding but they also offer routes to a higher knowledge and a perspective attainable only by the poet as hero, or – as Roberts depicts him in the *New Signatures* preface – as 'leader' (Roberts 1934, p.10). The poem suggests that only by going to the limits of the known can these poet-leaders hope to find the new perspectives needed; only they, with their energy and determination, can find new ways of addressing the political and ideological dilemmas of the age.

Mountains become the dominant trope within Roberts's poetry and Adam Smith notes the apparent incongruity that her husband 'found in the mountains the symbols and the language for his poetry' and that 'his austere, anti-romantic view of life, found expression in imagery which is more often associated with romantic poets,' an incongruity which she relates to personal and wider intellectual concerns relating to the experiences of this decade (Roberts 1958, p.35). A key distinction between his own mountain poetics and that of the Romantics is made clear though by Roberts in his 1939 paper for the Alpine Club. In this he praises earlier Romantic responses to mountains in poetry, suggesting that 'Wordsworth's lines on the Simplon, Shelley's *Mont Blanc*, and Coleridge's *Hymn before Sunrise* all contrive to express imaginative insight without falsifying or distorting the material vision' but he says that 'on the whole' mountain-inspired poetry 'shows all the vices of bad description... It expresses a kind of sham religion, a sentimental daydream in which brutal realities are not transcended but conveniently ignored' (Roberts 1940, p.28). Roberts goes on to classify these earlier examples as 'poetry of mountains' and he makes a crucial distinction between this and what he refers to as a 'poetry of mountaineering' (p.27). What this distinction flags is a movement away from visual and aesthetic responses to mountains and towards the human struggle experienced in the ascent and in the physical act of the climb. It is the poetry of mountaineering which becomes for Roberts such an important art form for his generation. While mountains, in their immensity and permanence, remain an important symbol within the human imagination,

precisely with feet walking on snow and the wintry moonlight above:

> Midnight, and the pale snow
> Crisp underfoot,
> A frost-encircled moon
> On Glaramara.
> Stone country cannot suffer
> Your loss or mine;
> The valley guards its sorrow
> At this New Year.
> And every wintry angel
> Looks to the hills
> Whose frozen comfort stays,
> Endures, compels.
> A country of stone dreams
> The ghost of a hill,
> A frozen tarn, the still
> Echo of bells,
> Bells in the midnight valley,
> Frosty stars,
> Blencathra, Gable, ghostly Helvellyn,
> And this New Year. (Roberts 1958, p.175)

This poem is written in the immediate aftermath of the Second World War and in the face of Roberts's awareness of his own mortality. There is a real sense here of what he refers to in an earlier poem as 'the bleak Inhuman north,' ('Shining Dark,' in Roberts 1958, p.75) as the desolate mountainous landscape appears to be wholly untouched by human concerns and human misery. Nonetheless the stony implacability of the fells and their apparent resistance to change offers some sort of counter to the ephemeral concerns of human life and perhaps some aid to endurance. The fells, like the stars, represent something fixed and certain against which we take our bearings. In the final stanza the individual mountains are referred to intimately by name and the sound of the bells echoing round the valley which is walled in by these familiar and enduring physical forms is both a requiem for that which is lost and a peal for the promise of the new year. There is the merest suggestion of hope offered by the stillness, which is a reminder of the peace that has followed the bloodshed, and in the significance of the precise temporal moment, the start of the first new year for peace-time Europe.

In his introduction to *The Faber Book of Modern Verse*, Roberts suggests that 'primarily poetry is an exploration of the possibilities of language' which 'does not aim directly at consolation or moral exhortation,' but he says that 'a poem may ... change the configuration of the mind and alter our responses to certain situations' (Roberts, 1936, pp.3 & 5). Both the climb and the act of writing the poem are important precisely because they can

173. Michael Roberts
at Tignes.
(Janet Adam Smith)

engender new mental and philosophical perspectives even in the face of death and human suffering. Adam Smith observes that for Roberts, writing is less an act of 'self-expression' than of 'exploration' (Roberts 1958, p. 20) and it is this exploratory and 'athletic' response to nature which allows him to find a new relevance for his generation in these Romantic landscapes. The climb upwards through new and difficult territory becomes in his poetry a powerful metaphor for the intellectual and political challenges which were faced both during and immediately after one of the most turbulent decades of the 20th century. These literary and physical mountain journeys explore the possibilities offered by new directions and become a means of attaining a clearer perspective on the geography of our lives.

References

Grubb, Frederick (ed.), *Michael Roberts: Selected Poems and Prose* (Manchester: Carcanet Press, 1980).

Hynes, Samuel, *The Auden Generation: Literature and Politics in England in the 1930s* (London: Bodley Head, 1976).

Nicholson, Norman, *The Lakers: The Adventures of the First Tourists* (London: Hale, 1955).

Raine, Kathleen, *The Land Unknown* (New York: Brazilier, 1975).

Roberts, Michael, 'Preface,' *New Signatures: Poems by Several Hands*, ed. by Michael Roberts (London: Hogarth Press, 1932), pp. 7-20.

Roberts, Michael, 'The Return of the Hero,' *London Mercury*, 31 (November 1934), 72-3.

Roberts, Michael (ed.), 'Introduction,' *The Faber Book of Modern Verse*, ed. Michael Roberts (London: Faber and Faber, 1936), pp. 1-35

Roberts, Michael, 'The Poetry and Humour of Mountaineering,' *Alpine Journal*, 52 (1940), 22-33.

Roberts, Michael, *Collected Poems* (London Faber and Faber, 1958)

ELIZABETH RAIKES

Kindred Spirits

Four Mountaineers and a Painter

A chance enquiry as to the relationship between Alpine Club member, the Reverend W H Hawker (1827-1874) and the artist and poet Edward Lear (1812-1888), has led to the answer to a mystery that has been unresolved for more than 100 years – the mystery being a partially-dated letter from Lear to an unidentified recipient.

William Hawker is well known by AC historians as an active member of the Club. He contributed several papers to the *Alpine Journal*, was a keen naturalist, a good sportsman, keen shot and fisherman. Edward Lear is particularly celebrated today for his nonsense rhymes. Children all over the world are familiar with *The Owl and the Pussycat* or the *Dong with the Luminous Nose*. He was also an entertaining writer and an accomplished oil and watercolour painter, specialising in landscapes. It was this latter occupation that brought him into contact with members of the Alpine Club.

Lear's letter, dated Wednesday 21 February from the Villa Emily, reads as follows:

Dear Sir
>*I should be glad to know any friend of Mr Freshfield's, and in your case, shall have the greatest pleasure in renewing our acquaintance. After 12 o'clock I shall be at home today till 4, & I hope you will look in – as I am sure my Kinchingunga will interest you.*
>
>*By a curious coincidence I was this very morning writing to Mr Douglas Freshfield – at London – not being aware he was at Cannes.*
>
>*He tells me you have been up Monte Viso: - I have many drawings of it, but never got nearer than the foot of the mountain.*
>
>*With hope of seeing you shortly, believe me.*
>>*Yours very truly*
>>*Edward Lear*

Could this letter have been sent to Hawker? The archives contain no record of a meeting between Lear and Hawker but that Lear was acquainted with Hawker is beyond doubt. In the spring of 1868 in Corsica, the land of the '*Helix Tristis* – the melancholy snail', Lear waited for the weather to clear and 'for the want of society and much else' spent the time writing out 'Mr Hawker's notes for use'.(1) In the words of Hawker, 'Corsica, as seen from the shores of the Riviera…is in reality entirely invisible, and is only seen by the medium of refraction or mirage. It is often so seen, and still better, is bodily seen from the heights above those towns; and it is undeniable, that dream-like beauty is the sight often presented at early morn of the far off island rising Venus-like out of the sea, her many snow peaks, like a diadem of pearls, catching the rising sun, and her base clothed with sleepy haze .' '...the sunset glow changes the pearl diadem for a tiara of rubies.'(2)

What mountaineer could not fail to be tempted by such an image? And, to a landscape painter like Edward Lear, reading these notes in the cold wet winter of the Riviera in 1867, it would have been irresistible. For what else does Hawker go on to say about Corsica but: 'the artist is abundantly rewarded by the amazing loveliness of the scenery.' If Lear had not read the notes before setting foot on Corsica, he would surely have come across Hawker within the small but rapidly growing and busy English community of the late 19th century French Riviera where Lear spent some considerable time between 1864 and 1868.

But if not Hawker, who else? The trail of Lear's encounters with the members of the Alpine Club starts earlier than 1868. From May to August 1861, Lear was wandering between France, Italy and Switzerland. Born the twentieth of twenty-one children, Lear was brought up entirely from an early age by his oldest sister, Ann. She was the rock in his life for more than 50 years. He wrote to her almost everyday of his adult life. When she died in March 1861 he was utterly bereft. He plunged into a profound period of depression, an illness he suffered from all his life and which he called 'The Morbids'. Salvation, or at least a sense of direction, came with a commission to paint the celebrated Villa Petraia in Florence. So a couple of days after Ann's gravestone was completed in May, Lear set off for the Continent. But his spirits remained stubbornly low: 'The past is past – the present seems nonsense, and the future darkness,' he wrote in his diary on 13 June.(3) Nothing was right. His 'boles' were always troublesome. In Florence he encountered 'very vulgar English'. In Courmayeur the 'flies were horrible', Pisa was a 'most offensive begging inferno', and as he grew nearer the mountain he found 'crowds of English, some 30 to 40 at table'. 'The bore of joining Swiss-English travellers, is, that all speak of "Passes and Peaks" and nought else.'

It was, though, to these 'passes and peaks' that Lear was headed. For a while, they did lighten his mood. He was impressed with Monte Viso: 'The plain and lofty Monte Viso are very grand, and the colour vastly rich... gleaming from high above cloud – looking more like a set of stars than anything mundane.' And not all the English turned out to be a 'bore'. In Turin he met Mr Blackstone, 'agreeable fellow and member of the Alpine Club'.(4) Blackstone apparently gave him advice about Courmayeur which Lear said was 'all bosh'. Yet just as it seems he was picking himself up, once again he plunged into the abyss. He felt 'a gloom about these Alpine valleys, I can't abide... the sense of never being able to get out-ness is paramount with me'. Verrex was a 'narrow gloomy valley', Monjovet 'horrid and gloomy indeed' and he didn't 'like Mont Blanc enough to stay longer'. Driven out by the crowds, the flies and the weather, he moved on to Lausanne on 3 August.

At the Hotel Gibbon, things seemed to be looking up. The scenery was 'very lovely' and there were 'nice intelligent children'. At supper he records meeting two Englishmen. But 'The Morbids' returned and later that evening he wrote in his diary that he was 'Unhinged and altogether upset. I do not know what to do.' But he did what he always did and got up the next morning, went out to draw and hid his feelings. He returned to the hotel in the afternoon and sat in the garden 'talking with the 2 men of last night – one's name is Mattheus (sic)'. It is unlikely that they would have regarded Lear as anything other than a jolly, enthusiastic and interesting man. Mathews, observed Lear, 'seems very regularly up in the Alps'. Mathews was, of course, William Mathews (1828-1901) founder member of the Alpine Club. Mathews' diary for 4 August confirms that he indeed did meet a painter 'named Edward Lear' at the Hotel Gibbon.

Rarely does Lear record the names of casual acquaintances in his diaries. Blackstone and Mathews clearly made an impression upon him. So, with Hawker, there are three potential recipients of Lear's letter. As a prolific letter writer, Lear was exceptionally good at staying in touch with people he encountered. He collected these people, adding to his circle of acquaintances at every stage of his life. It is clear from his letter that Douglas Freshfield (1845-1934), one of the most distinguished members of the AC, was part of this circle. But how did they meet? One could imagine that their paths may have crossed in the Alps in 1861. Freshfield would have been 16 and it is known that while still a pupil at Eton, he ascended Mont Blanc, and in the 1860s and 1870s made a number of first ascents in the Italian Alps. More likely, they may have met at Alfred Lord Tennyson's, both having a friendship with the poet over a number of years.

Certainly, Freshfield was familiar with, and seemed to appreciate, Lear's drawings. He describes Lear's drawings of the Abruzzi as 'striking'. (5) And it may not be too fanciful to suppose that Lear's book ('the best English work on Corsica '(6)) could have been the inspiration that sent Freshfield, with his guide and friend Francois Devouassoud, to Corsica in 1880. They were not disappointed. Devouassoud was an experienced mountaineer and not easily impressed. Yet, according to Freshfield, on a day when they were more than usually impressed by the granite mountains of Corsica, Devouassoud's view was that 'when *le bon Dieu* was building the Alps, he must have had a bit left over and have thrown it down in the Mediterranean to make Corsica '. (7) Despite the difference in age, Lear and Freshfield had much in common. Freshfield described himself as 'much a traveller as a climber' (8) and Lear was just as much a traveller as a painter and writer of nonsense verse. Like Lear, Freshfield was also an eccentric. While Lear travelled with his own bed and an Indian-rubber mat, Freshfield could be seen in the mountains with an umbrella in place of an ice-axe.

Could Lear's drawing of Kangchenjunga have also been the inspiration

74. Edward Lear (1812-88) *Kinchinjunga from Darjeeling, Himalayas*, signed with monogram and dated 1875; pencil, pen and ink, and watercolour, heightened with bodycolour; 241 x 391mm. *(Courtesy of Christie's Images)*

for Freshfield's pioneering circumnavigation of the mountain in 1899? Freshfield has described the mountain as being 'a row of roseate flames. They are not clouds. While he gazes they harden from the phantoms of a dream into definite forms'. (9) This ethereal nature had given Lear great problems when capturing the scene in 1874. 'Kinchinjunga is... so very godlike and stupendous, and all the great world of dark opal valleys, full of misty, hardly to be imagined forms... apt to become a wonderful hash of Turneresque colour and mist and space, but with little claim to forming a picture of grand effect.' (10) Capture it, though, he did. In the various versions of his painting, the mountain rises ghost-like above the tree-lined slopes and scarps above Darjeeling. His painting is nothing less than a fitting throwback to the 18th century tradition of the sublime.

Kangchenjunga is the key that unlocks the dating of Lear's letter. This soaring snow-covered peak in the exotic Himalayas captured the imagination of the British public in the 1870s. Lear accepted the invitation of his friend Thomas Baring, Lord Northbrook (then Viceroy), to join him in India. Having collected three commissions to paint the great mountain, Lear went out in 1873 and first set eyes on the mountain in 1874. At the time of the letter Lear was living in the Villa Emily in San Remo. He left there in 1880. He wrote the letter as he was putting the finishing touches to one of the paintings of Kangchenjunga, and one version is signed and dated 1877. In 1877, the 21 February happened to fall on a Wednesday. This date rules out Hawker who had died in 1874. There is no further reference to Blackstone and Lear. This leaves Mathews as the remaining contender to be the recipient of the letter.

Was Mathews on the Riviera and near San Remo in 1877? Lear knew that Freshfield was in Cannes. Most likely he received this news from the letter to which he was responding. Mumm's Alpine Register suggests that both Mathews and Freshfield were indeed in the area. The entry for Freshfield states that in the winter and early spring he was rambling in the *Alpes Maritimes* which rise immediately above the Riviera. The entry for Mathews states that 'In the winter of 1876-7, mainly for reasons of health, he spent seven months in Algeria.' He would have crossed to Algeria, most likely from one of the Mediterranean ports. A further clue that Lear was writing to Mathews lies in the reference to Monte Viso. Mathews made the first ascent of Monte Viso on 30 August 1861, a few weeks after his meeting with Lear at the Hotel Gibbon, and it is highly likely that their conversation would have covered Mathew's reason for being in the area. Lear, with his phenomenal recall of people and events, would have remembered this, and clearly Freshfield had communicated with him about it. While this is not absolute proof, it now appears beyond reasonable doubt that William Mathews was the recipient of Lear's letter and that Mathews was Lear's visitor on 21 February 1877.

Acknowledgements: The author wishes to thank Terry Hodgkinson, without whose original enquiry this mystery would never have been solved, and Glyn Hughes, Hon Archivist of the Alpine Club, for his interest and help in tracking down references without which the connections could not have been made. Lear's partially-dated letter and William Mathews's diary are located in the AC Archive.

Notes

1. Lear, E., *Journal of a Landscape Painter in Corsica,* London, Robert John Bush, 1870
2. Hawker, The Reverend W.H., 'Corsica', *AJ4* (May 1869), 269-282, 289-309.
3. Quotes from Edward Lear in this section come from *Edward Lear's Diaries, The private Journal of a Landscape Painter*, transcribed by Mario Graziosi from the Houghton Library, Harvard University, MSEng. 797.3 and published on the internet:
www.monsenselit.org/diaries
4. Frederick Elliott Blackstone was a member of the Alpine Club from 1859 until his death in 1892.
5. Freshfield, Douglas, W, *Below the Snow Line*, London, Constable & Company Limited, 1923
6. p60, ibid.
7. p49, ibid.
8. p v, ibid.
9. Freshfield, Douglas, W, *Round Kangchenjunga: a narrative of mountain travel and exploration*, London, Edward Arnold, 1903, p31
10. Murphy, R. (ed.) *Indian Journal, Watercolours and extracts, 1873-1875,* London, R, Jarrold, 1953, p63.

History

175. John Fairley, *Aiguille Verte et Dru*, watercolour, 210 x 280mm, 1993

ERIC VOLA

L'affaire Frêney

A Long-overdue Acknowledgement

August 29 1961: the 'Last Great Problem of the Alps', The Central Pillar of Frêney, is solved by Chris Bonington, Ian Clough, Jan Djuglosz and Don Whillans. But in French eyes the honours go also to René Desmaison, Pierre Julien, Yves Pollet-Villard and Ignacio Piussi.

Desmaison seemed unable to accept the facts of the respective Pillar ascents and set about denigrating the British achievement while inflating his own – a fiction in which he was supported by the all-powerful Lucien Devies, the veritable godfather of post-war French mountaineering. Only now, half a century after the landmark climb, has the record been put straight in the French mountaineering press.

176.   Southern flank of Mont Blanc showing Frêney pillars (centre).
(Chris Bonington Picture Library)

I became aware of Desmaison's claim to have at least shared the first ascent on reading a recent biography of him by Antoine Chandellier, a journalist on *Le Dauphiné Libéré*, a regional newspaper in the French Alps. Entitled *La Montagne en direct – La vie de René Desmaison* (Guerin 2010), the book gives René's version of the celebrated climb. In it Chandellier refers to Chris and Don as 'an employee of a tinned food manufacturer and a plumber and zinc worker', implying that no integrity could be expected of

247

such characters. Being a friend of Chris, I saw red and started a quest for the facts.

To understand the 'Frêney controversy', one must remember the context of the time. Most climbers did not have pennies or francs in their pocket to spare for local luxuries. The Brits camped at the Biolay and apart from Snell, a sports shop owner of American descent, and Maurice Simond, owner of the Bar National, they were regarded by locals as no better than scruffy beggars. This was also the case for many French climbing *sans guide*, and in our case our benefactors were Louis Jannin of the Hôtel de Paris, who rented us his top floor shabby rooms at bargain rates, and Denise Escande whose little chalet 'La Tirelire' was crammed with scores of us. Alpinism was heavy with nationalism and attracted widespread media coverage: The first ascents of Annapurna and Everest were comparatively recent. The 100,000-copy run of Maurice Herzog's *Annapurna: The First 8000m Peak* sold out in three weeks and its worldwide sales exceeded 10 million copies.

The man who validated René's account was Lucien Devies. For 30 years Devies was the unchallenged authority of French alpinism. His voice was paramount in affairs of the National Guides' Training Academy (ENSA) as well as the alpine associations. Louis Lachenal called him 'the De Gaulle of alpinism'. At the time of the controversy he was focused on the 1962 Jannu expedition, which proved a magnificent success, all the climbers, including Desmaison, summiting, along with two Sherpas.

Walter Bonatti was probably the first to set his sights on the granite tower at the head of the Frêney glacier on the south-east side of Mont Blanc. He made an attempt in 1959 and again the following year. The public at large learned about this 'last great problem of the Alps' in June 1961 when simultaneous French and Italian attempts ended in tragedy: Pierre Mazeaud lost three of his best friends, and Bonatti, his partner, the Italian guide Andreas Oggioni.

Three days later, Pierre Julien, an ENSA instructor, made an attempt with Ignacio Piussi. They failed on the first extremely difficult pitch on the Chandelle. Five weeks later Chris, Don and Jan asked Julien to join them. He declined. They then met Ian Clough and enlisted him. Meanwhile Julien had alerted Desmaison and Pollet-Villard, who were also ENSA instructors. The race was on.

Philippe Gaussot from the *Dauphiné Libéré* covered the event. His aerial photos show clearly Chris and Don on top of the Chandelle and the French party at its foot. Chris and Don were greeted with tea at midday on the summit of Mont Blanc by two journalists and were later interviewed in Chamonix. Desmaison's party reached the summit too late and spent the night at the Goûter hut. The next day, on reading the news, Demaison went berserk and requested a rewrite stating they had made the first ascent with the British. Gaussot refused. This triggered the 'Frêney Controversy'.

René wrote to the *Dauphiné* editor complaining about Gaussot's bias and 'lies' and managed to have another regional newspaper, based in Lyon,

177. Central Pillar of Frêney from the Col de Peuterey. *(Chris Bonington Picture Library)*

publish an account of 'his' first ascent with no mention of Chris's party. He gave his account to Devies who published it in the October issue of *La Montagne et Alpinisme* without checking with the British. René criticized the British party as 'irresponsible amateurs, slow, not waiting for them at the summit' and invented an account that was a travesty of the facts.

178. The French team, heavily laden, at the téléphérique station.
(Chris Bonington Picture Library)

They had all met in the Aiguille du Midi cable car on the afternoon of 26 August:

We were astonished of the lightness of the British equipment... Well, each one has his own conception of alpinism. We preferred heavier equipment, but efficient in case of bad weather.

René stated later that his competitors had a 24-hour lead. In fact, the British party spent the night at the Col de la Fourche bivouac while the French went to the Torino hut to fetch Ignacio Piussi. On the 27th, René and Pollet-Villard started from the hut at the same time that Chris and Don's party left the Fourche bivvi – that is at 1am, with three hours to catch up. Julien with Piussi got the first cable car from La Palud and departed at 6am, giving the British party a lead of eight hours, not 24 hours.

René reached the 'Bonatti-Mazeaud' bivouac after 2pm on the 28th to see Don belaying on slings below a *dièdre* and chimney that formed the crux of the route. The previous pitch climbed mostly free (French 6c) by Don was quite a feat by one of the very best climbers of the time. Don realized that his pegs were not wide enough and his wooden edges too wide for the corner crack, the crux. He decided to climb it free: a pitch today of French 7a+ if climbed free. He reached the overhung bottomless chimney but could not get established in it and couldn't let go with one hand to hammer in a rock peg in front of his nose. After a struggle, he fell off, losing his hammer, his cap and 'me fags in it'.

It was then that the French refused to lend the British some small wooden edges.

Unfortunately for René, who thought that the British would let them go ahead, now was the time for Chris to perform his best ever lead on rock. He decided to show the 'Frogs' a trick used by 'The Master', Joe Brown: taking some pebbles, he jammed two in the crack and with a sling around them trod delicately in the étriers. Reaching the bottom of the overhanging exit chimney, he was able to hammer in a peg, get ensconced in the chimney, wriggle up it and, with a 500m drop beneath, edge out of the chimney and on to the wall; strength fading, he pulled on to a narrow ledge. The difficulties were over. Don wrote that 'it had been a fine piece of climbing by him...' not a compliment he made often.

Don climbed up to Chris and fixed a rope for Ian and Jan to prusik up.

From René's account, it was now 5pm. He saw Chris on top of the crux and proposed to Djuglosz 'who speaks French' to end the competition for 'chivalric reasons' and because:

It would be regrettable to create such a competitive atmosphere for an ascent for which already four alpinists have died.

He concludes:

Have we done the first ascent of the pillar with the British? Have we only done the second or third ascent, as asserted by one journalist short of copy? Whatever, we did it. The controversies which were provoked to minimize our ascent have been made by men who are not alpinists and who have not understood the true spirit of alpinism. Yes, the men from below, and when I say from below, I don't mean from the plains, there are people who understand better than others those who climb a bit higher.

Following René's article and his attack on Gaussot, the latter asked the British to send their account to Devies. Chris's text was translated into excellent French by Etienne Nusslé from Geneva, then a journalist in London. Devies, who did not speak English, was impressed. He asked for a similar statement from the French climbers.

Here are the two statements:

On Alpine Club letterhead, Chris to Devies:

... Mr Desmaison's account is so inaccurate and gives such an erroneous impression of what really occurred that Don Whillans, Ian Clough and I have judged necessary to re-establish the facts as we lived them up there...

Some weeks ago, Mr Desmaison wrote to Don Whillans asking him to clarify those points. After having consulted Ian Clough and me, Whillans answered that we had not received any help or any equipment from the French party. It is therefore difficult for me to understand what made Mr Desmaison ignore this response in his article...

Statement on the first ascent of the Central Pillar of Frêney:

On the morning of the 28th of August, when Don Whillans and myself started to climb on the vertical wall above our bivouac…we saw the French party leaving the Peuterey pass. Later, René Desmaison and his friends went up quite fast on the snow couloirs between the Central Pillar and the Right Pillar of Frêney at around half its height.

Around 2pm they got up to our comrades Clough and Djuglosz who were still on the bivouac ledge. At this instant, we attempted to climb a corner to reach a chimney with no bottom splitting in two a horizontal roof clearly on the right of the Pillar. The crack in the corner was too wide for our pegs and too narrow for our wooden edges. Whillans then tried to climb it free climbing, but he fell off.

I then called Djuglosz and told him to ask the French party to lend us some of the narrow wooden wedges which they had. Our Polish comrade negotiated to no avail for quite sometime with Desmaison and Julien. They believed that we were on the wrong route and that they needed all their equipment. Consequently they did not give Djuglosz any wooden wedges or pegs.

*In an article relating to the 'first' ascent, René Desmaison claims that Whillans left all the pegs in place in the corner as **we** had taken their equipment and therefore had more than enough. The French climbers at no time were in a position to verify this assertion. In fact, Don Whillans took out almost all the pegs **we** placed in as **we** estimated they would be necessary to cope with the difficulties to come…*

The following day, Piussi was the first to join us. He asked me to lend him another rope in order to lower down to his French comrades the Prusik apparatus and take up their rucksacks. I gave him our two small 30m ropes which we had left, with the promise that they would be returned in Chamonix.

To conclude, we gave the French considerable aid in this first ascent of the Frêney Pillar and we are happy to have done so. However without the usage of the rope in the most difficult part of the climb, they would have arrived at least 24 hours after us. On the other hand, they did not lift a little finger at the time when their collaboration would have been most welcome.

Desmaison's team to Devies:

Statement from the French alpinists R. Desmaison, P. Julien, Y. Pollet-Villard on the First Ascent of the Central Pillar of Frêney

On Monday, the 28th, leaving the Peuterey pass where they had bivouacked, the French climbers R. Desmaison, P. Julien and Y. Pollet-Villard with the Italian alpinist I. Piussi went up the snow slopes below the Central Pillar of Frêney, and reached the base of the Pillar, on its left side. Traversing to the right, they gained the right side of the Pillar which they followed for 150m. Returning to the centre of the Pillar, they caught up with the British alpinists at 2pm.

At that moment, their intention was to overtake the English alpinists who were far too slow in their opinion and who since the beginning of the day had only climbed 30 to 40m, over difficult ground but partially equipped by I. Piussi and P. Julien during their first attempt.

The English alpinists then asked them for some equipment, estimating that they did not have enough. The French climbers first refused as they wanted to climb a

79. Don Whillans leading one of the hard pitches on the lower part of the Pillar.
(Chris Bonington Picture Library)

crack more direct and less difficult...

It is quite likely that I. Piussi and R. Desmaison who had done the two most difficult artificial climbs in the Dolomites – Torre Trieste and Cima Ovest – would not have taken more than three hours to climb up this crack. But they did not do it, in order not to create a competition that would have been particularly unpleasant. With the agreement of his three comrades, René Desmaison told Jan Djuglosz to take the equipment he believed necessary to continue the climb. Djuglosz then took pegs of different sizes belonging to the French alpinists and attached them to their rope and Clough hoisted them up. Did Clough give them to Bonington and Whillans? This, R. Desmaison and his comrades cannot confirm; the variety of the languages spoken by the various parties made it particularly difficult to understand each other.

At 5 pm, Bonington and Whillans managed to overcome the corner, then, after having traversed horizontally to the left, they came back to the centre of the Pillar and from there threw a rope to Clough and to Djuglosz. Clough ascended the rope near the aforementioned crack using prusik knots.

R. Desmaison and Piussi then handed the end of their rope to Djuglosz for him to fix it on the belay once up so that, the next morning, they could repeat the procedure to get up the remaining 40m.

Naturally the French and Italian alpinists used the fastest mean to get up those 40m since they had agreed to stay behind the English, not in order to benefit from their help but so as not to overtake them, as mentioned above...

On Tuesday the 29th, Piussi was the first to arrive at the last bivouac of the English alpinists. They were preparing to leave for the summit. It was only three pitches above and these did not present any particular difficulties.

R. Desmaison came up to Piussi, then, after having hauled up their rucksacks, P. Julien and Y. Pollet-Villard came up to join them. They arrived at the summit of the Pillar one hour after the English alpinists.

The French alpinists and their Italian comrade do not think it is necessary to point out the climbing record of each of them in order to understand that they needed no help from anyone to climb the Central Pillar of Frêney, having done previous ascents technically much more difficult.

The presence of the English alpinists on this ascent did not help the French gain 24 hours as they [the English] *seem to attest; on the contrary it caused them to lose half a day from the moment they had caught up with the English alpinists, on the 28th of August at 2 pm until the morning of the 29th when they at last left their final bivouac.*

Same ascent, two stories!

Devies replied to Bonington 15 weeks later, apologizing for replying in French:

…as I did not have around me anyone able to translate your letter in such an English to return the courtesy of the impeccable French of your letter…"

…As far as I am concerned, I see only one possibility to explain the misunderstanding. The Frêney Pillar was a Babel tower. Apart from Mr. Djuglosz, the climbers spoke only their mother tongue. The distance was great – 40m – between your party and the party of your friends from the Desmaison-Piussi team.

It is with a certain conception of Alpinism that Mr. Desmaison relinquished - and had his friends do the same - the attempt to 'make a race' on the Pillar and he believes that lending their equipment sealed an agreement of solidarity concluded with you through Mr. Djuglosz.

I believe without any doubt that if the French-Italian team did not have this type of spirit, they would have attacked the different route than yours as they had envisaged in the first instance.

I believe that those elements will make you reconsider the light in which you see the end of the ascent of the Frêney Central Pillar and I would hope that its ascent will not end with a confirmation of this misunderstanding, but with its dissipation and the reassessment of an International friendship spirit to which we are here very much attached to.

His final sentence in effect validated René's fiction:

It is in this hope that I am putting off publication of your report and that of the French-Italian team in the belief that their publication would serve no purpose and should not occur…

Bonington's final letter to Devies was in English:

…Like you I share a desire to see this affair ended. To me friendly relations between French and English climbers, and particularly between Desmaison, Pollet-

Villard, Julien and us, are by far the most important factor.

Repeating his claim for the last time, he concluded:

But in the interests of truth and our own honour I must repeat to you that Ian Clough definitely did not receive any pitons or karabiners from the French party. I shall not attempt to analyze Desmaison's motives and his statements. As I see it we have now reached a stalemate and the incident is best forgotten.

Devies had chosen to back his ENSA instructors (the French climbers) though in the past he had shown much fair play to the British and had close links with people like John Hunt and Douglas Busk. In 1951 he had made an agreement with Busk, representing the AC/RGS Everest committee:

During friendly conversations, it was agreed that due to their previous efforts, it was normal that the British should be first to organize an assault expedition on Everest. But the English agreed that if they did not succeed, it would be legitimate for the French to then take their chance. This is how the British obtained from Nepal the authorisation for 1953 and us for 1954, Switzerland getting it for 1952.

Devies had also agreed to let the British go to Kangchenjunga in 1955, changing his target to Makalu. How could a man of such integrity believe

180. Don Whillans (left) and Chris Bonington at sunset before an icy bivouac below the Chandelle. *(Chris Bonington Picture Library)*

Desmaison's fiction? Even to a layman, it seems extravagant, or at least very bizarre. After the French refusal to help when needed, after Don's fall resulted in a very risky lead from Chris, and after having overcome all the difficulties, why would Chris and Don accept unneeded help? The details of René's account do not fit. René stated that they were one hour behind, but photos show that this was more like five hours. Bonington, in the 1962 *Alpine Journal*, records that Clough and Djuglosz 'reached the top two hours later [than himself and Whillans], and the French were a good two hours behind them'.

181. Success is a summit sandwich: Bonington (left) and Whillans on the top of Mont Blanc after making the first ascent of the Central Pillar of Frêney. *(Chris Bonington Picture Library)*

In a letter to his friend Dominique Leprince-Rinquet, Devies wrote:

...I was in Chamonix between August and September and I know well, alas, the controversies around the drama, the attempts and the success and the split of opinions on the matter. As far as I am concerned, I have not ascertained a majority one way or another but exacerbations of rivalries which seemed to me contrary to the true spirit of Alpinism.

Yet he had published René's tale and the 'Four' had signed their story. Therefore, it was a matter of *parole contre parole* as he wrote to Pierre Mazeaud (13 January 1962):

....Objectivity is not going in one direction only. Compatriots have the same rights as foreigners. The word of some of them does not take precedence over the word of the others. And a misunderstanding is the most probable hypothesis...

and to René, two days after his last letter to Chris:

Do not worry about the past. The future of Jannu is facing you. It alone deserves your attention...

British readers may feel less bitter knowing that not everyone in France agreed with Devies. Pierre Mazeaud wrote to Devies stating that he would soon be forced to admit that:

The French-Italian first ascent was no more than an English Polish first ascent...

And later:

... I do not speak of the contradictions between Bonington's text published in the Observer of 17 September, to which I give full credit...

With Philippe Gaussot, Devies was very blunt: in a letter of just three lines he wrote that *La Montagne et Alpinisme* would never be the place for any such controversy. At the time *La Montagne* was effectively the official mouthpiece of alpinism in France, with no specialist rivals – and it was fully controlled by Lucien Devies. All newspapers' directors and owners knew of Devies's power – his industrial and political connections – and none would have dared to challenge him. Therefore as far as *Le Dauphiné Libéré* was concerned the 'Affair' was ended and Philippe Gaussot's articles forgotten.[1]

What remained was René's fiction published in *La Montagne et Alpinisme* and repeated throughout his books and importantly in the Vallot guide. For many years the only mountain guide-book in France, and copied by most non-French guide-books, the Vallot guide was also fully controlled by Devies. In it, the first ascent of the Central Pillar was attributed at par to both parties but with a 'plus' to René's party as Devies endorsed René's deliberately misleading statement of having completed the ascent in two days while the Anglo-Polish party took three days.

But, as the proverb reminds us, 'the truth will out'. Fifty years after the event, using the information I gave him and the *Dauphiné* archives, Antoine Chandellier has written an article in *Alpes Loisirs* (Oct-Dec 2011) giving the full credit for the first ascent of the Central Pillar of Frêney to Bonington, Whillans, Clough and Djuglosz.

Sources: *Dauphiné Libéré* archives – GHM *Lucien Devies* archives – *La Montagne et Alpinisme* October 1961 – Jean Franco *Makalu* p. 21 – Lionel Terray *Les Conquérants de l'inutile* p.326 – Antoine Chandellier *La Montagne en Direct* Guerin 2010 – Chris Bonington *Les Horizons Lointains* Nevicata 2011.

---

1 Philippe Gaussot was a journalist and author of noted integrity, which was sorely tested by Desmaison who repeatedly pressured him to change his initial story in *Dauphiné Libéré*. Although born in the north-east of France, in 1911, Gaussot loved the mountains and climbing. He participated in the Resistance in the Second World War and was a correspondent for national newspapers such as *Le Figaro, Le Parisien Libéré* and *France Soir.* However a few months after the war ended, he decided that he could not live in Paris any longer and chose Chamonix (also because of his pulmonary problems). He joined the regional newspaper, *Dauphiné Libéré*, in September 1945 and remained with it until his death in 1977.

ELISA VILLA, ALFREDO ÍÑIGUEZ & JESÚS LONGO

Unknown AC First in
Picos de Europa

Alfredo Íñiguez died on 30 March 2012 following a climbing accident.
His two co-authors wish to dedicate the article to his memory.

Exploration of the Picos de Europa in northern Spain is closely linked
to the name of John Ormsby, an early member of the Alpine Club,
who in 1872 in the company of a local guide, attempted to reach the Torre
del Llambrión, the second highest summit of the Picos. The pair missed
their objective but did get to the top of a nearby lower summit. Although
Ormsby gave an account of his trip in an article published shortly afterwards, 'The Mountains of Spain' (*AJ* 6, 57-74), the precise point reached
by both men remained unknown for more than a century. And probably
because Ormsby himself judged the adventure to be a failure, later historians never considered it a relevant moment in the history of climbing in
the Picos de Europa, nor tried to ascertain which summit he had climbed.

A recent analysis of the Ormsby's account has shown that his text
contains limited but quite distinct information, and fortunately enough
to allow an interpretation of the route that he followed in 1872. Several
hypotheses were evaluated, however after detailed fieldwork in the Picos,
only one survived.

Our conclusion is that Ormsby and his guide reached the summit of the
Tiro Tirso, the third highest peak in the Picos de Europa and unclimbed
up to that time. Moreover, as the ascent of the Tiro Tirso is much more
demanding than that of the Torre del Llambrión, for none of its walls
offers an easy route, Ormsby's 'failure' should really be considered a great
success, and one that sets him among the outstanding pioneers of early
climbing in the Picos de Europa.

Who was John Ormsby?

John Ormsby (1829-1895) was elected to the Alpine Club barely a year
after it came into existence. As an alpinist, his most famous achievement
was the first ascent of La Grivola in the Graian Alps, which he described
in the second volume of *Peaks, Passes and Glaciers*. A controversy followed
this climb, for some argued that he had reached the summit ridge but not
the highest point. In Ormsby's obituary (*AJ* 18, 33-36), his close friend Sir
Leslie Stephen, one of the earliest presidents of the Alpine Club, recalled
their joyful days of comradeship spent in the Alps, remarking on Orsmby's
great sense of humour and his enthusiasm for mountaineering. However it

82. View from the east of the amphitheatre encircling the Jou Tras Llambrión. As John Ormsby and his guide Eusebio went up the Jou Tras Llambrión walking towards the left, they reached the base of the north face of the Tiro Tirso (in the shade left of centre) instead of the Torre del Llambrión (in the centre). *(Elisa Villa)*

seems that the bitter debate over La Grivola deeply affected Ormsby; over time he lost interest in the glory of first ascents, preferring to wander the Alps in the company of peasants, listening with pleasure to their stories and legends.

Although nominally a barrister by profession, in practice Ormsby was a man of letters who gained prestige as an expert in Hispanics, and especially in the literature of Miguel de Cervantes. He learnt Spanish thoroughly, producing the best 19th century translation of the novel Don Quixote, and also translating from Spanish the anonymous medieval epic poem Cantar del Mío Cid.

His interest in Spain extended to its mountains, which he described briefly, but very accurately, in 'Mountains of Spain'. Although Ormsby visited the Pyrenees, the Sierra de Gredos, the Iberian Chain, and the Sierra Nevada, his most enthusiastic words were dedicated to the westwards prolongation of the Pyrenees, the Cantabrian Mountains. Within this chain, he spoke highly about the Picos de Europa, which he described as:

a compact mass of limestone rising in most places like a wall out of the valley below, and crowned by an array of peaks the like of which I have never seen out of the Dolomite country (…). The peaks rise so high and in such a lordly style above the valleys on either side, that it is difficult to believe they can be much under 10,000

183. The elegant *Western Arête* of the Tiro Tirso seen from the Torre del Llambrión. It was along the north face (left) of the Tiro Tirso that Ormsby and Eusebio looked painstakingly for a way to the summit of what they thought it was the Torre del Llambrión. *(Alfredo Íñiguez)*

184. Three routes from the Jou Tras Llambrión to the Tiro Tirso summit: **1.** *North Face Left Chimney*, **2.** *North Face Right Chimney*, **3.** *Western Arête*. *(Alfredo Íñiguez)*

feet; besides, without being actually snow-capped, they preserve a good deal of snow all through the summer; and then one is apt to fancy the valleys from which they spring much higher than they really are.

A trip to Picos de Europa

The beauty of the Picos de Europa captivated Ormsby to the extent of trying to climb one of their highest summits. His first attempt was 'on the fine bold crest which rises south-west of the town of Potes, in the Liébana'. In spite of the assertions of the Potes people, he soon found that this ridge (a part of the Eastern Massif) is lower than several other ridges further west in the Central Massif. However, from the distance, he found it impossible to establish which was the highest point: To the eye, looking at the Picos de Europa from any elevation, it would appear about as hopeless to go in search of the highest peak as it would to try to determine which is absolutely the tallest spine on the back of a hedgehog.

Back in the valley, Ormsby found out that several years earlier Spanish government engineers had discovered the highest point in the Picos de Europa to be the Torre de Llambrión, and that they had reached the summit, though not without difficulties. This information referred to an expedition under the leadership of Casiano de Prado, a Spanish engineer and geologist who, seeking to establish the topmost elevation of the Picos, had reached the Torre de Llambrión (2642m) in August 1856. The success of the Casiano de Prado team was only tarnished by the discovery that another peak, the Torre de Cerredo, hidden away inside the massif and so not visible from the valley, was slightly higher than the Torre de Llambrión. Apparently, this fact was unknown to Ormsby's informants, but it is worth remembering that the tiny difference in altitude between both peaks – only six metres – fed a controversy that lasted well into the 20th century.

Either way, for decades the Torre de Llambrión remained one of the main objectives in the Picos de Europa for any mountaineer, and Ormsby was no exception. Intent on climbing it, he left Potes and moved to the neighbouring Valdeón valley. There, in the village of Santa Marina, he met Eusebio Díez Escudero, who had been on the Casiano de Prado expedition, and took on his services as a guide.

Although Eusebio made every effort to take Ormsby to his objective, and Ormsby himself recognised that Eusebio was 'as active and plucky a rock-climber as anyone could desire for a guide', they did not succeed. After sometimes difficult climbing they found themselves on top of a ridge very close to the Torre del Llambrión and only a few metres lower, but, unfortunately, cut off from it 'by a mighty cleft some 1,500 feet deep'. The guide tried to console his client by saying that it came to very nearly the same thing, but Ormsby, in his *AJ* article, did not recognise his adventure in Picos de Europa as a successful climb. It seems obvious now that the memory of La Grivola, and the wish to demonstrate his honesty in his climbing achievements, determined this attitude.

Yet the peak Ormsby had bagged was nearly as high as the Torre del Llambrión, and, most important of all, in 1872, was still a virgin summit. Which peak was it? For more than a century nobody has tried to answer this question, although Ormsby's account contains one key piece of information: the existence of a deep gap between the unknown peak and the Llambrión ridge. And only one peak close to the Torre del Llambrión is separated from it by a deep cleft: the Tiro Tirso (2639m). If anyone ever thought that the Tiro Tirso was the outcome of Ormsby's ascent the idea was probably immediately rejected.

The present-day normal route to the Tiro Tirso, the *Western Arête*, which is thought by many to be the only relatively easy option, starts from the bottom of the cleft Ormsby mentions. Hence the *Western Arête* cannot have been Ormsby's route as his account clearly states that they only saw the cleft after reaching the summit.

Is there any other route to the Tiro Tirso summit that coincides with all the details contained in the brief description given by Ormsby? One of the authors of this article, Alfredo Íñiguez, undertook a thorough exploration of all the possible ways to the top of the Tiro Tirso, some of them little known by other mountaineers. He concluded that only one route, the so-called *North Face Left Chimney* fully matches Ormsby's account.

Based on the above, and on the account published in 1872 in the *Alpine Journal*, we feel confident that we can reconstruct the itinerary followed by Ormsby and his guide Eusebio.

Reconstruction of Ormsby's itinerary

The Picos de Europa are limestone mountains that featured enormous glaciers during the last Ice Age. Glacier abrasion, plus the subsequent intensive karstic processes, resulted in the intricate relief that Ormsby fully succeeded in describing: The interior of the massif is something in form like a very dilapidated honeycomb; a labyrinth of crater-like basins separated by walls bristling with aiguilles, all bearing the strongest possible family likeness one to the other.

Unfortunately, 16 years after the Casiano de Prado expedition, Eusebio's memory of the route to the Torre del Llambrión had weakened and he found the labyrinth far more troublesome than expected. Nevertheless, helped by sporadic views of the cairn left on top of the Torre del Llambrión in 1856, he managed quite well during the long approach to the peak. The main problems started when they were closer to the rock walls, their proximity causing Eusebio and Ormsby to lose all reference.

The Torre del Llambrión crowns a long semicircular row of peaks forming the amphitheatre of Jou Tras Llambrión (*jou*, pronounced hou, is a local term meaning 'depression' or 'hole'). In 1856 the Casiano de Prado team went up through this depression heading towards the right, where they had seen an easy way to the ridge. But this option, as they soon discovered, was not the best, and on their way along the crest they found a number of exposed moves. Because of this they looked for a safer descent route, finding one closer to the Llambrión summit – an inclined chimney connecting the ridge with the Jou Tras Llambrión. Seen from the bottom of the Jou, this route lies to the left of the ascent by the de Prado team.

Though by 1872 Eusebio had forgotten many details of the itinerary followed in 1856, he probably remembered well enough that the safer route was towards the left. Bearing this in mind, he approached the limestone walls too soon, coming up against not the Llambrión but the north face of

85. Alfredo Íñiguez descending the *Western Arête*. To the right of the ridge (looking down) is the *North Face Right Chimney* that Ormsby and Eusebio probably used in descent. *(Enrique González Barbón)*

the Tiro Tirso, where two obvious lines cut through the limestone wall: the *North Face Left Chimney* and the *North Face Right Chimney*. As the latter ends on the *Western Arête*, from where the true summit of Torre del Llambrión is visible, this route can be ruled out. Thus Eusebio and Ormsby can only have climbed the *North Face Left Chimney*.

The *North Face Left Chimney* consists of a relatively easy climb (Grade III-) up a chimney that ends slightly below the east ridge of the Tiro Tirso. In the uppermost part of the chimney the difficulties increase and to get the top of the ridge it is necessary to climb a Grade IV friction slab some 20m high. Their ascent of the slab is fine testimony to the courage of Ormsby and Eusebio. After the relatively safe (at least psychologically) chimney they were able to face, unroped[1], an exposed, vertical slab poised above an abyss. In addition, the slab must be tackled as a rising traverse, increasing in the climber the unpleasant sensation of being at risk of a fall to the very bottom of the Jou Tras Llambrión.

Once the friction slab has been overcome, the top of the Tiro Tirso appears some 60m further west. Beyond the summit, the Torre del Llambrión appears to be a prolongation of the main ridge; it is only when the Tiro Tirso summit is crowned that the huge gash between both peaks can be clearly seen.

1. The first use of a rope for climbing in the Picos de Europa is believed to have been in 1904 on Naranjo de Bulnes.

FRICTION SLAB

186. A more detailed line for Ormsby and Eusebio's route up the Left Chimney on the north face of Tiro as seen from the Jou Tras Llambrión. *(Alfredo Íñiguez)*

Each of these episodes can be traced through Ormsby's words:

Their progress through the chimney: *The rocks were often difficult and –without being actually dangerous to anyone furnished with head, heart, and hands – were in places decidedly ugly to look at.*

The Grade IV friction slab: *When the work grew serious, fairly struck, Eusebio declined to go farther, and owned to 'miedo' – the only time I have ever known a Spanish mountaineer to confess bodily fear. He, however, persevered...*

The moment when Eusebio gets to the ridge and sees the Torre del Llambrión peak: *... and at last he hailed me to come on; we were all right this time; he could see the cairn, and it was only a little way above us.*

The arrival at the Tiro Tirso peak: *A quarter of an hour's stiff climbing brought us to the top, and Eusebio sat down and groaned. We had gone up the wrong peak. Right opposite to us was the real Simon Pure only 200 or 300 yards away, but cut off from us by a mighty cleft some 1,500 feet deep.*

John Ormsby did not provide any detail about the way down, but as the easier *North Face Right Chimney* can be seen from the summit we guess that they took this route and so avoided the risky descent of the Grade IV friction slab.

Vindication of the first ascent of the Tiro Tirso by John Ormsby

The Tirso Tirso was not climbed again until 1906, when the German geologist and alpinist Gustav Schulze approached the peak from the south and mistook it for the Torre del Llambrión (again!). Schulze put up a new route along the very imposing southern wall of the Tiro Tirso and descended via the *Western Arête*. Until now, this climb has been considered the first ascent. However, our analysis of the text written by Ormsby, coupled with climbs 'on-site', enables us to state that although Schulze's

187. The 'friction slab', crux
of the 1872 ascent.
(Alfredo Íñiguez)

routes were both firsts,
the first ascent of the Tiro
Tirso must be assigned to
John Ormsby and Eusebio
Díez Escudero in 1872.

The Tiro Tirso was
therefore the fourth
summit of the Picos de
Europa to be climbed (or,
at least, the fourth that is
documented), following
the Torre de Salinas
(1853), the Torre del
Llambrión (1856) and the
Pico Cortés (1861). For the time, it was a difficult piece of pioneer climbing
and an achievement that warrants a place of honour in the history of the
exploration of the Picos de Europa for John Ormsby and Eusebio.

Acknowledgements: Many thanks are due to Robin Walker for his revision of the manuscript and to José Luis Moreno for opening his marvellous library up to us.

Bibliography
Íñiguez, A. (2010). Una primera ignorada: la ascensión de 1872 al Tiro Tirso, *Revista Ilustrada de Alpinismo Peñalara* 534, 209-213, Madrid.
Ormsby, J. (1872). The Mountains of Spain. *AJ* 6, 57-74.
Ormsby, J. (1862). The ascent of the Grivola, *Peaks, Passes and Glaciers* 2, 318-338, Longman, Green, Longman and Roberts, London.
Prado, C. de (1860). Valdeón, Caín, la Canal de Trea: ascensión a los Picos de Europa en la Cordillera Cantábrica, *Revista Minera* XI (234-235), 62-72, 92-101, Madrid.
Stephen, L. (1895). In Memoriam: John Ormsby. *AJ* 18, 33-36.
Villa, E. & Longo, J. (2010). Viajeros en los Picos de Europa (III). Pioneros británicos: John Ormsby, Mars Ross, H. Stonehewer-Cooper y William T. Elmslie, *Revista Ilustrada de Alpinismo Peñalara* 534, 204-208, Madrid.
Walker, R. (1989). *Walks and Climbs in the Picos de Europa* (Cicerone Press) p215.

C A RUSSELL

One Hundred Years Ago

Excellent snow conditions in the principal Alpine regions during the early months of 1912 were welcomed by ski mountaineers, including Arnold Lunn whose party completed ski ascents of the Lauterbrunnen Breithorn and other peaks in the Bernese Alps. In March Marcel Kurz joined forces with the Zürich doctor Willy Odermatt to make the first ski ascent of the Rimpfischhorn. Later in the year, in December, four guides from Zinal reached the summit of the Bishorn with the aid of ski.

The climbing season in the Alps was marred by some of the worst weather on record. In August an expedition of note was the first ascent of L'Isolée, the fourth highest point of Les Dames Anglaises, the group of rock pinnacles on the Peuterey ridge of Mont Blanc by the guided party of H O Jones and Geoffrey Winthrop Young. This success was however overshadowed by tragedy: only four days later Jones, his wife and their guide fell to their deaths while ascending Mont Rouge de Peuterey. In October Young lost another friend when Hugh Pope was killed while climbing alone on the Pic du Midi d'Ossau in the Pyrenees.

Following the completion of the Jungfrau railway the station at the Jungfraujoch was opened to the public in August and later that month celebrations were held at Saas Fee to mark the inauguration of the Britannia hut.

Many successful expeditions were completed in other mountain ranges. In Arctic Norway in July Carl Rubenson and Ferdinand Schjelderup of Stedtind fame and Harald Jentoft made the first ascent of Store Strandåtind (862m), a notable peak on the Kjerringøy peninsular. In the Caucasus Max Winkler's Bavarian team climbed the west, higher summit (5198m) of Dych Tau, traversed Gestola (4860m) and followed the crest of the Bezingi Wall to Lyalver (4350m) before completing other climbs, including the first ascent of Kentchat Bashi (4171m).

After leaving Srinagar early in June, Dr and Mrs Workman's party, including the surveyor Grant Peterkin and an assistant from the Survey of India, triangulated the whole of the Siachen glacier and fixed the heights of prominent neighbouring peaks. During two months of fine weather the party reached a number of points at the head of the glacier, including Indira Col (5776m).

In Garhwal C F Meade and his guides continued their exploration of the approaches to Kamet (7756m), reaching a height of some 7000m before being forced to retreat. In Kashmir Dr Ernest Neve and Kenneth Mason made the first ascent of the highest peak (5425m) in the Kolahoi group. To the east Dr Alexander Kellas undertook his fourth visit to Sikkim where

88. Kanchenjau (6919m), Sikkim. Alexander Kellas initially approached the peak from this south side in 1911, but eventually reached the summit plateau from the north in August 1912. *(Roger Payne)*

in August, accompanied by local men, he reached the summit plateau of Kangchenjau (6919m).

In July during an expedition to the Kilimanjaro massif Fritz Klute and Eduard Oehler made the first ascent of the highest point (5149m) of Mawenzi, which they named Hans Meyer Peak after the geographer Hans Meyer who with Ludwig Purtscheller had made the first recorded ascent of Kibo (5895m). In the Southern Alps of New Zealand in March the Australian climber Freda Du Faur and her guides became the first party to reach the summit of Mount Dampier (3443m). In Canada in June Howard Palmer and his companions made the first ascent of Mount Sir Sandford (3530m), the highest peak in the Selkirk range.

At home in the Lake District, Siegfried Herford and George Sansom produced a series of outstanding climbs on Scafell including, on the Pinnacle Face, *Direct from Lord's Rake to Hopkinson's Cairn*, and the first complete ascent of *Hopkinson's Gully*. Later in the year, with Walter Brunskill and H B Gibson they completed the *Girdle Traverse of Scafell*.

All in all, a year of considerable achievement in the mountaineering world.

Area Notes

189. John Fairley, *Climbers on the east ridge of Lyskamm,* oil on canvas, 255x610mm, 2008

Area Notes

COMPILED AND EDITED BY PAUL KNOTT

The Alps 2011	*Lindsay Griffin*
Scottish Winter 2010-2011	*Simon Richardson*
Afghanistan 2011	*Lindsay Griffin*
Pakistan 2011	*Dick Isherwood*
India 2010	*Harish Kapadia*
Nepal 2011	*Dick Isherwood*
China and Tibet 2011	*John Town*
Bolivia 2009-2011	*Erik Monasterio*
Argentine Andes 2010-2011	*Marcelo Scanu*
New Zealand 2010-2011	*Kester Brown*

LINDSAY GRIFFIN

The Alps 2011

190. Frêney face of Mont Blanc, showing the line of *Chronique de la haine
      ordinaire. (Luca Signorelli)*

The Alps remain the experimental laboratory for European climbers, a place to develop their skills and try out progressive ideas before using experience gained to tackle increasingly difficult climbs in the Greater Ranges. Autumn and winter are now the preferred time for the great ice and mixed faces, the 2011 autumn especially producing excellent conditions. Although this resumé deals with the innovative climbing that took place throughout the year, many other mountaineers were ticking notable repeats. The relative number of alpinists may be diminishing, but there still appears to be plenty operating at a very high level.

On **Mont Blanc** itself, two well-known lines, believed to be previously unattempted, were finally climbed. Italian Hervé Barmasse and the Spanish-Basque brothers Eneko and Iker Pou added a second route to the remote and very rarely climbed Left-hand Pillar of Brouillard. The smallest of the four pillars on the Brouillard Face was first climbed in 1971 by Poles, Ryszard Kowalewski, Janusz Maczka and Wojciech Wroz, who followed the left flank of the pillar on rock that is in parts quite friable (VI). They continued with 300m of mixed terrain up the broad rocky spur, common with the upper section of the Red Pillar, to the Brouillard Ridge, and from there to the summit. However, the obvious and most elegant line – straight up the crest – remained unclimbed. Barmasse and the Pou brothers completed 11 pitches up to F6c, more or less directly up the crest. They continued onwards to the vicinity of Mont Blanc de Courmayeur, where they bivouacked. The route was named *La Classica Moderna* (1000m to the summit; 350m of new climbing on the pillar), as their style of ascent resembled that used by Walter Bonatti on his historic climb of the neighbouring Red Pillar in 1959. As Barmasse points out, in those days the pioneers had to reach the summit of Mont Blanc in order to get home. This was the second climb in Barmasse's trilogy entitled 'Exploring the Alps', of which more below.

Aymeric Clouet, Pierre Labbre and Jérôme Para completed a winter *Peuterey Super-integral*, only the third known of its type. The first winter super-integral took place in 1982 and sealed a place in history for Renato Casarotto. Over 15 days the legendary Italian, completely alone, climbed the *Ratti-Vitali* on the west face of the Aiguille Noire, the *Boccalatte-Gervasutti* route on the south-west face of the Gugliermina, and finished up the Central Pillar of Frêney. This idea was repeated in winter 2003 by three French, who for their final route on the Frêney face substituted *Fréneysie Pascale*, the steep and discontinuous couloir between the Right Hand and Central Pillar. Clouet, Labbre and Para also opted for a different route on the Frêney face; the very steep corner system between the Hidden and Central pillars. In the past this corner was equipped with anchors for a rappel descent – albeit objectively-threatened – from above the difficulties on the Central Pillar of Frêney. However, it overhangs in parts and appears to have deterred any serious winter attempts until now. The climbing, in generally wide cracks or chimneys choked with old ice, was sustained, hard and mixed. The route has been named *Chronique de la haine ordinaire*.

Nicolas Potard made an important free ascent on the east face of the **Grand Capucin,** when he linked the 1968 *Lecco Route* with the 1991 Romain Vogler route *De fil en Aiguille* to produce *Le Tresor de Romain*. The link required two new pitches (F6a and F7a+) and the climb offers one pitch of F8a and another at F8a+. Potard, with Paul Dudas, added *Ciao Vinc* to **La Vierge** – the 'mini Grand Capucin' above the right bank of the

191. Aiguille Verte from the north, showing the ephemeral line of Les Cascades de Col du Nant Blanc *(Lindsay Griffin)*

Milieu glacier on the Aiguille d'Argentière. The 200m route is 7b+, 6c obl, with a wonderful 7b crack on pitch four. Both Potard's lines rely heavily on trad gear. The previously unclimbed south face of rarely visited **Pointe Sud de Fréboudze** was the goal of Philippe Batoux, Pierre d'Alboy and Lionel Daudet. Over four days in winter they put up *N'oublie pas la Saint Valentin* (500m, A2+, 6b and M4).

A strange climb, with serious death potential, was dubbed *Paranormal Activiti* by Spanish alpinist Pau Escalé. With various partners he made attempts to climb the huge sérac to the right of the initial spur on the classic 1929 route up the north face of the **Plan**, leading to the hanging glacier. The four rock pitches below the sérac wall itself were A2+ and A3; the sérac gave sections of WI6. However, on his final attempt, darkness caught him 50-60m below the top of the sérac, and he bailed. Incomplete lines, which reach no logical conclusion, are increasingly being given a name; climbers seemingly unable to admit 'defeat'. This one is no exception. It seems most unlikely there will be queues at the base to finish it off.

On **Les Droites**, Patrick Pessi, Sébastien Ratel and Remy Sfilio made a winter ascent of a line up the middle of the Bergland Pillar (climbed in 1969 up the left flank by Lackner and Messner), naming their 1000m route *Ecaille Epique* (ED M6, 90° and A1). However, for much of the way

192. North-west face (c.1000m) of the Mönch. **1.** *Haston-Eistrup Couloir* (1976),
2. *Dare* (solo 2011). *(Ben Dare)*

it appears to coincide with a little-known ascent in 1991 by Chris Dale
and Jim Kerr, who climbed in summer, and naturally in a different style,
to produce an ED2 route with difficulties of 6b. There will be differences
between the French and British lines, certainly in the lower half, though
there appears to be far less room for variation above the conspicuous tower
at mid-height. But the concept of climbing the spur direct is two decades
old.

Although not in 2011, mention must be made of two routes climbed from the Nant Blanc glacier by AC member Andy Parkin. Starting at the base of the classic Charlet-Platonov *Nant Blanc Face Direct* on the **Aiguille Verte**, Parkin, climbing solo, followed a series of icefalls and goulottes up the face to the left, exiting on the upper Grand Montets Ridge at the Col du Nant Blanc (just above the Pointe de Ségogne, the last rock on the arête before the summit). The 650m route – *Les Cascades de Col du Nant Blanc* (V/4) – lies wholly to the right of the Gugliermina and involves ice to 85°. Parkin had watched and waited 10 years for this route to come into condition, and his ascent took place during a spell of unusually hard freeze in early June 2009. He descended the same route, as glaciers on the far side of the mountain were quite open at the time, and the Nant Blanc has relatively few crevasses.

Prior to this he had soloed another new route well to the left on the **Petit Aiguille Verte**. The 350m line was discovered 'by accident', lies to the right of *Imassacre Directe*, and slants left to reach the north-west ridge not far below the summit. Graded WI4+, with rock at IV/V to finish, the route offers delicate ice climbing to 90°. Both these routes receive, and need, a reasonable amount of sun: normally it would be too cold in winter for ice to form.

The Grandes Jorasses was the first venue for an exceptional winter trilogy. Between 14 January and 12 March Patrice Glairon-Rappaz and Cedric Périllat Merceroz climbed the three great north faces of the Alps – **Grandes Jorasses, Eiger and Matterhorn** – by three difficult direct routes. This project, linking three of the hardest, and rarely climbed, *direttissima*, had not previously been done in one winter: 14-18 January, Grandes Jorasses via *Rolling Stones* (five bivouacs); 20 January - 5 February, Eiger via *Harlin Direttissima with 1938 Heckmair exit* (six bivouacs); 8-12 March, Matterhorn via *Cerutti-Gogna* (four bivouacs).

In the Ecrins massif there was an impressive series of multiple ascents by Yann Borgnet and Robin Revest, who linked three great north faces above the Glacier Noir, the theme being to celebrate the achievements of one of the massif's most famous partnerships; Jean-Michel Cambon and Bernard Francou. On day one they climbed the 1976 *Cambon-Francou Direct* on **Mont Pelvoux**. This sombre 1000m wall is TD+, F6a and mixed, and had possibly no more than two ascents before 2011. From the summit they descended the *Coolidge Couloir* (PD), climbed back up the Sialouze glacier to the *Col Est du Pelvoux*, and then down-climbed and rappelled the *North Couloir* (700m: D) to regain their bivouac site on the glacier at 10pm. Next day it was the 1975 *Cambon-Francou Directe de Droite* on the **Pic Sans Nom** (1000m: ED1: F6b, A1 and mixed), which climbs the great slabs to the right of the famous Jean-Marc Boivin ice route, *Raie des Fesses*. From the summit they climbed down the *North West Couloir* (AD) to the Coup de Sabre glacier, they again reached their bivouac site late; this time at 10.30pm. On the third and final day they climbed the easiest of their three chosen north faces, the 1981 *Cambon-Francou Direct*, aka *Pilier des Séracs*, on **Ailefroide Centrale** (900m: TD+: 5+, 60° and mixed). On the hanging glacier, they abandoned the original line, which climbs direct to the subsidiary summit of Pointe Forastier, and instead slanted right to finish up the *Costa Rouge Arête* (D) to the central summit. Descending the *South Face* (PD), they were in the Ailefroide campsite at 10pm.

Still in the Ecrins, over two days in May Hélias Millerioux and Romain Hocquemiller climbed a new line on the upper WNW face of the **Pic Sans Nom**. Millerioux had spotted this during two failed attempts to make a winter ascent of *L'éloge de la Fuite*, further right on the face. The 350m upper wall has a tricky mixed approach, above which the pair climbed four pitches to bivouac on the Chapoutot Ledge. Next day they climbed a further four difficult pitches to the north-west ridge, then followed the crest over more mixed terrain to the summit. *T'y as mis un bon piton* is ED1 F7a, F6c obl.

On the great north-west face of the **Olan**, one of the most serious rock walls in the Ecrins, Mathieu Detrie and Pierre Labbre put up *Chauve qui peut* (1100m, F7b or F6c+ and A1), which on the upper wall climbs direct up the face between the 1981 *Directe de Gauche* and the 1956 *Couzy-Desmaison*, to where the two more or less intersect on the middle terraces. After a short stretch on the latter, it climbs right of the *Directe* before joining it towards the top.

In the Valais Alps the **Matterhorn** came under the spotlight with a number of notable ascents on both north and south faces. Local guide and all-round Matterhorn guru Hervé Barmasse climbed the south pillar of Picco Muzio. There are other established routes on this pillar but they are not direct: Barmasse rectified this by first climbing 400m up the objectively dangerous snow gully, and then a further 700m of characteristically chossy Matterhorn rock (with difficulties up to 6c), solo. He made three bivouacs on the face. This line was the first in a trilogy named 'Exploring the Alps', in which Barmasse climbed new routes on three of the most famous (and thought to be very well-explored) mountains in the Alps.

On the north side, conditions during the autumn proved excellent, allowing several parties to complete the rarely climbed *Bonatti Direct* in one day. Olov Isaksson and Nikolay Primerov took bivouac gear and a large rack, crossed the rimaye at 5am and summited at 7pm, free climbing throughout up to M6. However, locals Patrick Aufdenblatten and Michael Lerjen travelled light, moved together above the Traverse of the Angels, and reached the summit in a remarkable 7hrs14mins. The previous fastest time on this route had been 25 hours, by racehorse Ueli Steck, solo. Given Steck's credentials, many felt an improvement on his time would be almost impossible for roped parties.

In 2008 Martial Dumas, Jean-Yves Fredricksen and Jean Troillet climbed an independent line up the centre of the north face for 400-500m to meet the classic *Schmidt Route*, which they followed to the level of the Shoulder on the Hörnli Ridge, before traversing left to gain this crest. Troillet had previously attempted this line with Sébastien Gay, who shortly after was killed in a ski-flying incident. Troillet dedicated the line to his friend and

193. The top half of the north-west face of the Piz Badile, showing the approximate line of *Sogni d'alta Quota*. *Ringo Starr* takes a parallel line to the left, finishing up the prominent left-facing dièdre. *(Lindsay Griffin coll.)*

Sébastien Gay was graded ED2/3, F5, A2 and 85° ice. In autumn 2011 Roger Schaeli and Robert Jasper made the second overall and first free ascent at M8, again finishing out left to the Hörnli Ridge (which at that height on the face is probably more difficult than continuing direct to the summit).

Barmasse's third new route in the trilogy took place on **Monte Rosa**, where with his father Marco, also a highly accomplished alpinist and guide, he climbed the wall left of the 1987 Italian route *Africa Nostra* on the remote and rarely visited south-east face of Signalkuppe (aka Punta Gnifetti). The pair took the logical approach of descending onto the glacier plateau below the face from high on the standard Italian route up the SSW flank. The 800m new route hits the south-west ridge just 15m below the summit (and Margherita hut), has pitches of 'UIAA VI', and was graded ED. With the completion of the trilogy Barmasse had achieved what he set out to prove; we should never take for granted that everything in the Alps has been climbed.

Moving east to the Bregaglia-Disgrazia, there were two new routes of note. The **Piz Badile** gained, arguably, its first really major new route in almost a decade, with the completion of *Sogni d'alta Quota* on the austere 650m north-west face. This new line breaches the obvious and previously unclimbed expanse of rock between the 1985 Italian route, *Ringo Starr*, and the classic but serious 1937 *Bramani Route*. It was completed over two days by Antonio Gomba, Andrea Marzorati and Corrado Trezzi, who climbed 18 pitches of primarily bolt-protected ground at F6b+, F6a obl. **Monte Disgrazia** gave up one of its secrets when, after a lengthy approach, Michele Comi, Stefano Mogavero, and guidebook authors Luca Maspes and Giuseppe Miotti made the first ascent of the south spur of the 3468m East Summit. This route was a prelude to the 2012 celebrations held to commemorate the 150th anniversary of the first ascent of this fine peak. The route was named *Via del 149* and is 600m high with difficulties of UIAA VII- on generally good to excellent rock.

On the huge granite wall of the **Qualido**, Swiss-based James Pearson made the first continuous free ascent of *Joy Division* (800m, 22 pitches, F8b). *Joy Division*, a combination of the three lines *Forse si, forse no* (1996), *Mellodrama* (1989) and *Melat* (1993) was climbed by local star Simone Pederferri over three days in 2004. After several attempts using a portaledge, Pearson, belayed by Nico Nastorg, completed the route with one bivouac on the good ledge above pitch 15. Pitch one (F8b) proved to be the crux, even though reports suggested the fourth pitch (also F8b) would be harder. Pearson also found the seventh pitch (F7b+) very demanding, a sustained, technical affair coming after six hard pitches.

On a different slant, American John Harlin completed the second *circumnavigation of the Swiss border*, a journey of around 2000km with a total height gain of 170,000m. Harlin started the project in 2010 but was stopped early in the trip by an accident. He came back in the autumn of that year to paddle and mountain bike the northern frontier, and in the summer of 2011 returned to the Liechtenstein border to continue east, south and then west, passing through the Rätikon, Bernina, Bregaglia and Valais before finishing over Mont Dolent. While he certainly didn't keep religiously to the frontier, for instance his crossing of the Bregaglia was made via the Roma Path to the south, this was certainly a weather-dependent feat of endurance.

There is little to report from the Bernese Oberland. In the on-going fascination with speed ascents, on 20 April, 27-year-old Dani Arnold surprised the world of alpinism by breaking Ueli Steck's record time for an ascent of the north face of the **Eiger**. Arnold arrived on the summit at around 11:30 in the morning, having taken just 2hrs 28mins, almost 20 minutes faster than Steck's record ascent in February 2008. This is particularly remarkable given that when Steck achieved this time he had climbed the route many times previously, including several solo ascents: Arnold appears to have climbed it only once before, roped. Speed ascents prove great technical competence and represent huge personal achievement, though their general contribution to the wider world of alpinism remains unclear. However, they are inspirational in showing what can be achieved in the mountains with a highly trained body.

Another notable solo came from Ben Dare, who climbed a partial new line on the c1000m north-west face of the **Mönch.** From low on the *Nollen Route*, he slanted left to reach the 1976 *Haston-Eistrup Couloir* well above its base. Following this through the crux narrows, he branched left into a prominent gully, cutting through the rocky face on the left. This led to the upper section of the south-west ridge, just below the summit. The grade was around TD. The gully was 60-75° with a few short vertical sections, and was followed by moderate mixed ground to the ridge.

A hard new mixed route was climbed in the Orobie Alps, where Tito Arosio, Yuri Parimbelli and Ennio Spiranelli made a one-day, winter first ascent of *Piantobaldo* (600m, WI4, M7, A1) on the north-west face of the **Presolana.** The route starts up the first two rope lengths of *Orobic Ice*, then continues for 11 independent pitches to the summit ridge of Presolana West.

In the Dolomites one of the most notable winter ascents came from Fabio Valsechini, who completed the first winter solo of *Via dei Cinque di Valmadrera* (1,350m: VI+ and A3) on the north-west face of the **Civetta.** First climbed in the winter of 1972 by the Rusconi brothers, this demanding route had seen only four previous ascents, including a summer solo in 2004. Valsechini made seven bivouacs on this huge, complex wall, and an eighth during the descent. An important first winter ascent came from Simon Gietl and Roger Schaeli, who climbed *Pressknodel* (400m, 7c) on the north face of **Cima Ovest di Lavaredo.** The route climbs the right side of the face, is committing, and has rather spaced protection. It was only first redpointed in 2010.

The Dolomites is an area where many fine new routes are still created adhering to good ethics. On the east face of **Piz Ciavazes** Simon Gietl and Simon Niederbacher put up *Das Privileg* (300m, nine pitches, F7b) using entirely natural gear (nuts, cams and pegs). Similarly, on the **Lastia de Gardas** above the San Lucano Valley, Pietro Dal Prà and Alessandro Rudatis climbed *In mezzo poco* (400m, F8a+) and *Gracias a la vida* (270m, F8a+), using largely trad protection. Only eight bolts were placed on *In mezzo* and there are one or two dangerous runouts. On both routes seconds need to have a lot of experience of dynamic belaying. On the south face of **Tofana di Rozes**, Tomaz Jakofcic and Luka Lindic spent four days establishing *Viki krema* (800m: F7a/F7b), and then freed it over two days. Again, the climb relies heavily on trad gear, with only 23 bolts *in situ.*

Belayed by his brother, the talented Austrian Hansjörg Auer returned to the **Marmolada** and on the **Ombretta** put up *Bruderliebe* (800m, 19 pitches, F8b/F8b+). Auer is a regular on the Marmolada and came to global prominence with his free solo of the *Fish.* His new route climbs the wall right of Igor Koller's *40 anni per il Falier* and was established ground up in eight days. The main difficulties are in the compact lower half; pitches above are no more than F6b. While using a mixture of trad gear and bolts, the climbing is generally quite run out.

SIMON RICHARDSON

Scottish Winter 2010-11

The 2011 season was a long one, starting early and continuing consistently cold from mid October to late March. There some were superb settled periods during December and January, and the large number of winter climbers operating at the highest level meant that the 2011 winter was one of the best in recent decades. It is difficult to single out specific performances, but Greg Boswell's magnificent run of routes including the first ascent of *To Those Who Wait* (IX,9), stands out. Guy Robertson also had a scintillating season with no less than five new IXs – his finest ascent was undoubtedly *Stone Temple Pilots* (X,9) on The Shelter Stone, climbed with Pete Macpherson. There were also some remarkable repeats, such as Andy Turner's forceful ascent of *The Hurting* and the second ascent of the legendary *Extasy* on Creag Meagaidh, together with the development of new crags such as Eilde Canyon in Glen Coe and Creagan Coire Cha-no on Cairngorm.

To Those Who Wait (IX,9)
Ever since the first modern mixed climbs were added to Ben Nevis 15 years ago, the impending crack-line on the right wall of Number Three Gully has been stared at in awe by hundreds of winter climbers. It had seen at least one serious attempt, but most had been deterred by its unremitting steepness. Enter 19-year old Greg Boswell and 20-year old Will Sim. Boswell is a relative newcomer to the Scottish winter scene and made headlines last season with second ascents of *Ship of Fools* (VIII,7) and *Pic'n Mix* (IX,9). Alongside these achievements, Boswell has amassed a career's worth of classic VIIs and VIIIs, many climbed on consecutive days. Will Sim's pedigree is more mountaineering-based with a string of major alpine routes climbed in fast times such as the second ascent of the *East Face Route* on Cerro Piergiogio in Patagonia.

On 31 December, the pair headed up *Number Three Gully* to take a look at the crack-line. It was a typically dreich Scottish winter day – the crags were black and dripping wet after the post-Christmas thaw and conditions looked hopeless. The forecast predicted a slow cooling through the day and they had chosen their venue wisely because not only is the *Number Three Gully* area one of the highest venues in the country but when winds start funnelling up from Coire na Ciste it hoars up remarkably quickly. After two hours of patient waiting the cliff was transformed with a thin layer of white frost. Sim led the awkward entry pitch and then Boswell set off up the meat of the route – the impending crack-line. Boswell's account of his lead on his blog, tussling with a delicately poised television-sized block, is palm-wetting reading, but eventually he pulled on to the plateau after

94. Iain Small pulling into the bulging crack-line on the third pitch of *Brave New World* (IX,8) on Ben Nevis during the first ascent. This four-pitch route lies between Kellett's *North Wall Route* and *The Past is Close Behind* on the North Wall of Carn Dearg. *(Simon Richardson)*

a remarkable on-sight lead. *To Those Who Wait* was graded IX,9 and was particularly noteworthy because it was climbed by such a young team.

Stone Temple Pilots (X,9)

Guy Robertson and Pete Macpherson pulled off a major coup on 28 January when they climbed a new direct line up the front edge of the Shelter Stone in the Cairngorms. Their new route, called *Stone Temple Pilots* (named after a 90s rock band), links the first three pitches of *Steeple* with the crux pitch of *Haystack*, followed by a new pitch into *Citadel* and a finish up *Spire*. The pair left the car at 2.30am and started up the lower *Steeple* corners at 5.20am, climbing the first big pitch in the dark and the next two as dawn broke. They continued up the crux of *Haystack* and then reached an impasse.

'We didn't have a guidebook and couldn't remember where *Haystack* went, and with the clock ticking it all began to get rather exciting!' Robertson explained. 'With no choice but to forge on, Pete opened a new hard pitch straight up then slightly left, eventually joining *Citadel* where this goes right to below the headwall. Then it was my big lead. Despite cramping biceps and only a couple of hours light left, I managed to drag myself up the penultimate pitch of *Spire* before Pete dispatched the last 5b crack – just in time for the darkness to envelop us.'

The pair graded *Stone Temple Pilots* X,9, making it the most difficult Scottish new winter route ever climbed ground up, although later Robertson commented: 'Whatever the grade, it's kind of irrelevant. The Stone has some of the most inspiring and challenging winter climbing this great country has to offer. For a well-balanced and keen team there's probably nothing anywhere else to compare!'

Ben Nevis

The first major new route of the season was *Apache* (VIII,9), climbed on 13 November by Steve Ashworth and Paddy Cave. The pair were part of a four-man Lakes-based team who spent three days staying at the CIC Hut and Ashworth had his sights firmly set on the impressive barrel shaped headwall to the right of *Sioux Wall* on Number Three Gully Buttress. Ashworth led the first pitch up the steep arête to the left of *Thompson's Route* and then handed the lead over to Cave for the crucial second pitch up the gently overhanging barrel-shaped wall. 'Paddy had to climb a steep blank section for a few metres to reach a crack,' Ashworth explained. 'Fortunately, the crack had good hooks, and it turned out to be one of those brilliant pitches that looks harder than it actually is!'

The following weekend, the spotlight fell once again on Ben Nevis when Pete Davies and Tim Marsh made the first ascent of *Catriona* (VIII,8) on Creag Coire na Ciste. This spectacular and unlikely-looking line follows the left arête of the corner taken by the modern test-piece *Cornucopia*. Later in the season, Iain Small and Simon Richardson made the first ascent of *Brave New World* (IX,8) on the North Wall of Carn Dearg. The highlight of this sustained four-pitch route was the final headwall, which overhangs at the top with no obvious line of cracks, and Small's on sight lead was the epitome of adventurous Scottish winter climbing.

Southern Cairngorms

Towards the end of the late December freeze, there was a remarkable addition to Creag an Dubh Loch when Gordon Lennox, Tony Stone and Iain Small made the first winter ascent of *Culloden* on the awe-inspiring Broad Terrace Wall. This summer E2, which overhangs for much of its 125m length, had been a winter objective for Lennox for a number of years. Small led the 5a summer entry pitch, before Lennox battled with the 5c summer crux. Finally, Stone led the steep finishing cracks to a delicate and serious finish, just reaching the plateau rim as darkness fell. The trio graded their on sight ascent IX,9, and many other steep summer crack-lines across the country must now be considered potential winter targets.

195. Guy Robertson climbing steep technical 8 mixed ground after pulling through the crux roof on the first winter ascent of *Crazy Sorrow* (IX,10) on the Tough-Brown Face on Lochnagar. *(Pete Benson)*

The big event on Lochnagar was the first winter ascent of *Crazy Sorrow* (IX,10) on the Tough-Brown Face of Lochnagar by Guy Robertson and Pete Benson. This rarely climbed summer route is graded E4 6a and the crux second pitch involves pulling over a big roof. It was first climbed in winter, after summer pre-inspection, by Alan Mullin and Steve Lynch in 2002. Unfortunately Mullin decided to abseil off without climbing the third pitch which leads to easier ground on the Tough-Brown Ridge, so as a result, *Frozen Sorrow* as Mullin called his 'route', was considered to be unfinished and therefore classified as an attempt.

When Benson started up the first pitch the weather was wild, but as he belayed under the crux roof of the second pitch the wind relented and the skies cleared. 'I had to give it everything to get over the roof,' Robertson said afterwards. 'But the protection was good so I decided there was nothing to lose by giving it a go.' The decision to classify Mullin's route as an attempt in the SMC Cairngorms guide was correct, as Benson then had to lead another demanding technical 8 pitch to reach easy ground and the crest of the Tough-Brown Ridge.

Other Significant Ascents

Arguably, the finest achievement in the North-West was the first ascent of *Godzilla* on the Giant's Wall on **Beinn Bhan** by Pete Benson, Nick Bullock and Guy Robertson. This new IX,8 takes a direct line into the upper two pitches of *The Godfather*. 'It's a super-direct, true winter-only line with awesome turf-dependent climbing and a really spectacular feel – the stuff of dreams,' Robertson said afterwards.

In December Martin Moran teamed up with Murdo Jamieson and Francis Blunt to make the first winter ascent of *Feast of The East* (VIII,9), a summer E1 5c on the Eastern Ramparts of **Beinn Eighe**. A few days later he roped

up with Jamieson again, to climb *The Wailing Wall* (IX,9) on the awe-inspiring left side of Haystack Gully. Moran returned to Beinn Eighe with Pete Macpherson to make the first winter ascent of *King of the Swingers* (VIII,10). Unfortunately, Macpherson took a small fall before the crux traverse of this summer E3 6b therefore losing the on sight. Also in December, Guy Robertson and Greg Boswell made the first winter ascent of *Mammoth* (IX,9) on **The Brack** in the Southern Highlands.

Repeats

Martin Moran and Pete Macpherson had an excellent start to the season with the second ascent of *The God Delusion* (IX,9) on Beinn Bhan. This touchstone route was first climbed by Guy Robertson and Pete Benson in December 2008 and (until this season)

196. Guy Robertson on the second ascent of *Extasy* (VIII,8) on Creag Meagaidh. The route was first climbed by Dave Hesleden and French climber Bruno Sourzac during the 2005 International Winter Meet.
(Pete Benson)

was widely regarded as the hardest route in the Northern Highlands. Moran and Macpherson used snowshoes for the approach and were full of praise for the first ascensionists after climbing the route in a 21-hour push. Big news from late January was the second ascent of *The Hurting* (XI,11) in Coire an t-Sneachda by Andy Turner at the end of January. Turner had attempted the route a few days earlier, but he took a small fall at one-third height so decided to return for a re-match with Phil Dowthwaite. Turner's successful ascent was a gripping battle of hard technical climbing with difficult to protect icy cracks, confirming the route's reputation as one of Scotland's most demanding winter pitches. Turner had made the first ground up ascent of *The Hurting*, and the next logical step was to climb it on sight. This advance was nearly fulfilled remarkably quickly, when Greg Boswell made two attempts on the route, falling tantalisingly close to the top, before finally succeeding on his third attempt.

At the end of January, well-known German climber Ines Papert visited Scotland with Austrian Charly Fritzer. They warmed up with ascents of *Daddy Longlegs* (VIII,9) and *Ventricle* (VII,8) in Coire an Lochain, before moving to the Ben and making the second ascent of Boswell's *To Those Who Wait* (IX,9). They then teamed up with Dave MacLeod to make the first ascent of *Triple X* (VIII,8), an icy mixed climb based on the summer route *Rolling Stones* on the East Flank of Tower Ridge.

The climax of the trip took place in Coire an Lochain where they both led *Happy Tyroleans* (IX,10) and Fritzer cruised *Demon Direct* (IX,9). The following day the weather was poor, but after climbing *Savage Slit*, the pair spotted an unclimbed line up the steep blocky wall between *Fallout Corner* and *War and Peace*. The result was *Bavarinthia* (IX,9), a superb two-pitch climb up an impressively steep wall. *Bavarinthia* was an almost unique event in Scottish winter climbing. Very few overseas teams have succeeded in climbing new winter routes in the Scottish mountains – two notable exceptions being *Raven's Gully Direct Finish* (Chouinard/Tompkins – 1970) and *Happy Tyroleans* (Schranz/Zak/Netzer – 2001).

Finally, Guy Robertson and Pete Benson made the second ascent of *Extasy* (VIII,8) on Creag Meagaidh at the end of February. This landmark route, which takes the awe-inspiring 300m-high wall between *Smith's Gully* and *The Fly*, was first climbed by Dave Hesleden and Bruno Sourzac from France, during the 2005 International Winter Meet.

New Venues

On the eastern side of Cairngorm overlooking Strath Nethy, Roger Webb, Iain Small, Sandy Simpson and Simon Richardson explored **Creagan Coire Cha-no**. Fifteen routes were climbed with pride of place going to *Arch Wall* (VII,7), *Anvil Corner* (VI,6) and *Smooth as Silk* (VII,7). Andy Nisbet also visited the cliff with John Lyall and came away with the first ascent of *Arch Enemy* (V,5). With a 2km approach, this is the most accessible winter cliff in the Cairngorms, and is likely to become popular with teams looking for an alternative to the Northern Corries.

The big event in Glen Coe was the development of a superb new ice venue rivalling the nearby Beinn Udlaidh for the quality and quantity of ice. **Eilde Canyon** was discovered by Simon Yearsley and Malcolm Bass on their way back from climbing the classic Sron na Lairig ridge earlier in the season. The narrow 250m-long canyon now has 10 new icefall routes climbed by Yearsley and Bass together with Dan Peach, Neil Silver, Simon Davidson, Tom Broadbent and Neil Carnegie. Pride of place goes to the beautiful ice formation *Zapatista* (V,5 – Bass), the steep *Central Amigo* (V,6

197. Malcolm Bass on the first ascent of *Zapatista* (V,5). This was one of 10 new routes at the new Glen Coe ice venue Eilde Canyon discovered by Simon Yearsley and Malcolm Bass. *(Simon Yearsley)*

– Yearsley) and the two-tiered *Andale Andale!* (V,5 – Silver/Davidson). Yearsley believes there is room for at least six more routes, so expect the canyon to get busy once it gets cold again.

LINDSAY GRIFFIN

Afghanistan 2011

In 2010 the High Hindu Kush and Pamir mountains of north-east Afghanistan, situated in that long finger of land known as the Wakhan Corridor, were visited by six climbing expeditions (half of which were British). In 2011 the number was less, but this remote area is gradually being re-visited by climbers, who report meeting nothing but kindness, respect, and incredible hospitality from the local people, in a wild region worlds apart from the on-going civil war.

Peaks in the Wakhan were hugely popular from the 1960s until just before the Soviet invasion in December 1979. The majority of expeditions were European, and would often reach the area overland – via the 'hippy trail'. They were enticed by generally easier access than found in other parts of the Himalaya-Karakoram, more stable weather than the Karakoram (which was closed until 1974), and the ability to climb unhampered, free from a restrictive permit system.

Why Afghanistan today? The answer lies in the incredible wealth of unclimbed peaks below 6000m and the opportunity to penetrate glaciated valleys that no climbers have previously visited. Many of these peaks can be ascended by routes of modest difficulty, making them suitable for small teams of less technically driven mountaineers, with pioneering spirits, operating in a very lightweight style. Today's access, via Tajikistan and a crossing of the Oxus to Ishkashim at the entrance to the Wakhan by a relatively-recently built 135m suspension bridge, avoids the now unsafe and more or less impractical route from the south.

Close to the entrance to the Corridor stands **Noshaq**, at 7492m the highest mountain in the country and second highest in the entire Hindu Kush. This was climbed twice during 2011 by its technically straightforward west ridge. On 4 August, Tim Wood, with local guide Aziz Beg, became the first Australian to climb the mountain. On the 13th, Krzysztof Garolyna and Krzysztof Mularski, carrying on a long tradition of Polish climbing in the region, also reached the top. These are the sixth and seventh known ascents since before the Soviet invasion.

Two more Poles, Klaudiusz Duda and Slawomir Kawecki, became the first to climb in the Mandaras group, a little east of Noshaq, since 1978. Snowfall thwarted their attempt to repeat the 1962 Polish route on **Koh-e-Nadir Sah** (M4, 6814m). Instead they made the first ascent of the south ridge of **M3** (6109m) at AD. This peak had been climbed previously: first in 1962 (Polish) via the north-west ridge, and twice in 1978 (Czechoslovak) – via the north-west and north-east ridges.

Becky Coles and James Kitson from the UK spent many months in Asia,

199. The 2011 Russian route on the W face of Latok III (6949m), showing portaledge
camps. *(2011 Russian Latok III Expedition)*

Four members of a Russian expedition, Alexander Odintsov, Evgeny
Dmitrienko, Ivan Dozhdev and Alex Lonchinsky completed the first
ascent of the west face of 6949m **Latok III** (in the Panmah Mustagh), in
capsule style and using eight portaledge camps over two weeks, nearly 20
years after this route was first attempted. They followed a line attempted by
two previous Russian expeditions, in 2000 and 2001; during the latter, Igor
Barihin died when falling rocks severed the fixed rope he was jumaring on.
The 2011 party recovered a bolt from that trip as a memento for his widow.
They again experienced significant rockfall and avalanche danger, and one
climber suffered a broken arm, but four climbers reached the summit on 25
June. This is clearly a route with significant objective dangers, at least in
its lower part.

A five member Korean party attempted the north face of **Latok I** (7145m)
from the Choktoi glacier. They spent five days on the face but had to retreat
from 5800m in bad weather and avalanche conditions. A Japanese team

200. North face of Latok I, showing the high point of the 2011 Korean attempt.

of three, the 'Giri Giri Boys', attempted a line to the left of the Korean one of 2010 but also retreated in falling ice, snow and rock. Several strong parties have attempted this still unclimbed side of Latok I over the last 35 years – an American team of Michael Kennedy, Jim Donini, Jeff Lowe and George Lowe reached 7000m on the obviously difficult but perhaps much safer north ridge in 1978. The summit of Latok I was first reached in 1979 by a Japanese expedition from the south-east (Biafo glacier) side, finishing up the east ridge.

Slovenians Nejc Marcic and Luka Strazar climbed a new route on the south-west flank of **K7 West** (6858m) in the Charakusa Valley, Pakistan. They completed the alpine-style ascent of *Dreamers of Golden Caves* (VI A2 M5, 1600m) in four days, between 6 and 9 September. This is probably the second route to reach the summit and the third ascent overall of K7 West. It was not a bad effort as their first climb in the Karakoram and earned the pair a Piolet d'Or. The name is translated from Slovenian – the 22-year-old Strazar explained 'We young guys are often without money, and thus often dream of golden caves.' Another party led by Rainer Treppte was unsuccessful due to avalanche danger on their proposed line. The big rock spike between K7 West and K7 itself remains unclimbed.

Two American parties also went to attempt K7 West this year, but both had to settle for difficult new routes on lower peaks. Kyle Dempster and Hayden Kennedy made the first ascent of **Hassan Peak** (6300m) just north of K6. The pair climbed the peak via its previously attempted west face, overcoming difficulties of WI5, M5 on their two-day ascent. Pat Goodman, Matt McCormick and Will Meinen climbed a1050m new route on a previ-

201. The 2011 Slovenian route *Dreamers of Golden Caves* on K7 West, showing bivouac sites. *(Dick Isherwood)*

ously unclimbed pillar, **Fida Brakk** (c5350m), which they named the *Jenga Spur* (V+, 5.11R, A0). The Charakusa valley continues to be a hot area for hard Alpine-style rock and mixed climbing.

In August a four-man Russian team established a new route on the northwest face of the **Trango Tower** (6251m). *No Fear* (VII 6B+ A3, 1120m), put up by Dmitry Golovchenko, Sergey Nilov, Viktor Volodin and Alexander Yurkin, is the first largely independent route established on the Trango Tower in more than a decade. They used three portaledge camps and much of the climbing was pegging.

A Russian/Ukrainian ladies team of Marina Kopteva, Galina Chibitok and Anna Yasinskaya spent 38 days establishing a new route on the northwest face of **Great Trango Tower** (6238m), *Parallelniy Mir* (VI+ 6b A3). They used nine camps on their route, which is at least the fourth line on this mile-high granite face.

HARISH KAPADIA

India 2010

I am grateful to the Indian Mountaineering Foundation, Lindsay Griffin, Rajesh Gadgil and several individual contributors, as mentioned, for information and reports.

If you'll pardon the cliché, whenever God closes a door he opens a window. This adage truly applied to the Indian Himalaya in 2010. There were not many expeditions to high peaks, perhaps reflecting higher peak fees and above all bureaucratic hindrance. However, there was much activity around small peaks, new regions and smaller teams. This may be an indicator for the future, as these expeditions are cost effective. Many did not mind meeting serious challenges below the height of 5500m, as peak fees are payable above this height. There were 40 foreign expeditions to India – a steep drop from the normal figure of around 65. Indian expeditions were 63, but unfortunately many were either to normal peaks or washed out due to bad weather. A flash flood hit the lower areas of Ladakh near Leh and elsewhere in remote valleys in early August. Rivers of mud destroyed houses, roads and fields. Aid from the army and government agencies poured in but it is never sufficient. Various organisations, including the Himalayan Club, raised funds to help.

Two new books were published in India. *The Siachen Glacier – The Battle of Roses* by Harish Kapadia covers the history of the glacier that has been the scene of conflict for the last 26 years. The history of the glacier, based on the author's several visits to trek and climb, is covered. *Himalayan Wonderland*, an earlier publication on Lahaul and Spiti by Dr M. S. Gill, was thoroughly revised and re-published with several additional maps and pictures.

The following were the major expeditions to the Indian Himalaya in 2010.

UTTARAKHAND
Arwa Tower (6352m)
Expedition: Dutch; leader, Sebastiaan Van der Smeede. The team approached the mountain from Ghastoli and entered the Arwa valley. They established base camp at around 4700m and placed two more high camps at 5350m and 5775m. They attempted the north-west buttress. Ice and snow on rock repulsed both the attempts made during the end of May and first week of June. They reached around 6000m.
Vasuki Parvat (6792m)
Expedition: British-New Zealand; leader, Malcolm Bass. This peak

located by the Chaturangi glacier is so named due to its shape as a serpent hood of a mythological figure, Vasuki. The alpine style ascent by the four-member British-New Zealand team of the unclimbed west face, traverse of the main summit and descent from the north-west ridge was a notable achievement. After establishing their base camp near the junction of Chaturangi and Vasuki Bamak glaciers at 4820m, they started their attempt on 3 October. During a continuous push, bivouacs were placed at 5400m, 5700m, 5900m, 6000m, 6200m, 6500m and 6700m on the west face. Malcolm Bass with Paul Figg reached the summit on 12 October. After traversing the summit ridge, they descended the NW ridge after a bivouac at 6250m and reached base camp on 13 October (see *AJ115* 18-30).

Kamet (7756m)

Expedition: German/Austrian/Swiss/French; leader, Herbert Wolf. This international team established their base camp at Vasudhara Tal and followed the traditional route to the summit via the Purbi Kamet glacier and Meade's col. Four high camps were established and the attempt took place from the summit camp at an altitude of 7080m. On 28 September the leader, with Oliver Amann, Nicolas Touboul, Bernd Mayer and Roland Brand, reached the summit.

Ekdant (6100m)

Expedition: Portuguese; leader, Daniela E.N. Teixeira. This two-member team from Portugal did not attempt Chaukhamba III as originally planned. Instead, they made two ascents in the area of Satopanth Tal. The leader with Paulo Roxo made the first ascent of the north spur of Ekdant (6100m) on 21 May and an Unnamed Peak (5115m) on 2 June. They have proposed to name this peak 'Kartik'. They also attempted Parvati Parvat but bad snow conditions foiled their plan.

Nithal Thaur (6236m)

Expedition: Slovenian; leader, Urban Golob. The team approached via Munsiyari, Lilam, Bugdiyar, Rilkot and Milam to Nithal Thaur (base camp) at 4200m. They followed the Milam glacier and established two high camps. Loose rocks and séracs on the south ridge of Hardeol stopped their attempt at an altitude of 5800m. They changed their objective and on 10 October, in an alpine style ascent, Boris Lorencic, Karel Zavrsnik and Matija Jost reached the summit of Nithal Thaur (6236m) by the south-west and west ridge.

Trisuli (7074m)

Expedition: Swiss-German; leader, Walter Josef Pfeifhofer; September-October 2010. Because of heavy rainfall and obstructed route, the team reached the base camp at Nithal Thaur very late in the season. While on the glacier at 4700m, mountain guide Michael Nellen stepped into a crevasse and dislocated his knee. Two high camps were established and the team reached 5700m before retreating due to lack of time.

Bhagirathi III (6454m)

Expedition: French; leader, Christophe Moulin with seven others. Two routes were simultaneously climbed on Bhagirathi III by this French team.

202. Ranglana (5554m) from the lower Obra valley. *(Harish Kapadia)*

On 23 September, Bletton Antoine, Gentet Frederic and Messina Dimitri reached the summit via the east ridge, which is the normal route up this peak. On 26 September, all team members reached the summit by a new route on the west face. They established one high camp at 5500m on each route.

Trisul (7120m)

Expedition: British; leader, Simon Hall; September-October. Approaching from the west, the team established three high camps on the mountain and placed the top camp at 6400m. Unfortunately, this remained their high point.

Nanda Ghunti (6390m)

Expedition: Indian; leader, Shyamal Sarkar. This large team attempted this peak named after the 'Veil of Nanda Devi'. On 13 August, Sukumar Roy and Dilip Banerjee reached the summit following the traditional route.

Nanda Khat (6611m)

Expedition: Indian Mountaineering Foundation; leader, Dr Anil Gurtoo. Nanda Khat is an oft-attempted mountain in Kumaun. The team followed the traditional route through Song, Dwali and Phurkia and established base camp at 4482m. They climbed via a new route on the north-east spur to the north summit to reach the main summit after establishing two high camps (5352m and 5325m). Dhruv Joshi, Tapka Norbu, Chetan Pandey and Bharat Bhushan reached the main summit on 22 June. No high altitude supporters were employed.

Ranglana and the Obra valley

Boris Korzh, Philip Leadbeater, Kunal Masania, Andrew McLellan and Jonathan Phillips, all from Imperial College, London, made three first ascents in the Obra valley, west of the Bandarpunch-Swargarohini group

in far western Garhwal. They were only the third group to climb in this area. The middle part of the Obra is dominated by Ranglana (5554m), which has been the main objective of several previous climbing teams. British climbers Gerry and Louise Wilson, with Harish Kapadia and seven friends were here in 2006, but did not attempt Ranglana due to poor conditions. Vinay Hegde, a leading Mumbai mountaineer, later made multiple attempts on Ranglana with a young team but poor conditions beat them back. In the same area in 2008, Derek Buckle, Toto Gronlund, Martin Scott and Bill Thurston were unsuccessful on the north-west ridge of Pt 5760m, but instead climbed Pt 5165m north of base camp, which they christened Lammergeyer Peak.

The Imperial College team battled slush in the upper valley to establish a high camp at 4900m, from where they made the first ascent of Pt 5480m via the south-west ridge (500m, AD-). Five members then climbed the valley's highest peak, Pt 5877m, thought to be known locally as 'Dauru', via the north-west ridge (700m, AD). Finally, the team climbed Ranglana (5554m). The five placed a high camp just below a col on the SW ridge and then next day crossed the pass. From here they descended slightly towards the Maninda valley before traversing to Ranglana's south ridge and following it to the summit (900m, D-).

HIMACHAL PRADESH
Ascents in Jiwa Nala (Kullu)
Five members of the Alpine Club made a successful exploratory expedition to the Indian Himalaya, where they climbed four previously virgin peaks. Derek Buckle, Michael Cocker, Drew Cook, John Hudson and Laura Millichamp visited the Jiwa Nala in the protected region of the Great Himalayan National Park. Located in Himachal Pradesh, the Jiwa drains west towards the Beas river, south of the famous tourist resort of Manali. It lies in the Banjar region, approximately 70km ESE of Kullu. The area, as far as is known, had not previously been visited by mountaineers.

While shepherds had occasionally grazed flocks in the past, the valley can only be accessed via two difficult passes and no permanent settlement has ever been established. Peaks at the valley head rise to 5445m. From a high camp just below the glacial snout, Buckle, Cocker and Cook accessed an upper glacier via a steep snow couloir and then made the first ascent of Snow Leopard Peak (5365m), climbing a mixed route on the south face at AD.

The expedition also made first ascents of Tribulation Point (5125m) and Sentinel Peak (5140m), which lie in the crenulated cirque south of Snow Leopard. After establishing a different high camp, they also climbed Snowcock Point (4890m), south of the main valley. (See *AJ115*, 31-38)
Singekang (6000m)
Expedition: Irish-British; leader, Alan Tees. This peak is located in the Singekang valley of Himachal Pradesh. This valley in Spiti was approached via Poh and Pomrang villages in southern Spiti. The team suffered poor

203. Raldang (5499m) seen from Kalpa. *(Harish Kapadia)*

snow conditions on Singekang and thus shifted their focus to a nearby **Unnamed Peak (5500m)**. They followed the west ridge and reached the summit on 12 November. The leader with Sandra Kennedy, Andrew Tees, George Carleton, Jeremy Windsor and Niall Boner reached the top.

Manirang (6593m)

Expedition: Howrah District Mountaineers and Trekkers, West Bengal; leader, Anal Das plus 11. Manirang is a high peak on the borders of Spiti and Kinnaur, first climbed by South African couple Dr and Mrs J. de V. Graaf in 1952 with the legendary Sherpa Pasang Dawa Lama and Tashi Sherpa. After reaching the base camp location at Spoana (4580m), the 2010 team established camp 1 at Sojana (5150m) and the summit camp at 5740m. Climbing via the south face, Molay Mukherjee, Kuntal Karar, Abhrajit Chatterjee with Norbu, Lakpa and Lopsang reached the summit on 3 August.

Ramjak (6318m)

Expedition: Punjab Police Adventure Sports Club; leader, HC Mohan Lal. Ramjak lies on the popular trek route from Manali, passing through the Shingo La to Zanskar. They followed the route taken by the earlier teams, ascending the eastern slopes to reach a col on the north ridge and turning south to climb the north ridge. On 14 July, the leader with Jagdev Raj Kodpha, Dina Nath and Aryan Singh reached the summit.

Raldang (5499m)

In July, Catalan Sílvia Vidal attempted an El Capitan-sized granite wall on this peak in the Kinnaur region. A picture of the face had originally been posted on the big wall website of John Middendorf, who had offered a hammer to anyone who could identify the location of this impressive formation. The most impressive view of this peak and face is obtained from Kalpa, directly to its west. As per the records, this pinnacle was climbed by Lt P. R. Oliver in 1931. It is clearly visible from many angles, especially from Kalpa, yet it was waiting to be climbed after almost 80 years.

Vidal established base camp at 3800m with porters. For seven days, she was never able to see the whole face due to cloud and heavy rain, and it took two days to find the foot of the wall. Access was via a complex and slippery ravine, in which she needed to fix ropes. After fixing the first three pitches of the face, Vidal set off for her 25-day solo stint. Two weeks into the route and above pitch 10 she reluctantly had to resort to drilling bat hooks through completely featureless sections. However, the crux A4 and A4+ sections were all natural.

Dome Peak (5650m), Point James (4965m), Miyar valley (Lahaul)

Expedition: Spanish; Anna Pfaff and Camilo Lopez. At the end of August, after a three-day trek, the pair established base camp on the grassy meadow below Castle Peak. They set off on 1 September for the south-east face of unnamed Peak 5650m on the north side of the Chhudong valley. After three-quarters height, instead of a traverse right to a gully, they opted for the headwall. Lopez led a steep face of 5.10, then Pfaff led two pitches of 5.10+, overcoming a loose section. Moderate 5.8 terrain led to the summit. They descended by 14 rappels through the night, along the way losing a rope, running out of slings, and almost losing their bivouac gear. They named the route *Lopez-Pfaff Direct* (IV 5.10+, 800m), and the previously virgin summit, Dome Peak. After this, the weather turned bad for 10 days. When it began to improve, Pfaff and Lopez tackled the nearby pyramid of 'Point James', which they believe to have been unclimbed. After climbing moderate terrain on an exciting ridge, they reached a head-wall. An exposed 70m pitch up a 5.10 finger crack through solid rock led to a roof, bypassed by a rightward traverse that proved to be the crux of the route. An unprotected overhang above a hanging belay led to the summit and completed the 600m south-east ridge at III 5.10c.

Shiva Shankar West (5510m)

From mid-August to mid-September, Lynn Lacobini De Fazio, Massimo Marcheggiani, and Bruno Moretti, from the Italian Alpine Club, explored the lush Saichu valley, the first of the Pangi's sub-valleys right of the Chenab. After braving floods and washed-out roads to reach the Saichu valley, two days' trekking took them to the narrow entrance to the Tarundi valley, leading to the east side of Shiva. As horses were unable to go beyond this point, base camp (3535m), was established much lower than desirable.

Taking advantage of a good weather window, they continued north upvalley, camping at 4165m, 4600m and 5080m, the last 20m above a col overlooking Sural valley and dominated to the west by Peak 5860m. Visible to the south-west was the huge north-east face and magic east pillar of Shiva. On 1 September they started up the face immediately east of the col, first climbing a 200m wall of crumbly shale in huge unstable blocks with difficulties up to UIAA V. Some of this was verglassed and they had to climb in crampons. Then they climbed a steep ice slope, followed by a snow shoulder that led to the 5510m rounded dome of Shiva Shankar West. This summit was first climbed in 2005 by Italian Diego Stefani, who named it 'Zero Point'. Continuing east would lead to the summit of Shiva Shankar (6011m) – the Horn of Shiva. All information suggests that the two Italian expeditions are the only ones to have climbed from the Tarundi valley.

Shiva (6142m)

Expedition: Russian; Andrey Muryshev with Evgeny Korol and Alexander Kornilov, and snowboarder Natalia Lapina; Aug-Sep 2010. Shiva was first climbed in 1988 by Junko Tabei. Climbing the north side of Shiva is problematic. It is divided into two parts by a central spur. In the lower section of the ENE face, huge hanging glaciers constantly discharge ice avalanches. Two fine ice couloirs rise almost to the summit but accessing them is difficult, and they were avalanching. The north face is only 50° and shorter, because it starts from a large and easily accessible ice terrace at c5000m. The group tried the central line starting at 5000m, but found the 45-50°snow wet, deep and unstable. When they returned after four days of bad weather, they found their equipment had been buried by a huge ice avalanche and the climbing was over.

Pangi Valley: mountaineering history; unclimbed objectives from the Saichu valley *(Bruno Moretti).*

Early history in the Pangi was made by Japanese Junko Tabei, who in 1988 made the first ascent of Shiva by the south-west face from the Parmar valley. In 2001 a Japanese team climbed Baihali Jot (6290m) by the north ridge. In 2002, an Indian expedition made the second ascent of Shiva, following the 1988 route. In 2004, Chris Bonington, Harish Kapadia, and friends trekked north up the Saichu as far as the confluence between Tarundi and Paphita valleys, then continued east up the latter to climb Jot Mund (5130m), Jambu Peak (5105m) and Pimu Peak (5480m) on the watershed with the Miyar valley. The following year Diego Stefani's expedition climbed Shiva Shankar West.

In 2007, Bonington returned, this time going up the Sural valley from the administrative capital, Killar. While he and Raj Kumar climbed Peak 5027m, the other three members of his British team, Rob Ferguson, Graham Little and Jim Lowther, attempted the north-west face of unclimbed Shiva Shankar (6011m), failing due to rotten rock. It was left to Japanese Kazuo Kozu, Hidetaka Lizuka and Reiko Maruyama, with three Indian porters, to make the first ascent of Shiva Shankar (aka Sersank Peak, because it dominates the Sersank pass to the north) the following year, via the same route attempted by the British trio.

Many challenges remain for future parties, the most notable being the eastern and northern aspects of Shiva [attempted by the Russians]. Equally interesting are the unclimbed icy north-west faces of Menthosa (6443m), Baihali Jot (6290m) and its satellites, the latter with elegant ice faces above the Saichu valley. No less intriguing is the south face of Shiva Shankar, though it has a disturbing array of séracs that get the sun's rays most of the day. East of the Italian base camp lies the confusingly named Baheli Jot (5600m) – a miniature Everest. The south-west ridge would provide good acclimatisation and an interesting exploratory climb.

LADAKH AND EASTERN KARAKORAM
Gulmothungos Rocks
The valleys from Ringdom monastery to Padam contain several rock pinnacles, peaks and passes. Photographs of these were published in the *Himalayan Journal*, vol. 66. These small valleys offer good climbs without need for much arrangement or planning. One such group of high walls is near the check post at Gulmothungos. After crossing the river a small valley of same the name is approached and it offers a wide variety of rock climbs. A team of young American rock climbers, led by Rushad Nanavatty spent an enjoyable three weeks in the summer of 2010 climbing challenging routes.

Barma Kangri (6515m)
Expedition: Japanese; leader: Masato Oki. Mari is located south-west of Pangong Tso in the Pangong range of the Ladakh Himalaya. Base camp was established at Kongma (4800m), a roadhead 23km from Chushul on the Tangtse road. The team made three high camps at 5400m, 6000m and 6100m. They did not climb Mari (6587m), their original objective, but instead climbed Barma Kangri (6515m). They ascended the south-east ridge and on 12 July, Rentaro Nishijima with Konchok Thinles and Pemba Sherpa reached the summit. On 17 July they were followed by Masato Oki with the same high altitude supporters.

Peak (5850m), and Peak (5995m) in Thanglasgo valley
Expedition: British-American-Finn; Christopher Horobin with Colin Bainbridge, Henry Latti (Finland), David Moseley, Matt Powell (USA) and others; July-August 2010. Lying north of Leh in the rain shadow of the Himalaya, this region has seen few parties operate outside the main trekking routes. Because of its proximity to the Pakistan border, the Indian military regard it as being particularly sensitive. The team had originally planned to attempt Telthop (6120m), but this was not possible due to difficult terrain where mules could not go. Hence they changed their plans for peaks above Thanglasgo. From Hundar, in the western Nubra valley, they accessed the main Thanglasgo valley. A three-day trek took them to Thanglasgo hamlet (c4600m) and the start of an unexplored valley to the east. A reconnaissance showed this approach to be long and difficult, with much moraine and a steep glacier. Later they caught sight of a peak at the head of the initial valley. It is marked on the map as 5850m and their Sherpas confirmed it as unclimbed.

From a base camp at Thanglasgo hamlet, they established a high camp

204. Gulmothungos Rocks, Ringdom valley. *(Harish Kapadia)*

in the valley leading to 5850m, and the day after crossed unstable moraine and a long glacier to reach the north-west face. This gave 300m of climbing up to 60° and led to the snowy, sometimes knife-edge, north-east ridge. Horobin, Andrea Bainbridge, Sarah Reynolds and Bob Shiels reached the rocky summit in deteriorating weather. The team then attempted the peak north of Shabib Chasser. The crest of the rocky south-east ridge gave climbing up to British Severe in standard, and after nine hours Reynolds, Shiels, and Horobin reached the summit, on which they recorded a GPS altitude of 5995m.

Lingsarmo (Pinnacle peak) (6995m)

Expedition: American-Canadian; Alison Criscitiello, Rebecca Haspel and Kate Harris. This three-woman team reached Nun base camp from Shafat village. After entering the Shafat glacier, they placed three high camps respectively at 5490m, 6130m, and 6270m ascending the Swiss face. They climbed to the col between Kun and Pinnacle Peak and on 16 August the leader and Haspel reached the summit.

Author's note: The historic first ascent of Pinnacle Peak was made in 1906 via the south-east ridge by American Fanny Bullock Workman with Savoye (her guide), and a porter. At the time it was the highest summit reached by a woman, and close to the human altitude record. The ascent is well recorded in the Workmans' 1909 book, *Peaks and Glaciers of Nun Kun*. The first editor of the *Himalayan Journal*, Kenneth Mason, created doubts about this ascent through his writings, although he never wrote explicitly that he doubted the ascent; 'Mrs. Bullock Workman claimed to have ascended

205. Nyegi Kangsang (6983m). *(Harish Kapadia)*

Journal he writes that it was, 'incomparably the hardest ascent we had in the Himalaya owing to the great steepness of the glacier work'. It is hard to imagine that Jopuno was climbed in 1883, but I would have thought that the west ridge would have been the line of choice in the pioneering days of alpinism. Nothing in his account fits the topography of Jopuno, and my current view is that he might have climbed the north-west glacier on Tinchenkang and mistaken this for Jopuno.

Lamalamani, Pk 5500m and Jopuno

Expedition: British-American; Paul Swienton with Geoff Cohen, Bob Hamilton, Dick Isherwood, Steve Kennedy, and Dave Ritchie. Inspired by Roger Payne and his accounts of the mountains of Sikkim, this team visited the Thangsing valley from 8-22 May. First, they attempted an obvious line on the west face of Lamalamani, going up to a col south of the final elegant snow arête of the north top. They left some gear in the boulders below the face and on the 11th began climbing the face in excellent weather. Overall, the route was c600m and AD+ and by following various degrees of difficulties, by noon all reached the summit.

On 14 May, Hamilton and Ritchie climbed an unnamed peak of 5500m between Jopuno and Lamalamani. The pair traversed steep snow and ice for a couple of rope lengths to reach a snow arête on the south face, followed this for a pitch, and then climbed two short pitches up mixed grooves to the summit block, which was gained by exposed moves. On the 18th, Kennedy, Hamilton, Cohen and Swienton left camp to repeat the west ridge of Jopuno. Above c5450m the ridge became icy and the section above was well covered in snow. They reached the foot of the looser black rock that forms the summit of the mountain. It appeared unlikely that the summit could be reached so they turned around.

Together with Tingchenkhang (6010m), Lamalamani and Jopuno have been designated 'Alpine Peaks' by the Sikkim authorities, and it is easy to arrange permits. All three offer good, medium-grade alpine ascents and could become classics of the Eastern Himalaya.

ARUNACHAL PRADESH
Looking for Kangto
Exploration in the east Kameng valley (Harish Kapadia)

The Himalayan range east of the high mountains of Bhutan starts getting lower as it enters Arunachal Pradesh. The Kangto range is the last high range, rising to 7042m, with its second peak of 6953m. The high peaks of Gorichen (6488m) lie to its west, while to the east of Kangto peaks are Chomo I (6878m), Chomo II (6710m) and Nyegi Kangsang (6983m). They stand along with many other peaks above 6000m and up to 6800m. The main peak, Kangto I, was climbed by a Japanese team in 1981 – approaching from the Tibetan Plateau in the north. However these peaks had never been approached from the south. Two expeditions to locate the approaches to its base camp in the south had failed due to difficulties of the terrain. In fact it was not known from where this peak can be climbed, where it could be approached from or the way to its base camp. There were no explorers to this valley during the last century or earlier. This group of peaks rises at the head of the Pachuk valley, in the East Kameng district of the Arunachal. It is on the McMahon Line, which is the international border. As there are no passes to Tibet from here, neither locals nor defence forces have ventured here. In the early part of the century, people used to trek to Tibet via the adjoining valley of Mago to buy salt. However, after the India-China war of 1962 this trail was not used. The approach is through thick forest, with scant trails and remote villages.

Harish Kapadia, Vijay Kothari, Atul Rawal and Geeta Kapadia travelled in the area from 18 October to 20 November. First, we travelled from Guwahati to Seppa (450m) and to Baming (1400m) by road. After four very tiring and hot days we reached Lada (1500m). A large Tourist Bungalow was being constructed. However, who would walk for three days in this hot valley to visit the bungalow was a question nobody could answer. Next day we woke by 4am to a clear sky and a magnificent view. From the ridge, on which Lada was located, we could observe the entire Kangto range. Such stunning and clear views are rare in these valleys as for about 10 months it remains cloudy, and for five of these months it pours. All the peaks: Gorichen, Kangto, Chomo, Nyegi Kangsang and a host of others were observed including a few in Tibet.

We trekked to the head of the valley, first to Sachong village attending the local church service with loud traditional singing. A priest, simply called 'Prembhai' – Brother of Love – with a long beard, was responsible for establishing such Catholic churches in the Kameng valley. Due to his efforts most villages were Christian and there was no large-scale drinking, no smoking and the people were god-fearing. Three days ahead was Bisal,

206. Kangto I (7042m) and Kangto II (6953m). *(Harish Kapadia)*

through similar terrain. Ahead of Bisal, on the left bank of the Pachuk river is Chalran Lake (4625m). The trail to the lake was over a sharp ridge and through a rarely used shikari trail. The main obstacle on the route was crossing the Pachuk river below Bisal where an old iron wire was hanging high between the two banks as the bridge was washed away. Shikaris would hang on the wire with an improvised harness and go across pulling themselves. It was scary and dangerous. So crossing the river to visit the lake was ruled out. We returned to Lada by a new route via the West Kameng valley crossing 'Lapung Pass' (2400m) (or Lupoi Pass as on the map), through a veritable paradise of forest, especially large areas of bamboo. We emerged at Khajlang (1500m) near a new dam, and returned via Nofra and Solari to reach Bomdila on the main road.

DICK ISHERWOOD

Nepal 2011

I would like to thank Elizabeth Hawley and the climbers named in this report for their help with information.

In October 2011, Park Young-Seok, arguably Korea's most accomplished high altitude mountaineer, died on the south face of **Annapurna** with two companions. He was making his second attempt on the prominent unclimbed line between the two pillars taken by the British and Japanese routes. The party reached around 6400m, climbing alpine style, and apparently died retreating in bad weather and stonefall. An extensive rescue effort failed to find their bodies. Park was the first Korean to climb all fourteen 8000m peaks. He has been widely quoted as saying, 'Mountaineers should be on the mountains... I will continue expeditions until death comes.' This line has some history – in 1992 Pierre Beghin and Jean-Christophe Lafaille reached 7400m, above the major difficulties, and were forced to descend by bad weather. Beghin died when an abseil anchor pulled out; Lafaille managed to descend alone despite an arm broken by rockfall. Ueli Steck made two attempts on it in 2007-8. As it is basically a depression in the face, it is not without objective danger.

There were 526 successful ascents of **Everest** this year, all in the spring and many on just 20/21 May in a good weather window, when it must have been awfully crowded up there. Apa Sherpa has now climbed Everest 21 times. The American guide Michael Horst climbed Everest and Lhotse in under 21 hours, thus becoming probably the first person to climb two 8000m peaks in a single day. He did use some oxygen and took a rest in his camp on the South Col midway. Babu Sunawar and Lakpa Tshering reached the summit of Everest by the standard southern route and descended to Syangboche airfield above Namche Bazaar by paraglider, circling over the summit and setting a world altitude record in the process. They subsequently kayaked down the Dudh Kosi and Ganges to Calcutta, naming their whole trip 'The Ultimate Descent, Summit to Sea'. A holy man from south-east Nepal, Bhakta Kumar Rai, who has a considerable past record of performing miracles, spent 32 hours on the summit, mostly praying for world peace. This is apparently another Everest record, but has not so far been accepted by the authorities in Nepal. Sixteen-year-old George Atkinson from Surbiton climbed Everest in the spring and became the youngest person to complete the Seven Summits. His record was however beaten later in the year by Californian Jordan Romero, who achieved the same feat at age 15. What will they do after they leave school?

The well-known Dutch mountaineer, Ronald Naar, died at around

207. The Gottlieb - Kellogg route on the south face of Pangbuk Ri (6716m). The black spot shows their advanced base camp. *(David Gottlieb)*

8000m on **Cho Oyu** in the spring season. He was 56 and had a long climbing record in many parts of the world. The cause of his death is not known – it does not appear to have been a fall.

In the spring Julian Freeman-Attwood, Nick Colton and Ed Douglas attempted the unclimbed **Gave Ding** (6571m), north-east of Simikot in the Changla Himal of far west Nepal. They reached 5900m on its south ridge before retreating in deteriorating weather. Julian promises a full article on his explorations in this area after his next trip in late 2012. In the post monsoon season Mick Fowler, Dave Turnbull, Jonny Ratcliffe and Graham Desroy went to **Mugu Chuli** (6310m), also known as **Gojung**), also in a remote part of far west Nepal but a bit further east than Gave Ding. Fowler and Turnbull made the first ascent of the peak by its west face at a standard of ED, taking four days up and three more down by a long traverse of the frontier ridge with Tibet. Desroy and Ratcliffe made a probable first ascent of an unnamed 5800m peak, also on the border. *(Fowler's account appears in this AJ on pages 3-15)* The highest peak in this group, **Koji-chuwa Chuli** (6439m) was climbed by a Japanese party in 2011. Also in the far north-west, Paulo Grobel and Jean-Pierre Arles climbed a new line on the north-west ridge of **Changwathang** (5960m) in late September. This peak has had at least two previous ascents by Japanese parties.

The Nepalese Government has announced that there will be no peak fees for mountains in the far west of the country – i.e. west of the Dhaula-giri range – until at least 2015, in an attempt to attract more parties to this remote region.

In Solu Khumbu a New Zealand party led by Ben Dare attempted new

)8. Andy Houseman on the west ridge of Kyashar (6769m) in the Hinku valley.
   (Nick Bullock)

routes on **Kyajo Ri** (6186m) and **Kusum Kanguru** (6367m), both trekking peaks. They reached around 6000m on the south-west ridge of Kyajo Ri but had to retreat after an injury to Dare who was struck on the hand by falling ice. His companions then attempted a route on the far left part of the south-west face of Kusum Kanguru, but turned back in poor snow conditions.

Andy Houseman and Nick Bullock tried a new route on the south pillar of **Kyashar** (Peak 43, 6769m) in the Hinku valley in the spring season – a line they had previously attempted in 2010. They found unsettled weather and lots of snow, abandoned this project and instead attempted the previously climbed west ridge, but retreated from around 6000m on very poor rock.

Americans David Gottlieb and Chad Kellogg climbed the south face of **Pangbuk Ri** (6716m) in the Rolwaling valley in alpine style over seven days in November. They graded the 1400m route VI WI5 M5. There was a good deal of rockfall on the route, one piece of which smashed Gottlieb's helmet. They bivouacked in a crevasse on the summit ridge and descended the opposite side of the mountain with 20 abseils, some of them long and precarious, then had a 10 mile walk back to their base camp.

In October, a three man British party led by Steve Holmes attempted

209. The Lunag peaks from the south. L-R: Lunag III, IV and V. *(Steve Holmes)*

Lunag V (6550m), north-east of Pangbuk Ri and near the Nangpa La. They abandoned the attempt in very warm and hazardous conditions – they were also troubled by Tibetan refugees crossing the Nangpa La and apparently willing to plunder their base camp.

In December 2010, three Korean climbers made a new mixed route on **Phari Lapcha East** (6017m). The route was technically difficult at 5.9 A3 WI5+ M5, with three bivouacs on the ascent and another on the descent. Sadly one climber died on the way down, apparently from a stroke – he had been unwell on the ascent.

Andy Parkin's impressive solo ascent of the north face of **Dingjung Ri** (6249m) in the Rowaling valley in January 2011 was reported in detail in *AJ115*, 290.

JOHN TOWN

China & Tibet 2011

Restrictions in the Tibetan Autonomous Region continue to make climbing or exploration very difficult. With the exception of the Nyenchen Tanglha West, which lies within the central region, within a day's drive of Lhasa, it seems to be impossible to get permits to travel or climb. Tamotsu Nakamura has continued to be successful in visiting the mountains around the lower Yigrong Tsangpo valley, but there is little hope for lesser mortals.

In 2012, matters have deteriorated further. Unrest in the Tibetan areas of Sichuan have resulted in the closure of the Qonglai Shan (Siguniang) and other regions, which do not normally require permits for travel and climbing. It remains to be seen how long these restrictions will remain in place.

QONGLAI SHAN

Li Lan, Yan Dongdong and Zhao Xingzheng visited the Siguniang National Park in August 2010 to make the first ascent of the west face and south-west ridge of **Abi** (5694m) in the less-known western sector of the range.

On the south face of **Siguniang** (6250m), Sun Bin and Li Zhongli completed *Liberation* (1100m), a route that slants through the 1992 Japanese south buttress to finish up the south-west ridge. Sun Bin had made three previous attempts on this line. Two French climbers Maël Baguet and Dimitri Messina had earlier completed a new route on the north-west face, following a spur to the right of the north couloir and the large rock buttress subsequently climbed by Russians, which rises towards mixed ground below the upper south-west ridge. There had been two previous attempts on the 1300m route, which the pair completed in a five-day round trip.

DAXUE SHAN

In October 2011, Jeff Shapiro and Chris Gibisch made the third ascent of **Mt Grosvenor** (6376m) via a new route on the W/NW aspect. Shortly afterwards, Dmitry Paramonov and Denis Shushko, two members of a larger Russian expedition, climbed more or less directly up the east face of Grosvenor to make the fourth overall ascent.

Yan Dongdong and Zhou Peng visited the Riuche valley on the western side of the Minya Konka range and made three new routes. They began with a one-day ascent of the 1000m north face of **Reddomain** (6112m), followed by the second ascent of **Jiazi** (6540m) via a new route on the c1500m west face. For their third route, on the 600m south face of **Xiao**

210. Yan Dongdong and Bruce Normand approach Sir Duk (6653m). Along with Guy McKinnon they climbed the gully on the left, angling right, up to the summit (AD). The rock ridge on the right would be a fine route and is probably unclimbed. *(Guy McKinnon)*

Gongga (**Little Konka**, 5928m) they were accompanied by female film-maker Li Shuang

SHALULI SHAN

On October 20 2011, Jon Otto, Liu Yong (Daliu), Su Rongqin (Asu), and Tim Boelter made the first successful ascent of **Yangmolong** (6060m).

This had been the subject of several attempts over recent years, concentrating on the southern aspect. This team followed a bold route over three days up the middle of the north face, which is divided in its lower part by a rock buttress and ridge.

LITANG PLATEAU

In October 2011, New Zealand climbers Yvonne Pfluger and Tim Church made the first ascent of **Nideng Gonnga** (5690m), via the western glacier and south face. Earlier, they were turned back from **Xiangqiuqieke** (5863m) due to locals' concerns about them climbing a holy mountain.

NYENCHEN TANGLHA WEST

In October 2009, Yan Dongdong, Guy McKinnon (New Zealand) and Bruce Normand (Scotland) based themselves in the Langbu Qu, the third valley system west of Nyenchen Tanglha Main (7162m). They climbed **Pt 6382m** and **Pt 6286m** (on the Mi Desheng map) at the head of the valley, and **Pt 6120m** (altimeter reading) above the west bank. They also made ascents of **Chorten Garpo (6380m)** and **Sir Duk (6653m)**, both by new routes. In May 2010, Yan Dongdong and Li Lan made the first ascent of **Dongxung (6095m)**, one of a cluster of 6000m peaks in the Beutse group lying south of the south-western end of the Nyenchen Tanglha. They climbed the south-east ridge in a 13-hour round trip.

CENTRAL TIBET

There has been little winter climbing in Tibet – unsurprising given the very low temperatures that prevail. In December 2010, Li Lan and Yan Dongdong made the first ascent of **Nojin Kangsang (7206m)**. The peak is straightforward and access is via the Gyantse-Lhasa road that runs over a spur of the mountain at just below 5000m. Night-time temperatures in winter on the mountain are likely to sink below -30°C. The pair placed a camp at 6050m on the SSW spur and then bivouacked in a snow hole at 6900m on the south ridge, before reaching the summit in the afternoon of 8 December. They encountered ferocious winds on the final section above the 7130m col.

HIMALAYA

Japanese Kazuya Hiraide and Kei Taniguchi, made the first south to north traverse of **Naimona'nyi, (Gurla Mandhata 7694m)** in West Tibet. They ascended the unclimbed south-west ridge, and completed it with four bivouacs, crossing the peak's previously unclimbed south summit **Naofeng Peak (7422m)**. They descended the original route along the north-west slopes, encountering a number of route-finding difficulties due to séracs.

Sources: Alpinist, Climb magazine, BMC.

ERIK MONASTERIO

Bolivia 2009-2011

211. Ancohuma (6430m) from Viluyo Jankohuma, showing the line of the 2011 ascent. Peaks from left to right are Nevado Piramide (5907m), Haucana (6200m)(flattish summit), Ancohuma (in centre), the Yacuma Peaks (5970m, 5953m, 6062m) and then Illampu (6300m). *(Erik Monasterio)*

Over recent years there has been little mountaineering information coming out of Bolivia. This may be partly due to the fact that there isn't an agency or an individual who is committed to collecting mountaineering information, particularly activity relating to new routes or notable repeats of established climbs. One of Bolivia's best known guides and archivist Alain Mesili has taken a break from climbing to concentrate on writing, and this may have further limited the flow of information. Unfortunately it seems that the total number of climbers to going Bolivia is decreasing, despite the country offering one of the most stable weather patterns in the mountaineering world and the scope for new route development remaining high. Most climbing activity in recent years has centred on the popular (often guided) peaks in the southern Cordillera Real; Huayna Potojsi, Kondoriri and Illimani, which are easily accessible for the capital.

In August 2009, Gregg Beisley and Andy Baker (USA) climbed a new route on **Maria Lloco (5523m)** via the south-east couloir, which involved three steep pitches of hard ice climbing after a long scramble/ snow climb on the lower slopes. Maria Lloco is a striking subsidiary peak just north

212. North face of Jankhopiti (5723m) (centre), showing the line of the 2011
ascent. Other summits in the photo remain unnamed. *(Erik Monasterio)*

west of Huayna Potojsi.

On 20 June 2010, Florian Hill of Austria, Robert Rauch of Germany
and Stefan Berger climbed a new mixed route up the south face of **Serkhe
Khollu (5546m)**, in the southern Cordillera Real. They named the route
Chamaka. The route was climbed in eight hours and followed a discontinuous ribbon of ice, 3m wide and averaging 80°. Between 24 and 31
July 2010, Hill and Rauch climbed an impressive new route on **Illimani
(6438m)** and added to the challenge by immediately traversing over four
more peaks. On 25 July they climbed *Deliver Me* (VI WI6 M6+, 1700m) on
the south face of Illimani, in a 21-hour push. The next day, after reaching
the summit, they continued traversing the Illimani massif, heading east.
Hill said they climbed Pico Likho Linkho, Pico Layca Khollu, Pico Central
and Pico Sur – about 5km of mountainous terrain – over the three days that
followed. They arrived back in base camp on 31 July.

In June 2011, Beisley and Baker climbed a new route to the summit of
the south face of **Huayna Potojsi, Pt. 5600m**. This involved nine pitches of
ice/ mixed climbing and descent via the south-west ridge, in a round trip
of 16 hours. In late July 2011, Isabel Suppe and Robert Rauch climbed a
new route on **Serkhe Khollu**. The route called The *Birthday of the Broken
Leg* (TD+/ED) is reported to climb 500m up the south-west face before
meeting with the normal route on the summit ridge. Once they joined the
normal route the pair began their descent, avoiding the 45min walk to the
summit.

In September 2011, after a five-year break from mountaineering, Erik
Monasterio travelled home to Bolivia and joined Kiwi expat Gregg Beisley
for two weeks of intensive climbing. Gregg and his family work as missionaries in the city of El Alto, Bolivia. On his backyard Gregg has set up
what must the highest bouldering wall in the world, at 4000m. After Erik
repeatedly failed on the easiest problems the pair decided to tackle bigger,

easier and potentially achievable objectives, and headed into the northern Cordillera Real mountains.

They approached the isolated eastern valleys of this mountain chain from the town of Cocooyo and over a nine-day period climbed three routes. On 1 September they climbed a new route on the north face of **Jankhopiti (5723m)**, which involved an easy glacier approach and five pitches of rock climbing, straight up the steep face (F6b/20). They called the route, which was climbed in a 16-hour round trip from their base camp at 4800m, *Via Santiago*. Two days later from the same camp they climbed what may be a new route on Pt. 5540m (DAV Map), **Viluyo Jankohuma**, via the southeast ridge, in an eight-hour round trip. After a rest day the pair set up a low(ish) high camp at 4900m, from where they climbed the highest peak in the area, **Ancohuma (6430m)**, in 16 hours of sustained and at times complex climbing. The route was climbed up the north-east ridge onto the north ridge and summit. Erik, hardly acclimatised after only a week at altitude, staggered onto the summit in a whiteout before receiving assistance from Gregg to get down to the col at 6200m, where he found his legs and sufficient air to get back down to camp. Although there is significant scope for new routes, the eastern aspect of the northern Cordillera Real has been all but abandoned by expeditions over recent years and there have been no reported climbs on Ancohuma from this side for a decade; since Erik's last visit to the peak (15 years ago) the characteristics of the climb have changed significantly with the appearance of penitentes and loose rock on the summit ridges, making it now a more serious undertaking.

This year has seen significantly more snowfall than usual and some of the traditional ice routes (which had disappeared through climate change) re-formed. On 13 September, Monasterio and Beisley climbed the longest, most sustained route in Bolivia – the west face of **Huayna Potosi (6088m)**, in a single push to the summit in eight hours. They climbed a variation of the direct route, *Via del Zorro*. The 900m route involved zigzagging around a series of bergschrunds before taking the steepest, direct line to the summit. This route is a variation of the *West Face Direct Route*, first climbed by Mesili, Faure, Challeat and Levy in September 1978. Beisley and Monasterio had previously climbed the west face via another (ridge) route 15 years earlier and were delighted to have one final weather window in the season to climb back up memory lane.

MARCELO SCANU
Argentine Andes 2010-2011

This report is ordered from north to south by province.

Jujuy

On 27 May 2010, Martín Altamirano and Martín Castillo, both Argentineans, made a new route to the summit of **Morro Von Rosen** (5450m) in the Chañi group. They departed from 4700m and finished the route at 5400m on the ridge leading to the summit. They spent six hours ascending the 14 pitches, the most difficult of 6a, and called the route *Guanuqueando*. The last 300m were very steep. They descended on scree.

Salta

On 12 January 2010, Adrián Gandino, Ariel Seghezzi, Gerardo Casaldi and Emilio González Turú opened a new route, *West route* or *Luracatao route*, on the important **Nevado de Cachi** (also known as Cerro Blanco). The next day Guillermo Martin reached the 6380m summit solo from a slightly different line. The route was attempted in 1904 by Federico Reitchert, known as the father of Argentine mountaineering, nearly reach the summit.

The sacred mountain of **Cerro Acay** (5716m) was first ascended by the Incas for religious purposes (by the easy route). On 13 February 2011, Argentine Gustavo González and a friend from Salta left from a 5000m camp at an ancient mine. They crossed a col and switched to the snowy south ridge. At 5500m, González descended 50m and climbed a 200m ice and mixed couloir, very exposed and steep (he stated up to 80°). He finally climbed a little rock wall to a ridge that took him to the summit where he joined his friend. He called the route *Como llegar a rozarte el alma*. From the summit they descended in a storm and got lost. When the sun reappeared, they re-ascended 500m to the summit to find easier terrain.

Catamarca

The Cordón de los Arrieros is a very little visited range on the Argentinean-Chilean border, between **Ojos del Salado** (6864m, the second highest American summit and the highest volcano and active volcano on Earth) and Cerro Solo. This zone has the highest 6000er density outside Asia. On the first days of December 2011, Argentines Glauco Muratti and Adrián Petrocelli ascended three of the four summits of the ridge. They ascended virgin **De los Grillos** (5768m) and **De las Chullpas** (5898m) (both are official heights from IGN / ex IGM). They also summited **De los Arrieros** (5860m) where they found documents from 1955 and 1956

ascents made by the Asociación Tucumana de Andinismo, Argentina, which had been very active exploring in the area.

On the first days of 2011, North American Jonathan Kreiss-Tomkins ascended with a partner a high volcano east of mighty El Muerto. They made an absolute first ascent of this volcano erroneously called El Muertito (the little Dead One) by some sources. It was named Cerro Sin Nombre (Unnamed Peak) by a Polish expedition in the 1930s and later as **Cerro Nevado** (the Snowy One) by Argentine climbers. It has an official Argentine height of 5988m and lies on the Argentine-Chilean frontier; it was considered the highest virgin peak in the Americas. In the crater, they found a bizarre lagoon that had a strange beetroot juice colour, maybe due to algae.

John Biggar and party climbed the peak of **Cerro Medusa North-east** (6046m) in one day from the El Arenal base camp on the Argentine side of Ojos del Salado at 5500m. Medusa North-east is a summit with over 200m of prominence that appears in the list of subsidiary peaks in the 2005 edition of Biggar's guidebook *The Andes – A Guide for Climbers*. It is about 5km north-east of the higher peak of Medusa. Biggar had overlooked it in the past despite having visited the area about six times and written the guidebook. There is no record of a previous ascent of this peak (and apparently no mention of it anywhere other than the Biggar guidebook). After a week of heavy snowfalls at base camp, the group was unable to climb Ojos del Salado as planned. Instead, on 29 January 2010, Biggar climbed Medusa North-east, with two clients Thom Rankin and Barry Woods. Their route from El Arenal took them around the east side of Cerro Medusa (6120m) then along an undulating ridge to the summit of the north-east peak. The ascent was little more than rough walking over snow and rubble, but the summit area was very small (only a few metres square) and there was no cairn or cache.

In January 2012, Argentines Sandra Odriozola, Christián Chávez, Matías Barberis, Pablo Barberis, Federico Barberis and Marcelo Scanu explored the Puna high mountain desert. On 15 January, they camped at c4200m in a little-explored range that runs parallel to the border with Chile. On the 17th, all the team ascended a summit unofficially named **Cerro Ponta Ladina** (c4859m by Google Earth, 26°49'23.92"S 68° 0'21.59"W) by its west ridge. They found a trigonometric cairn that was perhaps erected by the well known German geologist Walther Penck in 1910. On 19 January, the Barberis brothers ascended **San Francisco** (6016m) on the border with Chile and Odriozola, while Chàvez and Scanu climbed a virgin summit christened **Cerro Camila** (c4932m by Google Earth, 27°1'40.16"S 68° 0'26.94"W) by its north ridge. Near camp, they found Inca ruins and an apparent section of the Inca trail.

On the 20th, the group rejoined in Las Grutas and took some water before travelling by vehicle to a depression north of **Bertrand** (4730m). Conditions were harsh here with high winds and hot days but cold afternoons and nights. On the 21st, the Barberis brothers made an ascent of Bertrand's

north summit (5188m by official map) by a new route on the north face. On the 23rd, the remaining three climbers left for Bertrand's 4.5km diameter, 400m deep crater aiming to ascend the last virgin summit on the crater rim. Scanu had made the first descent in 2008 with José Luis Querlico. They took 4l of water each and erected a tent in the deepest part (26°49'32.21"S, 68° 9'37.18"W, c.4850m). Tiny plants survived beneath the rocks, and even a few butterflies. On 24 January, they ascended to a col and hence to the virgin summit (c5187m by Google Earth). The summit was a huge pointed rock covered by bird excrement.

After this, they attempted **Pabellón** (5331m by official map), with Scanu reaching the summit by the south ridge/face late on 26 January. After this, the team retreated in un-typical snowfall and rain. Later, they found that Matías Marin, not knowing about their expedition, also ascended some virgin peaks in the zone. A point of note in this area is that many people believe there is a difference of 40-50m between heights on the official map and GPS readings. The above GPS records used the Campo Inchauspe datum as used on Argentine maps.

La Rioja

John Biggar led an important expedition with clients and an Argentine guide to the high barren zone of the **Cordón de los Pioneros**, a line of volcanoes north of mighty Bonete Chico (6759m). They found no trace of any previous ascent, despite a claimed earlier ascent of one of the summits by an Italian party. They erected base camp at 5300m on the western slopes of the volcanoes, from which they made all the climbs. On 5 December 2011, they ascended **Peak 6152m** (Argentine maps, 6190m by GPS). The next day the party split into groups, ascending **Peak c6100** (6155 GPS), **Peak 6144** (6162 GPS) and **Peak 6200** (6240 GPS).

San Juan

Argentine Fernando Daneri and Edgardo Liberman, from Panamá but resident in Buenos Aires, ascended a new route on the 6770m **Cerro Merc-edario** in November 2010. They called the route *A Contramano*, 1300m AD. The alpine style climb started in Laguna Turqueza, a rare turquoise lagoon at 4200m. They erected a camp at 4800m and started ascending the Paduszek glacier on the east face. They found 40-50° ice, some scree and then snow and ice to El Diente 6300m, with cold and windy conditions. They continued to the summit by the normal route.

The team of Argentines Javier Giuliani, Fabrizio Oieni and Juan Manuel Leániz were active in January 2011 in the Cordillera de la Ramada. The highest peak is Mercedario but the most attractive is **Pico Polaco** (c6000m). They camped at Pirca de Polacos and climbed a nice icefall (100m WI4) near the col between Mercedario and Cerro Negro. After this, they made a new route on the south-east face of Pico Polaco. The pair crossed five berg-schrunds and took the obvious couloirs (40°), trying to climb fast because of falling rocks. At 5500m, Oieni gave up and Giuliani continued alone

219. South side of Pico Ansilta 4 (5116m) showing the line of *6 Hermanos* on the south-east spur. *(Gabriel Fava)*

up bad ice and snow and a vertical icefall. Finally he reached the summit (*Acecho Felino*, 1100m, 90° max) and descended the south ridge.

On 19 September 2010 (southern winter), Frenchman Henry Bizot and Argentine Gabriel Fava ascended a new line on the south-east spur of **Pico Ansilta 4** (5116m) in the Ansilta range, north of Mercedario. They called it *6 Hermanos*, 700m, AD+, 55° ice. They were supported by the climber Santiago Scavolini.

Mendoza

The **Nevado Excelsior** (5773m) is the highest mountain in La Jaula range. It is also called Mogote Central. It has had three ascents overall: The first in 1964 by its north-east ridge, the second in 1979 by the south-east face and the third in 1985 by its south face. In November 2011, Argentines Mijel Lofti and Pablo González ascended it by a new route, a line near its west ridge, which had less ice than in earlier years (in 2009 González had attempted this route). On 2 November, they departed with no ropes, nuts or helmets. The pair took the Río Tupungato route and camped at Quebrada Fea (2900m), and at 4000m on the slopes of Enanos Blancos. On the 5th they climbed 30-45° slopes with some easy rock before switching to the ridge to avoid the west glacier. They could see Aconcagua from the summit.

Rodrigo Maique and Sebastián Ruiz made a new route on the east face of **Cerro Plata** (5968m) in the Cordón del Plata (it doesn't exceed 6000m as ancient maps stated). They set off on 22 September 2011, walking the Quebrada de la Angostura route towards the east face. After acclimatising on 25 September, they departed at 3.30am through penitentes and scree. The channel splits into two: the right one is the route opened in the '80s by

220. East face of the rock tower Torre La Yaya, Tierra del Fuego. Beltrame and Rodríguez descended this side of the tower. *(Mariano Rodríguez)*

Alessio and Mon; Maique and Ruiz took the 40° left branch, first with iced scree and afterwards with 55° snow and ice linking with the ridge, and took the east ridge to the summit. They descended via a shallow couloir. They called their route *Faltó la Gorda*.

During the southern hemisphere spring 2011, Argentines Diego Molina and Hernán Ortega made a very interesting route on the very little known **Cerro Manantiales** (c5100m) in the valley of the same name. From Tunuyán they went to the Refugio Portinari, erected in the Perón era, then to Refugio Scaravelli (3000m) camping in an ancient ruined hotel at 3900m. They first ascended 500m 55° at the steepest on the south face, then 180m of hard ice 70-75° ending in mixed terrain on the south-east face. They continued up 100m more of 60° deep snow. The bad conditions and cold feet made them retreat at a foresummit. They made four rappels with Abalakovs. They think it was a first ascent of the south face, which is nearly certain because it is rarely visited. They called their route *Direct a la cubetera*, rating it 700m D 60° WI3-M2.

In September 2011, Argentines Luciano Fiorenza and Pablo Pontoriero opened an important new route on the east face of **Cerro Vallecitos** (5475m) in the Cordón del Plata. They called it *De paso.... cañazo* (1000m MD WI4 M3). The first part was 60°, then they found a couloir and small icefall zone. At 5000m, in the middle of the face was the crux, which involved two pitches of ice and one with snow and mixed terrain. A final 60° couloir led to the ridge. They reached the summit (central) with an impressive view of Aconcagua. They claim this summit as the highest; they also reached the south summit after a 20m rappel and a traverse of the

221. Tronador (c3500m) showing the lines of *Finito Sur* (red line) and *Jeneración Descartable* (blue line). *(Luciano Fiorenza)*

exposed ridge. This last summit is the one with the cross, and is very often climbed by other routes: Vallecitos, by the easier route, is the first summit for many climbers. The pair descended the normal route, making a 14-hour round trip.

Aconcagua 2010-2011

There were fewer people visiting Aconcagua and the weather was poor, with many days with snowfall. Unfortunately, there were six fatalities, as in the 2008-2009 season, and 197 rescues, 46 of them complex. Although the number of rescues was smaller than in recent years, the cost was higher, mainly because of the helicopter use. The climbing fee has been raised; more than 2 million dollars was collected. On the other hand, cleaning in the park was completed and two more huts have been constructed – one at 3800m in the Quebrada de las Vacas, and another at 6000m. The late Italian climber Senin's family donated the latter after she died on the mountain in the 2009 tragedy. Another positive development is that more climbers and trekkers are accessing the mountain by the Quebrada de las Vacas, now it's 37% against the historic 20%. Plaza de Mulas and the normal route are less crowded.

Because of the Spanish crisis especially, there were 600 fewer people trekking and 300 fewer climbers compared to the previous year. From a total of 6298 visitors (85% non-Argentineans), 3498 tried the summit and 2800 went trekking. 33,000 persons went to Laguna Horcones in the park's entrance, and 80,000 went to the park below 3000m.

On 3 February, the Peruvian guide Holmes Pantoja Bayona broke Aconcagua's climbing record from Laguna Horcones (2850m) to the summit and back in 20 hours and 35 minutes (4112m in 13 hours). The previous

222. Top pitch of the Beltrame/Rodríguez route on the north face of Torre La Yaya, Tierra del Fuego. *(Mariano Rodríguez)*

record was that of well-known Willie Benegas in little more than 23 hours.

Rio Negro

Argentines Tomy Aguiló and Luciano Fiorenza ascended the c3500m mountain **Tronador** near Bariloche in the Argentine-Chilean South Andes, by a new route they named *Finito Sur* (550m, 80° mixed terrain, 5sup rock) in October 2010. They reached the highest peak, the Pico Internacional or Anón. On 2009 Fiorenza with Jorge Ackerman and José Bonacalza made a variant to reach the *Clausen (Normal) Route*, they named it *Jeneración Descartable* (300m, 85°).

Tierra del Fuego

The Argentine section of Tierra del Fuego has also very interesting mountains. One of these is a rock tower **Torre La Yaya**, located in the Valle (valley) Carabajal, some kilometres from Ushuaia, the world´s southernmost city. It can be accessed in a four-hour hike crossing the Río Olivia and the Lago Arco Iris. Despite being so near to a major city, it was unclimbed until 6 November 2009, when Sebastián Beltrame and Mariano Rodríguez climbed a 150m line on its north face rated 5+/6a, four rope lengths on mostly good rock. They descended a snow and ice couloir on its east face in three rappels.

New Zealand 2010-2011

This report covers developments in the New Zealand mountains from November 2010 to December 2011.

Darran Mountains

Summer 2010/11 activity included lots of the usual low elevation rock climbing, plus a few new routes 'up high' in the Darrans. Ben Dare and Guy McKinnon managed to climb a 'proper' alpine line on the south face of **Mt Tutoko** in November 2010. The grade V/3+ climb starts from the Age glacier and joins the upper section of the south-west ridge before avoiding the final headwall on the ridge by cutting out onto the west face before heading to the summit. On **Mt Talbot**, Dave Bolger and Rupert Gardiner climbed *Walking the Dog* in April. The route starts about 70m to the right of *Neal's Climb* and ascends impeccable coarse grey diorite for four pitches of grade 18 followed by a final pitch of fun grade 14. Daniel Joll, Rupert Gardiner and Erika Tovar established a new traditional route in ground-up style on the upper north face of **Mt Moir**. The aptly named *Old School* (5 pitches, grade 20) is situated in good company between the *Denz-Herron* and *Denz-Hudson* lines of the 70s. Dave Vass, Rich Turner and James Spears did a new route on the south-east face of **Karetai.** *More Drugs, More Threesomes* consists of six pitches straight up the middle of the face. Matteo Scoz and Carl Schiller found two new lines on the north-east buttress of **Sentinel**. *UraeU* is grade 15 and *New Born* is grade 13. Nick Cradock, Murray Ball and Dave Shotwell continued their work in gifting NZ climbers with moderate well-protected multi-pitch rock routes in the Darrans by bolting three 160-230m slab routes on the Shotwell Slabs in the upper Hollyford Valley.

The annual NZAC Darrans Winter Meet has been the focal point for winter climbers and climbing in Fiordland the past few years and 2011 was no exception. During the meet, in June, Steve Fortune and Bret Shandro made the first ascent of *Behavioural Therapy* on the right-hand end of the Psycopath Wall under the north face of **Mt Talbot**. Two new lines were climbed directly above the Homer Tunnel. *Night Vision* (Ant Morgan, Jimmy Harrison, Al Walker) is a 500m route up an open groove system in the middle of the face and *Tunnel Vision* (Reg Measures, Anthony Garvie, Tim Steward) takes a deep gully line.

Wakatipu

New route activity has continued at a cracking pace on the **Remarkables**, thanks mainly to Daniel Joll and his many and varied partners. Daniel and

223. Guy McKinnon on the summit slopes of Mt Tutoko, having just completed a new route on the south face with Ben Dare. *(Ben Dare)*

Rupert Gardiner climbed the nine-pitch *Thursday's Fool* (14/M4) on the south face of Single Cone in late May. Soon after that, Daniel climbed *Sunset on Single* (16/M6) with Erika Tovar and then *Double Ds* (16/M5) with Danny Murphy on the same face in early June. Continuing with his run of first ascent success, Daniel recruited Craig Jefferies later in the season to establish *Searching for Sumo* (M5), on the west face of Double Cone, and then adding Danny Murphy to the team, the trio climbed *Consolation Prize* (M6) on the same face. Toward the end of the winter season, Daniel and Danny climbed *Recessionary Downgrade* (M5) on the Telecom Tower, and then Daniel and Jamie Vinton-Boot established what is currently the most difficult traditional mixed line in the country. *Under Pressure* (M8) is also on the Telecom Tower and was climbed third try in the ground-up style by Daniel, followed immediately by Jamie.

224. Daniel Joll on the first ascent of *Under Pressure* (M8), West face of The Remarkables.
(Erika Tovar)

During the summer months Queenstown resident Stanley Costa was busy up the Dart Valley, putting in a number of new multi-pitch rock routes on Mount Chaos. The rock is apparently very good—similar to schist, but with more structural integrity.

The Remarkables also saw some summer activity. Ben Dare, Danny Murphy and Anna Ruotsi climbed the south-west spur of Single Cone for its first ascent. The route constituted seven pitches with a crux grade of 17. Ben then did a second new route in the area, this time on the south face of Single Cone with Andrew Finnigan, seven pitches again and with a crux one notch up at grade 18.

Aoraki Mt Cook and Westland

Three new routes have been established in Aoraki Mount Cook National Park in the past year. Just one new route was completed during the 2010/11 summer. Ben Dare and Mike Rowe found some untouched rock

225. Elke Braun-Elwert on the Hillary Ridge of Aoraki Mount Cook, having just completed a 13-pitch new ice and mixed line on the south face called Pounamu. *(Marty Schmidt)*

on the south face of **Malte Brun** in February, with a crux grade of 17. The 2011 winter new route tally was also just one. Steve Fortune and Greig Hamilton made the first ascent of the south face of **Mt Sibbald** from the Godley Valley in June.

In October 2011, Marty Schmidt and Elke Braun-Elwert climbed 13 pitches of new terrain on the south face of **Aoraki** which they then linked into the South/Hillary Ridge. They named their route *Pounamu* and it is grade MC5 (Mount Cook grade 5). Also in October, Jamie Vinton-Boot and Matt Thom added a direct start to the Central Gullies on the south face of Mt Hicks. *Generation Y* is graded MC6- and takes in seven pitches of previously unclimbed terrain.

Over to the west, Stuart Holloway and Felix Landman climbed *Path of Manolin* on the right side of the Abel Janszoon Face of **Mt Tasman** in January 2011. Also in January, Paul Hersey, Jamie Vinton-Boot, Shelley Hersey and Kester Brown climbed two new rock routes on the west side of **Mt Walter** and Daniel Joll, Erika Tovar and Rupert Gardiner climbed a new route on the west buttress of Mt Haast.

On to winter, and the Fox Neve saw two new routes, thanks to Jono Clarke and Jamie Vinton-Boot. *Technospectacle* (IV, AI5, M7) takes a line of most resistance on the west face of **Conway Peak** and is probably the most technically difficult route in the NZ mountains. They climbed *Supergroove* (III, AI4, M6) on the Marcel Face of **Mt Haast** shortly after. Jamie and Jono then recruited Thomas Adamson to establish a direct start to *Swimming with Sharks*, also on the Marcel Face.

Hopkins Valley and Ben Ohau Range

In January 2011, Jamie Vinton-Boot soloed the first ascent of the south-

226. Jamie Vinton-Boot on the first ascent of the west rib of Mt Walter, Westland National Park. *(Kester Brown)*

west face of **Mt Williams**, the hardest bit of which was grade 16. When winter arrived, Jamie with Paul Hersey climbed *Don't Drop the Chandelier* (M5, WI4) on the SW face of **Peak 2200m**, *Honey Badger* (WI3) on the west side of **Rabbiters Peak** and *White Strike* (WI3, M4) on the west side of the **Dasler Pinnacles**.

In Bush Stream, Jamie teamed up with Nick Hanafin to make the first ascent of *Deformed on Palpation* (WI4+), on the south face of **Mt Brown**. Ben Warrick and James Farrant also had a poke up Bush Stream, coming away with first ascent honours with their route *Cool Running* (WI4) in The Portal area.

Marlborough

David Manning, Kieran Parsons and Vaughan Snowdon climbed a new route on **Pinnacle** in March. The route was horrible – mossy, wet and hard to protect. The crux was grade 15 and it is called *Not for Rock Jocks*.

Ruapehu

Jono Clarke and Diane Drayton climbed a number of new mixed routes in the Mangaturuturu Cirque during the winter. Clarke climbed *Reach Exceeds Grasp* (M7), which is on the first wall seen when arriving in the valley, along with *Roadrunner* (M6/7) on the left end of the main wall. Drayton put up *Nervous Connections* (M5) on the same wall as *Reach Exceeds Grasp*. All routes are fully bolted.

Mount Everest Foundation Expedition Reports

SUMMARISED BY BILL RUTHVEN

The Mount Everest Foundation was set up as a registered charity following the ascent of Everest in 1953 and was initially financed from the surplus funds and subsequent royalties of that expedition. It is a continuing initiative between the Alpine Club and the Royal Geographical Society (with the Institute of British Geographers).

The foundation's prime object is the promotion of 'exploration' in mountain areas: this is mainly geographic, but also includes the application of other exploratory disciplines in these areas, such as geology, botany and zoology. It has now distributed well over £900,000 to almost 1600 British and New Zealand expeditions, mostly to ambitious young climbers.

In return for supporting an expedition, all that the MEF asks is a comprehensive report. Once received, copies are lodged in the Alpine Club Library, the Royal Geographical Society, the British Mountaineering Council and the Alan Rouse Memorial Collection in Sheffield Central Library. Donations to assist the work of the MEF are very welcome, so if you have previously benefited from MEF grants, why not include a bequest to the Foundation in your will?

2013 will see the 60th anniversary of the first ascent of Mount Everest, and plans are in hand to celebrate this milestone with a major event in the Royal Geographical Society on 29 May. See our website [www.mef.org.uk] for more information nearer to the date.

The following notes summarise reports from the expeditions supported during 2011, and are divided into geographical areas.

AMERICA – NORTH & CENTRAL

British Mount Hayes (USA) Guy Wilson with Chris Johnson and Neil Warren, April-May 2011.
This team hoped to make the first ascent of the west ridge of Mount Hayes (4216m), the highest peak in the remote Eastern Alaska Range. However, when they arrived in the area and discussed their plans with local climbers, they learned that although not generally reported, the ridge had actually been climbed in the 1970s. Apparently this situation is not atypical of the region, where a number of first ascents by local climbers have gone unreported, allowing subsequent parties the pleasure of making 'second first ascents'. The British team decided to stick with its plan but due to unseasonable snowfall was unsuccessful. Nevertheless, they climbed two neighbouring mountains, firstly Skarland (3145m), by its SE ridge – the

second ascent of the peak. Though not steep, it proved precarious due to poor snow. The trio had hoped to ski from the summit but at 2800m they met hard ice so left their skis at this point and climbed to the top. Their subsequent ski descent from 2800m was superb. With time running out Warren and Wilson turned their attention to Mount Geist (3268m) and in a 22-hour round trip made what was possibly the first ascent of a new direct route up the 1000m NE face, descending by the north ridge. The overall grade of the ascent was considered to be TD+.   MEF Ref 11/08

British Yukon (Canada) Glenn Wilks with Jonathon Wakefield, May-June 2011.
This two-man team was making a return visit to the Yukon with the hope of exploring and making first ascents of peaks of 3000m to 4000m close to the confluence of the Walsh and Denis glaciers. Unfortunately, they struck a period of extremely bad weather, making it impossible for the ski plane to land in the chosen area. They therefore relocated to a spur of the Stairway glacier that they had visited in 2009, in the hope that conditions would be more reasonable. Unfortunately they weren't and although they did manage to make the (probable) first ascent of Peak 3450m, they also spent several days confined to camp, before calling for early evacuation. MEF Ref 11/12

Glacier Bay Climbing (USA) Paul Knott with Vaughan Snowdon (NZ), April-May 2011.
Mount Orville (3199m) is a fine looking peak rising from the Johns Hopkins glacier, and although it was once climbed from the south, the climbers who made the ascent were killed while descending. This team hoped to make the first ascent of the NE spur-N ridge, which rises 2800m over a distance of 8km. They were dropped by ski-plane into deep powder snow at c1200m on the west shoulder of Mt Abbe (2667m), which gave them easy access to the 8 km ridge. On the fourth day of their attempt they reached a fore-summit at c2460m giving a fine view of the upper mountain, but from here the route appeared to be extremely serious – rocky on both sides, with a very exposed cornice-encrusted knife-edge arête. With a weather front approaching, they decided to call it a day, and reversed the terrain climbed so far. Later they attempted an unclimbed 2257m snow summit south of Mt Abbe, approaching from the NW and reaching a fore-peak at c2280m. Further progress would have entailed a steep drop off and the ascent of a steep couloir covered in unstable powder snow, so they elected to retreat, escaping the region by ski-plane just ahead of a forecast storm.
MEF Ref 11/20

Foraker/Lacuna (USA) Graham Zimmerman (NZ/US) with Mark Allen (US), May 2011.
This team planned an exploratory climbing trip in the Central Alaska Range. From the Kahiltna base camp, they skied 27km up the previously unexplored NW fork of the Lacuna glacier (south of Foraker) and

attempted an unclimbed top marked as Peak 12,213 (3723m), south of The Fin. Their first attempt was via its SE ridge, but after climbing c750m at up to M5 and AI2, they were forced to retreat due to storm conditions. After a return to Kahiltna and an ascent of the west ridge of Mt Hunter (4441m) they renewed their assault on Peak 12,213, this time via the south buttress, left of the previously attempted ridge. Here they were more successful, climbing the buttress and couloir above (M6 A1 AI2) to join the SE ridge about 1000m above its base. But once more bad weather forced a retreat. Their third attempt was via a more direct line up a couloir in the centre of the south face. With more amenable snow and ice conditions they reached their previous high point in just five hours continuing up a corniced crest to the summit, and regained their camp after a 20-hour round trip. They named the route *To the Center* (1370m, AI2 and cornices), and the summit 'Voyager Peak' after a NASA satellite.   MEF Ref 11/23

British Columbia (Canada) Adrian Dye with Neil Mackenzie, Aengus Mccullough and Kenneth Wright, August 2011.
Sittakanay Peak (2415m) was chosen as the objective of this team, as according to the Canadian Mountain Encyclopaedia it was unclimbed. It was felt that the most promising route would be via the SE ridge, although there are several other possibilities. Unfortunately, the Juneau region experienced the worst summer weather in years, with high winds and rainfall records for August being broken, resulting in widespread flooding. Although there was little chance to venture very high, the team managed to carry out a thorough reconnaissance of the area, taking plenty of digital images that should prove invaluable to future visitors.   MEF Ref 11/26

AMERICA – SOUTH

Cordillera Oriental (Peru) Matt Balmer with Dan Fitzgerald and James Wake, May-June 2011.
Although first climbed in 1957, Huaguruncho Chico (c5300m) apparently still awaits a second ascent; this team hoped to achieve that by completing a route on its south face previously attempted by Barton and Houseman in 2006. They reached approximately 5150m before being forced to retreat by poor weather and dangerous snow conditions. However the expedition did record some success, as during the acclimatisation phase they climbed a new route on the south face of Huarancayo Sur (c5200m). The route, which they have called *Boys Don't Cry* (350m, Scottish V, 4) gave them the second ascent of the peak, but was followed by an epic descent in thick cloud and failing light that forced an unplanned snow-hole bivouac 50m below the summit. MEF Ref 11/16

British Cordillera Carabaya (Peru) Tom Ripley with Hamish Dunn, August-September 2011.
The Cordillera Carabaya range in Southern Peru is remote and rarely

visited, offering a good opportunity for exploration and first ascents. Unfortunately, when this pair arrived at the nearest town they could find nobody who understood where they wanted to go. Eventually they met an English-speaking catholic priest who kindly drove them to the road-head and arranged two donkeys for the approach to base camp. Although they had planned to acclimatise on lower peaks before tackling their prime objective, after being snowed in for a few days they decided to 'get on with it' and set out to climb the 600m south face of Chichicapac, at 5614m the second highest summit in the range. The obvious line was threatened by séracs, so they climbed a direct route up the centre until forced left at the headwall. After 10 hours on the face they reached the summit in early evening and then made a rapid descent of the west ridge. Difficulties were sustained at Scottish IV/V, with two crux pitches of VI, and they gave the route an overall grade of TD. Although there are few unclimbed peaks in the area, the team felt that there were plenty of unclimbed technical routes awaiting first ascents.   MEF Ref 11/24

HIMALAYA – INDIA

Imperial College Raru Valley Jonathan Moodie with Jonathan Bull, Robin Jones, Kunal Masania, Joe Prinold, Virgil Scott and Dominic Southgate, August-September 2011.
The side valley of the Raru in the Zanskar region is little explored but reputed to have 35 unclimbed peaks between 5600m and 6300m. The team's first objective was Lama Jimsa Kangri, the summit of which (recorded at 6276m) was reached by two different routes. However they were disap-pointed to find a cairn and other evidence of a previous ascent, probably from the north. An attempt on an unnamed 5700m peak on the south side of the valley was abandoned at 5570m due to difficulties and fatigue. In all they attempted seven routes, (including three first ascents) and reached four summits. MEF Ref 11/28

HIMALAYA – NEPAL

British Far West Nepal 2011 Julian Freeman-Attwood with Nick Colton and Ed Douglas, April-May 2011.
The mountains of West Nepal are far less frequented than the rest of the country; during visits in 2007 and 2009, Freeman-Attwood made a number of first ascents that alerted him to the tremendous scope of the area for true exploration. On this third visit, to an unexplored valley in the Changla Himal (even further west), he hoped to make the first ascent of Gave Ding (6571m). There appeared to be two possible routes to the summit, either the west ridge to a fine rock spire, or the south ridge to the East Peak. They attempted the second of these, reaching 5900m before realising that the summit ridge was much longer than had previously been thought, giving them no chance of reaching the summit before nightfall. With the weather

increasingly threatening, an abseil retreat was undertaken. There followed a period of extensive snowfall, denying any further attempt.

MEF Ref 11/01

NZ Solu Khumbu Alpine-Style Ben Dare with Steven Fortune and Mike Rowe (March-May 2011)
The prime objective of this team was to climb new routes on the NE face of Kyajo Ri (6186m) and SW face of Kusum Kanguru (6367m), both designated as 'trekking peaks', and hence subject to reduced peak fees. Initially, they tried to climb Kyajo Ri via its SW ridge but they abandoned at 6000m due to poor snow conditions and injury to Dare, who was struck on the hand by falling ice. With Dare safely evacuated to base camp, the remaining pair then attempted the NE ridge, on which they reached 5700m before avalanche risk made further progress extremely hazardous. Moving to Kusum Kanguru, they found the SW face almost devoid of snow and ice, but a sustained snowfall soon changed that and in fact forced them to abandon their attempt due to the unseasonal weather and high level of avalanche activity. However, they did manage to climb a (probable new) route up the far left of the face to the NW ridge below the West Peak. This provided 1000m of slow mixed climbing up to an approximate grade of M5. In view of the snow conditions they did not attempt to continue up and over the West Peak to the Central summit. MEF Ref 11/09

British Kyashar Andy Houseman and Nick Bullock, April-May 2011.
Kyashar (6769m) – previously known as Peak 43 – lies above the village of Tangnag in the Hinku valley; its summit was first reached in 2003 via the west ridge and face. In 2010 Houseman attempted the 1800m south pillar with Tony Stone, reaching a snow ridge at 5700m (about the same point as two earlier Czech teams) where they abandoned the climb because Stone was suffering from altitude sickness. On this return trip the weather was unsettled, with so much snow that Houseman and Bullock did not even attempt the pillar but attempted a new route on the easier west ridge. They climbed a rock buttress at 5800m, however above that the climbing was 'sketchy' on very poor rock, so the attempt was ended at 6000m. This expedition received the Nick Estcourt Award for 2011. MEF Ref 11/11

British Mugu Mick Fowler with Graham Desroy, Jonny Ratcliffe and Dave Turnbull, October 2011 *(see account page 3)*.
The main objective of this strong team was an unclimbed peak in the province of Mugu in Far West Nepal, marked on maps as Mugu Chulu (6310m). Although the area had been previously visited by climbers from Spain and Japan, none of the 6000m summits had ever been reached. On arrival in the remote Kojichuwa valley below the mountain's west face, they discovered that the peak was known locally as 'Gojung'. Over a period of four days Fowler and Turnbull climbed the West Face (at a grade of ED) to the summit, taking another three days to traverse the frontier ridge over

Pt 6246m and descend by abseil and complex glacial terrain from the foot of the south ridge of Kojichuwa Chuli. Meanwhile Desroy and Ratcliffe made the (probable) first ascent of an unnamed 5800m peak on the Nepal/Tibet border to the west of the Kojichuwa La, which gave fine views of Tibet and Kojichuwa Chuli.   MEF Ref 11/19

Lunag Massif Steve Holmes with Neil Phillips plus Matt Welborn as base camp manager, September-November 2011.
The first ascent of Jobo Rinjang (6778m) by US climbers Gottlieb and Puryear in 2009 inspired these outdoor instructors to explore the Lunag mountain range further in the hope of making first ascents and traverses of other peaks in the area. Although part of the Khumbu region, the Lunag range is little visited, and hence still offers some unclimbed peaks. The team took eight days to reach base camp, and then spent a further five carrying out a reconnaissance of the unclimbed Lunag V (6550m). After being pinned down by a week of bad weather, they managed to reach 5400m on Lunag V. Holmes then achieved a solo ascent of the south pinnacle of Nangpa Goteya (5700m). This expedition also received a Mark Clifford Award.   MEF Ref 11/25

CHINA AND TIBET

Zhongdian (China): Hilary Greaves with Philip Rowsell and Mark Smith plus Timothy Bond in support, December 2010-January 2011.
The leader of this team of cave divers had visited the Zhongdian mountains of Yunnan on several previous occasions; this time it was hoped that by diving resurgences in the Yangtse valley they might be able to find a way into the large cave system which must exist. For once logistical arrangements went smoothly, and they were ready to dive within five days of leaving UK. All four resurgences were explored, but all were left at underwater limits of exploration. The most notable success was in Hei Shui Dong (Black Water Cave) in which they explored some 200m of new passage, including two sumps. Progress beyond a third sump was stopped due to lack of time and manpower, but no doubt a return trip is already being planned. [See also www.hongmeigui.net]   MEF Ref 11/06

British Eren Habirga (China) John Town with Iwonna Hudowska, Tadeusz Hudowski, Jerry Lovatt and Richard Wojtaszewski, August-September 2011.
The Eren Habirga and Borohoru mountains form a heavily glaciated part of the Tien Shan, and stretch about 480km from near Urumchi NW to the Kazakhstan border. The ranges contain more than 20 attractive peaks over 5000m and several hundred over 4000m, only one of which is known to have been climbed. The leader had made a reconnaissance of the eastern area in 2010; returning, he set up a base camp at Ak-Tash, hoping this would give access to about 10 unclimbed peaks with a wide range of diffi-

culty. Unfortunately, the weather 'put on a mercurial performance of bewildering variations in visibility and temperature' and although several peaks were attempted, no summits were reached. Note: Iwonna Hudowska was awarded the Alison Chadwick Memorial Grant for 2011. MEF Ref 11/27

CENTRAL ASIA

Sarychat/Fersmana (Kyrgyzstan) Gareth Mottram with Charlie Evans, Edward Lemon and Hannes Granberg (Sweden), July-August 2011.
This was a follow-up to an expedition in 2009 (MEF Ref 09/27) which was dropped off 25km short of the intended spot in the central Western Kokshaal-too and thus lost valuable time (and weather) ferrying gear, subsequently only managing two days climbing in a month. Not put off, the team returned in 2011 determined to explore and make some first ascents. Their principal objective was a fine snow pyramid, Fersmana III (5210m) at the head of the Sarychat glacier. After acclimatising with an attempt on Sentinel Peak via a gully on the east flank of Pik Lyell (4864m), they split into two pairs to follow different lines on Fersmana III. Granberg and Mottram climbed a continuous icy ramp to the main ridge, while Evans and Lemon hugged the rock further right. Both routes then crossed the final rock band on the summit ridge by mixed chimneys at AI4 and M5. Both pairs then followed the same line up the final 300m, snow steepening to 55/60°, passing the summit sérac on the left, and descended their lines, regaining camp 28 hours after setting out. Both routes were c1200m in length and provisionally graded ED1 due to high altitude technical difficulties with significant risk of avalanche and rockfall. They decided to rename the peak Eggmendülüük, a Kyrkyz word meaning Independence. Granberg and Mottram later climbed scree gullies and a ridge in poor condition to reach two adjacent tops above base camp – Pik 4631m and Pik 4685m, which they named Pik Georgina and Pik Annika respectively.
MEF Ref 11/14

Kyrgyz Djangart (Kyrgyzstan) Richard Tremellen with Alex Brighton, July-August 2011.
The Djangart area is a sub-range of the Tien Shan in Kyrgyzstan, midway between the Inylchek glacier and the Western Kokshaal-too, and has a number of unclimbed peaks c5000m. The pair hoped to climb a number of these, including the highest, Pt 5318m. Their plan to hire mules to carry gear over the 4200m Djangart pass did not work out, so they established a base camp in the Kaichi valley, considerably increasing the length and complexity of walk-ins to their chosen peaks. An attempt on Peak 5318m was abandoned at 4750m due to avalanche conditions, however the pair succeeded in making the first ascents of Pt 4765m (1200m AD) and Pt 4950m (*The Phoenix*, 1200m, AD), for which they have proposed the names Peak Emma & Peak Laetitia respectively. MEF Ref 11/17

Tajikistan and Afghanistan First Ascents Becky Coles with James Kitson (also Mark Redhead in Tajikistan only), July-September 2011.
Strictly speaking this was two expeditions running back to back. The first part was in Tajikistan, where it was hoped to make the first ascent of the last unclimbed 6000m peak in the little visited Muzkol range of the SE Pamirs. Unfortunately high winds delayed the team's summit attempt, and then snow conditions prevented them getting above a col at 5500m. Although some bad weather was experienced in Afghanistan, conditions soon improved, and Coles and Kitson were able to achieve their aim of exploring the Raig Jurm valley in the Wakhan Corridor, including reaching a 5730m summit on the border with Pakistan. They assumed that this was a first ascent and named it 'Raven Peak', however subsequent investigations suggest that the peak was climbed in 1972 by an Italian team who named it Koh-e-Sauze. MEF Ref 11/18

Aberystwyth University Kamchatka (Russia) Colin Souness and Henry Patton, August-September 2011.
The Kamchatka Peninsula in far eastern Russia boasts 160 volcanoes, of which 29 are still active. Photographs of an ash-covered glacier near to one of these – Klyuchevskaya Sopka (4721m) – show an incredible similarity to high resolution satellite photographs of the surface of Mars, tempting these two post-graduate glaciology students to undertake a study of surface structures and morphology, in the hope that it would lead to a better understanding of conditions on Mars. Valuable observations were made of the unique glaciers, leaving them sufficient time to climb Avachinsky Sopka (2741m) and Ushkovsky (3954m). They were unable to climb Klyuchevskaya Sopka due to the danger of rockfall following a recent eruption. While in the area they met and worked with a group of Russian geoscientists from the Russian Academy of Sciences (Moscow). MEF Ref 11/21

NZ Women's Wakhan Corridor (Afghanistan) Pat Deavoll with Christine Byrch, July-August 2011 *(see account page 16)*.
Koh-e-Baba-Tangi (aka Jade Peak, 6516m) is the highest point in the eastern sector of the Afghan Hindu Kush, and was first climbed in 1963 by an Italian team via its west ridge: all subsequent attempts have failed to reach the summit. In his guidebook *Peaks of Silver and Jade* (2007) Carlo Pinelli comments that the NW ridge 'seems to be particularly attractive... a varied and hard route but probably not too dangerous, alternating sections of rock, mixed and ice'. This was therefore the route chosen by the two New Zealand sisters. Difficult terrain around base camp meant that attempts to acclimatise were limited to spending a couple of nights at a col c5200m. Once on the route itself, Deavoll led the steeper pitches with the less experienced Byrch following, sometimes using jumars. Camps were established at 5000m and 6000m and they reached the summit on the fifth day. To give a more aesthetic end to the climb, they decided to traverse the

mountain and descend by its west ridge where they were surprised to find traces of the first ascent nearly half a century ago.   MEF Ref 11/22

FAR EAST

Shan Plateau (Myanmar) Imogen Furlong with Chris Densham, Fleur Loveridge, Philip Rowsell and Pete Talling (all UK) plus Joerg Dreybodt (Germany) January-February 2011.
Although much of Myanmar (formerly Burma) is closed to foreigners, this party of cavers managed to obtain permission for a return visit to the Hopong region (east of Taungyi) not only from the local authorities but also from the local monasteries. On a reconnaissance trip in 2010 they found 25 cave entrances and explored 10, surveying 3.5 km of passage. On this trip they logged 37 new entrances, and explored 11 (nine in the Hopong area and two in Kutcai) mapping a total of 4.78km of passage. However, there is still plenty of scope for future visits.   MEF Ref 11/05

Mulu Caves (Malaysia) Tim Allen with Jane Allen, Sam Allshorn, Mark Brown, Kevin Dixon, Andy Eavis, Pete Hall, Matt Kirby, Ian Lawton, Liz Lawton, Dr Gina Moseley, John Palmer, Mark Richardson, Robbie Shone, Meg Stark, Hugh St Lawrence, Richard Walters and Mark Wright, February-March 2011.
Despite 18 previous 'Mulu Caves' expeditions to the Gunnung Mulu National Park in Sarawak, apparently there still remains plenty of work to explore and map the extensive cave system. With the advantage of new technology, this team undertook some ambitious technical objectives, including a 3D laser scan and panoramic photography in the enormous Sarawak Chamber, plus radio location and exploration of new passages. All the major objectives were achieved, and although full analysis of the results will take some time, the team surveyed more than 15 km of 'new' passage of which about 13 km were in Whiterock Cave. Total lengths are now Whiterock 80.4 km and Clearwater 189.1 km, making the latter the world's eighth longest system.   MEF Ref 11/04

CORRECTION

In the MEF notes in the 2010/11 *Alpine Journal* (vol 115, 322), against the entry for the British Apolobamba Expedition, (MEF Ref 09/30), I stated: 'They also attempted routes on the north face of Canisaya and on the SW face of Charquini, but failed on both.' It is now understood that Griffin and Wyatt made a successful traverse of Canisaya (5706m) climbing up the NW face and descending the WNW ridge. Although most of the route was around PD, they felt that a 100m section through séracs at the top of the face was AD+. I would like to express my sincere apologies to Messrs Griffin and Wyatt for the error, and congratulate them on their success.

Reviews

234. John Fairley, *Finsteraarhorn*, watercolour, 177x253mm, 2004

Reviews

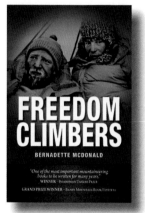

Freedom Climbers
Bernadette McDonald
First issued by Rocky Mountain Books, 2011.
Issued in the UK by Vertebrate Publishing, 2012,
pp 256, £12.99

Polish photographer David Seymour (born David Szymin) apparently once remarked that in great photography '...all you need is a little bit of luck, and enough muscle to click the shutter'. He was being modest, for clicking the shutter in the way that Seymour and his contemporaries did took considerable strength and vision. There are similarities between the making of a photograph and the writing of history or biography. At their most effective and aesthetic, the photographer and the writer seek not only to collect facts and display them, but they also strive to give shape and meaning to an image or a story in a way that puts them at the very core of the thing being described. Simply 'seeing' something is not the same as photographing it; likewise, dry chronology and recitation of facts do not make for good history or biographical writing. To succeed demands *real* muscle.

It takes the reader only a few pages to realise that *Freedom Climbers*, the latest book by acclaimed Canadian mountain writer Bernadette McDonald has what it takes. *Freedom Climbers* is the ambitious and sweeping history of post-WWII Polish Himalayan alpinism, one that contains factual information and pulls it together into a great story. That it won both the Grand Prize at the 2011 Banff Mountain Book Festival and the 2011 Boardman Tasker Prize is in itself sufficient endorsement. A meaningful, must-read book, it follows the key members of a driven tribe of alpinists who occupied the forefront of a renaissance in climbing as they struggled and succeeded in pioneering routes on the world's highest peaks in bold style. A good many of them lost their lives in the process, in the service of their dreams, their ambition, their search for a liberation from the oppression and limitations of their own country – and at times of themselves.

Simultaneously describing and capturing the zeitgeist of those days is not an easy task. As Churchill said: 'History with its flickering lamp stumbles along the trail of the past, trying to reconstruct its scenes, to revive its echoes, and kindle with pale gleams the passion of former days.' This was McDonald's challenge, the seeds of a complex tale which were first sown through her personal exposure to several of *Freedom Climbers* main characters during her years in the world of mountain culture and film/book festivals. One single event also served as principal catalyst, a festival gathering and after-party in Katowice. There she listened as the remaining members of that tribe reminisced and told their stories, many of which were unknown in the West. McDonald felt as though she was witness to the end of an era; a golden age had passed.

Any good drama, real or fiction, has a cast of lead and supporting characters. *Freedom Climbers* is no different. McDonald intentionally devotes most of her attention and spotlight to arguably the three most significant Polish climbers: Wanda Rutkiewicz, Jerzy Kukuczka, and Voytek Kurtyka. This is not just because they were among the most famous and accomplished, but also because of the contrasts and commonalities they represent, and how their individual stories also serve in telling the broader story of the community as a whole. And so in each life story, and throughout the book, McDonald subtly and effectively layers the themes of suffering, faith, pride and ingenuity that have defined the Polish nation and its people for hundreds of years.

Rutkiewicz, Kukuczka, and Kurtyka all describe the freedom they realised upon first discovering climbing. This is not uncommon for all of us, but set against the oppressive government system of the Iron Curtain and the slow recovery from WWII, it must have felt like revelation. Brilliant expedition organizers like Andrzej Zawada would come to play a critical role in recruiting talent, building national pride and recognition (which kept the state happy), and enabling the dreams of many climbers. Unlike in many Western countries, climbing in Poland was not some counter-culture escape; the state had successfully crushed most aspects of normal self-actualisation, and often wasn't even providing the basics, so the communal and structured climbing system in Poland became *the* place of social connection and fulfilment – something quite absent in a lot of other areas of Polish life at that time.

How this plays out with each character in McDonald's book makes for interesting reading and reflection. In Rutkiewicz, we have a life shaped by tragedy in the death of her brother while playing with a grenade in the rubble following WWII, and her father's brutal murder when she was a young woman. A study in contrasts, McDonald shows the duality of Rutkiewicz's simultaneous desire for love and acceptance, and in the same moment, desire to compete with and alienate many who tried to get close. She is a person who seems lost in life, everywhere except the fleeting moments on the heights. Her story is in some ways the loneliest, a national hero who was one of the best female alpinists in history, a dreamer whose search finally ended with her death on Kangchenjunga in 1992.

Kukuzcka's determination and hard work were legendary in a culture where such qualities were already in abundance. He applied these traditional values to the problems at hand – whether negotiating contracts for chimney painting as a means of income for club expeditions, dealing with the setbacks of the deaths of partners, or pushing past altitude illness and severe cold. One of the most impressive Himalayan climbers the world has ever known, Kukuzcka was the second man to climb all 14 eight-thousand metre peaks, most by difficult new routes and several in winter. McDonald shows that if Rutkiewicz's faith was that of independence and acceptance, where many didn't know what to expect of her, Kukuzcka's was a faith of dogged determination and adaptability. When adaptability didn't work, all-out suffering often did. Sadly, the continuous exposure to hard, high climbing caught up with him when a rope broke high on the south face of Lhotse in 1989.

Kurtyka would follow a different path than others. Elite, intuitive, and artistic, he would come to define his freedom not just by slipping past the Iron Curtain to pursue his climbs, but by the style and aesthetic qualities of the experiences he had. One of the principle architects of the Himalayan alpine-style movement, his bold ascents included the east face of Dhaulagiri, Shining Wall on Gasherbrum IV, Broad Peak traverse, the east face of Trango Tower, and many others. He's also known for the chances he didn't take, his cautionary sixth sense. The style and attitude of these climbs, including the specific nature of their partnerships (often with iconoclastic Western climbers such as Alex MacIntyre) defined the alpinist's art in their purity of line and rejection of large bureaucratic expeditions. McDonald shows how Kurtyka saw that the desire to climb at all costs contained a trap that could constrain. Ever the intellectual, he took freedom to another level, and is still alive today.

Freedom Climbers is a magnificent book. As Henri Cartier-Bresson did when he 'craved to seize the whole essence' in a single picture, Bernadette McDonald has managed likewise to trip the writer's shutter at the decisive moment when fact and art intersect, thus giving events their 'proper expression' as the master photographer would say. And ultimately as we witness the lightning that was the golden age of Polish Himalayan alpinism, we see a little bit of ourselves, our own motivations, and the freedom we all seek in the mountains.

Jon Popowich

Wind From a Distant Summit
Pat Deavoll
2011, Craig Potton Publishing (NZ), 2011, pp 264, NZ$39.99

Climbing difficult first ascents in the greater ranges, in alpine style, is generally considered the most committing and demanding form of mountaineering.

Those involved in this high-risk pursuit form a small elite, made up of mostly men. This makes Pat Deavoll's slick and candid memoir unique. Here is a book, not about Everest or being a celebrity, but a quiet, true climber's quest to pioneer new territory, told from a female perspective.

However, perhaps more impressive than her many difficult ascents, and

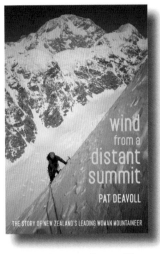

wind
from a
distant
summit

PAT DEAVOLL

THE STORY OF NEW ZEALAND'S LEADING WOMAN MOUNTAINEER

her flair as a writer, is this woman's courage in her battle with depression and her willingness to share these dark experiences with the reader. To tackle the peaks that she does is a huge test of self-belief, but considering her issues around lack of self worth, they seem all the more impressive. Clearly, the respect she gains from the wider climbing community, particularly in New Zealand, is of huge importance, so much so that during her Karim Sar expedition of 2009 (*AJ* 115, 3-10*)* she is terrified of returning home with no summit.

Learning to climb in the New Zealand Alps, Deavoll develops resourcefulness and resilience. It is a world apart from much of today's western European Alps. On many of the adventures she recounts, she and her partner are often completely alone, the approaches long, the rock not always perfect, and the weather prone to quickly turning vicious. Certainly, the wildness and the solitude of her native mountains are perfect preparation for future expeditions to Pakistan, China and India.

Deavoll clearly enjoys all disciplines of climbing and has dedicated more than 30 years to perfecting her art. This leads to what she describes as one of the 'happiest days of my life' after climbing *Deprivation* on the Moonflower Buttress of Mount Hunter, Alaska, with Marty Bear in 45 hours non-stop. Any route on this steep, 1500m wall – known as the 'El Cap of ice and mixed climbing' – has become a holy grail among top alpinists. To climb this route so quickly is simply world class.

Climbing in alpine-style and attempting unclimbed routes sometimes brings failure, but for Deavoll, following her ideals has been worth it. 'It's the journey and the trying that matter: the heart that goes into the attempt rather than the summit,' she says.

Deavoll is open about other darkness too; the impact of losing her friend Karen McNeill in Alaska; an artificial knee, the breakdown of personal relationships. She also weaves in fascinating ideas from the psychology of risk in an attempt to explain why some people are drawn to such a high-stakes game.

This prose is packed with drama – the narrow escapes, the storms, tension among partners – but it also contains wonderful contemplative descriptions of the natural world she travels through. By the end of the book Deavoll has learned to cope with depression. The self-esteem from other top climbers respecting her climbing achievements contributes to this, along with the self-recognition that for her, peace and serenity are gained from being in high places. It is a fine book.

Andy Cave

Fiva: An Adventure That Went Wrong
Gordon Stainforth
Golden Arrow Books, 2012, pp224, £9.95

'So you had an epic then?' The question, delivered in a flat Lancastrian accent to the Stainforth twins, must have seemed a statement of
the obvious taken to absurdity. The tattered pair
were two days late back at camp, they'd hardly
eaten in that time, had fallen hundreds of feet,
been hopelessly lost, Gordon had smashed his
left knee – it looked, he says, like a Jackson
Pollack abstract done on the side of a beach
ball, and worse still, it was turning gangrenous
and starting to smell. Yes, this is the story of an epic. A more pertinent
question would have been, 'Why aren't you dead?'

Fiva (pronounced 'fever') is the name of a 6,000-foot route on Store
Trolltind in the Romsdal region of Norway. Stainforth's subtitle, *An Adventure That Went Wrong*, speaks for itself; it also carries the flavour of laconic
self-mockery that makes this book such a delight. The boys' plight – they
were just teenagers at the time – was dire, yet in retelling it Stainforth
cannot resist drollery. His attitude to life (and death) epitomises that quip
about the difference between Americans and the English: to Americans life
is serious but not hopeless; to the English life is hopeless but not serious.

The Stainforths are as English as they come, two former public school-
boys from Knebworth in Hertfordshire; and, back in 1969, they were
wonderfully naïve: 'We've climbed a couple of quite big mountains in
the Alps with guides, and we've done dozens of rock climbs (last year) in
North Wales and now we're going to tackle the biggest rock wall in Europe
– *OK?*'

It's not a novel and both Stainforths are still alive and climbing so we
know the book has a happy ending. However it unfolds as such a gripper
that it would be churlish to go into detail over the plot.

Epics, of course, are standard fare of mountaineering narratives; what
elevates *Fiva* is the manner of Gordon Stainforth's telling of it. As with his
superb photographic books – notably *The Cuillin* and *The Peak* – there is a
sense of much careful forethought as to character of the final product. He
didn't just sit down and trot out an account, dramatic though it would have
been. The book is written in the first person present tense, a bold move that
has been skilfully carried off, and employs a smaller type size for the voice
of his brother John when distant at the far end of the rope. Echoes from the
cliffs and voices in Gordon's head, spaced out with exhaustion, pain and
hunger, are also cleverly conveyed.

For those of us of a similar age (the twins were born in 1949) there is also
a good deal of gear nostalgia, Norwegian sweaters, Millarmitts, MOAC
wedges and so on. Most glorious of all though is Stainforth's evocation of

the late 1960s through his zany use of song lines and titles. Looking over an abyss he turns a whiter shade of pale, without quote marks, which adds to the fun; Louis Armstrong, Del Shannon, the Beatles and more are drawn in. Gordon could be scripting a climbing version of *The Singing Detective*.

Fiva should, as publicists like to say, appeal to climber and non-climber alike. If there were any justice in the publishing world it would be a best seller, eclipsing '*the Void*'. But I can hear a doleful Gordon Stainforth adding, 'there isn't'. If so he'll have to settle for the accolade of 'a future cult classic'.

Stephen Goodwin

Triumph and Tragedy
The Life of Edward Whymper
Emil Henry
Matador 2011, pp460, £17.99

Shadow of The Matterhorn
The Life of Edward Whymper
Ian Smith
Carreg Ltd 2011, pp 336, £25

Whymper's Scrambles With a Camera
A Victorian Magic Lantern Show
Peter Berg
Alpine Club 2011, pp148, £16.00

The multi-faceted life of Edward Whymper has only been the subject of one serious biography in the English language, namely that by Frank Smythe, published as long ago as 1940 and never reprinted. Coinciding with the centenary of Whymper's death, two attempts to repair the situation arrived during 2011 and both have added usefully to Smythe's work. However, though they may have had similar aspirations, the two resulting works are very different.

Emil Henry is essentially both a non-mountaineer and a non-historian, though part of the stimulus to his interest in Whymper was a guided ascent of the Matterhorn back in 1984. In fulfilling what is clearly something of a passion for him, he has produced a successful historical biography here, albeit at the 'popular' end of the spectrum. Not that there is anything wrong with that: bringing Whymper's life to the attention of the modern generation in such a thoroughly engaging and well-written way is certainly no bad thing. However, his relative lack of contact with mountaineering history and European history more generally has produced a book that would have benefited from a level of editorial input that was apparently not forthcoming.

To concentrate on the errors in the book to the detriment of its good side would be unfair. However, a couple of examples will perhaps help to encourage readers to do their own research if they have doubts at any point:

p xv Rather than the 14 cited, more than 30 peaks over 4000m were first climbed in the Golden Age and the Primus, far from being available for mountain bivouacs in this period, was not invented until 1892.

p 65 Mont Pelvoux is not the highest peak in the Dauphiné. Mr Henry himself correctly identifies it as the Pointe des Ecrins on page 126.

p 84 Val Tournanche was at one time in Savoy (Savoie refers to the French part of the region) but was only part of France from 1792 to 1815. Austria did not rule this area at the time of Carrel's birth (1829). It did control Lombardy, but Val Tournanche was not part of Lombardy. The 'King' (sic) of Sardinia was not in any sense self-appointed.

p 257 Mummery was not 'Alfred' and Haskett Smith, not Mummery, is generally regarded as the father of rock climbing.

On the plus side, Mr Henry has done much to improve the somewhat dismissive treatment given by Smythe to the last 10 years or so of Whymper's life, which included his marriage, the birth of his daughter, his divorce and no less than six trips to Canada, as well as his lonely death in Chamonix. As compared to some of the earlier ones, the final two chapters are notable for the limited references to Smythe and they are all the better for that, though one has to say that even when re-presenting Smythe, Mr Henry does it with his usual pace and style.

In general production terms the book looks good, though some of the illustrations could have done more justice to Whymper's wonderful originals. The author has rightly included maps of the key areas, as aids to orientation for the lay reader. However, they should either have been rendered in more legible form or replaced by modern maps.

All in all, with the caveat noted above, this is a very enjoyable, non-specialist account of Whymper's life. However, the more demanding reader will have to turn elsewhere for a more reliable work.

In contrast to the life of Whymper reviewed above, Ian Smith has provided a biography that takes us some way beyond Smythe and stands as a worthy tribute to the memory of the great, if flawed, man 100 years after his death in Chamonix in 1911.

Although of course not of itself any kind of quality assurance, the sheer comprehensiveness of references (more than 1000) and bibliography (more than 300) is extremely impressive. More impressive still is the fact that Mr Smith's researches have not only covered the more obvious sources, such as the ACL, BL, NLS, RGS and the Scott Polar Research Institute, but have also uncovered relevant material in such diverse places as Leeds, Zurich, St Andrews University, the Bodleian and the Greenland National Museum in Nuuk. If for no other reason, we are in Mr Smith's debt for

guises. The preface makes clear Rupert had not planned to write this book at this time. Yet diary entries over nearly four decades and impressive archived photographs document his mountaineering experiences with a menagerie of AC, ASC and Eagle Ski Club companions in meticulous detail, allowing us to share the range and scope of his development as climber and ski-tourer.

Six months prior to the publication of this book, Rupert was diagnosed with terminal pancreatic cancer. He was just 55 *(obituary p418)*. There is a wide range of reaction to such shattering news. Entirely in character, Rupert's response was to devote his remarkable energies to writing his mountain autobiography to share with as wide an audience as possible. His journey is perhaps classic, from reading mountain adventure books as a boy, through adolescent exploration of local landscapes, to growing confidence in his abilities on rock and ice faces, extensive ski-touring and climbing around the world and latterly Munro'ing closer to home.

Embedded in accounts of his day job as a seismic geologist across four continents, the acquisition of mountain skills and the development of lasting friendships, the book charts Rupert's love affair with all things pertaining to the mountain. It is a remarkable itinerary with chapters devoted to most areas of Britain and the Alps, as well as Arctic Norway, Greece, the Pyrenees and the first British ski traverse of the Corsican High Level Route in 1994. Additional exploits include climbs in South Africa, the Karakoram, Indonesia and Japan, and ski-tours in Iran, New Zealand and Greenland. Each experience is illustrated by accomplished photography with vivid descriptions of challenges and triumphs, occasions of failure to achieve objectives and the often damp, uncomfortable realities, but always rescued by awe-inspiring scenery and the many natural wonders encountered. The book's sense of purpose to inspire others to connect with mountains by mapping his own relationship with high places is delivered with honesty and fervour, and often enhanced with dry humour. The contemporaneous diary and reflections with added geological, historical and architectural detail further enrich the book and make it appealing to all. The chapters set in the Scottish hills and in the Alps are typical, seemingly capturing each strenuous but gleeful step, with vibrant succinct observations to create scenarios easily appreciated by those who have been there, as well as those who have yet to venture beyond the ski lifts or even the armchair.

Despite Rupert's renowned enthusiasm to get 'onward and upward', almost bouncing from the page at times; his deep curiosity and ability to reflect on and evoke his surroundings, whether wonder at a rock formation, its texture and smell, snow crystal subtype, rare alpine flower or length-ening shadows, enables the reader to join his many companions in reliving, with vivid immediacy, times shared in the hills. The decision on an early Alps trip, that 'the others had different objectives' so he would continue alone, provides insight into his 'own man' approach. At times self effacing, at others increasingly aware of his own impatience and well able to 'say it as it is', particularly if he felt slowed down or worse if there was 'faffing' with kit, Rupert demonstrates an infectious enthusiasm which friends and companions came to expect and enjoy. It was not all plain sailing and we are gripped during his 1984 Greenland expedition by his epic return to camp in very cold blizzard conditions whilst helping his frostbitten companion. The book also describes the development of many lifetime friends, including his evolving relationship with Jay, culminating in their marriage and enduring partnership when climbing and touring together.

There is poignancy to Rupert's focus on his earlier mountaineering accomplishments as being 'most memorable' and they are the most thoroughly detailed. Nicely paced with unpretentious and relaxed style, the book has a sense of gathering momentum with greater brevity in the descriptions of trips towards the end of the book, perhaps suggesting Rupert's determination to complete his story. His candid approach to communication, relationships, and both flatland and mountain life, are particularly evident in his moving epilogue, where he reflects on spirituality and meaning, while struggling with the certainties inherent in conventional beliefs. That he chose to channel the last of his energies into documenting his experiences is what is most uplifting and moving about this book, particularly for those of us privileged to have joined Rupert at altitude on one or more occasions.

Rupert writes of the Dolomite hotelier remarking that he and Jay have 'returned much richer through experience' from their trip and this can also be said of the experience of reading Rupert's account of his life and times in the hills.

Rodney Franklin

The Challenge of K2: A History of the Savage Mountain
Richard Sale
Pen & Sword Discovery, 2011, 256pp, £19.99

An extraordinary number of books have recently appeared on the subject of K2, but the phenomenally well-read Richard Sale has possibly produced the best-researched history to date with *The Challenge of K2*. The last comprehensive biography of the world's second highest is now more than 15 years old, and in the intervening time there have been significant incidents both on and off the mountain, the latter best exemplified by formal acceptance of Walter Bonatti's version of events on the first ascent in 1954.

Previous omissions have come to light and no stone seems left unturned. For example, take the fascinating story of Italian Roberto Lerco, who in 1890, two years before Conway's expedition to the mountain, may well have climbed the Abruzzi Spur as far as House's Chimney, though was far too modest to speak about 'such a humble attempt'. Details of his Baltoro journey have been pieced together from letters to a German friend, which are now housed in the National Library of Israel.

The book continues from those early escapades, with prodigious detail through the years, to the claimed ascent by Christian Stangl in 2010. Then there are pages of the inevitable K2 statistics; all ascents, deaths and comparisons with other 8000ers etc. More than 30 pages of comprehensive notes, forming part of the appendix, are interesting reading in their own right. The text has an academic feel, but for those interested in a comprehensive history to (almost) the present day, *The Challenge of K2* is indispensable.

Lindsay Griffin

Prelude to Everest
Ian R Mitchell & George W Rodway
Luath Press, 2011, pp285, £20

This timely collaboration between a mountaineer with a grasp of neglected history and a scientist with a keenness for climbing deserves to re-establish Alexander Kellas, the Scottish scientist and Himalayan pioneer, among the great high altitude mountaineers. *Prelude to Everest* by Ian Mitchell and George Rodway lifts Kellas out of obscurity and puts his achievements into proper focus. It is a memorial to an exceptional mountaineer.

Kellas died in 1921 while taking part in the first reconnaissance expedition to Everest after at least 10 first ascents in Sikkim and the Garwhal and adding significantly to the sum of knowledge surrounding the effects of high altitude on human performance. He emerges from this biography as a solitary, unheroic individual, unsung and overshadowed by his contemporaries but who, as a climber aged 40 and despite poor health, discovered a natural ability and obsession for high altitude mountaineering.

Kellas was born in Aberdeen in 1868 and attended Heriot Watt College, Edinburgh, before graduating in chemistry at University College, London, where a study of inert gases saw him measuring the argon contained in peas and mice. A shy young man, he was already contemplating the possibility that he would not emerge among the front ranks of scientific research. But an early love of the Scottish mountain country made him a strong and determined Munro bagger, extending his expeditions from the Cairngorms to the Alps where, in 1905, he climbed Mont Blanc with his brother, Henry.

A series of visits to Sikkim followed; small, lightweight expeditions with only the local Sherpas for company. He dismissed the idea of employing alpine guides in the Himalaya where, he believed, they would probably be useless. On Pauhunri (7125m) he unwittingly broke the world summit altitude record and produced an academic paper entitled 'A consideration of the possibility of ascending the loftier Himalayas'. Unlike such contemporaries as Mummery, Collie, Younghusband and Longstaff, Kellas left no detailed accounts of his adventures but he was probably the first climber to provide scientific evidence of the positive effects of using supplementary oxygen at high altitude, thereby opening the way to Everest.

The authors trace Kellas's mountaineering and scientific life in a comprehensive and well-researched way. George Mallory's first impression of him was unheroic but affectionate. 'Kellas I love already,' he wrote to his wife. 'He is beyond description Scotch and uncouth in his speech... He is very slight in build, short, thin, stooping and narrow-chested, his head made grotesque by veritable gig-lamps of spectacles and a long, pointed moustache. He is an absolutely devoted and disinterested person.'

John Noel, the expedition photographer, paid fulsome tribute to Kellas as 'a pioneer in every sense' who with the help of the Sherpa people conquered virgin peaks one after another with an ease and rapidity that astonished the world. 'He would emerge each year from his chemical research work at the hospital. He did not tell the newspapers when he set out to climb a mountain higher than any climber had ever tackled before. He just went unobserved...'

Kellas was a natural choice for inclusion into the 1921 Everest reconnaissance although he was strongly opposed by Percy Farrar, president of the Alpine Club, who had earlier criticised the Scotsman's climbing abilities, insisting, 'Kellas has never climbed a mountain, but has only walked about in deep snow with a lot of coolies, and the only time they got on a very steep place they all tumbled down and ought to have been killed.'

Although Kellas wrote very little about his expeditions, he did create an impressive photographic record as his ambitions to climb even higher summits progressed. Three times he explored the possibility of a route up Kamet (7756m) in the Garhwal, frustrated when the delivery of oxygen cylinders intended for the climb was delayed after they were classified as explosives. As Kellas became more obsessed by the prospect of Everest, physical illness was added to a fragile mental state; he suffered from aural hallucinations and was already exhausted when he began the long trek to the mountain. Mallory wrote that he died 'without one of us anywhere near him' after insisting that everyone should go ahead. Two summits were named after him and one, Kellas Rock Peak (7071m), a near neighbour of Everest, still bears his name.

Ian Mitchell, an award-winning mountaineering author long aware of the historical importance of Alexander Kellas, and George Rodway, an active mountaineer and Honorary Research Fellow at University College London's Centre for Altitude, Space and Environment Medicine, have combined to produce a fascinating and important account of Kellas's life with a 60-page appendix covering his work on high altitude physiology. Kellas concluded that Mount Everest could be ascended by a man of excellent physical and mental constitution in first rate training, without 'adventitious aids'. Some 58 years later, Reinhold Messner and Peter Habeler proved him right.

Ronald Faux

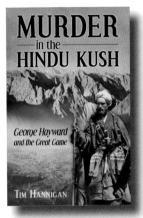

Murder in the Hindu Kush: George Hayward and the Great Game
Tim Hannigan
The History Press, 2011, pp254, £18.99

What a pity Richard Sale didn't have the benefit of this fascinating book when he was writing *The Challenge of K2*, reviewed in this same *AJ*. Lindsay Griffin describes *The Challenge* as 'possibly' the best-researched book on K2, but it seems that when researching the early exploration of the savage mountain, Sale either did not look in quite the same places as Tim Hannigan or did not rate what he found there. Perhaps the two authors should confer.

Sale credits Francis Younghusband with the being 'the first European known to have seen K2 from the north', on his extraordinary 1887 journey from Peking to Srinagar via Kashgar and Yarkand. However, to be fair, Sale is far from categorical about this and does wonder if there might be a precedent. Hannigan supplies one (and perhaps there are more).

On a freezing (-15C) morning in November 1868, the RGS-sponsored explorer George Hayward scrambled to the top of a crag near the source of the Yarkand river in what was then known as Eastern Turkestan (today's Xinjiang) and from 19,000ft looked upon 'a dizzying expanse of mountains'. Far to the south stretched the Karakoram where one mountain towered above all. Hayward tilted his artificial horizon, directed his compass, and calculated it was 28,278ft tall.

Surveyors in western Kashmir had already spotted the mountain that would become known as K2 and Hayward had no way of knowing he was looking at the same peak. In his notebook he recorded it simply as 'Snowy Peak', however he had the height right to within 30 feet – a remarkable achievement given his immediate vicissitudes as a fugitive in wild and lawless mountains in the grip of winter. Younghusband could of course be described as the first European to *know* he was looking at the north face of K2.

Hayward was a pawn in the 'Great Game' between the Raj and the Russian Empire. True, he mapped the source of the Yarkand and spotted K2 from the north, but he was pipped into Yarkand and Kashgar by Robert Shaw, and kept under house arrest there, and in July 1870 was murdered, still short of his primary objective, the High Pamirs.

Murder in the Hindu Kush was rightly shortlisted for the Boardman Tasker Award in 2011. It is Hannigan's first book – borne of a visit to the western Himalaya as an 18-year old with his climber father Des Hannigan – and he has done well grappling with the ethnic and political complexities of the region, every bit as tangled and brutal in the 19th century as they are today. Comprehending the geography of 'Hayward country' would have benefited from some far better maps than the naïve sketches included here.

The odds were always against George Hayward but that, in large part, is what must have endeared the increasingly suicidally obsessive to Tim Hannigan and makes his story such an engaging read.

Stephen Goodwin

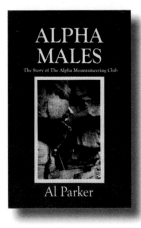

Alpha Males:
The story of the Alpha Mountaineering Club
Al Parker
Fastprint, 2010, pp 274; available in hardback or paperback (£16.99 or £10.99) direct from Al Parker Tel: 01457 855240

Richard's climbing improved week by week and pretty soon he and I were climbing at the same standard. Around this time we got to know a group of climbers from the Rotherham area, some of whom were coal miners. They were a tough bunch with some good climbers in the group. One climber who was outstanding was Len Millsom who later did the first ascent of Millsom's Minion at Stanage. When we first met them Len climbed all manner of things in pit boots with metal studs in the soles. I remember he once traversed from Robin Hood's Cave to the Balcony Cave wearing pit boots and with a lighted primus in one hand!

Al Parker recalling early days at Stanage.

All climbers thrive on stories and this lovingly produced volume is chock full of them. Al Parker was a founder member of the Alpha in 1956 and has put together an enjoyable and often very funny account of the history of the club's heyday from 1956 to 1970. The role of the Alpha in the development of British climbing at this time is of great significance, and Parker recounts all the deeds and misdeeds, all the triumphs and not a little loss and tragedy. Within these pages are to be found all the usual suspects; Al Parker himself, Richard McHardy, Pete Bamfield, Bob Brayshaw, Les Brown, Paul Nunn, Pete Crew, Barry Ingle, Martin Boysen, Tanky Stokes, Gerry Rogan, Paul Ross and Clive Rowland to name but a few. The Alpha was never a large club, normally having only 20 to 30 members at any one time. Membership was by invitation only and was desired by many, but not everyone got invited, not even the famous. The organisation of the club was kept to a minimum and usually only extended as far as a riotous annual dinner and a small and widely respected badge.

The Alpha began with a small group of lads getting together in a barn at Edale in November 1956. All in their mid to late teens, they set about forming what would soon become a huge element in the development not only of gritstone, but of climbing in both Wales and the Lakes over the next decade. Sterling deeds were also done in Scotland, the Alps and further afield. By the mid-60s the Alpha was a byword for excellence in climbing, with a reputation the envy of many. Particularly interesting here are the accounts of the club's early years, as this group of keen youngsters found their way towards becoming a group of highly competent mountaineers. Not all the early members were naturally talented, a good example being Richard McHardy. From an unpromising beginning with a serious fear of heights, Richard was destined over the next decade to become one of the boldest rock climbers and accomplished alpinists of his generation. In truth, the club became a 'who's who' of top British climbing talent, from both the Manchester and Sheffield sides of the Peak. The overall improvement and development of ability within the club was impressively rapid; many of the members were soon in the vanguard of British climbing both at home and abroad, particularly in the Alps. Parker relates adventures, punch-ups and accidents from Chamonix, Zermatt, the Dolomites and the Bregaglia. The sixties was a period of huge consolidation for British climbers in the Alps and much of that story is told here. The alpine tales are not without sadness and are a reminder of the price paid by some at this time.

Al Parker's book belongs on your bookshelf alongside Don Roscoe's wonderful *Llanberis North*, Hugh Banner and Pete Crew's 1963 Cloggy guide and the now revered (and rare) *The Black Cliff*. More than anything this book goes some way to recording the heartbeat of Peak and Welsh climbing in particular in the period 1959-1966 when modern rock climbing in Britain really arrived. It is a valuable comment on the social context of climbing at that time: the privations of the 1950s were past; young, energetic, ambitious men were busting out of the northern cities and the economic and social constraints of the postwar period were no longer going to hold sway. A whole new climbing scene emerged, of which the Alpha were key players, whereby the sport became democratic and far more welcoming. Just as the verve, energy and lust of the music of the Beatles (a soundtrack of the great years of the Alpha) was the result of hopes, expectations and cravings that had built up in the social straitjacket of Harold Macmillan's Britain, so the drive, ability and ambition of the Alpha's members were central to defining the character of climbing in Britain as we understand it today. Those of us who have come later have stood on the shoulders of groups like the Alpha and have greatly benefited from the knowledge both of their triumphs and misfortunes.

In some quarters the sixties is a much maligned period in our climbing history, but some very hard and bold things were done back then, long before modern footwear, chalk, reliable protection and the huge benefits of indoor training all winter. It was not only a period of healthy consolidation of ability but also a time when a lot of myths and shibboleths were laid to rest and when British climbers stopped being also-rans in the Western Alps.

Humour is never far from the surface in Al Parker's writing, but this is balanced with tales of hard lessons learned on the mountains and the loss of friends by illness or accident as the years have passed.

Alpha Males puts you right there, whether it's a sunny Friday night and you're bombing down to Wales on the back of someone's borrowed motorbike en route for the delights of The Pass, Cloggy or Gogarth, or in describing the majesty of the Mont Blanc range as seen for the first time by skinny young lads from Manchester with their precious fortnight's holiday ahead of them. Hugely enjoyable, this book is essential reading for anyone who wants to understand the core of our climbing culture and how it has evolved over the past 50 years.

Steve Dean

Itching To Climb
Barbara James
Matador, 2009, pp 204, £8.99

The combination of compunction and physical disability is perfectly suggested by the title of this book, in which Barbara James describes the impact of debilitating eczema and allergies on a determinedly active and adventurous life. From her early introduction to the strenuous delights of Snowdonia, instigated by a thoughtful and inspirational teacher, James 'found the route to a lifetime pursuing – or being dropped into – work and play that was mainly the prerogative of men.' This double challenge – her rebellious body and the rigid social demarcation of the late 1950s – served only to spur her on to achieve remarkable and varied ambitions.

A brief teaching career, cheerfully abandoned for the energetic outdoor life she so enjoyed, paved the way to James's immersion in climbing, instructing and outdoor centre management in Snowdonia, principally at Ogwen Cottage and Plas y Brenin. Her accounts of these pursuits are leavened both with an unobtrusive but wryly enlightening examination of the social mores which permeated them and uncomplaining accounts of the physical discomforts she was forced to endure as a result of severe allergic reactions to pollens, synthetic fabrics, animals and her own sweat. James was always doubly disabled – by her sex and by her health – but, in turn, these factors made her doubly determined to succeed.

James's singlemindedness is woven through every facet of her private and working life: her interests and abilities in the field of outdoor education were furthered by the acquisition of new skills and qualifications in skiing and mountain rescue and the emotional and financial damage of a traumatic divorce was resolutely overcome when she began work as possibly the only woman civilian to be employed by the MoD to train soldiers. Even her holidays were often groundbreaking; she was captivated by the Falkland Islands when she visited them soon after the conflict and it was after this visit that she celebrated her 50th birthday by getting her Private Pilot's Licence.

She has left a thoughtful and indelible imprint on whichever environment she has found herself living and working in, from Snowdonia to Tenerife; alive to local needs and issues, led by a combination of common sense and pragmatism, energetic and resolute in overcoming her own difficulties and urging manufacturers to come up with practical solutions for those similarly afflicted. *Itching To Climb* provides readers with meticulously detailed descriptions of the development of outdoor education, unquenchable enthusiasm for conveying knowledge and understanding of mountaineering history – celebrated in her involvement in the Rheged 'History of Mountaineering' Exhibition – and an opportunity to become acquainted with a remarkable woman who has reacted with self-effacing humour and quiet resilience to the problems and opportunities with which life has presented her.

Val Randall

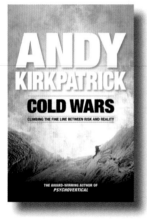

Cold Wars: Climbing the fine line between risk and reality
Andy Kirkpatrick
Vertebrate Publishing, 2011, pp 276, £20

Cold Wars is the second volume of autobiography from Andy Kirkpartrick, whose first, *Psychovertical*, won the Boardman Tasker prize in 2008. Title apart, (and the subtitle of this latest is no better), *Psychovertical* was a tremendous book, chronicling the author's climbing escapades through his 20s, and formed around a series of chapters describing his ascent of *Reticent Wall*, one of Yosemite's hardest multi-day aid climbs.

'But you are so young', comments a German lady at a publicity event for *Psychovertical*, clearly unconvinced that at such a tender age there can yet be enough to say. Andy hasn't got the nerve to inform her that he plans not only a volume two but a trilogy.

Andy has the ability to conjure up a character in a couple of lines. This is something that did not strike me so forcefully with *Psychovertical*. On the other hand, what's missing here is the awareness of place, the sense of wonder at the natural world that was so well conveyed there. Reading his chapters on Reticent Wall one could feel the grainy texture of the granite, the fine detail of the exfoliations up which he hooks, the mind concentrated and focused in the most microscopic way by his fear.

It is inevitable, as Andy well knows, that *Cold Wars* will be compared to its predecessor. Something that I don't recall in the first volume, but that irritated me here, is his impressionability vis-à-vis 'names'. This may be a technique of course. The book dovetails seamlessly with *Psychovertical*, beginning with Andy back in camp hours after topping out on El Cap, where he is now deemed enough of a success to hang out with the other top dudes. And so it continues, sporadically, throughout the book; a social climbing which, given Andy's hair-raising performances, is no more than his just deserts and which introduces us to a succession of apparently celebrity climbers – 'apparently', because this reviewer had never heard of half of them, and none came over as nearly as interesting as the author.

As I say, this may be technique, as may Andy's supposed dire incompetence – forgetting things, dropping things, getting in a mess generally. There is no doubt that this makes the book more gripping and entertaining than it might otherwise be, just as it has always struck me that climbing films would be so much better if the stars weren't all so damned good. Mild VS (just, for a few feet) climbers on E4; now, there's entertainment. But I was on the Boardman Tasker panel when *Psychovertical* was discussed, and we all wondered whether, the book's structure being so brilliant, it mightn't have had significant input from a very experienced editor. Andy has since assured me that this was not so, that he did it all himself. We must believe him, of course, and do the same here: assume the incompetence is genuine. In any case, if it is not exaggerated that only makes his climbing successes all the more remarkable, and his cleverness as a writer all the more impressive.

Not only does this volume follow *Psychovertical* seamlessly in time, but the climbing is also much the same. Here is a series of adventures, each of which contains at least one epic, that are geographically quite narrow-minded – mainly the Dru and Patagonia – and always played out in winter. Andy is driven by an urge to reach the top of the game that requires him to attempt the hardest climbs in the most punishing conditions that is reminiscent of Joe Tasker. He does not succeed in conveying just how hard his climbing escapades are, and perhaps this is the drawback of the stand-up comedian that he is, the slap-stick humour that infuses every page – it just becomes impossible to credit that things are really as serious as they appear to be. But he does convey the sheer cold. I found myself shivering on several occasions – a remarkable achievement. And the man is genuinely funny.

Andy loves to play the clown, but though I suppose even here I'm open to his formidable persuasive talents, I don't believe he's in any way the dimwit he likes to portray. The whole book just smells too strongly of talent. It is wonderfully entertaining, almost un-put-down-able.

Even so, if it was just a book of climbing adventures I would have been satiated well before the end. After all, we've all done these sorts of things, felt these sorts of things, if at a less exalted level. What raises it into a different league is that it's not ultimately about hard climbing at all – it's about escaping from it. Andy is a father and husband, and gradually the psychological forces at war in his head – and this, not climbing, is the real cold war of the book – begin to turn in favour of his children. This was all there in embryo in volume one, so there is nothing entirely new here, but that is precisely why it's so effective, and why *Psychovertical* and *Cold Wars* really form a single piece of work. What we are seeing over the course of both volumes is a gradual realignment of competing forces. The metamorphosis takes several years – for Andy to climb down gracefully – but something of its inevitability infuses every chapter. Perhaps the best, the most poignant, describes his ascent of the *Lesueur Route* on the Dru with a partner he doesn't know but who comes strongly recommended. And the man's a guide, after all. After a shaky start, this stranger – who seems not to have quite the right gear, to be oddly lacking in confidence, to have weird gaps in his expertise – just gets stronger and stronger, and has emerged well before the top as the climbing hero, with Andy very much the junior partner. The writing is almost frighteningly honest here.

'I can't do it,' I said, looking back at him. 'I can't do it. Please will you lead it?' I felt shame saying those words but they came easily enough. I'd have given everything I had not to lead that pitch.

Not only that, but Andy has by this time discovered a misunderstanding, and the explanation for those weird gaps: the stranger – who's never named – is indeed a qualified guide, but a walking guide. Andy has taken him onto a route way beyond anything he's ever done. 'On paper he was going to die. In reality he had found his calling.'

Whilst for Andy, by this time, in the end, the children have won, and soon he's skiing the sun-kissed slopes, not slogging up to the Dru for yet another epic. The vignettes of his family are without exception moving. There are others too that have nothing directly to do with climbing but paint a picture wonderfully – that of being a film-set extra brings the glamour of that world nicely down to earth. And anyone who thinks being a professional speaker is glamorous should perhaps read his description of the *Alpinist* magazine party in Colorado, which came over as a yearningly empty, lonely experience.

This notion that as a well-known climber Kirkpatrick would always disappoint is so wrong. He should forget – perhaps he already has – those celeb climbers who so impress him. He is both cleverer and more interesting than they. There is some unevenness, but *Cold Wars* confirms that Kirkpatrick is a writer, not just a climber who writes. It would be interesting to see him tackle a novel – a kid's novel perhaps. Meanwhile, what has he got left to put into volume III? If it's of the standard of its predecessors he will have created one of the most important of modern climbing autobiographies.

Phil Bartlett

Into The Silence: The Great War, Mallory and The Conquest of Everest
Wade Davis
Bodley Head, 2011, pp680, £25

This colossal work deals with the three 1920s Mount Everest expeditions against the backdrop of the First World War and the twilight years of the British Empire.

A decade in the making, the book's strength lies in the serious and

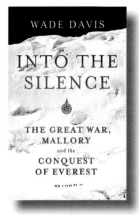

WADE DAVIS

INTO THE
SILENCE

THE GREAT WAR,
MALLORY
and the
CONQUEST
OF EVEREST

thorough research that Davis has undertaken into the history of the early expeditions and the records of the individual members in the Great War. A clue to Davis's fascination with the war lies in the dedication to his grandfather, Captain Daniel Wade Davis, who served as a medical officer in France with the Royal Army Medical Corps from 1915-16 and thereafter in England with the Canadian Army Medical Corps until the end of the war. Certainly his respect for the work carried out by the surgeons and medical staff on the Western Front shines through.

Davis does not spare the reader, describing at times in disturbing detail the sights, sounds and smells of the battlefield. One of the grimmest of all tasks for the doctors after the battle of the Somme was to pick their way around six acres of stretchers holding the wounded and the dying, deciding who could be helped. At its best Davis's descriptions are worthy of Edmund Blunden as he writes of the sheer, gargantuan horror of the slaughter and the senselessness of the loss.

Davis sees the conquest of Everest as an attempt to wrest something glorious from the annihilation of the war. The summit would prove that although beaten to both Poles the British could master the heights. In a wholly constructed conceit Everest became the third pole. Davis details the diplomatic shenanigans involved in negotiating between the factions that had every interest in keeping the British out of Tibet and away from the mountain.

We are reminded that the first expedition, in 1921, had as its goal not just the summit of the mountain but also the mapping of a hitherto unknown region. Its success was not the height record but the unravelling of the geography of the Everest region. In a matter of weeks, '12,000 square miles of unexplored territory had been mapped on a quarter inch scale and a further 4,000 miles revised with greater accuracy.'

However, it is the men, rather than their achievements that are the focus. Davis brings to the fore the characters involved in planning and executing the expeditions. He weaves colour into the black and white tapestry that has illustrated the familiar but long-gone world of the early 1920s Mount Everest expeditions. Using private letters and diaries as well as official accounts he breathes life and energy into men whose names have faded into the shadows of the legend of Mallory and Irvine.

We read of the achievements of Lieutenant Colonel Edward Norton, who took part in almost every one of the great battles – Aisne, Marne, Ypres, Loos, the Somme, Arras and finally the German Spring Offensive of 1918 – being 'mentioned in despatches three times, he was awarded the Military Cross, appointed DSO, and honoured with every medal for gallantry and combat, save the Victoria Cross.' That he survived was a statistical miracle. Or Dr Arthur Wakefield, whose experiences in France were so shattering that they changed him forever. Operating as a surgeon on the Somme in July 1916 he witnessed the complete decimation of the Newfoundland regiment he had helped to arm from his own family money. As a colonial doctor since 1908, he had known and treated most of the men and boys before the war. Of the 810 men who went over the top on 1 July only 35 survived physically unscathed. Or Dr Howard Somervell, also operating as a surgeon in France, who with Norton would set a high altitude record of 28,126 feet without oxygen in 1924, a record that stood unbeaten until 1978. It is hard not be drawn to some of the larger than life characters in this book: General Charles Bruce, who was to lead the 1922 and 1924 expeditions, was described by a friend as having 'the energy of a steam engine plus a goods train'. He was reputed to have slept with the wife of every man in his regiment. Henry Morshead, veteran of 1921 and 1922, ultimately murdered under mysterious circumstances in Burma in 1931, was an explorer, a man of action. Yet it was Mallory, gallant, enduringly youthful and attractive, who would get closest to the summit of Everest. Davis's portrait of Mallory is not as powerful as his descriptions of the First World War. There is almost a reluctance to be too intrusive. I found myself asking whether he had really got into Mallory's head, but perhaps Mallory was so elusive that nobody could. Where I disagree with Davis's thesis is in his suggestion that Mallory was prepared to sacrifice Sandy Irvine in order to obtain the summit come what may. The title of Davis's last chapter: 'The price of life is death' suggests that Mallory chose to die and took Irvine with him and I am not convinced of that.

Julie Summers

A Day to Die For – 1996: Everest's Worst Disaster, the Untold Story
Graham Ratcliffe
Mainstream, 2011, pp 334, £11.99

Everest & Conquest in the Himalaya: Science and Courage on the World's Highest Mountain
Richard Sale and George Rodway
Pen & Sword Books, 2011, pp 240, £19.99

The Everest disasters of 1996 are among the most scrutinised events in mountaineering history. Numerous books have recounted how five members of commercial expeditions – three guides and two clients – died after being hit by a storm on the south-east ridge on 10 May. The most ambitious in its scope and research is *Into Thin Air* by the climber and journalist Jon Krakauer, which became the second most successful mountaineering book in history, behind only Maurice Herzog's *Annapurna*. Collectively these accounts can be read as a morality tale whereby the excesses of commercialism bring the hapless participants to their fate.

Now a new contender has stepped forward to re-examine what occurred.

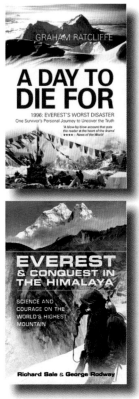

British climber Graham Ratcliffe arrived on the South Col around 6.30pm on 10 May in readiness for his own summit attempt. As he lay in his tent that night he was unaware of the dramas being played out nearby. He was understandably shocked when he learned of the deaths – and, as he tells it, remained troubled in the years since, wondering whether he could have helped the stricken climbers blundering around on the South Col at the height of the storm.

Mountain accidents are often the outcome of a succession of incidents and causes, none of them decisive in themselves, but combining to the point where they achieve critical mass. Ratcliffe focuses on one crucial element, the storm which hit Everest while the south-east ridge was awash with climbers making their descent. The two leaders of the commercial expeditions, Scott Fischer and Rob Hall, already stand accused, by Krakauer and others, of distorting their decisions through competition to get their clients to the summit. Ratcliffe goes further, contending that they made their summit attempts in the full knowledge that a storm was forecast. As an aside, he also charges that they recommended to Ratcliffe and his colleagues that they make their summit bid on 11 May, when the storm was due to be at its height.

There could hardly be a graver charge against professional guides than that they deliberately led their clients into danger; and it is worth pointing out that since both Fischer and Hall died on Everest – Hall because he refused to abandon a client – they are unable to sue for libel. They have in addition been unable to present their view of events. However Ratcliffe has a third figure in his sights: David Breashears, leader of a US IMAX expedition, who Ratcliffe says was receiving forecasts which he was sharing with Scott and Fischer. Breashears wrote his own book about the disasters and Ratcliffe also attacks both him and Krakauer for not examining what forecasts the expeditions were receiving in their accounts of the disaster.

There is some truth in the second charge, and Krakauer appears to offer a hostage to fortune by referring to a 'rogue storm' hitting the mountain. But for the first charge to stick, Ratcliffe needs a smoking gun – and he has not found one. After a 10-year search, he established that Breashears and a Danish team, led by Mal Duff, were receiving forecasts via email sent over a satellite phone and printed in base camp. Breashears was receiving forecasts from the Met Office in London, the Danes from the ECMWF (European Centre for Medium-Range Weather Forecasts). The Met Office forecasts covered a six-day period and in forecasts for 5 and 7 May, Ratcliffe relates, 'the storm on May 11 was apparent'. The forecasts to the Danish team, according to Ratcliffe, predicted 'a steady increase in the wind from 8 May onwards' and 'indicated the strength of the winds on 11 May quite clearly'.

It is in light of these that Ratcliffe levels his charge of negligence to the point of recklessness against Hall and Fischer. But for a charge of such gravity, the evidence is a long way short of conclusive. Ratcliffe has not produced the forecasts themselves, nor any data concerning wind strength and direction. Ratcliffe has made at best an inferential case which he attempts to strengthen by eliding his summary of the forecasts with retrospective accounts, obtained from the respective forecasting services, of what actually happened. In addition, Ratcliffe places enormous weight on an article he recalled reading in 1997 in which one of Hall's team was quoted as saying: 'We went on the 10th of May because we knew the weather was going to go bad the next day.' This particularly riled Ratcliffe, as his team had scheduled their attempt for 11 May at the commercial teams' suggestion. But despite years of searching, and even offering a reward, Ratcliffe was never able to find the article containing the crucial quote.

There is a further problem with Ratcliffe's proposed scenario, namely that the forecasts he describes do not reflect what happened on the mountain. Krakauer tells how the weather deteriorated on the afternoon of 9 May, with a full storm in progress by nightfall. But at 7.30 pm the wind had all but disappeared. As is evident from Krakauer, the decision to make the summit attempt seemed straightforward, and he and the rest of the Hall team set off at 11.30pm in near-perfect conditions. The weather remained clear until around 4.30pm on 10 May, by which time the climbers should have been at or near the South Col on their descent.

That was not what happened. A myriad of factors combined to slow the climbers. Through misunderstandings ropes had not been fixed on the most difficult sections, there were jams at notorious bottlenecks such as the Hillary Step, and teams were delayed by their least experienced members. Worse, the team leaders ignored their own turnaround deadlines. As a result notional safety margins were eroded so that when the storm did return the laggards were fatally exposed. Three died above the South Summit: Hall, his guide Andrew Harris and client Doug Hansen. Fischer died around 350 metres above the South Col, possibly suffering from a cerebral oedema. Hall's client Yasuko Namba died on the South Col.

In relating his account, Ratcliffe suffered from the difficulty that he was unable to include any comment from those he criticises. Fischer and Hall were dead; he approached Breashears and got no reply. Breashears says now that he must have overlooked Ratcliffe's enquiry in the volume of letters and emails he habitually receives. When I contacted him, however, he delivered a forthright statement co-signed by his team member Ed Viesturs. Breashears insists that neither he nor any team members had seen any forecasts predicting a storm of the intensity that hit Everest. The Met Office forecasters had warned that their forecasting was poorly developed and not to be relied on as the primary source of weather information. Breashears adds that the forecasts were just one element in their decision making, alongside daily forecasts on Radio Nepal and their own observations of cloud formations, indication of wind on other peaks, and barometric changes – 'skills and techniques that had served experienced mountaineers very well during long and demanding Himalayan careers'.

Breashears and others have also pointed out that in any case in 1996 climbers placed far less trust in forecasts than today, when up to the minute forecasts can be received on laptops. Breashears also insists that it was unthinkable that Hall or Fischer would have deliberately risked their clients' lives. 'Hall and all the team leaders wanted successful and safe ascents. Ed and I have acknowledged publicly that mistakes were made high on the mountain on that fateful day, but ignoring important weather information that would place one's team members, long-term climbing friends and others at risk was not one of them…'

Richard Sale and George Rodway also touch on 1996 in their book, *Everest & Conquest in the Himalaya*, but without drawing any conclusions. Much of the book consists of a useful summary of major ascents and accidents on Everest and elsewhere. It is at its best when it fulfils its brief of relating success in mountaineering to scientific advances. The summaries of early work on high-altitude physiology, giving all due credit to figures such as Alexander Kellas and Griffith Pugh, are the most illuminating part of the book.

Peter Gillman

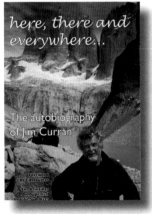

Here, There and Everywhere
Jim Curran
Edgebrook Publishing, 2012, pp 388, £30

Back in my student days in Sheffield I went along with a group of mates on a dank winter evening to an unpromising venue to hear Jim Curran speak about a mountaineering expedition he had recently returned from. While I cannot recall Jim's exact trip, his talk painted a compelling picture of far away exotic mountains and he kept us entertained with liberal doses of what I would learn was his trademark self-effacing humour.

Later I would come to know Jim socially as a big-hearted, generous and supportive man – a natural storyteller and pub raconteur second-to-none. Now at what he acknowledges is nearing the end of his life he has sat down and written a comprehensive autobiography, lavishly illustrated with many photographs. As such, it is a warm book about a life lived to the full; it feels very much like Jim wrote it predominantly for himself and appears to leave few stones unturned. For a time he struggled to come up with a suitable

as the second son of wealthy parents. Their bemused confession that 'we didn't know what to do with you' seems to set the pattern for relationships throughout his life and points up the concerted rebellion against protocol which he mounted from an early age.

Dawes is an engaging raconteur, describing vividly a childhood holiday in Vienna spent in Hitler's bedroom, an early attempt at rallying in a Porsche Carrera touching 100mph down the long drive at the family home, a succession of travelling misadventures and a plethora of impromptu parties. His writing is a breathless, cinematic rush that embodies his self-confessed hyperactivity, his inability to leave unclimbed any promising new route on the walls of home and school.

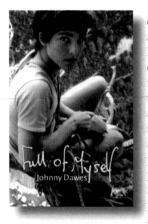

The narrative loses momentum when Dawes chronicles his many remarkable climbs. Although his accounts are often poetic, they are many and overloaded with the sort of technical detail only fully comprehensible to climbers. This closes down the initial impact of the book; it begins expansively but then loses its grip on a wider audience. Oddly, the aftermath of his stunning ascent of *Indian Face* – the stuff of instant appeal to climbers and non-climbers alike – is never fully expanded on. Similarly, he provides tantalising snippets about famous climbing personalities, then goes no further. This will surely frustrate those who are familiar with the prominent players of the time and fail to enlighten those who are not. Conversely, the quality of the photographs and the informative nature of their captions is consistent throughout, translating some of the more incomprehensible climbing terminology into the immediacy of impressive action.

Full of Myself is, however, not merely a roller-coaster ride of outrageous stories and equally outrageous climbs. There is an undercurrent of uncertainty which begins early in his life and, later, a deeper and more persistent melancholy. Uneasy at family parties, bullied at Uppingham, his public school, unable to tolerate 'the herd', he often feels isolated, both from his friends and his love of climbing, by a deep vein of unhappiness he attempts to understand, in part, through the construction of the narrative.

This book is more than an account of an unusual climber's life. It marks something of a watershed in the sport, looking back at a time before sponsorship and a preoccupation with training and competition threatened to overtake the love of the rock and the audacity of the challenge. 'Climbing can show us how rock and we are kin and make us at the end good friends,' he says.

Dawes's writing may occasionally lose its way in the twists and turns of his hectic thoughts but what never falters is, again, admirably pinpointed in George Smith's foreword – 'the gallantry of his assaults on the unknown'.

Val Randall

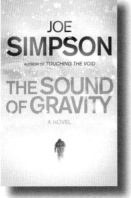

The Sound of Gravity
Joe Simpson
Jonathan Cape, 2011 pp 234, £16.99

This is the second novel by Joe Simpson who was perhaps somewhat surprised to discover himself as a writer at the famous first attempt. Since *Touching the Void* owed much to the editorial advice of the late Tony Colwell, to whom the present book is co-dedicated, Simpson would not have known whether he was a one-book wonder, especially since the very structure of the two-voiced form was Colwell's idea. It was therefore a rather bold move to attempt a novel for his second book. With *The Water People* Simpson might have been testing himself as 'a real writer', as it were – someone who was not dependent upon having a gripping personal survival story to tell, but a writer with a shaping imagination and a range of characterisations at his finger tips. The result was a creditable first novel that I thoroughly enjoyed reading. Now comes something rather different – so different, in fact, that readers who come straight from *Touching the Void* will find a writer who has, in many ways, produced a contrasting kind of book at a very different stage of his life. *The Sound of Gravity* is slower, more philosophical, deeply introspective and driven by a mature devotion to love.

But if the opening chapter is a gripping read in the old Simpson survival mode, it's actually about not gripping enough: a man lets his wife fall through his hands after she slips on their bivvi ledge. Except that she has noticed that in unclipping herself from their belay to take a pee she has also unclipped him. In fact, she has released herself from his grip to save him, which he will never know. The first section of the novel is about the man's survival of a storm and his descent to search for the body that he finds in a crevasse into which he has fallen. More accurately, it is about the ebbs and flows of emotions, thoughts and memories of a lover who has lost what he thought he could keep safe.

Actually, the male climber has been unnamed in the first section, so it takes the reader some time to realise that the Patrick who has occupied the hut every summer for the last 25 years in the second section is the same man. And the reason for this long-term vigil is only fully revealed in the novel's final pages. In between there are compelling characterisations of a series of visitors to the hut: the terminally ill climber, the mixed bag of a village rescue team, the arrogant macho climber who pushes his girlfriend, Cassie, into a state of blank hypothermia. Patrick, a grumpy old bachelor by this time, insists that the girl stays behind at the hut as her boyfriend pushes on through a building storm that lasts several days and dramatically rips apart the hut. Patrick's methodical preparation for this eventuality is punctuated by a melting of his reserve that leads to a tender sex scene amid the storm that is Lawrencian in its significance. Cassie returns to the hut later and tracks Patrick across the glacier to its snout where she finds him collecting, in a wooden chest stored there, the bones and clothing of his wife in 'a mixture of revulsion and love'. The novel's final sentences are a powerful and fully earned redemption in which Cassie says, 'You have her. We can take her home now.' Some may find the first section over-written, and the cynics, of whom Simpson would have been one in the past, may find a romantic redemption hard to swallow, but even hoary old alpinists are allowed to find love in the harshest of conditions. *The Sound of Gravity* is another bold statement by a mature and compelling writer who has yet again extended his reach, both emotionally and stylistically.

But I can't help smiling at the memory of the gnarly younger Simpson limping into the Byron from Siula Grande and grunting, 'I'm *not* going to write about it', and then later, 'I'm *not* going to give talks about it'. It's rather wonderful to consider where a little article for *High* magazine might lead.

Terry Gifford

Straight Up
Himalayan Tales of the Unexpected
Steve Berry
Himalayan Kingdoms, 2012, pp 166, £12.99

Steve Berry is the MD of Mountain Kingdoms, one of the UK's foremost trekking companies, an outfit that, at least to all outward appearances, runs with smooth efficiency, conveying its clients from Heathrow to the Himalaya and back, all creature comforts assured. Fascinating then to read of the young Berry's first muddling steps, pain and elation in equal measure, on a shoestring learning curve in the mountains that would eventually form the bedrock of his business.

Self-published, *Straight Up* is really the story of Berry finding himself, not just as a climber, expedition leader and pioneer of trekking of Bhutan, but also emotionally. The book is dedicated to Berry's father, Roy, 'who gave me my love of mountains', however as Steve and his brother Richard gasp towards the summit of Nun (7135m) in Ladakh comes a searing piece of self-examination and indictment of Berry Snr's influence:

I really never thought we would make it, but of course it had to be done. I had failed at school, I had failed to enter Hamble to train as a pilot, I had been arrested at the age of nineteen for possession of cannabis, I had been kicked out of my dad's best friend's engineering company, and I had smashed up my mother's car on more than one occasion. At the root of it all was a hate, love relationship with the Old Man, more hate than love in fact. Now I was going to show him.

I was going to say, so an everyday story of growing up in the 1960s and 70s, but maybe your experience was different.

The Berry boys took their punishment and made the first British ascent of Nun, 'finishing the job' for Major Roy Berry who had attempted the peak with Tom Stobbart in 1946 while soldiering in India. If the relationship with the Old Man was tortured, Berry's frustrated love life, or should it be lust life, sounds even more so. Indeed his pursuit of the late Ginette Harrison while attempting unclimbed Gangkar Punsum (7570m) in Bhutan contains rather more confessional detail than some may care for. But then as Berry says, he's told his story 'warts and all'. And what a story it is.

Stephen Goodwin

Hearing Silence
Edward Williams
Book Guild Publishing, 2011, pp80, £9.99

Fifty years a member of the AC, and here's a first book of poems from Edward Williams. They have the ring of the real thing, finely crafted and informed by years of learning from the masters: 'Fine fragile hairy clasps now unfolded, / Flowed to sheltering fronds on sturdy stems.' We can watch a 'Bracken Forest' come alive before our eyes in lines such as these, which might seem to out-Hopkins Gerard Manley. Indeed, Hopkins' preoccupation with the glorious detail of the natural world and its elusive source is an appropriate point of reference for these poems, although Williams seems more certain about that source: 'God's so pure and palpably perfect presence'. Against Hopkins' doubts, or 'loneliness, sorrows unspeakable ... inner ineptitude, disappointments', Williams finds that daffodil spikes through the frost and drab cold represent 'hope: a call to trust in holy care'.

It is his own vulnerability as a mountaineer that unsettles him as he faces the approaching storm and threat of avalanche: 'But what could I do, / Though I knew full well / The dangers of this place? / Only increase my pace.' In one poem titled 'Memory Gap', he reveals that he's quite right to be anxious about ineptitudes, beyond just the inner kind. 'At fourteen thousand feet, with all the world aglow, / The sun shone warm and clear, woolly clouds below', but the poem's title is revealed, in the last line, to refer to 'a blank about the fall'. At such times, as in the poem 'Avalanche', the poet is wise to seek to 'retain my prosaic poise'. Alpinists of a certain age will enjoy the crack of canvas, the roar of the Primus, the tinkle from crampon straps and the smell of stew from a billy on a wood fire. But some things do not change: the sense in the mountains of being 'betwixt mortal and eternal life'. That's just where Edward Williams' poems delight in negotiating, detailing, reflecting upon, a creative life.

Terry Gifford

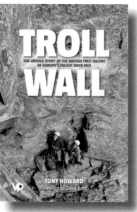

Troll Wall
Tony Howard
Vertebrate Publishing, 2011, pp 208, £17.99

The term 'big wall' can be applied to many faces, having no minimum requirement in height, verticality or difficulty; no European norm with which to categorise a route as being more than simply a 'climb'. It is perhaps only those who attempt the ascent that can really judge those special, defining qualities. For me a big wall is a route that weighs down on the climber, its difficulty beyond gymnastics, its sheer height and history enough to intimidate all but the bravest, or most ignorant.

Of the many walls I've tried (I'd like to say climbed, but then that's the nature of big walls) the one that I believe stands out as offering the true definition of a big wall is the Troll in Norway. It has a status much like that of the Eiger in the 1930s: probably unjustifiably dangerous to try, being loose (looser than the Eiger), wet (imagine a kilometre-high wall in autumnal North Wales) and hard (every hard Lakes mountain route one on top of the other). The Troll is no place to climb, and nothing is in the climber's favour; and therein lies its appeal – well, to a certain type of climber.

Knowing what I know about the Troll Wall added an extra element to reading Tony Howard's excellent book, a simple story well told, a classic *Boy's Own* adventure; only not one by Oxbridge graduates penning romantic prose about easy holiday summits but Northern lads taking on what I'd rate as the hardest unclimbed objective in Europe at the time – and climbing the bugger! Being a Northerner, it's no surprise that it's taken Tony Howard nearly half a century to get round to sharing the story with the rest of us; one of the most important British ascents of the last century; up there with the Frêney Pillar, Annapurna south face and the Trango Tower, but I for one am glad he eventually did.

Having been on the Troll Wall three times with all the best gear on the planet it's hard to imagine how any climber without such modern gear as belay devices, jumars, portaledges, haul bags, cams, or even a harness, would find the courage to attempt to be the first to climb such a thing, let alone by a line up the middle of the steepest, baddest piece of rock you could image. As I said, the Troll is no ordinary wall, not a scaled up crag such as the walls of Yosemite or the Dolomites, nor a gnarly alpine face like the Jorasses or Dru (which are just slabs really), oh no. If it was a crag scaled up, it would be one that even Gary Gibson wouldn't touch; covered in grass, its cracks full of mud, loose and dangerous 'stuff' hanging everywhere; and if it was to be compared to an alpine face, just take the Eiger and turn it upside down, making every slab a leaning overhanging wall, every ledge a roof (just make sure all the loose stuff that falls off is collected and piled back on any ledges you do find in order to retain the ambiance). Add to this weather that would make a Welshman weep and a vertical height four times higher than Canary Wharf and you should get the picture, an objective that is pretty much a climber's worst nightmare.

One of the most fascinating things about *Troll Wall* is that it documents the cusp of a new age, the dawn of American climbing technology with the jumars, pulleys and steel pegs, that would revolutionise all such climbs in the future. Unfortunately for Tony and his team, they were just a few months, or even weeks too early to reap the benefits of this advance, unlike the Norwegian team on the wall at the same time who had the latest gear from the US. Instead they had to carry 240 soft steel pegs, a range of home-made nuts on slings, not to mention homemade leather harnesses and bivvi gear, all carried – often on lead – in 50lb sacks. The difficulty and sheer hard work and grit it took to climb the wall 'old school' style only serves to make the ascent even more incredible.

I expect if this book had come out after the ascent in 1965 it would now rank as a classic alongside *The White Spider*, indeed Tony's tale reads very much like the first ascent of the Eiger 1938 route, full of hazard, friendship and vertigo as well as the simplicity and drive of the rope. The book is a real page-turner as bit by bit Howard, John Amatt and Bill Tweedale push and push and push for the top, forever driven, forever barred by some new obstacle, the story always moving, devoid of any ego or bullshit. It's a story told by a man aware that he will be judged by his peers, so it's one not of heroes but of mates. Tony's reluctance to showboat is the root of it having taken so long for the story to be told in full, that and the fact that Tony is a pioneer of the 'Gone Climbing' lifestyle, leaving the manuscript to languish in his loft since the first ascent. The upside is that it is not one written by an older man looking back at his young self, but his young self telling it how it was half a lifetime ago, giving the account a freshness that brings the climb back to life.

What I enjoyed most of all, however, was reading of Tony's life either side of the Troll Wall; tales of working on whaling boats, 'out there' expeditions to the far North, and journeys to the warmer climbs of the desert. I got the impression of a man who was unafraid of life, as bold in living as in climbing. Reading the short chapters that book end the ascent of the Troll, I wanted to know more and entertained the hope that age might slow Tony enough for him to sit still and bang out a few more such memoirs. However at 70 he is still climbing (and looking) like a man half his age, so I guess *Troll Wall* will probably be our lot.

Andy Kirkpatrick

Woman on The Rocks:
The Mountaineering Letters of Ruth Dyar Mendenhall
edited by Valerie Mendenhall Cohen
Spotted Dog Press, 2009, pp 349, US$18.95

In Appendix E, Valerie Mendenhall Cohen recounts her mother's thoughts about the letters – in excess of 900 pages of them – which spanned 50 years of her climbing and mountaineering experiences. She felt they were like 'a series of novels in which I am the heroine… like having a sort of verbal journey back into the Past'. They are, unquestionably, both of these things, providing both an idiosyncratic perspective on the way in which climbing developed in California in the 1930s onwards and a personal view of the role of a female climber in this patriarchal landscape in which women were excluded from all-male climbing expeditions.

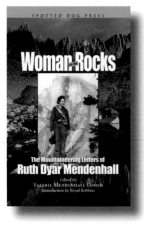

Ruth Dyar Mendenhall's introduction to climbing came as a result of joining the Sierra Club Ski Mountaineers in order to 'meet new people and have fun'. And have fun she certainly did. Her early letters are shot through with the enthusiasm for physical exercise and the sheer joy of being in the mountains, which lasted throughout her life. Indeed, it is clear from her first trips that she is incapable of understanding those who never travelled to the peaks she found it impossible to live without: 'I don't know how people get along without climbing mountains.'

Her use of language is delightfully anachronistic and her descriptions of her fellow climbers candid and forthright – 'Howard cannot yodel, but can howl in a wondrously fooey way just like a pained cow.' – effortlessly enveloping the reader in the climbing environment and the companionship it spawned. She writes with the same breathless energy she brought to her climbs, cataloguing the hardships endured with a pride born out of a love of total immersion into the landscape and a fiercely competitive nature; she is scathing about another female climber who 'had to wait for Brinton to tell her practically every move to make with hand or foot'.

Ruth's skill, nerve and determination enabled her to make 21 first ascents with her husband, John Mendenhall, often with homemade or adapted equipment. Many of her early climbs on mixed ground in the Sierra Nevada were made in crepe-soled tennis shoes, yet she makes light of difficulties and physical deprivation alike. Her home life was equally energetic and her standards as exacting. She wanted to be seen to succeed in this realm, just as she did on rock. Her children were left behind with grandparents in their early years when they were too young to accompany their parents on expeditions, but as soon as they were old enough they were made a part of the outdoor life of physicality, challenge and emotional fulfilment which was at the very heart of Ruth's and John's lives.

Woman on the Rocks provides an entertaining and insightful portrait of a charismatic and committed climber who cheerfully ignored the barriers erected to dissuade her sex from participating in climbing and mountaineering, and who wrote with wit and irreverence, puncturing the posturings of the men often less at ease than she on rock but who sought, in vain, to keep her from it.   *Val Randall*

Desert Towers
A Hundred Years of Adventure on the
Sandstone Towers of the Colorado Plateau
Steve 'Crusher' Bartlett
Sharp End Publishing, 2010, pp 352, US$49.95

Like its subjects, this lavish book is monu-
mental. *Desert Towers* was shortlisted for
the 2011 Boardman Tasker Award and the
fact that Bartlett came away empty-handed
underlines a downside of the BT in having
just a single winner with the emphasis on a
'literary' work. They do things differently at
Banff, with half a dozen different award categories. *Desert Towers* walked
away with the 'mountaineering history' prize at Banff, though it could
equally have taken the 'image' prize.

The BT judges don't have that flexibility, which is a pity, for the 2011
panel was certainly impressed by *Desert Towers*. A peek into Bernard
Newman's judicial notebook gives a flavour:

I was totally blown away by this book. Everything about it is on the grand scale:
the breadth of climbing history, the scope of the writing, the characters contributing
and profiled, the style and audacity of the climbing and of course the star of the
show: the exquisite desert landscape.

The production values reflect the subject: large hardbound format, superb repro-
duction and printing, and most importantly informed and skilful photo editing. The
group photos, always the soul of a climbing history, span the decades and show that
'cool', like sex, is nothing new. Once you dip into it, the only thing that will make
you put it down is the ache in your forearms!

Counting against the BT chances of *Desert Towers* was the fact that it is
in part an anthology. Many of the 30 or so essays have been culled from
American magazines and journals – like Don Wilson on the first ascent of
Spider Rock or Fred Becky on Moses – great for conveying the actuality
of the climbing and likely to be 'new' to most readers, certainly in the UK,
however they are not original.

The sections by Bartlett himself however are both original and engaging,
particularly his charting of Native American history, notably that of the
Navajos for whom many of the most iconic monoliths are sacred. One of
the most cinematic of the fabulous photos in this book is of Eric Bjornstad
and Fred Beckey in 1965, stood by a convertible of the era, gazing across
to Shiprock. But climbing is banned on the Navajo Nation, and as Bartlett
observes: 'For modern climbers Shiprock is so far off the radar screen it could
be in Namibia instead of New Mexico.' (And for more reasons than the ban.)

Later, weighing the ban, Bartlett concludes that in some ways the current
climber-access situation suits everyone: the Navajo Nation sees almost no
climbers, and for the self-selected elite who do attempt the illegal towers
the possibility of arrest can be looked on as just one more hazard.

It is choice irony that this superlative history of a uniquely American aspect of the climbing game should be the work of an Englishman who learnt his rock climbing trade in the Peak District. But Bartlett went native decades ago and as John Sherman says in the Foreword: 'He may talk funny, but Crusher is a desert rat through and through'.

Stephen Goodwin

**Exploring Greenland:
Twenty years of adventure in the great arctic wilderness**
Jim Gregson
Vertebrate Publishing, 2012, pp160, £20

This book in landscape format is a beautifully illustrated record of the author's various summer trips over a period of 20 years to explore not 'Greenland', as the title suggests, but a limited area of the mountains of the central east coast of that island, mostly made possible by access with a ski-equipped Twin Otter aircraft organised through the initially developing but now ubiquitous Tangent Expeditions.

Each visit is the subject of a separate chapter covering mountain ascents and ski journeys, the chapters linked with shorter notes covering general issues such as ice, weather and fauna. While most of the action is in the higher alpine regions bordering the Inland Ice there are two sections on travelling in the ice-free areas in the interior of Scoresbysund which provide an interesting contrast.

Jim has obviously fallen under the spell of the Arctic and transmits his feelings well. Having been on similar expeditions to the areas covered I found it easy to empathise with his enthusiasm after a good mountain day and with his frustrations caused by bad weather and delayed pick ups, but I wonder if other less committed readers will appreciate all the detail without a map to which locations and routes can be related.

Throughout the body of this book the photographs and text provide enduring images of the wonderful mountain, glacier and ice cap world of this part of Greenland, for which it is easy to share the author's affection. To those, like the author, who are already committed to the Arctic this book will be a great affirmation of their addiction. To those not yet so affected it will surely encourage them to join the ranks.

Derek Fordham

Tasmanian Summits To Sleep On
Kevin Doran
Desdichado in support of Bookend Trust, 2011, pp 128, Aus $44.99

This book is an engaging collection of the author Kevin Doran's expeditions

over 30 years accompanied by Ossie Ellis and others on ascents of the main peaks in the Tasmanian wilderness, with the added commitment of sleeping on their summits. The excellent photographs show their routes in all seasons, revealing the strange and lonely landscape of Tasmania's mountains, most of which involve two or three day approach walks and have seriously rocky summits.

The author dedicates this book to the memory of Ossie Ellis. He says in the introduction: 'He befriended me when I was a newly immigrant mountaineer in Tasmania and we became climbing and bushwalking companions for nearly thirty years. He could float a plan for an expedition and I'd probably routinely go along with it.'

Ossie Ellis was an important figure in Tasmanian climbing and became a co-founder of Pencil Pine Lodge, which later developed into Cradle Mountain Lodge, situated just north of the Cradle Mountain-Lake St. Clair National Park.

Kevin Doran was born in England where he trained as a doctor; he has climbed mountains in various parts of the world and has lived in Tasmania since 1971.

For anyone familiar with Tasmania, this book will no doubt bring back strong memories, and for those who aren't the book reveals the surprising richness and variety of the mountains of this unique island, a territory so near to mainland Australia but yet so different.

Julian Cooper

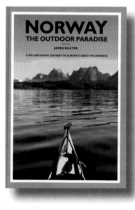

Norway The Outdoor Paradise: A ski and kayak odyssey in Europe's great wilderness
James Baxter
Scandinavian Publishing, 2012, pp448, £29.95

This is the story of James Baxter's remarkable eight and a half month journey, in which he skied the length of Norway from south to north (*Norge på langs*) and then kayaked back round the coastline to finish in Oslo, clocking a total distance of 6213 kilometres. Whilst many Norwegians have done the ski trip and a few have kayaked the north to south coast route, nobody is known to have done the two expeditions consecutively without any break. Undoubtedly, this is one of the finest achievements by a British traveller since the days of Empire. For James this great journey was the consummation of a lifelong

and exploration. For those intrigued by the names given to mountains, glaciers and other prominent features on topographical maps of Antarctica the book will provide interesting insights as to how these were derived.

Derek Buckle

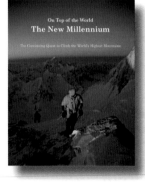

On Top of the World: The New Millennium
Richard Sale, Eberhard Jurgalski & George Rodway
Snowfinch Publishing, 2012, pp 248, £30

This handsome volume provides a welcome anti-dote to the depressing reports from 'Circus Everest' in May 2012 accompanied by photos of endless columns of punters gasping their way up the Lhotse Face. Crowds have been the Everest story for more than a decade. Meanwhile, as Sale and his collabora-tors remind us, amazing things have been going on elsewhere on 8000-metre peaks – siege style on super-hard technical routes or fast and light when the weather windows open. It's been the era of the likes of Christophe Lafaille, Denis Urubko and Simone Moro.

One wonders if Richard Sale ever sleeps. He has authored or co-authored three of the books reviewed in this *AJ*. For this one he was joined by high altitude physiologist and author George Rodway and 8000m data compiler Eberhard Jurgalski. Together they have produced a sequel to John Cleare's and Sale's *On Top of the World*, published in 2000, covering the history of the 14 big peaks up to the end of 1999. *New Millennium* essentially picks up the story, with just brief revisits of 20th century pioneering plus a re-evalua-tion of the first ascents of K2 and Broad Peak.

Jurgalski's tables are simultaneously fascinating and sobering. One table lists climbers who have summited 10 to 13 of the 8000ers; its footnotes are a roll call of those for whom pursuit of the final big ticks cost their lives. It cannot escape notice that AC member Alan Hinkes is not included in the table of climbers who have summited all 14 8000ers. According to Jurgalski, Hinkes's ascent of Cho Oyu is not recognised: 'Hinkes certainly reached the summit plateau, but may not have reached the true summit.'

New Millennium muses on the numerous adventures waiting on the 8000m peaks for alpinists with vision and commitment, starting with Everest's west ridge alpine style, and also on ethical questions. The latter include the possibility of climbers tackling routes beyond their abilities when the idea of 'extreme rescue' by helicopter has taken hold, and 'doping', whether by supplementary oxygen or, say, dexamethasone taken as a prophylactic, potentially allowing alpinists to ascend higher, faster. The 21st century has also brought a crop of fine new images, used effectively here to comple-ment the story of alpinism at its most tenuous limits.

Stephen Goodwin

Ascent: The Vertical Life
2011 & 2012 issues
From the publishers of Rock and Ice magazine,
US$12.95

Early copies of the journal *Ascent* retail for about
£10 in the second-hand bookstore I frequent in
Carlisle: hardbacks a little more, softbacks a little
less. I see that I paid £6 for the 1989 volume, by
which time the slim magazine of the late 1960s
had grown into a book of more than 200 pages.
Inscribed inside the cover of that 1989 *Ascent*
is a *'Merry Christmas'* greeting to Andrew from
David and Linda. No surnames are given and I
have no idea as to identity of these people, but
I would have shared the opinion offered in the
accompanying message:

> *I've aways enjoyed American books on mountain-*
> *eering – they seem to have kept the spirit of amateurism*
> *which is sometimes lacking in the massive expeditions.*

Would David and Linda, or any of us, express
the same sentiments today? The re-emergence of
Ascent after an absence of 13 years provides an opportunity to look at what
has changed in this stable of mountain writing, what it reflects, and perhaps
what has not changed.

First, let us be glad that *Ascent* is back. The fact that Steve Roper and
Allen Steck, the founding editors back in 1967, have both written essays for
the new incarnation must be a welcome seal of approval for the revivalist
work of the editorial team at *Rock and Ice* magazine and publisher Duane
Raleigh.

Ascent began life in July 1967; West Coast climbing's contribution to the
'Summer of Love' sweeping their home cities. The 'far out idea' – Roper's
words echoing the argot of the time – was to showcase good writing and
high-quality photography. And so it did. Published by the Sierra Club and
featuring early work by writers such as David Roberts, Doug Robinson and
Galen Rowell, *Ascent* set the standard for journal writing for two decades,
but gaps between issues lengthened as Steck and Roper ran out of steam.

As Roper puts it in an essay entitled 'Genesis' in the 2011 volume, they
called it a day in 1999, after 14 issues, because: 'The glossy climbing magazines paid a lot more than we could… and we simply couldn't attract the
best writers. Photos all looked the same and the prose we received didn't
seem to have the spark it once did. Steck and I became jaded in our waning
years.'

Roper's words certainly strike a chord with this journal editor. It goes
back to David and Linda's words about 'the spirit of amateurism' – and
'amateurism' in its proper French origin of doing something for love, and

not in the corruption whereby an 'amateur' climber is often equated with a bumbler. The Sierra Club never paid Steck and Roper more than $100 each per issue – 'mainly used to score our "editing wine"' – and contributors received just a token honorarium, starting at $25.

That sense of a journal put together by friends at wine-soaked after-dinner editing sessions at Steck's Berkeley home is gone from the new *Ascent*. The emphasis is still on art and stories well told – 2011 features, among others, Geof Childs, Tommy Caldwell, John Long and Doug Robinson; 2012 Reinhold Messner, Renan Ozturk, Dave Pagel and Colin Wells – but there is a slick professionalism too. As J J Cale sings it: 'Money talks, you'd better believe it.'

So the old *Ascent's* stodgy subtitle, 'the mountaineering experience in word and image' is replaced by 'The Vertical Life', with more market appeal to our vanity, and there are pages of glossy advertisements. I am not knocking 'ads; there are a good many at the back of this *AJ*; bills have to be paid, and maybe the odd bottle of wine purchased too. It's just different.

For the past decade, the literary and photographic aspirations of *Ascent* have guided that other US publication, *Alpinist*. Although the new *Ascent* is an annual event and *Alpinist* a quarterly, they are competing on the same territory. Raleigh's *Ascent* falls in appearance between *Alpinist* and *Rock and Ice*. Surely the market is getting a little crowded, or have American climbers an insatiable appetite for this stuff, and the deep pockets to sustain it? (Not dirtbags after all.) I haven't sufficient knowledge to judge the economics, but as a journal editor I am aware that the number of good mountain writers is worryingly finite and, as Roper observed, there is a danger of photos looking all the same. That said the new *Ascent* has got off to a cracking start, and good luck to it.

Stephen Goodwin

Climbing Dictionary:
Mountaineering slang, terms, neologisms & lingo
Matt Samet
The Mountaineers Books, 2011, pp 250, US$ 14.95

What use is a climbing dictionary? OK, it might be useful to a non-climber as a glossary, but shouldn't actual climbers know these words? Maybe, but you would have to be well-travelled to know all the 650 words explained in this US-centric publication.

Samet's highly entertaining little book puts in mind that famous misquotation: 'England and America are two countries divided by a common language.' How many UK climbers would get a reference to 'Jimmy Deans'? It's swollen-knuckle fingers brought on by too much crack climbing; Deans was the creator of a popular brand of breakfast sausage, and also a country music singer (remember 'Big Bad John'?)

'Jimmy Deans' type of knowledge might be regarded as optional for your US road trip, but any American partner would appreciate it if you knew what he meant when he yells 'Up rope!' It translates as 'take in slack', or probably when said with feeling: 'Tight rope!'

And what about a 'Hawaiian'? Any idea? Well think the 1970s TV programme *Hawaii Five-O*, then *Five-O* equals fifty and the word, coined at Smith Rock, Oregon, means a fall of 50ft or more. Thus I can say, last year I did a Hawaiian and survived to tell the tale.

So the fun of delving into the climber's argot would be the main reason for owning Samet's dictionary (zanily illustrated by Mike Tea). Two more would be that it might help translating American climbing magazines, even one or two terms in Andrew Bisharat's article in this *AJ*, and secondly – an editor's gripe this – that climbers are not always the best spellers in the world.

Stephen Goodwin

Spirit of Adventure:
An Anthology of Mountain and Wilderness Tales inspired by the K2
pioneer Henry Haversham Godwin-Austen
Edited by Catherine Moorehead & David Dunmur
Moyhill Publishing, 2011, pp 303

This anthology celebrates the adventurous spirit of Henry Haversham Godwin-Austen (1834-1923), the great military mountaineer of the Victorian era who pioneered the exploration of K2 (8611m).

For a time the world's second highest mountain was eponymously his until it reverted to the more prosaic K2 as the second peak to be officially measured in the Karakoram. Although his name still resounds on the approach glacier to the mountain, it was Godwin-Austen's old school, the Royal Grammar School, Guildford, one of Britain's ancient independent schools, that sparked the idea for this collection of essays and recollections by 30 former pupils and teachers who inherited his powerful interest in climbing mountains and exploring wilderness.

What is refreshing about this anthology of mountain adventure is that there are none of the usual suspects, only an eclectic selection of individuals from a broad spectrum of day jobs; criminology to aerospace, software engineering to management consultancy, with a shared theme of time spent among mountains. The wanderings range around the world from serious ascents, such as Mike Norris unsupported and oxygenless on Cho Oyu, via an assortment of adventures in a variety of Alpine regions to simple days out enjoyed among unthreatening hills.

Guildfordians clearly remain an adventurous lot and this collection of their stories reflects the legacy Godwin-Austen left to his old school, handed down as a torch that still burns brightly.

Ronald Faux

The Climbers' Club Journal 2011
Editor John Yates
The Climbers' Club, 2011, pp 170

How many CC traditionalists, I wonder, received the Club's 2011 *Journal* with a gnashing of teeth as they took in its radically different format and the fact that their bookshelves might not be deep enough for it to sit alongside previous volumes? Praise should really be the first response. Journal editors regularly ponder redesigns but I cannot recall one as total as this transformation of the *CCJ*. The wider page format has allowed for dramatic use of photographs, wide margins and double columns of text giving a clean, open feel to the pages. And thereon are chronicled the adventures of Club members as active as their predecessors, from Mugu to Madagascar, via the Craig Cwm Du and Harrison's Rocks – as bold, almost, as John Yates, his editorial team, and the late Tim Oliver who did much of the ground work for this attractive reincarnation. Reviews of other club journals are not normally carried in the *AJ* but here is an endeavour that deserves saluting. Congratulations! *SG*

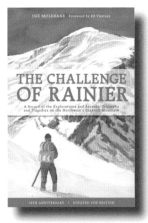

The Challenge of Rainier
Dee Molenaar
The Mountaineers Books, 2011, pp 432, US$24.95

This 40th anniversary reissue of Dee Molenaar's classic history of Mount Rainier (4392m) in the Pacific Northwest, Washington state, includes restored illustrations and a new foreword by Ed Viesturs who was a Rainier guide during the 1980s. Molenaar's professional association with the mountain began in 1940 and it is a mark of both the allure of Mount Rainier and Molenaar's enthusiasm that he has once again met the challenge of updating this history when, as he says, most of his early climbing companions have hung up their nailed boots and now use their axes for garden work. *SG*

Mountain Heroes: Portraits of Adventure
Huw Lewis-Jones
*Conway, in association with Polarworld, 2011,
pp 288, £30*

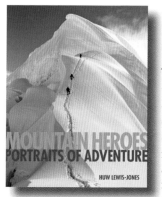

Welcome to the Big Book of Beards. Ruskin takes the prize with a flowing, Old Testament cascade that, like the piled hair of Gertrude, Countess of Groan, could hide numerous nesting birds. Scots Andy Nisbet and Adam Watson are contenders, and so might be Cory Richards, looking traumatised on Gasherbrum II, but his growth is too encrusted in ice and snow to be sure.

My apologies to Huw Lewis-Jones for being flippant when he has, in fact, produced something rather magnificent with this collection of portraits of the great and the good of mountaineering, plus a few young pretenders and a handful of *real* mountain people – that is those actually at home there. Perhaps it was his title that irritated me. 'Heroes' has become tabloid-speak, a word devalued. It should be reserved for those who rush into burning buildings to save complete strangers, or for Greek myths. And to be fair I doubt any of Lewis-Jones's subjects would regard themselves as heroes.

Steph Davis (first female ascent of the *Salathé Wall*, 2005) exudes a more grounded sense of self when she tells Lewis-Jones of her delight in the mountains. 'Spending time in wild places will always remind you that in the great scheme of nature, the universe and geological time, you are just the tiniest smidge of all the other energies at play. And I think this really good for people to remember.'

While it is the portraiture that makes the initial impact and feeds the desire to own this book, it is the writing that provides the sustaining meat. Those national treasures, Bonington and Scott, bookend *Mountain Heroes* with Fore and Afterwords, there is a thought-provoking essay by Jack Ives and AC hon member Bruno Messerli on the environmental, cultural and political pressures on mountains, a fascinating four-way discussion between Lewis-Jones, Gordon Wiltsie, Glen Denny and Cory Richards entitled 'Photography Now', plus a short essay for each of the mountaineers portrayed.

Naturally, many of the portraits have been taken on mountainsides, showing their subjects at their gnarly, steely-eyed best; it comes as a surprise then to turn over a page and by the dateline 'Hathersage, 2009' see Ron Fawcett in the bath, naked except for a pair of yellow rubber washing-up gloves. Every picture tells a story, but you have to cross-refer to the text to have this bizarre scene explained: Big Ron was so dedicated to his climbing that he used to wear gloves in the bath to preserve the tough skin on his hands.

Lewis-Jones says he will consider the book a success if people enjoy its rich photography, pause awhile on the writings and are perhaps inspired to head off to see something of the beautiful mountains with their own eyes. Only a dullard would not be so inspired by *Mountain Heroes*. Lewis-Jones can count it a success.

Stephen Goodwin

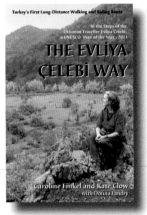

The Evliya Çelebi Way
Caroline Finkel and Kate Clow, with Donna Landry
Upcountry (Turkey) Ltd, 2011, pp 160 plus map, £17.99

Evliya Çelebi's 17th century work *Seyahatname* (Book of Travels) is one of the longest travel accounts in world literature. You wouldn't want to carry its 10 volumes in your pack across the mountains and plains of Anatolia, not least because some have never been translated from Ottoman Turkish. However there is no need: this comprehensive guidebook provides not only all the practicalities but fascinating insights into the culture, past and present, of this little-visited area of Turkey. Evliya (1611-1685) passed this way in 1671 after setting out from Istanbul on a pilgrimage to Mecca. The Evliya Çelebi Way follows the early stages of that journey through north-west Anatolia. Running 600km long from the Sea of Marmara via Bursa, Kütahya and Afyon to Usak and Simav, it is described as Turkey's 'first long-distance walking and riding route', though in fact the walking route is little more than half that length – omitting sections across the plains. The book follows the style of earlier books produced by Kate Clow, creator of both the Lycian Way and St Paul's Trail and reflects once again her love of the Turkish countryside and desire to promote a sustainable form of 'soft' tourism in these backwaters. *SG*

The High Atlas
Treks and climbs on Morocco's biggest and best mountains
Hamish Brown
Cicerone, 2012, pp 224, £17.95

Do not be misled by the title. This is not a conventional guidebook. Rather, AC member Hamish Brown has brought together the fruits of almost half a century of wandering in the mountains of Morocco to produce a work of inspiration. The necessary background for planning a trip and getting to grips with the bureaucracy, culture and language is all here, but when it comes to the itineraries, Brown is not so much guiding your every step as telling how it was for him, encouraging you into diversions to take in, say,

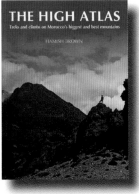

ancient rock art, gossiping as if you'd met him on the trail somewhere and he was passing on his top tips.

The book features 48 routes spread across the full length of the Atlas. Each has a sketch map and panel of essential detail, notably 'commitment'. Many are multi-day trips or peaks to be tackled in the course of a longer trek. The strength of the book though is in Brown's discursive route descriptions and excellent photographs, combining to create an alluring portrait of the mountains and Berber people.

Brown lays great emphasis on the use of local guides, indeed the book is dedicated to one, his friend El Aouad Ali, who was a key figure in Brown's 96-day traverse of the Atlas, undertaken in 1995 and described in his book *The Mountains Look on Marrakech*. Contact details for Ali, in the Western Atlas, and guides for other ranges are listed in a useful set of appendices.

The generous format of *The High Atlas* means this is not a pocketbook guide, however Brown is willing to produce the relevant area for any of the featured hills, at A4 or A3 size, for anyone who asks. But give him sufficient notice: Brown spends months at time in Morocco, still adding to the rich store of experience that has been poured into this inspiring book.

Stephen Goodwin

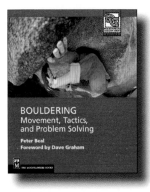

Bouldering
Movement, Tactics, and Problem Solving
by Peter Beal
Foreword by Dave Graham
The Mountaineers Books 2011

If, in the scope of human endeavour, Himalayan mountaineering is a celebration of the vast, then bouldering is a celebration of the minute. By it's very nature bouldering involves short, intense experiences, but having said that its exponents can be just as obsessive, often in the long term, about their goals as those with their mind's eye focussed on some vast unclimbed wall in the Hindu Kush.

I once asked Alex MacIntyre how he coped with being frightened for long periods of time in the big mountains? 'It's addictive, you become addicted to fear. . .' Well, bouldering is certainly addictive and (depending on the size of the boulder) the fear is of failing.

Now I am (was) what's touchingly referred to by modern climbers as an 'Old School' boulderer (i.e. our problems have holds), but the desire, the addiction stays with you into old age and structural infirmity. Recently at the climbing wall Jan and I were watching some young people attempting, with varying degrees of success, a ludicrously overhanging problem on well spaced and tiny holds. I felt myself irresistibly drawn in, and began shuffling towards them. 'Bernard, no. BERNARD – NO!' warned Jan, like a sober wife pulling a stroppy husband away from confrontation. 'It's not worth it.'

So it was with a feeling of curiosity tinged with envy that I picked up this latest training tome from The Mountaineers Books. Maybe it would convince me, as I've often jibed, that that there's more to bouldering than taking your shirt off and wearing a woolly hat.

Basically this book is a bouldering *Know The Game*. There's an introduction by those twin gods of bouldering Dave Graham and John Gill. There follows a detailed history of bouldering which contains a nod towards Fontainebleau and Britain before 'Bouldering as we know it today began to emerge in the 1960s in the United States though the efforts of one individual, John Gill.'

The meat of the book is a comprehensive and detailed analysis of every aspect of bouldering from hold types to diet, rock types to skin care. There's a slightly anachronistic section entitled 'Women and Bouldering' which does, however, contain a valuable message regarding eating disorders.

I was predictably drawn to the section 'Bouldering and The Older Climber' in which, amidst a wealth of sound and encouraging advice, the use of pads was recommended to improve your grade: 'I regularly encounter older boulderers who started before pads *even existed*. . . [my italics]. Oldschool insinuations of cowardice or cheating associated with pad use are usually uttered by those who have quit the sport, often, ironically enough, because of injuries.' That's told me then.

Bernard Newman

Eden Valley & South Lakes Limestone
Ron Kenyon, Nick Wharton & John Holden,
ed. Stephen Reid
The Fell and Rock Climbing Club, 2012, pp 456, £18

On Wednesday evenings in late spring the jackdaws of the Eden Valley, east of Penrith, can find themselves disturbed by half or dozen or so climbers grubbing up the somewhat esoteric cliffs that, I see from this guide, have been described as 'Cumbria's best kept secret'.

The personnel of this motley group may vary from week to week, as does the choice of crag, but each will be a member of the Eden Valley Mountaineering Club and Wednesday is their night for 'getting out'. The ritual round usually begins around Easter on the sandstone of Armathwaite, above the River Eden, wends around the valley via places like the limestone-atop-sandstone cake of Jackdaw Scar and ends as daylight lengthens and attention switches to the more conventional crags of the Lake District.

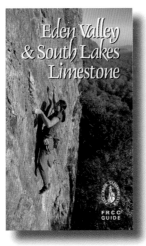

Eden Valley
& South Lakes
Limestone

FRCC
GUIDE

Regulars have hardly needed a guidebook, which is just as well since the last definitive one to include the Eden Valley and its surroundings was *North of England Rock Climbs*, published in 1992 and long out of print. What we have had, for years it seems, are printouts of Ron Kenyon's ever-developing notes for each of the Eden crags – and Ron himself as our tireless ringmaster.

By now I have given away a personal connection that should disqualify me as a reviewer. My excuse is that this guide was only published in June 2012, indecently late to recruit any reviewer, and secondly it is hard to think of anyone sufficiently familiar with the Eden Valley who isn't *ipso facto* part of the EVMC circle. However I shall confine myself to detail rather than judgement.

In his introduction, series editor Stephen Reid speculates on who will buy this latest addition to the FRCC guides, including, as it does, a large area of Cumbria that has not featured in the club's definitive guides before and does not lie within the Lake District National Park (therein, of course, lies some of that 'secret' charm). As Reid says, those leading F6c and above will buy it for the South Lakes Limestone section authored by Nick Wharton, and particularly for the sport climbing at Chapel Head Scar. Others might want to keep it handy for when rain envelopes the central Lake District.

The new guide follows the pattern established under Reid's regime of clear colour photodiagrams, a comprehensive history, first ascent lists, numerous action photos and all the customary 'useful info'. A disturbing feature is the number of crags where climbing has been forbidden by the landowners. It is galling to see the three star route *Merry Monk Direct* (HVS) on Lazonby Crag described as 'one of the finest lines in the Eden Valley' when in fact climbing here has been forbidden for many years. The place is also forbidding! More grievous perhaps is the recent ban on access to The Hoff, a friendly little eruption of vertical conglomerate in a meadow near Appleby – an early playground of Leo Houlding no less. All the routes on banned crags have been included, but with a warning in red print that this is to maintain the historical record only and in case access is allowed in future. We live in hope.

One aspect of Eden Valley intelligence the guide does not include is which pub to retire to when fading light, falling rain or failing strength brings an end to the evening's exertions. Maybe the pubs, unlike the crags now, should remain 'secrets', but I'll let you into just one: a few minutes above Jackdaw Scar at Kings Meaburn, the White Horse Inn serves a fine pint to wash away the dust of old birds' nests and a crumbly cliff.

Stephen Goodwin

Eastern Crags
Al Davies and Nick Wharton, ed. Stephen Reid
The Fell and Rock Climbing Club, 2011, pp 498, £18

It was with a mixture of nostalgia and a sense of urgent revisit that I dived into the elegant 2011 edition of *Eastern Crags*, the new authoritative guidebook to the climbing in that less climbed side of the Lake District. The book covers an area stretching from Windermere in the south to Ullswater in the north, and includes some of the greatest trad cliffs in Britain such as the North Buttress of Dove Crag, Raven Crag Thirlmere, and Raven Crag Threshwaite Cove.

I first climbed in the area as a teenager and remember being completely awestruck by the quality of isolation combined with the outstanding climbing to be found on the best cliffs in this hidden corner of north-west England. I recall one particular day when Kevin Avery and I climbed the classics *Fear and Fascination* and *Bucket City* on Dove Crag: when I reached the top of the latter the mist came in over the summit of Fairfield, smudging out the fading light, and my ropes vanished down into the swirling cloud. Just as I was preparing to abseil off, a raven swooped past, then circled, croaking as I descended. It remains one of the best day's trad climbing in Britain I can remember.

As befits such a singular and charismatic region, *Eastern Crags* combines a classic design style with clear and informative route descriptions, detailed modern photo-topos, and excellent diagrams and maps (the latter being of great importance in an area where many of the cliffs are invisible from any road or inhabited place). It is refreshing that the authors have retained the traditional size of these guidebooks – which makes them much easier to carry on long routes than the larger A5 format guides – whilst including all the information demanded by the contemporary user.

It is particularly commendable that French grades of many of the harder (E5 and above) trad routes are given. This is of significant value to prospective on-sighters, and ought to become a standard principle in all British climbing guides. Providing this kind of information obviously requires a significant degree of local knowledge, and that is one of the tremendous strengths of this book. Both the level of authorial expertise and the extensive history section in *Eastern Crags* also illuminate some of the problems of selective guidebooks, whose authors are often unable to provide important details of the harder routes, or to create a sense of a region's climbing history due to the limitations of copy space.

Eastern Crags is a marvellous guidebook to one of the UK's finest climbing areas, and the clarity of its composition, its sense of place and history, and the level of local knowledge it brings to the reader remind us all what real British climbing guidebooks should actually look like, and what they are actually for.

David Pickford

Skye: The Cuillin
Mike Lates
Scottish Mountaineering Club, 2011, pp 324, £25
Skye: Sea-cliffs & Outcrops
Mark Hudson
Scottish Mountaineering Club, 2012, pp 336, £25
Skye Scrambles
Noel Williams
Scottish Mountaineering Club, 2011, pp 400, £25

Befitting its status as the most alpine-like part of the British Isles, Skye probably contains more exposed climbable rock than the rest of the country put together. Such is the vastness of the climbing potential that, despite our information-saturated society, only a fraction of the best lines are well known, and many of the low technical difficulty climbs hardly at all.

Faced with such an overwhelming amount of climbing terrain, the SMC has decided the only answer is to take a radical approach – implementing a three-pronged strategy to overhaul the documentation of the island's recent climbing exploration. The result is a trio of guidebooks devoted to the Cuillin, the coastal and sub-alpine cliffs and to the scrambles.

The Cuillin are admirably covered in the flagship volume of the set. The range is notoriously complex, and sometimes confusing even to aficionados. But the copious use of full-colour topos, allied to local expert Mike Lates's clear and unambiguous prose, helps nullify the background noise generated by a chaotic concertina of hard-to-pronounce peaks and corries. These improvements, partly enabled by the enormous advance in colour printing technology, mean the current volume marks an enormous leap forward compared to the last edition published 15 years ago.

Not only are there far more climbs recorded, in better, clearer detail than ever, but the guide remains slim and lightweight (still just 390g) ensuring it can easily be carried up into the remote mountains – which is after all its primary purpose. But it also works well in its secondary role – as an armchair research tool – thanks to an array of colour action and landscape shots peppering the text.

Skye Sea-Cliffs & Outcrops meanwhile is destined to become a long-overdue boon to those long-suffering visitors to the island whose Cuillin ambitions are all too often rained on. Within its covers is a staggering collection of

SCOTTISH MOUNTAINEERING CLUB
SCRAMBLERS' GUIDE

holiday-salvaging short routes, massively expanded now they have been liberated from being shackled to the mountains in guidebook form. Usually set in delectable lowland situations, most of which have largely been the secret playground of locals until now, the range of enticing climbs recorded is likely to be revelatory even to visitors who thought they were familiar with the island.

At the other end of the technical spectrum, the latest edition of Noel Williams's scrambles guide reveals an enticing cornucopia of 200 easier climbs and scrambles, plus some outstanding walks, which might easily detain the visiting climber for an entire lifetime. In addition, the book contains the most authoritative description of the Cuillin Main Ridge Traverse. All its potentially confusing sections are carefully and clearly described together with extremely useful technical sketch maps annotating the crux areas and potential emergency escape routes.

Skye Scrambles also develops a welcome trend in recent SMC publications by expanding their compass beyond the narrow focus of climbing or hillwalking information. Thus there are expansive and authoritative chapters on the geology, archaeology, history and natural history of the Cuillin range, all attractively illustrated.

For the curious mountain explorer they offer excellent primers on the environment in which all the climbing activity takes place. All in all, *Skye Scrambles* represents an exemplary holistic approach to describing the mountaineering experience of a range in its broadest sense.

It is difficult to see how any climber might think of visiting Skye without any of these guides from now on.

Colin Wells

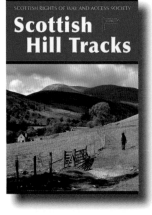

Scottish Hill Tracks
Scottish Rights of Way and Access Society
Scottish Mountaineering Trust, 2011, pp 252, £18

First published in 1947, this is the fifth edition of Scottish Hill Tracks. With 344 routes, it is a unique resource for walkers, cyclists, riders and runners wishing to explore the network of paths, old roads and rights of way which criss-cross Scotland's hill country, from the Borders to Caithness. Divided into 24 sections, each with a detailed colour map, this new edition has been fully revised and features more than 100 colour photographs of the routes.

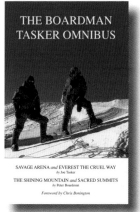

SAVAGE ARENA *and* EVEREST THE CRUEL WAY
by Joe Tasker
THE SHINING MOUNTAIN *and* SACRED SUMMITS
by Peter Boardman

Foreword by Chris Bonington

The Boardman Tasker Omnibus
Peter Boardman and Joe Tasker
Bâton Wicks, 2012, pp 873, £22

The re-issue of this omnibus edition of books by Peter Boardman and Joe Tasker, coming 30 years after their disappearance on the north-east ridge of Everest, serves as reminder not only of their tragic loss to family and friends but also of the loss to mountaineering literature of two outstanding talents from whom so much more eloquent writing might have been expected.

Each wrote two books that captured the excitement and commitment of high altitude climbing in the 1970s: Boardman's *The Shining Mountain* and *Sacred Summits* and Tasker's *Savage Arena* and *Everest the Cruel Way*. The quartet was first published in omnibus form in 1995 – a classic collection that has sold some 20,000 copies and now gone out of print in hardback.

Ken Wilson at Bâton Wicks is to be commended for keeping the literary legacy of Boardman and Tasker to the fore with this new edition of the *Omnibus*. It has a fresh cover, additional photographs at the start of each component book and an updated history of the mountain literature prize founded as the pair's memorial, with lists of entries, shortlists, winners and judges. Keeping the price affordable in a trade paperback should also help keep alive the writing of this talented pair. *SG*

The Boardman Tasker Prize for Mountain Literature 2011

Winner: *Freedom Climbers* by Bernadette McDonald, *Rocky Mountain Books, Canada*
Others shortlisted:
Desert Towers by Steve 'Crusher' Bartlett, *Sharp End Publishing*
Murder in The Hindu Kush by Tim Hannigan, *The History Press*
Shadow of The Matterhorn by Ian Smith, *Carreg*
The Sound of Gravity by Joe Simpson, *Jonathan Cape*
There were 25 entries.
Judges: Barry Imeson, Bernard Newman and Lindsay Griffin.

In Memoriam

The Alpine Club Obituary	Year of Election
	(including to ACG)
Alasdair Andrews	1984
George Band OBE	1953
Anthony (Tony) Bertram	1967
Alan Blackshaw OBE	1954
Walter Bonatti	Hon 2007
Peter Fleming	1976
Robert Folkard	1983
Alistair Gordon	1993
Arthur Grout	1976
Rev James (Jim) Harrison	1985
Rupert Hoare	1984
Jagdish Nanavati	1966
Alan Oliver	1966
Tim Oliver	1983
Roger Payne	1981
Guy Randle	1995
Wg Cdr Stewart Ward	1968
Michael (Mike) Westmacott	1952
Jocelin Winthrop Young OBE	1955

As usual, the Editor will be pleased to receive obituaries for any of those above not included in the following pages.

George Band, BMC Buxton Conference, 1994.
(Bernard Newman)

George Christopher Band OBE
1929 - 2011

With the death of George Band in August 2011 followed by that of Mike Westmacott in June 2012 the 'family' of British mountaineers who forged close bonds in the 1950s, notably on the crowning 1953 Everest expedition, suddenly seems much depleted.

George was the youngest of the climbers taken to Everest by John Hunt, and though Hunt, Tenzing Norgay and Edmund Hillary died some years ago, he tirelessly kept the Everesters' show on the road at anniversary galas, countless lectures and through charitable work. Until illness laid him low, Mike Westmacott would be there too, a quieter presence out of the limelight.

On Everest, George played an important role in forcing a route through the Khumbu Icefall, but his greatest mountaineering achievement came two years later on another Himalayan giant. On 25 May 1955, he and Mancunian Joe Brown became the first to stand – almost – on the summit of Kangchenjunga (8586m). In deference to Sikkimese beliefs, they stopped several yards short of the summit cone, leaving its sacred snows undefiled.

Everest and Kangchenjunga confirmed George as one of the top alpinists of his day and also provided the nexus for a network of climbers, their families and friends that in essence would constitute the British mountaineering establishment for the next half-century.

George was born on 2 February 1929 in Taiwan, then under Japanese control, where his parents were Presbyterian missionaries. He was educated at Eltham College, south London, and Queen's College, Cambridge, where he read Geology, followed by Petroleum Engineering at Imperial College, London. A member of the Cambridge University Mountaineering Club, of which he became president, he was at the forefront of a mainly Oxbridge set pushing the standard of British climbing in the Alps.

George had other qualifications that appealed to Hunt besides a 1952 season in the Alps which included a string of first British or first British guideless ascents. National Service in the Royal Corps of Signals appeared to make him a natural for radio duties and when George pointed out he had actually been a messing officer, Hunt responded, 'Better still, then you can also help... with the food.' At base camp, to vary the daily 'compo' diet, this, on one occasion, entailed George holding the tether of a yak as it was shot and then gutting it.

'At least there was no shortage of cold storage around,' he recalled in

235. George Band on mess duties during the 1953 Everest expedition. *(Alfred Gregory/Royal Geographical Society)*

Everest: the Official History (HarperCollins, 2003). 'To celebrate, we had scones for tea and then a tremendous supper of yak brains and liver, followed by jam omelette. The following night it was yak tongue.'

George's cheery writing style tends to obscure the committing nature of some of the climbing he did on Everest and elsewhere. He spent a week in the hazardous Khumbu Icefall, along with a small group of other climbers, weaving between ice walls and bridging crevasses, opening the way into the Western Cwm, the great glacier trench that leads to the final ramparts of Everest.

A bout of flu obliged George to descend to the valley to recuperate, but he returned to help ferry loads up the Cwm and on to the Lhotse Face, as well as performing his radio duties, monitoring weather reports, and dishing out rations. His high point was escorting a group of Sherpas to Camp VII at 7300m. He was at advanced base camp with Hunt and others for the emotional moment when Hillary and Tenzing were escorted in, having, as Hillary put it: 'knocked the bastard off'.

Three days later, on 2 June, back at base camp, George tuned in the radio to the Overseas Service and the team listened to the Coronation of Queen Elizabeth II. Then came an additional announcement: 'Crowds waiting in the Mall also heard that Mount Everest had been climbed by the British Expedition.' The climbers were dumbfounded that the news had got back so soon – a scoop for James (now Jan) Morris of *The Times* who accompanied the expedition. George recorded in his diary: 'A lively evening. Finished off the rum. Sick as a dog!'

Back home, the Everesters were feted as heroes; George returned to Cambridge for his final year and five days after his last practical examination was at London airport bound for Pakistan and an attempt on 7788m Rakaposhi in the Karakoram. The CUMC team, led by Alfred Tissières, reached a feature called the Monk's Head (6340m) on the south-west spur before being thwarted by days of fresh snow. George told the story in engaging style in his first book, *Road to Rakaposhi* (1955). As remarkable as the climbing was the team's decision to drive a Bedford Dormobile the 7000 miles from Cambridge to Rawalpindi and back, via Damascus, Baghdad and Teheran. Three climbers drove it out, and the other three, including George, drove it back. He hoped the journey through 10 countries would be sufficient to learn how to drive, but failed his test twice on return.

George wrote the preface to *Road to Rakaposhi* while on the 1955 Kangchenjunga expedition. Led by Charles Evans, a Liverpool surgeon, it was a very different affair to Everest: compact and low key with much less national pride at stake. In fact as the climbers would be exploring new and dangerous ground there was no expectation they would reach the top; the expedition was a 'reconnaissance in force'. It was also a more socially mixed team than on Everest, exemplified by the pairing of George with Joe Brown, then a jobbing builder and rock-climbing phenomenon.

George was on messing duties again. He recalled being popular at first, but there were few villages en route and the craving for meat, eggs and fresh vegetables became strong. 'I was constantly reminded that "Just in case you're getting swollen headed, Band, the grub's bloody awful."'

Ascent would be via the 3000m Yalung (or south-west) face of Kangchenjunga. Hunt had predicted, correctly, that the technical climbing problems and objective dangers would be of a higher order than on Everest. At base camp George lay in his tent marking off avalanches on his tent pole with a pencil. After 24 hours he had counted 48 thundering down the face. Allowing that he had slept for a third of that time, George calculated avalanches were occurring every 20 minutes. 'The lower icefall was horrific and we were absolutely extended,' he recalled. 'But then we saw this little gully up on the left that seemed to circumvent seven-eights of it. Charles suggested Norman [Hardie] and I have a crack and hey presto!'

The team endured screaming winds and blizzards, but eventually George and Joe pitched their tent on an inadequate ledge at 8200m. Next day dawned fine – 'the God of Kangchenjunga was kind to us,' wrote George – and after a couple of pints of tea and a biscuit the pair set off for the summit. Shortly before the top they came to a wall broken by a vertical crack – an irresistible temptation to Joe. Cranking up the flow on his oxygen bottle, he disposed of the highest rock pitch ever attempted, though it would have been a modest Very Difficult grade at sea level; George followed, and there, 20 feet away and five feet higher, was the summit snow cone. They respectfully left it untrammelled.

Next day two other climbers, Norman Hardie and Tony Streather also reached the same point. Sadly, on return to base camp the climbers learnt that one of the Sherpas, Pemi Dorje, had died of cerebral thrombosis. To the Sherpas, it seemed, the God of Kangchenjunga had demanded a sacrifice after all.

Lecturing and writing kept George independent until 1957 when he pleased his parents by getting 'a proper job', beginning a long career with Royal Dutch Shell, initially as a petroleum engineer. At the end of the 1950s, while working in Texas, a millionaire offered to fund his next big

236. Khumbu Icefall, Everest 1953: George Band leads a group of Sherpas at 'Nasty Crevasse' across a ladder bridge between camps II and III. *(Charles Wylie/Royal Geographical Society)*

climbing trip. George was forced to decide which direction his life should take. When he asked Shell for more leave, he got a very similar letter to the one received by Chris Bonington during his junior days with Unilever. But whereas Chris, as he explained in his autobiography's title, chose to climb, Band would later quip: 'I chose to work.'

Oil and gas development took George to seven different countries – some, like Venezuela offering climbs on the side – before returning to England where, in 1983, he was appointed director general of the UK Offshore Operators Association. Home was in rural Hampshire where he and Susan raised three children.

After retirement in 1990, George returned to his first love of mountains – immersing himself in the affairs of bodies including the Alpine Club, the British Mountaineering Council, the Royal Geographical Society (serving as president of all three) and the Himalayan Trust, the charity founded by Edmund Hillary to provide education, health care and other aid to the Sherpa people of Nepal. He took over as chairman of the UK arm of the Trust in 2003 and worked ceaselessly as its ambassador even as his health was failing. George authored two more books, the Everest history and *Summit: 150 Years of The Alpine Club* (2006), also for HarperCollins, and led adventurous treks in the Himalaya for the company Far Frontiers, of which he was also chairman. In 2008 he was appointed OBE for services to mountaineering and charity.

George served as AC president from 1987 to 1989 and chairman of the council of Trustees of the Alpine Club Library from 1993 to 2005. He was also a regular and valued contributor to the *Alpine Journal*, well connected and informed, and able to turn round lucid copy, plus photographs, at short

237. George Band high on Kangchenjunga on the 1955 first ascent.
(Joe Brown/Royal Geographical Society)

notice. I already miss those 'George Band here' phone calls, re-assuring on the matter in hand and then diverging into mountaineering gossip.

News of George's cancer came as a shock to the mountaineering community. While other Everesters had aged and many passed on, George Band seemed to defy the years, energies matched by his affability. When the Alpine Club celebrated its 150th anniversary in Zermatt in 2007, George was in his element. For the media, AC leaders and their mountain celebrity guests made a mass ascent of the Breithorn, the 4164m snow summit above the resort. George had climbed it in 1963 during the club's centenary celebrations, via the tricky Younggrat. Fifty years later he reached the summit again, albeit by the easier standard route, but at aged 78 a testimony to George's unquenchable enthusiasm for the mountains.

Stephen Goodwin

Roger Chorley writes: In the summer of 1952 George suggested we team up for the Alps. I readily agreed. I had more alpine experience but George was considerably superior on rock. To help matters along financially – we were both Cambridge students – an American millionaire funded us to help with his theories of the Pleistocene ice age. For us this meant digging a tunnel in the glacier under the summit of Monte Rosa, the highest peak in Switzerland – a somewhat weird but very well paid job. We climbed on our days off, and one of our earliest big routes was the Cresta di Santa Caterina on the Nordend of Monte Rosa.

In those days the Brits – us that is – were keen to repeat as unguided amateurs some of the great routes of our forefathers. There was great cachet in doing 'first British guideless' climbs. The first ascent of the Cresta di Santa Caterina was a Ryan-Lochmatter route. This was a quality assurance of a fine but difficult route. Ryan was a gentleman mountaineer and F Lochmatter – the 'incomparable Franz' to use (I think) Geoffrey Winthrop Young's accolade, possibly the finest guide in alpine history.

We started for the route in the early hours of the morning. And the fact is we did not find it very difficult and we were back at the hut by lunchtime. A few weeks later I bumped into a Zermatt guide who said: 'Oh you were the couple who said they had done the Santa Caterinagrat. It can't be true, because you couldn't have been back by lunchtime.'

I'm not sure that I ever told George this story. It doesn't matter, but it does underline the fact that George, even in those days, was a considerable mountaineer. Over that fantastic summer George amassed a fine record of great routes, of 'first British guideless' ascents. It was a summer of exceptionally good weather and George used it to the full. It is not surprising that John Hunt spotted him when selecting the Everest team for 1953. 'Not surprising', but nevertheless bold – George was by a long way the youngest member of the team.

Michael Westmacott
1925 - 2012

Mike Westmacott in Derbyshire, 1970s.
(Ian Roper)

When several hundred breathless people reached the summit of Everest in May this year they did so thanks in no small measure to the labour of an unsung group of Sherpas known as the 'Icefall Doctors' whose job it is to maintain a passageway through the chaos of ice cliffs and crevasses of the Khumbu Icefall. 'Mike' Westmacott was in essence the prototype Icefall Doctor. While the final assault was underway in 1953 that would see Hillary and Tenzing to the 8850m summit, it was Mike and his team of Sherpas who were charged with keeping open the expedition's vital line of supply and return.

In 1953 the Icefall was still relatively unknown territory and much feared. The 1951 reconnaissance expedition led by Eric Shipton had penetrated to the lip of the Western Cwm and in spring 1952 the Swiss rigged a rope bridge across the giant crevasse that bars the top of the Icefall and entered the Cwm for the first time. Though Raymond Lambert and Tenzing Norgay got tantalisingly close, reaching almost 8600m, fatigue and bad weather finally forced them back.

As the Swiss were trying and failing on Everest – a second attempt in the autumn reached just over 8000m – young Michael Westmacott was embarking on his career as a statistician and enjoying a highly successful climbing season in the Alps. Everest hadn't seriously entered his head. That summer, with friends, he had spent three weeks in Switzerland and succeeded on a clutch of classic routes that would still be the envy of alpinists today, then finished with a traverse of the Matterhorn.

'As we made for our doss at Satfelalp, Dick [Viney] said 'We've had a marvellous day's climbing, Mike. Nothing like in the Himalayas – all slog, slog, slog – but wouldn't you give anything to go to Everest next year?' He was right, but I don't think it had occurred to me before to do anything about it.

The quote comes from a short recollection Mike wrote for the *Alpine Journal* on the 40th anniversary of the Everest ascent. Mike was the most self-effacing of men and first person accounts of his climbing emerged only in understated journal accounts and interviews. He was one of the few main players of 1953 not to write a book of his experiences.

238. John Hunt (left) and Mike Westmacott paying off porters, Everest 1953 *(Alfred Gregory/Royal Geographical Society)*

Born on 12 April 1925 in Babbacombe, Torquay, and educated at Radley College, Oxfordshire, Mike's first climbing adventures were scrambles on the limestone and sandstone cliffs behind the Torquay beaches. His father had been invalided out of the Royal Navy and would take the family for picnics among the tors of Dartmoor. But Mike was still years from catching the climbing bug and first had the excitement of service as a junior officer in King George V's Bengal Sappers and Miners, building bridges in Burma with 150 Japanese PoWs under his command. Then came Oxford, where he studied Mathematics, adding a further year of Statistics, and joined the university mountaineering club – initially more for the comradeship than to satisfy any great yen. His first rock climb was of Napes Needle in Wasdale, done in floppy tennis shoes on a cold day in December 1947.

The OUMC was on the cusp of a post-war mountaineering renaissance and together with its Cambridge counterpart would provide many of the leading climbers of the 1950s. Both George Band (Cambridge) and Mike had been president of their respective university mountaineering clubs and at the time John Hunt was selecting his Everest team both had just enjoyed excellent alpine seasons. Mike speculated that they might both have owed their Everest places to the good weather in the Alps in 1952.

Mike had been climbing with Anthony Rawlinson and Dick Viney; together in a 22hr 30min day they had climbed the east ridge of the Dent d'Hérens, one of the longest arêtes in the Alps, more than 2km long, 'sustained, exposed and committing'; Mike and Rawlinson went on to do the Weisshorn Schalligrat and the Cresta di Santa Caterina on Nordend. (Band and Roger Chorley had done the first British guideless ascent of the latter route earlier that same season – see page 400)

Mike was by this time employed as an agricultural statistician at the Rothamsted Experimental Station, for example analysing the effect of feeding penicillin to pigs. Returning from the Alps he had put in his Everest application as a long shot and some weeks later was delighted to receive an invitation for an interview at the RGS. Hunt was certainly impressed by the young man's alpine record, but as an ex-Sapper, Mike had other valuable skills. He was given responsibility for structural equipment, notably the ladders needed for bridging crevasses. As kit was being tested on the approach march, Mike assembled one of the sectional ladders between two large boulders. Hunt noted 'an alarming sag' in the middle but Mike's Sherpa assistants soon gained confidence as they crawled along it.

Mike joined Hillary, Band and others in forcing a route up the maze of the Icefall. Grisly names like 'Atom Bomb Area' and 'Mike's Horror' reflect the hazardous nature of the beast – the latter being an awkward crevasse negotiated by Mike in what Hunt praised as 'a fine feat of icemanship'. Higher on the mountain he helped push the route and carry loads on the Lhotse Face, but was dogged by sickness and reluctantly had to retreat having reached a height of about 7000m, just below Camp VI. He spent the succeeding days in the Icefall, engaged on the risky task of keeping a route open as the ice continually shifted. However he was back up at the camp at the head of the Western Cwm when Hillary and Tenzing returned triumphant.

Handshakes over, Mike accompanied *Times* correspondent Jan (then James) Morris, down through the Icefall in order to get the news back to London in time for the coronation of Queen Elizabeth II. It was late in the day and, as Westmacott recalled for the BBC, 'not the most sensible thing I've done from a mountaineering point of view. By the time we got to the bottom we were very tired indeed and it was getting dark.' Morris had already noted how much the Icefall had changed – 'messier and crumblier than ever before... its ice bridges soggy and ominous. Michael Westmacott had been working inside this horrible place for 10 days... I have often thought of Westmacott since, immured there in the icefall, and marvelled at his tenacity.'

Though few of the expedition members realised it at the time, the Everest experience would shape the rest of their lives. A dinner invitation to the young celebrity (though he would never have described himself as such) led to Mike's courtship of Sally Seddon, then studying at the Royal College of Music, and a long and happy marriage; together they climbed together in the Alps, North America and throughout the UK, often with other Everest friends. Mike left Rothamsted to work for Shell as an economist. During a spell for the company in the USA, in 1964 he and Sally joined a lightweight expedition to an untouched range of granite peaks in northern Alaska, the Arrigetch, where they made eight first ascents. In 1956 he went to Peru with a party including George Band and made the first ascent of Huaguruncho (5748m); and in 1968 he and Sally went to the Hindu Kush where with Hugh Thomlinson they made the first ascent of Wakhikah Rah (5681m) – 'three rock pinnacles on a beautifully sculptured snow ridge. It was one of the most beautiful summits I have known,' he wrote .

Most of Mike's years with Shell were spent working in London and living in Stanmore. He retired in 1985 and in 2000 the couple moved to the Lake District, close to friends and the best rock climbing in England. Mike had joined the AC in 1952, served as honorary secretary from 1967 to 71, president from 1993 to 95 and rightly became an honorary member. He was similarly active in the affairs of the Climbers' Club.

Mike's most public legacy to mountaineering must be the development of the Himalayan Index, an initiative of the Alpine Club Library, the council of which he chaired from 1984 to 1992. Aided by a small team, he created a computer database that now lists more than 4,000 peaks of above 6,000 metres and their climbing histories – an invaluable resource to expedition planners and available on the internet. Mike's labours on the Index led to him probably holding a record for the most nights spent in the AC bunkhouse. One of the few compensations I recall for a night in that cheerless basement was the pleasure of breakfast with Mike – and sometimes Sally too – in a café round the corner from Charlotte Road.

Mike died on 20 June 2012 after more than two years of debilitating illness. Next year will be the 60th anniversary of the Everest ascent and family and friends of the 1953 team will gather at an AC event at the Pen y Gwryd Hotel in Snowdonia, venue of many happy reunions. The absence of Mike Westmacott and George Band will be strongly felt, but there will be great lives to celebrate.

Stephen Goodwin

Alan Blackshaw. *(Ken Wilson)*

Alan Blackshaw OBE
1933 - 2011

For hillwalkers and climbers learning their craft in the late 1960s and 70s, the name 'Alan Blackshaw' meant just one thing, except to those who knew him personally, and that was 'Blackshaw's Mountaineering'. This compact and compendious manual contained advice on everything from buying your first hiking boots to leading hard rock routes in the Alps.

Mountaineering: From Hill Walking to Alpine Climbing (Penguin Books 1965) was the training 'bible' of its day. The Americans had *Freedom of the Hills*, a bulky volume produced by a large team of experts, and the Brits had 'Blackshaw's Mountaineering' – or just 'Blackshaw' – written in his spare time by a civil servant in the then Ministry of Power. My own 1977 edition runs to 556 pages. By then Alan was Director General of the Offshore Supplies Office with responsibilities for the development of the North Sea oil industry. A capacity for detailed work on several different fronts was just one of the talents of this courteous man: a warm and generous friend and host, yet resolute in causes and disputes – of which he pursued several.

Alan Blackshaw was born in Liverpool on 7 April 1933. His father was a docker and his mother had a corner shop on the dock road where the infant Alan slept under the counter. His first sight of the hills came during the Second World War when, aged six, he was evacuated to a farm in the Black Mountains. Welsh was the only language spoken. After returning home, he won a scholarship to Merchant Taylor's School, Crosby, and then an Open Scholarship to Wadham College, Oxford, where he gained an MA in Modern History and honed his skills as a climber. 'Night climbing' on the dreaming college spires and rooftops was, and maybe still is, one of the illicit pleasures of student life for a minority at Oxford. One Eights Week, he and Hamish Nicol, another leading light in the Oxford University Mountaineering Club (OUMC), installed a neon sign on the top of Trinity Tower, flashing on and off 'Bloody Trinity' in revenge for some since forgotten transgression.

Climbing had been discovered through cycling. Given a bike for his 14th birthday, young Alan cycled from Liverpool to Land's End and back. The following year he set off for John o'Groats. While pedalling through Glencoe he met a bunch of climbers and did his first route. One of them sold him a pair of nailed boots and a hemp rope. The die was cast: Alan entered the world of the impecunious climber, hitchhiking, dossing in barns, climbing on crags such as Gimmer in the Lake District and Clogwyn D'ur Arddu, North Wales. In 1951 a place in a Workers' Educational Association party introduced him to the Alps and the climbing paradise of the Chamonix valley. Alan's best season in the Alps was summer 1955 when with various partners he made first British ascents of the north face of the Aiguille de Triolet, south face of the Aiguille du Géant, Republique Arête of the Grands Charmoz and south face of the Pointe Gugliermina, all in the Mont Blanc-Chamonix area, where later in life he would buy an apartment, and the north face of Piz Badile in the Bregaglia. Oxford days over, he was doing National Service and became an officer instructor in the cliff assault wing of 42 Commando, Royal Marines.

Alan was at the top of his climbing game and might have been expected to

239. Alan Blackshaw during an 800km ski traverse from Sulitjelma on the Arctic Circle to the North Cape in 1979. *(Mike Esten)*

graduate to the Himalaya where the 8000m peaks were being scaled. But in the summer of 1956 British mountaineers, and particularly the OUMC set, were shaken by the deaths of Tom Bourdillon and Dick Viney on the Jägihorn in the Bernese Alps. Bourdillon had been one of the bright stars of the OUMC and had reached the south summit of Everest in 1953. Alan recalled: 'It was a terrible shock and we had to think very deeply about mountaineering, the ethical issues involved, and the question of obligations to families and civil society. I came to realise that the very hard forms of mountaineering no longer held quite the same appeal for me.'[1] (*AJ* 2005) That still left plenty of scope: he went on expeditions to the Caucasus (1958) and Greenland (1960) with John Hunt and continued as a mountain warfare instructor in the Royal Marines Reserve until 1974. In a foreword to 'Blackshaw's Mountaineering', Hunt wrote: 'I know of no one with whom I feel more confidence and comradeship on a rope.'

In fact the feat for which Alan is best remembered did not come until 1972 – his leadership of the first British continuous ski traverse of the Alps, more than 400 miles in 49 days from near the Grossglockner in central Austria to the southern fringe of the Ecrins where the snow ran out. Later in the 1970s he skied Scandinavia from end-to-end in sections.

Traversing the mountains on skis remained a passion almost until his final months. Work and places of play had drawn closer in 1974 when Alan moved to Scotland to set up the headquarters of the Offshore Supplies Office in Glasgow for the growing oil and gas industry. He had been principal private secretary to three ministers of power, including Tony Benn, and held other senior posts, however decided to leave the Civil Service at the end of the 1970s to concentrate on writing and updating his mountaineering manual.

1. *AJ 110*, 263-276

This bold career move was unfortunately timed. 'By a freak of fate', as Alan termed it, his resignation coincided with a parliamentary investigation into what was alleged to be mis-spending on North Sea oil grants; certain newspapers incorrectly concluded this was why Alan had left. Although he was exonerated by the government and awarded compensation, the legal wrangling dragged on. Eventually he obtained libel damages against the *Daily Telegraph* – upheld in the Court of Appeal in 1983 – and the *Daily Mail*.

The Civil Service's loss was the mountaineering community's gain, though a new manual was a casualty of those four traumatic years. While earning a living as a management consultant, Alan threw himself into the clubs and councils side of the outdoor world, voluntary work that culminated in the presidencies of bodies such as the British Mountaineering Council (1973-76), Eagle Ski Club (1980-82), Ski Club of Great Britain (1997-2003), and the Alpine Club (2001-4). He was made an OBE in 1992.

Most notable perhaps was his service on the world representative body for mountaineering, the *Union Internationale des Associations d'Alpinisme* (UIAA). Increasingly concerned about issues such as sustainable tourism, he was a key player, on behalf of the UIAA, in the United Nations International Year of the Mountains in 2002. However in 2005 he resigned as UIAA President after just one year in the top post amid bitter faction fighting.

Causes and disputes were a speciality. He could be a dogged opponent, as Scottish Natural Heritage discovered when he challenged their somewhat feudal view on rights of access to the hills. Alan advocated a 'freedom to roam', and in alliance with Dave Morris of Ramblers Scotland helped secure access laws that are the envy of walkers and climbers south of the border. The Land Reform (Scotland) Act 2003 was a big feather in his cap.

Yet conviviality was as much a part of Alan's life as controversy. Home was on the edge of the Cairngorms, a comfortable house at Newtonmore where visitors were always assured of a warm welcome from Alan and his wife Elspeth, a GP in nearby Aviemore. Diagnosed with non-Hodgkins lymphoma in 2007, he remained doggedly active between bouts of treatment and late in 2010 crewed on a 36ft yacht sailing across the Atlantic from Tenerife to Brazil. Only days before his final admission to Raigmore hospital, Inverness, he was still engaged in busy email correspondence on mountain issues.

I will miss the arrival in the post of those heavy A4 envelopes – or their email equivalent – with pages of forensic argument that signalled Alan on another mission. However his biggest impact on my life came in late 2003 when he pressed me to take on the editorship of the *Alpine Journal*. Alan was the Alpine Club president at the time. Having done the editor's job himself for three volumes (1968-70) he knew what was involved, but being a skilful persuader he rather underplayed it.

Stephen Goodwin

Doug Scott writes: I first became aware of Alan Blackshaw 50 years ago when checking out climbs in the Alpine Climbing Group Bulletin that Alan had edited. In it were lists of routes British climbers were doing including some by Alan and his fellow alpinists – routes that might be possible for myself and friends in the Nottingham Climbing Club to do; the *Cassin Route* on the Badile, Dent de Geant south face. It was a useful, if not essential publication, before the plethora of magazines available today

He went on to edit the *Alpine Journal*, introducing a modern format with integrated black and white photos and an index – most useful for those researching information. He persuaded younger climbers to contribute, including myself, giving encouragement and advice – advice about many things, as when I was bemoaning national park and council bureaucrats. 'Don't write them off,' he replied, 'bureaucrats don't mind what they do, as long as they are doing something, so get in there first and programme them to do what is really needed.'

Alan's contribution to the world of mountaineering owed much to his appreciation of the traditional British climbing scene from which he drew great strength. He was very proud to have been president of the AC as I was and Chris Bonington and everyone so privileged right back to 1857. He wrote: 'The fact that the Club is so firmly within the world of mountaineering for its own sake – with practically no links with commerce or officialdom – is perhaps its greatest strength.'

As with many of you here I would from time to time receive even weightier reports usually on matters of access – the Cuillin mountain range of Skye comes to mind and then the Cairngorm Funicular railway project was another, not to mention The Land Reform (Scotland) Act of 2003. Alan derived so much pleasure from the time he spent in wild places on rock, snow and on the oceans that he naturally wanted the same for everyone. He sought rights of access also as a means not only to lift one's state of being, but as a means to conserve the remaining natural places. He pursued this quest all the way to the UN where he was a member of the UN Inter Agency Group on Mountains. Alan wanted it set in stone that there is a 'Fundamental Human Right to the Enjoyment of Nature'.

Another of the many 'causes' that Alan took on was that of the ownership and copyright of the Everest photos. They had been lodged at the RGS who had proceeded to claim them and benefit from sales. Alan swung into action producing a report on the matter one hundred pages long and in two volumes. This proved to be good background material for Martin Scott to subsequently bring about a compromise between the MEF and the RGS.

Hiroo Saso sent this message from the president of the Japanese Mountaineering Association Tadao Kanzaki and Fumio Tanaka, the former president: 'Alan was a good friend to us and we acknowledge his great contribution to the UIAA and to the mountaineering community of the world. We shall never forget his gentle smile on the floor of UIAA meetings.'

The Japanese, as in a haiku brush stroke, evoke an impression in that one sentence of Alan that we all recall – Alan's gentle smile that survived all the extreme challenges he faced throughout his life – physical, intellectual and emotional.

Walter Bonatti at the BMC Buxton Conference 1984.
(Bernard Newman)

Walter Bonatti 1930 - 2011

Walter Bonatti could have made the first ascent of K2. He was the most talented member of the Italian expedition that climbed the world's second highest mountain in 1954, but at 24 he was also the youngest, relegated to a disappointing support role that nearly cost him his life. With the local Hunza porter Mahdi, he had to carry up oxygen cylinders for the chosen summit pair, Achille Compagnoni and Lino Lacedelli, who at the last minute pitched camp some distance from the agreed site. After a long exhausting day, arriving at nightfall, Bonatti was unable to reach the re-sited camp and it was too late to descend to a lower camp, so was forced to spend a night in the open, without tent or sleeping bag at 8100m. It was a hideous ordeal, made worse by Mahdi's delirious attempts to hurl himself from the precarious snow ledge, but both men survived, descending to safer altitude at first light. Meanwhile, aided by the vital oxygen cylinders, Compagnoni and Lacedelli reaped glory for themselves and for Italy, reaching the summit late that evening.

The K2 experience left Bonatti embittered. Not only was his heroic sacrifice unacknowledged: the summit pair blamed him for the fact that they ran out of oxygen near the top, suggesting that he had stolen some of it. The accusation was patently absurd – Bonatti had neither mask nor adaptor to deplete the cylinders; Compagnoni and Lacedelli were simply too slow – but the slur rubbed salt in the wounds of a man who, despite being one of the greatest mountaineers of all time, was quite thin skinned and prone to controversy.

Born on 22 June 1930 into a poor family near Bergamo, Walter had a tough adolescence around his home town during the Second World War and it was only in 1948, aged 18, that he discovered climbing, on the limestone pinnacles of the Grignetta, near Lecco. From then onwards, as he later wrote in his autobiography, *The Great Days*, 'I was devoted heart and soul to rock faces, to overhangs, to the intimate joy of trying to overcome my own weakness in a struggle that committed me to the very limits of the possible.' With a lesser climber, that might sound like posturing hyperbole, but with Bonatti the words rang true. He was bold and imaginative, with a resilient streak of asceticism. Right from the start he was repeating the hardest existing routes in the Alps and in 1951 he opened climbers' eyes with his first ascent of the east face of the Grand Capuçin – a beautiful, forbiddingly steep wall of compact granite in the Mont Blanc massif.

After the K2 debacle of 1954, as if in search of catharsis, he resolved to push himself even harder. The result was the first ascent of the spectacular south-west pillar of the Dru, familiar to every tourist who has ever gazed across the Mer de Glace from the railway station at Montenvers. On the first day Bonatti accidentally sliced off the tip of a finger with his piton hammer. He also dropped his stove, so was unable to melt snow for water. At that stage most people would have packed it in, but he continued with his self-imposed task, for six days, quenching his thirst with two cans of beer, climbing alone up some of the steepest, hardest rock attempted at that time. After each rope length he had to descend, removing the pitons he had hammered into the rock, then climb laboriously back up the rope. On day five, faced with an insurmountable overhang, he tied a bundle of pitons and wooden wedges to one end of the rope, hurled it over the roof, then swung free over the thousand metres void, praying that his improvised bolas would hold in the jammed blocks of granite above. It did, and he survived to complete what became known as the Bonatti Pillar.

In 1956 Bonatti made the first complete ski traverse of the Alps. In 1958 he returned to Pakistan as a member of Riccardo Cassin's expedition to Gasherbrum IV (7925m). The final section up the north-east ridge gave some of the hardest climbing ever achieved at that altitude. Bonatti led every pitch, supported by Carlo Mauri and it was only 28 years later, in 1986, that the mountain was climbed again, when Tim Macartney-Snape found Bonatti's original abseil piton on the summit block.

Elsewhere in the world's greater ranges, Bonatti made the first ascent of Rondoy North in Peru; but his real legacy lies in the Mont Blanc massif, above his adopted home of Courmayeur. Earning his living as a mountain guide, he knew every nook and cranny of the range and in his spare time he was always exploring new corners, stretching his own personal limits. With Cosimo Zapelli in 1963 he made the first winter ascent of the Walker Spur, on the great north face of the Grandes Jorasses. On the same face, with the Swiss climber, Michel Vaucher, he made the first ascent of the Whymper Spur. He was the first to dare to tackle the high remote Grand Pilier d'Angle on Mont Blanc, creating two routes with Zapelli and one with Toni Gobbi. It was also on Mont Blanc, in July 1961, that he survived one of the most epic disasters in alpine history.

Bonatti and his two Italian companions joined forces with four French climbers to attempt the unclimbed Central Pillar of Frêney. It would be the highest, hardest rock climb on the highest peak in western Europe, but after a long, committing approach they were caught by a ferocious electric storm near the top. After three nights huddled on a ledge, Bonatti realised that continuing was impossible and retreat by their approach route too dangerous. The only other option was a long, highly complex descent down an untried route onto the chaotically broken Frêney glacier. The storm barely relented, and in whiteout conditions Bonatti had to draw on all his instinct and experience to find a way down. Four of the team died from hypothermia and exhaustion, but without Bonatti's leadership it is doubtful whether anyone would have returned alive.

After operating for nearly two decades at the highest level, Bonatti decided cannily to retire from extreme alpinism. Ever the showman with a sense of history, he chose for his swansong an extremely hard new direct route up the north face of the Matterhorn. He climbed it alone, over six days, in the winter of 1965 – the centenary of the first ascent of the mountain. Aeroplanes filled with journalists circled the mountain as he emerged from the face to stand and wave beside the summit cross. Thereafter he concentrated on his own journalism, travelling the world as a freelance photojournalist, drawn particularly to the wild empty spaces of Patagonia.

In 2009 the Italian Alpine Club finally accepted Bonatti's version of what happened on K2 in 1954. Meanwhile, in 2007, he had been made an honorary member of the Alpine Club and invited to the club's 150th anniversary celebrations in Zermatt. There, beneath the Matterhorn, scene of his greatest triumph, he was the star guest – a charming charismatic man who gave no hint of the former controversies that had dogged his otherwise fulfilled long life.

Stephen Venables

Mirella Tenderini writes: During the last few years of his life Walter was bestowed a series of recognitions which he received with an almost naïve emotion: the first 'lifetime achievement' Piolet d'Or, awarded in Chamonix in 2009, the first honorary citizenship of Mont Blanc and honorary membership of the British Alpine Club among others. Walter was perhaps the best known and most popular mountaineer in the world. His books have been translated into countless languages and the first two, *On the Heights* and *The Great Days,* have been an inspiration for three generations of mountain lovers.

For Walter's postwar generation, mountaineering was a means of redemption from a life of mediocrity and deprivation and the achievement of self-assurance and respect. His climbing career began on spires of the Grignetta (2177m) that dominate the eastern branch of Lake of Como – the forcing ground which bred formidable figures such as Riccardo Cassin – and at age 19 he had already repeated most of the classic ascents of his predecessors, including Cassin's route on the Walker Spur of Grandes Jorasses, the *Ratti-Vitali* line on the west face of the Aiguille Noire de Peuterey, and the *Bramani-Castiglioni Route* on the north-west face of Piz Badile. In 1951 he accomplished the epochal climb of the east face of Grand Capucin, applying Dolomite aid techniques to the great walls of Mont Blanc and showing the possibility of climbing vertical or even overhanging granite in the kingdom of ice and snow. He distinguished himself also by accomplishing the first winter ascents of the north face of Cima Ovest di Lavaredo and of the

Furggen Ridge of the Matterhorn, where he completed the classic route with a variation along a new direct line.

Walter's abundant success stimulated several young climbers to follow his tracks and played an important role in the development of rock climbing in the high Alps. When, in 1954, he was chosen to be part of the Italian expedition to K2, he was not only the youngest member of the team but plainly the strongest, and his presence upset some of his companions, especially those chosen for the summit, who feared he might take their role off them. They played a dirty trick on him and what was worse the leader of the expedition, Ardito Desio, refused to listen to Walter's version, accepting that of Compagnoni and Lacedelli, which became the official one.

It was a deplorable episode that scarred Walter's inner being so deeply as to torment him for more than 50 years, until the Italian Alpine Club officially re-examined the lamentable affair, corrected the falsified version and restored Walter's truth. That incident had an enormous impact on Walter's life: the utter injustice he had to endure for a long time frustrated him deeply. On the other hand it gave him a strong impetus; his want of revenge urged him to dare the impossible in order to assert himself in front of the whole world. His six-day solo ascent of the south-west pillar of the Petit Dru (1955), with an epic no-return pendulum, captured the imagination of mountaineers and even non-mountaineers and reached the front pages of daily papers and magazines, launching his popularity in Italy as a national hero.

Walter's success gained him many supporters, particularly among the new generation of young and ambitious climbers, but also gave rise to jealousy and even open hostility. In Courmayeur, where he had moved in 1957 to be near Mont Blanc and to earn his living as a guide, he was generally considered an outsider and – with a few exceptions – he was spared no criticisms when accidents occurred, as in the case of the tragedy of the Frêney Pillar in 1961 when he lost his friend and faithful partner Andrea Oggioni. Soon afterwards he moved to Chamonix on the other side of Mont Blanc and continued his high level activity.

In 1965, at the zenith of his career, Walter decided to leave the stage after accomplishing a final, theatrical exploit: a new direct route on the north face of Matterhorn in winter and solo. He had given up guiding a few years earlier, however had written two very successful books and gave lectures illustrated with slides. He was a good photographer and a fascinating narrator, and soon received a proposal to work as a photojournalist for *Epoca*, one of the most prestigious weekly magazines in Italy. For some 15 years he travelled to the remotest places in the world, from the Yukon to Cape Horn, writing articles and photographing surviving wild places.

He quit *Epoca* when changes in the magazine management interfered with his freedom of choice. He went on writing books and delivering lectures. And he never stopped climbing mountains: with no publicity, just for his own pleasure. He also built his own house and tended his garden, like an ancient Roman hero, to live peacefully with Rossana Podestà, the movie actress who shared with him thirty years out of the limelight. Together with her and a few close friends he continued his travels to distant places. During those years, far from competition and rivalries, his bitterness dissolved showing the best side of his generous personality and the fidelity to his own ideals which he enunciated in his books and practised his whole life: those ideals which made him a myth and an example for younger generations.

lasdair Andrews. *(John Monks)*

Alasdair Ian Andrews 1939 - 2011

Alasdair Andrews was born in 1939 in Edinburgh where he lived all his life. Following National Service he joined Ferranti Ltd working in the accounts department. He had a long and successful career with the company, ending as Company Secretary, and retired in 1998 having worked there for 39 years.

Aside from his work, the two great interests in Andrew's life were music and mountaineering. At school he was a gifted chorister and he nearly became a professional singer. However, although he elected for a safer career, he continued singing. In 1975 he was a founder member of the Edinburgh Practice Choir, and then in 1979 he joined both the Edinburgh Festival Chorus and what became the Scottish Chamber Orchestra Chorus. He sang with all three choirs for more than 30 years, and many of their members sang at his Service of Thanksgiving.

He seldom missed a rehearsal. Evidence of this is that his Alpine meets always had to finish before the end of July so that he could start rehearsing for the Festival. His climbing friends had an opportunity to hear his singing voice on a wet day in the Valais when we visited the church in Ernen and he decided to test the acoustics by giving us a splendid rendering of the climbers' version of *Om Mane Padme Hum*.

But it was as a mountaineer that I knew him. Like many of us his love of the outdoors started as a Scout and as a member of the YHA, and then he joined the Junior Mountaineering Club of Scotland. Once at work he became a leading member of the Ferranti Mountaineering Club, a very active club in those days, becoming club secretary and organising many of the Club's meets. After his first trip to Switzerland in 1968 he joined the ABMSAC and in 1984 was elected to the Alpine Club.

It was through the ABMSAC that we met. In 1974 we found ourselves sitting next to each other at the Club's Northern Dinner at Glenridding. We discovered we had a mutual love of the Scottish hills and he suggested that I come up to Scotland for a weekend with other friends. He borrowed a cottage at Fearnan by Loch Tay which subsequently became the base for many of his early meets. The weekend was a great success and included a traverse of Meall nan Tarmachan in winter conditions. This led him to start organising Scottish weekend meets for the ABMSAC. He arranged meets for us all over the Highlands and we used to joke about his encyclopaedic knowledge of Scottish bunkhouses. These meets were soon an established feature of the Club calendar. As is to be expected in Scotland, the weather was not always kind but the meets were always enjoyable occasions thanks to Alasdair's unfailingly cheerful personality and his knack of livening up any party.

The ABMSAC's annual calendars illustrate his energy. In 1997 he organised no fewer than 10 meets, with similar numbers in other years. He was elected president of the ABMSAC in 2003, and on demitting office was made an honorary life member in recognition of his service to the Club.

But his enthusiasm did not wane and he continued to organise meets, some hotel based, others trekking from hut to hut, always in different areas of the Alps, Dolomites or Pyrenees. These were joint AC/ABMSAC meets, and a number of AC members participated in them. It was on the first of his treks in 1999, the tour of Monte Rosa, that he met his wife Pamela, also an AC member, and they organised the next 12 years of meets together. In his last year he attended meets in Scotland, Fiesch and Bhutan, and was already making plans for the following year's meet in the Val d'Aosta. Even at the July meet at Fiesch those of us with him saw no sign of the cancer which claimed him so quickly.

Alasdair would be the first to agree that he was no North Wall tiger, but he had an enormous wealth of experience as a mountaineer, with a creditable list of peaks to his name. He had also climbed all the 284 Munros which is no mean achievement.

What we will miss, and Pamela most of all, is not just his energy in organising meets, but his personality. He was one of the most charismatic people I have known, always full of laughter and jokes, and a good person to have around when the ground was steep or the going turned rough.

John Dempster

Alistair Gordon 1943 - 2011

Alistair Gordon was born in Aberdeen in 1943. His father, Bill, was a baker, a reserved occupation. Bill had been sent to Fort William where he lodged while the family, including Alistair, remained in Aberdeen. Later, the Fort William connection became the high point of Alistair's childhood because the family Bill had lodged with invited the family back for summer holidays. It was the start of Alistair's life-long love of the hills.

In his early teens Alistair finally persuaded his parents to buy him a bike and this was his passport to freedom. Weekends and holidays were spent youth hostelling with friends and cousins. Then, in 1958, the music teacher

Alistair Gordon

at Aberdeen Grammar School started a hill-walking club and that was the start of his Munro bagging career, at the age of 14.

At 16 he started work as an apprentice quantity surveyor and once qualified decided to head for the bright lights of London and got himself a job working on the of the Museum of London project.

Later in life, wanting more fulfilment, he studied for 10 years to gain an honours degree from the Open University. This enabled him to become a chartered surveyor with the RICS. All of this was fitted in around work and climbing.

Once in London he had plenty of spare time, outside work, so he joined an evening class in rock climbing. It was here where he met several people who together went on to join the London Mountaineering Club (LMC) and become lifelong friends. Thereafter most weekends were spent, travelling 4-up in his mini, to Wales or the Peak District, with occasional visits to Harrisons Rocks and to Scotland for the snow and ice.

It was in his early LMC days that I met Alistair and after climbing together for a few months we made our first ventures to the Alps. Chamonix and camping in Snell's field was the usual fare. Over three seasons in the early 1970s while we climbed at a modest standard we did plenty of routes and gained much experience. Even today after nearly 30 years I can still remember the day we climbed the aiguilles Mummery and Ravanel: we had traversed Les Courtes from the Couvercle hut the day before and stayed for another route; the ascent was uneventful until we got to the top of Aiguille Mummery when we noticed that cloud was building up, so we did not linger on the summit. By the time we gained the summit of the Ravanel the weather was very threatening with lightning over the Aiguille Verte. We quickly arranged to abseil down the east ridge and set off. Unfortunately when we tried to recover the ropes after the first abseil they would not move. At this point Alistair, with no discussion, had his prusiks on the ropes and was heading back up to free them. It was a long prusik and with lightning now around him he calmly sorted out the ropes before descending again. This was typical of Alistair and was just one of the fine virtues that made him a great climbing companion and good friend.

In 1974 our regular partnership came to an end when Alistair, answering the call of the mountains, found a job in Fort William. In the early 1980s we made several more trips together to the Alps for both summer climbing and spring ski-touring. It gave me great pleasure when he asked me to propose him for the AC when he at last decided to join the Club in the early 1990s. My last walk with Alistair was near his home in Matlock about a year before he died. He said he was not very fit, he had just finished some chemo, but I still struggled to keep up with his long strides. It brought back the memory of the Alps and of him tirelessly climbing a snow slope with me needing three steps to his two.

He was based in Fort William for four years, climbing whenever it was fit – sometimes he would be up and down the Ben four times in a weekend – and whenever it was foul weather there was always a Munro to do, usually alone, on the grounds that it kept him out of the pub. He joined the Lochaber Mountain Rescue team but had to keep it secret from his boss who, at the job interview, had bizarrely asked for assurance that he would not join. Even with his active local climbing scene Alistair always made time to climb with friends from London who made the trip to Fort Bill. His Fort William days ended in 1978 when he resigned from his job after his boss refused him unpaid leave for the trip of a lifetime to climb in the USA and Canada.

With no money on his return from the North America trip he took the first job he could get and late 1978 arrived in Matlock where, almost on arrival, he joined the Derwent Mountaineering Club. However, this initial encounter with the club was interrupted when work took him to Hong Kong for 6 months. This did provide him with an excellent opportunity to fit in a trek to the Annapurna Sanctuary. Once back in Matlock he soon became one of the club's most enthusiastic members, taking part in all its activities: climbing, walking, running and finding his other great passion – caving. He was fascinated by the notion that you can squeeze through a little hole in the ground and enter a whole parallel universe where new discoveries are still being made. Through the club he met his wife to be, Ruth, and friendship gradually grew into love over the following five years. He was never one for hasty decisions. While in Matlock, the Carsington Reservoir project began and that brought him long-term employment. He often looked back with amused surprise that a short-term expedient had led to a long-term job, a house, a wife, a cat, alarmingly even nieces and nephews, 'and suddenly half your life is away'.

As an only child, Alistair was always comfortable in his own company and was utterly self-reliant. He was reserved and did not easily speak of his feelings. Integrity was central to his character, written right through him like the words in a stick of rock. For him it was important to achieve whatever he set out to do in style and so in his climbing he never really fulfilled his potential. It wasn't enough for him to scrabble to the top, heart in mouth, he wanted to savour the experience. He embraced new ideas such as modern protection, climbing walls and bolted limestone to continually push his climbing standard. Even in his 60s he was still improving until the utterly unexpected blow of the lymphoma struck him almost as soon as he retired and overshadowed the last three years of his life.

Alistair was a true mountaineer and will be keenly missed by his wife, Ruth, and his many friends.

Pete Stokes

Reverend Jim Harrison
1930 - 2011

Jim Harrison. *(Rupert Hoare)*

Jim Harrison died suddenly but peacefully on Saturday 23 July 2011 whilst reading in the library of the Savile Club, London. John Moore and I had been fortunate to have dined with him on the previous two evenings. He was a reticent man and rarely spoke about his family, achievements or his childhood. My thanks go to his family and friends for filling the gaps in my knowledge of his life.

Jim was born on 3 May 1930 and raised in Edinburgh with one sister. He attended the Royal High School but contracted TB necessitating time in a sanatorium; this prevented him from taking his Highers. He worked for a while in a newspaper office and then emigrated to Canada where he did work for a Montreal newspaper, the RCA record company and also BBC radio. He then returned to Scotland and re-entered education, studying for his Highers. It was here that he met Maud who was his English teacher, and so began a loving partnership that lasted until Maud's death in 2007.

After Highers, Jim gained a degree in English and entered teaching. He and Maud then returned to Canada and both taught in Nova Scotia and Alberta. At this time he felt a call to the ministry and so returned to Scotland where he attended Seminary for a year. In 1972 he left again for Canada where he attended the Knox College, Toronto; here in 1975 he graduated with a Master of Divinty degree and was ordained by the Presbyterian Church of Canada. He became a minister for a year and a half. Jim then returned to Scotland where he taught Religious Education in the East Lothian School system for many years and was an adviser in RE to the Edinburgh schools. He was also a lecturer in English and Communication at Napier University. Jim continued working for the BBC as an independent interviewer, and gave the morning 'Thought for the Day' on many occasions.

Jim took up skiing and climbing in Canada and continued with his ski-mountaineering back in the UK, becoming a member of the Eagle Ski Club in 1980. He was vice-president of the ESC from 1991 to 1997 and president from 1997 to 2000. He attended and arranged many Eagle Ski Club meets in Scotland. These included the popular Dinner Meets, where he would give a Robert Burns grace in his inimitable style and was also an amusing after dinner speaker. He toured regularly in the Alps with, amongst others, Walter Mann and Mike Bennet. He had enormous respect for the leadership and skiing skills of Walter Mann. His accomplished photographs have graced a number of ESC journals.

Jim presided over the 75th Eagle Ski Club Anniversary Dinner at Maloja in 2000 with his typical entertaining style and memorable literary quotations. He was made an honorary member of the Alpine Ski Club in 1995, served as secretary from 1996-2002 and joined the Alpine Club in 1991.

In 1996 Jim was elected a member of the Savile Club and enjoyed frequent visits to London. He had a wide circle of friends many of whom, like myself, enjoyed warm hospitality at his home in Edinburgh. His humour was epitomised for me by a quote from the 1983 *ESC Journal*. When cheerily greeted one morning in the Franz Senn hut in the Stubai Alps before an early start he replied: 'It may be God's good morning but He doesn't have to get up!'

Jim did not suffer fools gladly but was a kind man whose modest charm, conversation and mischievous sense of humour will be greatly missed by all his friends.

Robin Chapman

Rupert John Stephen Hoare
1956 - 2011

Rupert Hoare. *(Jay Turner)*

Rupert Hoare's tragically early death on 20 September 2011 from pancreatic cancer deprived his widow Jay, his family, friends, colleagues and climbing companions of an exceptional man and a mountaineer to whom the hills were an inspiration and the force that shaped his aesthetic and spiritual values.

At Winchester, Rupert excelled academically and at gymnastics. Rock climbing under the aegis of two dons, John Durran and Tony Ayres, came naturally. *The Romance of Mountaineering,* written by another Wykehamist don, RLG Irving, who had introduced Mallory to mountaineering, particularly captured Rupert's youthful imagination and inspired him to join the British Schools Exploring Society's 1974 Expedition to Arctic Norway. That autumn, he went up to Exeter University to read Physical Geology having set his career sights not on banking but on the type of scientific research that allowed scope for travel and adventure. His university weekends were mainly spent in British hills, while on long vacations he made a second expedition to Arctic Norway and also visited South Africa where he climbed in the Drakensburg and had lunch with Desmond Tutu.

At Exeter, Rupert's principal climbing partner was Simon Mumford, later his Best Man. At Rupert's funeral Simon recalled select Rupert mnemonics that had found their way into the family lexicon. Thus, 'PMD' or 'Prudent Mountaineering Decision' covered those rare instances when Rupert decided on tactical retreat after coming across someone even more competitive than himself. After cutting their teeth in the Dauphiné, they crowned their first alpine season with an ascent of the Chardonnet's North Buttress.

Rupert's first overseas posting to Gabon in 1977 was followed by seismographic assignments to both Libya and Australia as party chief. In between, he trekked in Nepal, climbed Norway's Romsdalhorn and bushwacked his way through the Tasmanian wilderness to climb Federation Peak and, much later in 1992, Frenchman's Cap. On return to England, he joined the oil exploration company LASMO and the London Mountaineering Club, subsequently becoming its president. For the next nine years, he climbed most weekends throughout Britain, once with Mick Fowler to traverse the Needles. In the Alps, he did ambitious classic routes in the Oberland, Pennine Alps, and Bernina, principally with John Evans with whom he made his third visit to Arctic Norway in 1986 to climb Lofoten's Stetind, 'the most remarkable natural obelisk in the world'. Two years before, Rupert had been a member of Derek Fordham's 1984 Greenland Expedition. While attempting the south ridge of Mount Forel with David Waldron, a severe storm precipitated an epic retreat. Rupert's selfless gesture of giving his spare gloves and socks to a badly frostbitten David averted potential disaster. That same year, he was elected to the Alpine Club.

An early convert to ski-mountaineering, he attended a training course at Chamonix in 1981 and completed his first Haute Route a week later. During the 1980s when snow conditions in Scotland were exceptional, he was a leading player on Eagle Ski Club weekend Highlands meets, made possible by British Rail's excellent overnight sleeper services. He was a most valued member of the team that completed three stages of the Pyrenean High Route and the pioneer ski-tours that we did together in Spain's Picos de Europa, Sierra de Gredos and Cordillera Cantabrica. In 1990 he was on the Eagles' 1990 expedition to the Kulu Himalaya.

In 1990, Rupert's LASMO posting to Malaysia and Indonesia opened a new career window and unusual mountaineering opportunities. While on leave, he and his future wife Jay bagged Kinabalu and a string of Indonesian volcanoes before Rupert went on to traverse the Japanese Alps. In 1992 he joined the Eagles' Southern Alps ski-tour when, during a rare period of settled weather, they climbed Hochstetter Dome and Mount Aylmer; skied the Tasman Glacier; and then climbed mounts Grey and Lendenfeld before rounding up Rupert's 'best ever winter holiday' with an ascent of Mount Aspiring's north-west ridge.

Returning to Britain in 1993, he and John Evans did their last alpine season together and, in that same year, he became engaged to Jay. For the next 18 years they climbed together almost every summer in the Alps and Dolomites, developing a mutual love for alpine flora and also exploring the mountains of Mallorca, Spain and Greece. During the winter, there were Alpine Ski Club expeditions to Iran and Turkey; ski-tours in the Ötztal, Ortler, Oberland, Queyras, the Italian High Level Route, the Ecrins; the Corsican High Route and a ski ascent of Mt Blanc.

Rupert became president of the Alpine Ski Club in 2002 and an honorary Member in 2011.

In 1995, he joined WesternGeco with whom he was to spend the rest of his working life. The commercially successful investment projects he initiated and his pioneering work in North Sea Basin oil exploration earned him the plaudits and respect of both clients and colleagues and the gratitude of a generation of post-graduates. Professor John Underhill, president of the European Association of Geoscientists and Engineers, has written that, 'Without Rupert's foresight and him going out of his way to be helpful and accommodating, geoscientific understanding of basins would never have seen the light of day.'

Rupert's and Jay's decision to move to Aberdeenshire in 2002 assured them of the freedom of the Scottish hills at all times and seasons. Jay completed her Munros tally in 2008: Rupert was only 16 short before his death. Although they continued to make regular visits to European ranges, and did their last ski-tour together in 2009 on the Lyngen Peninsula, the Scottish highlands now claimed their deepest affections. Rupert's climbing biography *Mountain Views – A lifetime's enjoyment, (see page 349),* lovingly describes the many Scottish adventures and best days they shared together. On 29 April 2011, when his health was fast fading, he still managed to climb his last hill, Bennachie, within sight of their home at Hatton on Fintray.

Rupert's death on 20 September 2011, though inevitable, seemed inexplicably capricious. Although the most competitive of climbing companions, his mountain judgements were never rash and he had seemed physically indestructible. On the last leg of the Pyrenean High Route, a dramatic airborne leap into pinewoods followed by a five-metre fall onto boulder scree would have finished most men. Rupert just picked himself up, slightly shaken. On Aonach Mhor in 1994, an Ordnance Survey map inaccuracy resulted in his walking off a cornice during a white-out. Somehow, he survived a 75m free-fall and another of 200m down a steep snow slope sustaining only a severed anterior cruciate ligament. He was back in the hills that autumn.

In 2001, it was Rupert's super-charged effort getting back to the Sella Hut on Monte Viso to raise a helicopter to pick up Alan Wedgwood, unconscious with a smashed pelvis and bleeding profusely from a severed artery, that saved Alan's life.

When Rupert began to write his mountaineering testament *Mountain Views* he knew that he had only nine months to live. That last phase, made bearable by Jay's devoted love and care, was characterised by the same qualities that had held the respect, admiration and love of all who knew him. Whether in his work or in the mountains, his courage, enthusiasm, meticulous planning and technical competence were always balanced by a disarming modesty, selflessness and generosity of spirit. His artistic talents were reflected in his outstanding photography for it was in the mountains that he found beauty's most obvious manifestation.

John Harding

Jagdish Chandulal Nanavati

Jagdish C. Nanavati 1929 - 2011

What was said about Beethoven was also true for Jagdish Chandulal Nanavati (JCN): 'Talent is what a man possesses, genius is what possesses a man!'

He had a rare talent for the study and enjoyment of mountains in all their aspects. But once he was interested in a climb, or a problem with it, he became a man possessed and would pace in his garden till late, sit at his table burning the midnight oil, poring over maps and old articles. Much correspondence followed by hours of talking on the phone to gather authentic information. He used all his time, knowledge and talent to sort out truth from falsehood. And he would not rest till a problem was solved.

It is hard to go into details of expeditions he studied. However, some of the well-known peaks and claims of ascents that he studied included Nilkanth, Nyegi Kangsang, Kokthang, Matri, Sudarshan Parvat ... the list is endless. In the case of Gya, he later accepted and proved that the ascent was actually made though he had thought otherwise to start with. I learnt of his exactness in 1969 when we retreated from about 100 feet short of the summit of Tharkot after being carried down by an avalanche. The morning after our return JCN phoned to say that 'it will be appropriate to say that you were 125 feet from the summit and not 100'. We subsequently declared we were 150 feet short – after all, who would want to join issues with JCN?

His standards were high and many of us found it difficult to match his expectations. He was, as someone put it aptly, 'the inquisitor of mountains from Mumbai'. Studying maps, drawings and observations gave him enormous pleasure and through his incisive mind he solved many problems. He did not need to go to the mountain. By studying a mountain and details of its ascent, he could conclude whether it had been truly climbed or whether the climbers had made a mistake. He must have disproved ascent claims of more than 20 peaks, and in a few cases proved that peaks had been climbed when the climbers were not sure. It was not that he forced his view as the last word about a claim. He would prove it with detailed studies and present it with logic, almost like a detective. In most cases climbers disagreed with his conclusions; after all, who wants to accept that their claim of climbing a peak is false? So through letter after letter and proof after proof he would make them understand their folly, and if they still refused he would stand by his finding. Later as the Ombudsman of the Himalayan Club, he decided without favour or fear that the Club-sponsored expedition to Nilkanth had failed to reach the summit.

JCN lost his father when he was 12 years old and was, therefore, a self-made man. He met his wife Mandakini while in college; he was so much in love and roamed around with her on a motorbike that he failed final exams twice. After their marriage in 1949 she was the balance in his life as her practical wisdom perfectly offset the lofty ideals of JCN. Whenever we had difficulties we ran to her. She survives him with a family of four children and many grandchildren.

Early in his life JCN met Swami Anand, a learned ascetic who lived at Gangotri who introduced him to the Himalaya and its climbing stories and also gave him many maps. This was the beginning of a love affair. JCN made many treks in the local hills, the Sahyadris and the Western Ghat. It was a pioneering effort as the sport was unknown then. He was at home in the hills, whistling, shouting, cycling; his wit was legendary, he was always full of stories and full of questions. We enjoyed many trips together but his questioning was one trait that I could never fully satisfy – he wanted to know everything about everything and this was beyond my knowledge and patience. He was very fond of my son, Lt Nawang Kapadia who died in Kashmir at the young age of 25. JCN got on fabulously with him. On a trek they always shared a tent and Nawang's eyes would light up while listening to JCN's stories. They would talk until late at night and suddenly JCN would start his loud and famous snores. JCN could never speak of Nawang after his death without tears welling in his eyes.

He completed his mountaineering course at the Himalayan Mountaineering Institute, Darjeeling, in 1958. On his return he arranged with Brigadier Gyan Singh, the Principal of HMI, to send three instructors to Mumbai to conduct rock-climbing courses for the benefit of city dwellers. When the Himalayan Club was not interested in sponsoring it, he formed a 'Mountaineering Committee' that organised the courses. This small committee was converted into 'The Climbers Club'. After a decade of running these courses, for which he had explored the places near Mumbai and arranged everything, he fell out with the Club as they unfairly wanted to pass censure against an expedition sponsored by the Club to Bethartoli Himal in 1970. Four climbers died in an avalanche; it was a *vis major* but the Club wanted to blame the leadership and members. After a year of protracted arguments, JCN resigned as president of the Club when the committee published their prejudicial views. Many members, including myself, also resigned with him.

This resignation was surely an act of God. It was about the same time that the Himalayan Club moved from Calcutta to Mumbai as there were no volunteers to run it at the former. Soli Mehta asked JCN to take over the reins of the HC. As the statistics show, he served as hon secretary of the Club for 23 years, then as the president for eight years and finally as president emeritus. He literally reconstructed the Club from ruins to a pinnacle. He was the face of the club, organised its files and finances, his office was used as the HC office, and he was encouraging to youngsters. When Soli Mehta, hon editor of the *Himalayan Journal*, was posted abroad, I remember a handsome JCN walking into my house and requesting me to be the editor. I was a novice and from then until his last days he was helpful and a guiding light for the *HJ*.

JCN organised local talks and programmes in Mumbai and invited famous foreign climbers to speak to youngsters, thus encouraging the sport of mountaineering. In 1978, for the golden jubilee of the HC, he organised a five-day festival at the prestigious Jahangir Art Gallery in a prime area of Mumbai. A photo exhibition was arranged with daily talks by a well-known speaker. It was always a packed house and people lined up an hour early to gain entry. No wonder, as that extravaganza had speakers such as Pertemba Sherpa, Dr Salim Ali, H.C. Sarin, Joginder Singh and others. The HC has never looked back after that event.

I was surprised to learn, after his death, that JCN was an ardent fish collector. He had 40 fish tanks in his compound – a rare thing for he was a Jain – strictly vegetarian and would not even eat garlic and onions. Another love he had was for roses – which he tended in his garden and talked about in detail. He cultivated 100 different varieties of roses and photographed them while listening to music – all his passions. At the same time he was much engaged in social work, running his family school, college and hospital. With his upbringing he was also involved in many activities associated with Gandhian institutions, though he knew that these institutions were dying.

After the accident on the Bethartoli Himal in 1970 and the acrimony that followed, JCN did not venture to the Himalaya until 1982. But when he did return, it was with great pleasure to Kumaun, where we undertook a long trek in two valleys. One could sense in him the same exuberance and love for the Himalaya. In 1984 and 1986, with many youngsters, we went to the Ruinsara valley in Garhwal and the Baspa valley in Kinnaur. These trips brought out best in JCN as he spread maps to teach the youngsters, taught them how to walk methodically, camp manners and much more. His wards were taught how to enjoy mountains without bravado, safely and with knowledge. He had a way with the youngsters.

He climbed no high peaks, for that matter not even a small peak. He did not explore major ranges or undertake heroic adventures. But still, in the world of mountaineering, he became a legend and a Guru to many of us. Not only the youngsters but the even the Himalaya benefited from his wisdom, observations and studies. The Himalaya, like many of us, will miss him.

Harish Kapadia

Tim Oliver. *(Phill Thomas)*

Tim Oliver 1956 - 2011

It was a great shock to learn that my good friend Tim had taken his own life in his home in North Carolina. Tim was elected to the Alpine Club in 1983, however his big contribution to mountaineering was through the Climbers' Club, notably digitisation of 110 years of climbing history in the club journal.

Tim's appearance on the South Wales climbing scene was about 40 years ago at the age of 16. He was a fresh-faced youngster preparing for his GSEs, but with the extra energy and enthusiasm to take up climbing at such a busy period in his life. He gelled well with the active local climbers and climbed extensively around the UK and in the Alps.

Tim's academic career went well and led him to university in Plymouth, where he studied marine biology, and then on to work in a London hospital. In London, he met his future wife and eventually went to live in her home area of North Carolina. There he gained his PhD and worked on the staff of several leading universities.

After he left Cardiff we saw less of Tim, but he continued to visit several times most years and maintained good contact with his friends and family. Tim continued his involvement in climbing, caving and kayaking, often teaming up with his old South Wales friends. One notable occasion was with Mike Harber when they established a new route on Huascaran.

Tim was not a talented climber, but he loved adventure in a variety of forms. I jumped at his invitation to join him kayaking in the Appalachians mountains with his local canoe club. It was great paddling in great company. That trip continued with mountaineering in the Cascade mountains of Washington State. During that trip Tim told me of his plans for a kayak trip down the Colorado River and invited me to join him.

Tim eventually pulled the trip together and we went when his permit was issued 10 years later. He did the same again two years later when my 'back-up permit' was issued. This was typical of Tim who was a very self-disciplined and organised person. These were fantastic trips when we soaked up the atmosphere of the Grand Canyon for days on end.

These trips in Tim's company have left life long impressions on me, together with a host of other memories. He was probably best known within the CC as one of the members who was keen to maintain the historic atmosphere of Helyg, the club's hut in the Ogwen valley, and more recently for taking over the editorship of the *CC Journal*. He had a great love of climbing traditions and climbing literature and had eagerly taken on this new role.

My deepest sympathies go out to his partner Wendy, mother Beryl and brother John. He will be mourned by his many friends. Such a sad loss.

Phill Thomas

David Medcalf writes: I was aware of Tim Oliver before I took over as CC archivist – I had seen his name in the Newsletter associated with 'some project' regarding CC Journals, but I didn't know, or think, much about it. I wasn't in the job for long before realising how very useful this 'project' was going to be, for me and for many others. The project, of course, was the digitisation of the journals, in a form that made searching 110 years of Climbers' Club history straightforward and very fast.

Without Tim's knowledge of imaging, scanning and the state of the art processes that were becoming available in the United States, this project would never have got off the ground. I was pleased to meet Tim and Wendy a couple of years ago on one of his regular trips back to Wales and I hope I was successful in letting him know how important his project had turned out to be. We owe him a debt of gratitude.

Stewart Ward (right) with Chris Bonington in Aden on route to Annapurna II in 1960. *(Chris Bonington Picture Library)*

Stewart Ward
1930 - 2011

Stewart Ward, who died on 17 May 2011 aged 81, joined the Alpine Club in 1968 having been proposed by Jimmy Roberts with whom he had climbed on two Himalayan expeditions. Brought up in a Lancashire village and leaving school at 14, he had become an apprentice draughtsman with Leyland Motors until his 'call-up' for National Service in the Royal Air Force. A shortage of aircrew at the time enabled him to apply for a commission, which in turn took him to Canada for his initial training and where he seems to have found his metier as a navigator, later to spend most of his flying career in Bomber Command.

Ward's introduction to climbing had come in Norway on a meet with Norwegian Rover Scouts but it was another 10 years before he ventured further afield, to the Pyrenees. 1959 saw him on an RAF Mountain-

240. Stewart Ward load carrying up fixed ropes on Annapurna II in 1960. cf. the cover of the Annapurna II expedition book.

ANNAPURNA II

CAPTAIN R.H. GRANT.

eering Association meet in Chamonix, climbing with Norman Ridley (AC) before, in 1960, he was nominated as the RAF representative and 'Oxygen Member' on the British-Indian-Nepalese Services Himalayan Expedition led by Lt. Col. J.O.M. Roberts. Their objective was Annapurna II (7937m). With a team of six British Service climbers, including a young Christian Bonington, plus two each from the Nepalese and Indian Armed Services and nine Sherpas, Jimmy Roberts regarded the expedition as being rather top heavy; moreover few of the team had climbed with or even knew each other. Nevertheless, in spite of this potential drawback their efforts were crowned with success, Bonington, Dicky Grant and Sherpa Ang Nyima reaching the summit after a four-day ascent in far from perfect conditions while Ward, with two others, together with the very experienced Sherpa Tashi, climbed Annapurna IV (7525m).

Happily for Stewart Ward the expedition bug had bitten at a time when all three Services were exhibiting a growing enthusiasm for such adventurous activity. In successive years he led RAF parties to Lyngen in northern Norway and to the Vatnajokull Ice Cap in Iceland. Then in 1965 came further opportunity in the shape of the RAFMA expedition to the Dhaula Himal, post-monsoon, to climb Dhaulagiri IV (7661m). Led by John Sims, one of the RAF's most experienced mountaineers, the expedition again included Jimmy Roberts who, in making a reconnaissance of the lower slopes some few years previously, had detected what seemed a feasible route up this hitherto unclimbed peak. Unusually for those days, the expedition was able to charter a light aircraft and fly from Pokhara to an airstrip close to the site of their base camp. At first all went well in spite of strong winds and very cold weather. In little more than a week three camps were established up to 6220m. However, snow conditions were decidedly suspect and the following day while climbing above the highest camp two Sherpas were avalanched and swept down some 100 metres. They survived unhurt, just short of a huge crevasse, but prevailing conditions left Sims with little option but to abandon the climb. Ward and Roberts, both sick, had meanwhile descended to the lower camps. Subsequently other members were able to climb Ghustung, a minor summit nearby, but then found themselves trapped for several days by heavy snowfall. Having exhausted their supplies they eventually escaped to return to base camp, in Roberts' view, 'lucky to survive'.

If 1965 was perhaps a disappointing year it still held compensation for Stewart. He completed the RAF Survival course and, not long after, met Elizabeth, the young WRAF officer who was to become his wife. Married life and in due course the demands of a growing family inevitably left fewer opportunities for mountaineering but he continued his involvement in RAF Mountain Rescue to the end of his service. Earlier he had on occasion been seconded as an instructor to both the Eskdale and Ullswater Outward Bound Schools and his interest in the personal development of young people persisted throughout his life.

Following retirement from the RAF in the rank of Wing Commander he was appointed Chapter Steward at Gloucester Cathedral and was also Chaplain to the local Air Cadets Squadron. Never seeking the limelight, he preferred a 'supporting' role; as Church Warden and Reader in his Gloucestershire village, he is remembered with respect and affection, not least for his 'fabulous sense of humour'. He died peacefully at his home after a long illness throughout which he was nursed by his wife, herself the Priest in their Cotswold parish.

John Peacock

Alpine Club Notes

241. Chris Bonington and Doug Scott, honorary members of the Alpine Club.
(Chris Bonington Picture Library)

NEW HONORARY MEMBERS

Chris Bonington and Doug Scott were appointed honorary members of the Alpine Club in 2011. Both entered the AC via the Alpine Climbing Group, Chris joining the ACG in 1959 and Doug in 1962. Both served as the group's president – 1968 and 1975 respectively – and subsequently as AC president, Chris from 1996 with Doug succeeding him from 1999 to 2001. The pioneering records of these two giants of mountaineering in the second half of the 20th century need no further elaboration for AC members.

ALPINE CLUB CLIMBING FUND

The following grants were made to expeditions that took place in 2011:

British Mugu Expedition 2011 Western Nepal, 1-31 October. Mick Fowler (leader), Graham Desroy, Dave Turnbull and Jonny Ratcliffe.
Climbing as pairs the teams completed two separate objectives. Mick Fowler and Dave Turnbull succeeded in making the first ascent of Mugu Chuli (Gojung, 6310m) via a stunning line on the west face while Graham

Desroy and Jonny Ratcliffe were forced by bad rock to retreat on their primary objective of an unclimbed 5400m rock peak before making the first ascent of a non-technical 5800m peak on the Tibetan border west of Kojichuwa Chuli. *(see report pages 3 to 15)*

British Cordillera Carabaya Expedition Cordillera Carabaya, Southern Peru, 12 August - 14 September. Tom Ripley and Hamish Dunn.
Climbing in alpine-style Tom Ripley and Hamish Dunn successfully made the first ascent of the south face of Chichicapac (5614m), which they graded at Alpine TD.

British Eren Habirga Expedition Tien Shan, Xinjiang, China, 13 August - 11 September. John Town (leader), Jerry Lovatt, Iwonna Hudowska, Tadeusz Hudowski and Richard Wojtaszewski.
Plagued by bad weather and poor snow conditions the team were thwarted in their plans to make first ascents of various 4800 to 5200m peaks in the Ak-Tash valley, although Tadeusz and Iwonna successfully climbed a rocky 4300m peak near to their base camp in between spells of inclement weather.

FIDS Cordillera Oriental Expedition Peru, June 2011. Matt Balmer (leader), Dan Fitzgerald and James Wake.
The team successfully made the first ascent of a new route on the south face of Huarancayo Sur (c5200m) taking a prominent icy gully on the face but were forced to make an unplanned bivvi high on the face before descending safely the following day. A later attempt on Huaguruncho Chico failed on account of poor snow conditions.

British Mount Hayes Expedition Alaska, 25 April - May. Guy Wilson (leader), Neil Warren and Chris Johnson.
After making a successful ski-assisted ascent of Mount Skarland (3145m) via the south-east ridge the team climbed a new mixed line on the NE Face of Mount Geist (3268m) graded at Alpine TD+.

British Far West Nepal Expedition 2011 Changla/Gorakh Himal, Nepal, Mid April - end May 2011. Julian Freeman-Attwood (leader), Nick Colton and Ed Douglas.
After a long walk-in, an early arrival of the monsoon resulted in the party aborting their attempt on Gave Ding (6571m) at around 5900m when it became evident that it was prudent to retreat. They did, however, manage to get good views of the Gorakh Himal in which none of the mountains have yet been climbed.

42. L-R: John Cleare (mountain photographer), Peter Rowland (new Hon Keeper of the Photographs), Anna Lawford (retiring Hon Keeper), Hywel Lloyd, Harry Melville (conservation and scanning). *(ACL)*

ALPINE CLUB LIBRARY ANNUAL REPORT 2011

Hywel Lloyd, Chairman of the Council of Trustees of the Alpine Club Library writes: Established in 1858, the Alpine Club Library cares for the Alpine Club's collections, now comprising: 40,000 books; 25,000 sets of archives (diaries, letters, newspaper cuttings); 300 artefacts (ice-axes, oxygen sets).

Following a visit and guidance from the British Library's National Preservation experts, the storage of books, archives and photographs has been extensively re-arranged and improved. Damp problems have been greatly reduced, air circulation optimised, and humidity is now continuously monitored. Many items have been inserted into acid-free sleeves and stored in conservation boxes. Jerry Lovatt, Glyn Hughes, Barbara Grigor-Taylor and Tadeusz Hudowski have worked hard to do this.

Interesting library acquisitions this year include the diary of Peter Oliver on the 1936 Everest Expedition, which is well illustrated with his own drawings and maps, and a set of diaries 1943-1957 by Eileen Healey, telling her story of climbing in the UK, the Alps and then on Cho Oyu. Of more intrigue is the log of Bill Crace who was lost in an avalanche on Nanga Parbat in 1950. His diary came to us having been frozen solid. With funds from his family we used a specialist to separate the pages and we have now successfully scanned the diary to reveal the story up until the fatal day.

Since 1858, shortly after the invention of photography, the library has received many photographs from members. We now have 40,000 – from glass plates and prints to transparencies. We need a complete catalogue; digitisation has to be the route. A sub-committee under Roger James is working hard to gain a grant to enable this. We also aim to show-case 5000 selected images on the website. Meanwhile, the photograph team has been enlarged and is testing various methods.

From the left: John Cleare (mountain photographer), Peter Rowland (new Hon Keeper of the Photographs), Anna Lawford (retiring Hon Keeper), Hywel Lloyd, Harry Melville (conservation and scanning). Not shown are Sue Hare (reproduction sales) and Martin Hewson (scanning and cataloguing).

Meanwhile, working with the Royal Geographical Society to produce a book, *Mountaineers – Great Tales of Bravery and Conquest* for Dorling Kindersley, the team provided 280 photo images each with a detailed caption; this was quite a task with very tight deadlines. One review compliments '... a wealth of striking photographs'.

The Himalayan Index has been compiled holding 8,000 details of ascents and attempts (it is also on the website). New entries continue apace as Sally Russell fills gaps, adds latest detail, and is extending it into new areas in China.

Your donations of surplus second-hand books continue to arrive; some are retained to augment the collections; all spares find new owners via our published lists; none are thrown away. One member's surplus is another member's marvellous find so please keep donating surplus books.

Just to remind everyone, the library is open for certain (as certain as we can make it) 10am to 5pm every Tuesday and Wednesday. On a Tuesday with a lecture it stays open until 7pm. It is closed during August and the week Christmas to New Year. On Thursdays it is open by appointment– call 0207 613 0745. Catalogues of books and archives are via the AC website.

Of course, none of all this would happen without many tireless volunteers. The Trustees made 'Exceptional Service' awards to three volunteers who have retired, after many years of dedicated work. The engraved glass mementoes went to Richard Coatsworth, Hon Treasurer for more than 10 years, Anna Lawford, Hon Keeper of the Photographs for more than 10 years and Michael Westmacott for service over 25 years including as Chairman (1984-92) and as Curator of the Himalayan Index. Their efforts, and those of all our other library volunteers, will be appreciated by everyone in the Club.

LETTER TO THE EDITOR

Awards and Recognition

Sir,

I read with interest Doug Scott's article 'Awards and Recognition in Climbing' in the 2010/11 *Alpine Journal.*

In 1972, at the time of The Olympic Games in Munich, the German Alpine Club (DAV) organized a meet attended by climbers from many countries, including the then USSR. The Soviet delegation was made up mostly of members of its team for climbing competitions, which took the form at that time of speed climbing on top ropes.

Four British climbers attended this gathering; Ed Cross, Malcolm Howells, Mike Butler and myself.

One day during this event we were all taken by bus to a crag near to Munich where the Russians demonstrated their style of competition climbing. This made little impression on our group and after watching for a while we wandered off, preferring to climb at this well-situated limestone cliff.

Before the end of the meet, during which we managed to climb in the Wetterstein and the Karwendel, and watch some of the Olympic events, the DAV organised a debate on 'Competition and Climbing'. This was a major event held in the Löwenbrau Beer Hall in Munich. (No, it was not a beer hall putsch!) Because of the great interest in Germany in mountain activities, this debate was televised live by German television.

The Hall was full to overflowing with hundreds of climbers present from many countries. I spoke last in this debate and shortly afterwards a vote was taken on whether climbing should embrace competitions. There was no support for competitions except from the USSR delegation.

I think before the debate all of the speakers knew the history of climbing and the Olympics: the fact that Baron Pierre de Coubertin, founder of the modern Olympics, had envisaged mountaineering being an Olympic Sport, and the award previously of Olympic medals to the 1922 British Everest Expedition, the Schmid brothers (Matterhorn north face) in 1932 and later to the Dyhrenfurths for their explorations in the Karakoram. Several members of the Olympic Committee of that time were present at the debate.

When I returned to the UK I wrote up these events in the BMC's publication of that era *Mountain Life*. Both Alan Blackshaw and Roger Payne who subsequently investigated the background and history of the Olympic movement for the UIAA were aware of these facts.

In the 1980s attempts were made to hold climbing competitions in Britain on outdoor cliffs. There was strenuous objection by the BMC, and on one occasion we had to take a strong line to stop a competition being held at Malham Cove in Yorkshire. Our objection was on the grounds of ecological damage and safety. Eventually it was seen that such competitions were best held on artificial walls, where the problems of crowd control, safety and fairness to all the competitors could be better ensured. The BMC then agreed to support such developments.

With regards to the Piolet d'Or, I was confused by Doug's article: does he really think it a good or a bad thing for the future of mountaineering? I am with Voytek Kurtyka, who declined the Piolet's career award. I think it is an unnecessary bauble, bringing values into mountaineering that the sport just does not need.

Olé Conquistador, you're a winner of a Piolet d'Or,
Olé Conquistador, what can you use a gold axe for?
Maybe social climbing?

Yours sincerely
Dennis Gray
Ruskin College, Oxford.

Contributors

PHIL BARTLETT has been walking and climbing in mountains for 50 years. He is increasingly interested in exploratory expeditions rather than technical tests that he fails. His study of mountain literature and philosophy, *The Undiscovered Country*, was published in 1993. His other interests include the violin, mountain paintings, and how to sculpt a peaceful existence.

ANDREW BISHARAT is senior editor of *Rock and Ice* magazine. His book *Sport Climbing: From Top Rope to Redpoint, Techniques for Climbing Success* won the 2010 National Outdoor Book Award. You can find more of his writing at eveningsends.com

DR PENNY BRADSHAW is a Senior Lecturer in English at the University of Cumbria. She is Programme Leader for BA English and for a new MA in Literature, Romanticism, and the English Lake District. Penny works and publishes primarily within the field of Romanticism and is interested in the work of female Romantic poets as well as in the legacy of Romanticism within post-Romantic regional literature. Email: penelope.bradshaw@cumbria.ac.uk

KESTER BROWN is the managing editor/designer of publications for the New Zealand Alpine Club. He produces the club's quarterly magazine *The Climber* and the annual *NZ Alpine Journal*. He is a rock climber and mountaineer of many years' standing and lives at Taylors Mistake beach, NZ.

DEREK BUCKLE is a retired medicinal chemist now acting part-time as a consultant to the pharmaceutical industry. With plenty of free time he spends much of this rock-climbing, ski-touring and mountaineering in various parts of the world. Apart from climbing, his greatest challenges are finding time to accompany his wife on more traditional holidays and the filling of his passport with exotic and expensive visas.

ANDY CAVE loves all styles of climbing from Himalayan exploration to bouldering, as long as it's fun. He has a PhD from the University of Sheffield in linguistics and anthropology. His books *Thin White Line* and *Learning to Breathe* have won five literary awards between then and been translated into German, Italian and French. He is a motivational speaker and IFMGA mountain guide.

PAT DEAVOLL works as the Events and Activities Manager for the New Zealand Alpine Club. Apart from short distractions into rock climbing and kayaking she has been mountaineering for 35 years. Over the past ten years she has taken part in 10 expeditions to the greater ranges and has made first ascents in Alaska, Canada, China, India, Pakistan and Afghanistan. She will be heading for her second expedition to Afghanistan in mid 2012.

GRAHAM DUDLEY is a Resource Manager working in Aberdeen. Experience has been gained climbing and ski-mountaineering in the Alps, Africa, Canada, Caucasus, Alaska, Arctic Norway and Greenland.

JOHN FAIRLEY was Honorary Editor of the *Alpine Journal* from 1983 to 1987 and was Transceiver Manager for the Alpine Ski Club for 10 years. A Chartered Electrical Engineer throughout his working life, he worked on digital television, automation and telecoms but on retirement has devoted his time to painting mountains and people. He has climbed and painted in the Himalaya and in the Altai as well as in the Alps. He has exhibited at the Alpine Club and one of his paintings is in the Bob Lawford Collection. More pictures can be seen at www.johnfairley.co.uk

MICK FOWLER works for Her Majesty's Revenue and Customs and, by way of contrast, likes to inject as much memorable adventure and excitement into his climbing ventures. He has climbed extensively in the UK and has regularly led expeditions to the greater ranges for more than 25 years. He has written two books, *Vertical Pleasure* (1995) and *On Thin Ice* (2005). In December 2010 he was elected president of the Alpine Club.

STEPHEN GOODWIN renounced daily newspaper journalism on *The Independent* for a freelance existence in Cumbria, mixing writing and climbing. A precarious balance was maintained until 2003 when he was persuaded to take on the editorship of the *Alpine Journal* and 'getting out' became elusive again.

LINDSAY GRIFFIN lives in North Wales, from where he continues to report on the developments in world mountaineering. An enthusiastic mind still tries to coax a less than enthusiastic body up pleasant bits of rock and ice, both at home and abroad.

ULYANA HORODYSKYJ is a PhD candidate at the Cooperative Institute for Research in Environmental Sciences (CIRES) at the University of Colorado. She is a well-travelled field geologist, having worked on all seven continents. Her next expedition to the Himalaya is slated for November/ December 2012. When not travelling, researching or climbing mountains, she writes about science for the public, most regularly for the *Ukrainian Weekly* newspaper.

ALFREDO ÍÑIGUEZ was a climber and a member of the Grupo de Alta Montaña Español (Spanish High Mountain Group). His main activities took place on the limestone walls of the Picos, especially in the imposing

Naranjo de Bulnes Peak. Off the rock, he pursued his passion for alpinism through writing articles and stories in his popular blog. He died in March 2012 following a climbing accident.

DICK ISHERWOOD has been a member of the Alpine Club since 1970. His climbing record includes various buildings in Cambridge, lots of old-fashioned routes on Cloggy, a number of obscure Himalayan peaks, and a new route on the Piz Badile (in 1968). He now follows Tilman's dictum about old men on high mountains and limits his efforts to summits just a little under 20,000 feet.

HARISH KAPADIA has climbed in the Himalaya since 1960, with ascents up to 6800m. For more than three decades his name was synony-mous with that of the *Himalayan Journal,* which he edited until 2010. In 1993 he was awarded the IMF's Gold Medal and in 1996 he was made an honorary member of the Alpine Club. He has written several books including *High Himalaya Unknown Valleys, Spiti: Adventures in the Trans-Himalaya* and, most recently, *Siachen Glacier: The Battle of Roses.* In 2003 he was awarded the Patron's Gold Medal by the Royal Geographical Society.

PAUL KNOTT is a lecturer in business strategy at the University of Canter-bury, New Zealand. He previously lived in the UK. He enjoys exploratory climbing in remote mountains, and since 1990 has undertaken 14 expedi-tions to Russia, Central Asia, Alaska and the Yukon. He has also climbed new routes in the Southern Alps and on desert rock in Oman and Morocco.

JESÚS LONGO is a radiologist and mountaineer whose stressing hours in the hospital are counterbalanced by the time spent in the solitude of the most remote spots of the Picos de Europa. He shares Elisa Villa's interest for the scientific and alpine history of these mountains, and he has a special yearning to 'dive' into libraries or the web in search of ignored old texts about them.

ERIK MONASTERIO is a Bolivian/ New Zealand psychiatrist and climber, currently living and working in NZ. Erik has climbed all over the world, but specializes in the Andes, where he has done more than 40 new alpine routes over ice, rock and mixed ground. He is engaged on research into personality characteristics and accidents in climbers.

MARTIN MORAN is a British Mountain Guide and runs a moun-taineering business, www.moran-mountain.co.uk based in Lochcarron, Wester Ross, Scotland. He has led 25 expeditions to the Indian Himalaya over the last 30 years. Many of these have tackled new peaks in remote areas with clients. He is author of the Alpine Club's guide to the 4000m peaks of the Alps.

SIMONE MORO is an Italian alpinist with a particular calling to 8000 peaks in winter. In 2009 he made the first winter ascent of Makalu (8463m) with Denis Urubko in true alpine style and two years later the pair, plus Cory Richards, repeated the feat on Gasherbrum II. His book *Cometa Sull'Annapurna* tells of his 1997 winter expedition to Annapurna during which his companion Anatoli Bukreev died.

ANINDYA 'RAJA' MUKHERJEE works as a mountaineering expedition guide and trek leader in the Indian Himalaya where in the past decade or so he has participated in or led more than 25 expeditions. He has also climbed and trekked in Tanzania, Greenland, Iceland, the Caucasus, and the European Alps. Above all, his passion lies in exploring the lesser known valleys, glaciers and mountains of the Indian Himalaya.

TAMOTSU NAKAMURA has been climbing new routes in the greater ranges since his first successes in the Cordillera Blanca of Peru in 1961. He has lived in Pakistan, Mexico, New Zealand and Hong Kong and has made 30 trips to the 'Alps of Tibet' – the least-known mountains in East Tibet and the Hengduan mountains of Yunnan, Sichuan, East Tibet and Qinghai. In 2010 he retired as editor of the *Japanese Alpine News* but continues as contributing editor. He received the RGS Busk Medal in 2008 and has recently been awarded the 4th Japan Sports Prize.

BERNARD NEWMAN started climbing the day England won the World Cup, so you'd think he'd be better at it by now. He joined the Leeds University Union Climbing Club in 1968 when Mike Mortimer was president, and was closely associated with that exceptional group of rock climbers and super-alpinists which included Syrett, MacIntyre, Baxter-Jones, Porter and Hall, without any of their talent rubbing off. One-time geologist, editor of *Mountain* and *Climber*, Bernard is now a 'freelance' writer, editor and photographer. He is a vice-president of the Climbers' Club.

BRUCE NORMAND is from Scotland but lives in China where he works as professor of physics at Renmin University (People's University) in Beijing. Author of more than 20 first ascents and new routes on 6000m peaks in the Trans-Himalaya, he has also climbed K2.

ROGER PAYNE was killed in an avalanche on Mont Maudit on 12 July 2012. A former general secretary of the British Mountaineering Council, he was a passionate climber and explorer of mountains and had undertaken more than 30 expeditions, making many first ascents. He was an international mountain guide with a keen interest in sustainable development in mountain regions and had recently been advising the government of Sikkim. A full obituary will appear in the next *AJ*.

DAVID PICKFORD is Editor in Chief of *Climb* magazine. He has established many new rock climbs around Britain and across the world. A prolific photographer and writer, he is still working on more direct lines from his desk to the front door.

ELIZABETH RAIKES is Chief Executive of Torbay Council in Devon. She took up the post following careers in the Women's Royal Naval Service, teaching and chartered accountancy. She studied Archaeology and History at Southampton University and has never lost her love of unravelling the mysteries of the past. Most of all she enjoys walking the footpaths of Corsica.

PAUL RAMSDEN lives the somewhat schizophrenic lifestyle of a mountaineer funded by his work as a health and safety consultant. Since ascents of the classic alpine north faces in his teens he has continued to climb in most of the world's greater ranges. He puts his success down to a very tolerant wife and family.

SIMON RICHARDSON is a petroleum engineer based in Aberdeen. Experience gained in the Alps, Andes, Patagonia, Canada, the Himalaya, Caucasus, Alaska and the Yukon is put to good use most winter weekends whilst exploring and climbing in the Scottish Highlands.

C A RUSSELL, who formerly worked with a City bank, devotes much of his time to mountaineering and related activities. He has climbed in many regions of the Alps, in the Pyrenees, East Africa, North America and the Himalaya.

BILL RUTHVEN was made an honorary member of the Alpine Club in 2004 for his service to mountaineering as honorary secretary of the Mount Everest Foundation. Before being confined to a wheelchair, he had built up more than half a century of mountaineering experience, which is invaluable to him in his MEF work He is always happy to talk to and advise individuals planning an expedition.

MARCELO SCANU is an Argentine climber, born in 1970, who lives in Buenos Aires. He specialises in ascending virgin mountains and volcanoes in the Central Andes. His articles and photographs about alpinism, trekking, and mountain history, archaeology and ecology appear in prominent magazines in Europe and America. When not climbing, he works for a workers' union.

JOHN TOWN is a retired university administrator. He has climbed in the Alps, Caucasus, Altai, Andes, Turkey and Kamchatka, and explored little-known mountain areas of Mongolia, Yunnan and Tibet. He is old enough to remember the days without satellite photos and GPS.

ELISA VILLA is a mountaineer and university lecturer in Geology, who is never as happy as when she is searching for microfossils at a high altitude outcrop. A great deal of her professional life has been dedicated to the study of the Picos de Europa, trying to understand their geological history. Over time, she found equally fascinating the history of alpinism in these mountains.

ERIC VOLA is a French climber who lives in Chamonix and Marseille. He spent three years at University College, London, and climbed in the early 1960s with Chris Bonington, Nick Escourt, Don Whillans, Gunn Clarke, Martin Boysen and other Brits. In recent years he has translated British mountaineering books, including a selection of Chris Bonington's best stories, Ruth Hanson's biography of Maurice Wilson (royalties to CAN) and *Learning to Breathe* by Andy Cave.

PHIL WICKENS studied biology at Imperial College in London, England. After completing his PhD in plant pathology he worked for two winters and three summers as a field guide for the British Antarctic Survey, and currently works as a freelance guide, lecturer and photographer in the polar regions. He has led numerous climbing and skiing expeditions to remote areas, including the Alpine Club's expeditions to the Pamirs and Antarctica.

FREDDIE WILKINSON is a New England-based professional climber, mountain guide and writer. He has made numerous first ascents in Alaska, Patagonia and the Himalaya. His writing appears in the *Huffington Post*, *Rock and Ice*, *Alpinist* and the *AAJ*. His first book, *One Mountain Thousand Summits*, an analysis of the tragic debacle on K2 in 2008, was published to acclaim in 2010.

DAVE WYNNE-JONES used to teach before he learnt his lesson. He has spent over 30 years exploring the hills and crags of Britain and climbed all the Alpine 4000m peaks. By the 1990s annual alpine seasons had given way to explorative climbing further afield, including Jordan, Morocco, Russia and Ecuador, though ski-mountaineering took him back to the Alps in winter. Expedition destinations have included Pakistan, Peru, Alaska, the Yukon, Kyrgyzstan, Nepal, India and China with a respectable tally of first ascents.

Index 2012

A

Abbe Mt (2667m), Alaska 330
Abi (5694m), China 311
Ackerman, Jorge 95, 323
Aconcagua 320-2
Adams, Dave 302
Adamson, Thomas 327
A Day to Die For – 1996: Everest's Worst Disaster
by Graham Ratcliffe, review 362
Afghanistan, art 16-26; 270, 336
AFGHANISTAN Notes 287-8
Aguiló, Tomy 323
Aiguille Noire 272
Aiguille Verte 245, 273, 275
Ailefroide 275-6
Alan Rouse Memorial Collection 329
Aletsch glacier 213-4
Alexandrov glacier 56
Allen, Jane 337
Allen, Mark 330
Allen, Tim 337
Allshorn, Sam 337
Alpha Males: The Story of the Alpha Mountain-
eering Club by Al Parker, review 355
Alpine Convention, article 210
ALPS Notes 271-9
Amann, Oliver 294
Amundsen, Roald 180
Ancohuma (6430m), Bolivia 314, 316
Andrews, Alasdair, obit of 413-4
Andvord Bay, Antarctica 187-8
Ang Phula Sherpa 205, 207-8
Annapurna 248, 307, 362, 372, 416, 425-6, 437
Annequin, Jean 40
Antarctica 53; art 177-190; 196, 202, 379
Antoine, Bletton 295
Aoraki, Mt Cook 326-7
Apakidze, Gia 104
ARGENTINE ANDES Notes 317-23
Arles, Jean-Pierre 308
Arnold, Dani 278
Arosio, Tito 279
Arralang valley, West Sikkim 124
Arunachal Pradesh 305
Arwa Tower, Uttarakhand 293
Asa (5800m), Sichuan 139
Asatiani (3820m), Georgia 110-11
Ascent: The Vertical Life review 381-2

B

Baguet, Maël 311
Bahini group, West Sikkim 124-9
Baihaizishan (5924m), Sichuan 141
Baihali Jot (6290m), Himachal Pradesh 299
Bainbridge, Andrea 301
Bainbridge, Colin 300
Baker, Andy 314
Ball, Murray 324
Balmer, Matt 331, 430
Banck, Mt (710m), Antarctica 188
Band, George , obit of 396-401
Banerjee, Dilip 295
Barberis, F, M & P 318
Barbón, Enrique González 263
Barihin, Igor 290
Barma Kangri (6515m) 300
Barmasse, Hervé 272, 276
Bartenschlager, Dominik 103
Bartlett, Phil, his article 77-87; review 358-60
biog 434
Bartlett, Steve 'Crusher', reviewed 375-6
Barton, Bob 223
Bass, Malcolm 285-6, 293-4
Batoux, Philippe 273
Bauer, Paul 120
Baxter, James, reviewed 377-9
Bayona, Holmes Pantoja 322
Beal, Peter, reviewed 387-8
Bedin, Mikael Dubois 302
Beg, Aziz 287
Beghin, Pierre 307
Beinn Bhan 284
Beinn Eighe 284
Beinn Udlaidh 285
Beisley, Gregg 314-5
Bekauri, Nana 103
Belgian Antarctic Expedition 186
Bell, Julian 231
Beltrame, Sebastián 323

Ashagongge (5783m), Sichuan 138
Ashworth, Steve 282
Atkinson, George 307
Auer, Hansjörg 279
Aufdenblatten, Patrick 276
Avachinsky Sopka (2741m), Kamchatka 336
Azerbaijan 99-101, 110

Ben Nevis 280-2
Benson, Pete 283-5
Berger, Stefan 315
Bergland Pillar, Les Droites 273
Berg, Peter, reviewed 346-9
Bernese Oberland 158-62, 278
Berry, Steve, reviewed 370
Bertrand (4730m), Argentina 318
Bezingi Wall, Caucasus 266
Bhagirathi III (6454m) 223, 294
Bhushan, Bharat 295
Bhutia, Barap 129
Bhutia, Kunzang 128
Bidara (3174m) Mt, Caucasus 104
Biggar, John 318-9
Bin, Sun 311
Birch, Steve 32, 34, 39
Bisharat, Andrew, his article 88-95, biog 434
Bishorn 266
Bizot, Henry 320
Blackshaw, Alan, obit of 405-409
Blaser, Willy 131
Blunt, Francis 284
Boardman, Peter 79, 82, 248, 393
Boardman Tasker Omnibus (The) review 393
Boardman Tasker Prize 2011, 393
Boelter, Tim 312
Bolger, Dave 324
BOLIVIA Notes 314-6
Bonacalza, José 323
Bonatti Direct, Matterhorn 276
Bonatti Route, Petite Jorasses 147
Bonatti, Walter 272; obit of 409-413
Bond, Timothy 334
Boner, Niall 297
Bonete Chico (6759m), Argentina 319
Bonington, Chris 79; in art 247-57; 299, 399,
408, 425, 429, 439
Borgnet, Yann 275
Boskoff, Christine 138
Boss, Emil 130
Bossi, Umberto 214
Boswell, Greg 280, 282, 283, 284, 285
Bouldering by Peter Beal, review 387
Boustead, Captain 118
Bradshaw, Penny, article 229-237, biog 434
Braithwaite, Paul 428
Brand, Roland 294
Braun-Elwert, Elke 327
Bregaglia 225, 228, 277, 278, 356
Brighton, Alex 335

British Antarctic Survey 180, 183, 200
British Columbia 331
British Mountaineering Council (BMC) 51,
79, 87
Broadbent, Tom 285
Broad Peak 202, 289, 343
Brown, Hamish, reviewed 386-7
Brown, Joe 400
Brown, Kester 270, 327, 328, biog 434
Brown, Mark 337
Brunskill, Walter 267
Buckle, Derek, in art 52-58, his art 179-190,
296, review 379, 428, biog 434
Budalstinden, Norway 168
Bull, Jonathan 332
Bullock, Nick 284, 309, 333
Burke, Mick 92
Byrch, Christine, in art 16-26, 288, 336

C
Caffin, Roger 197
Cairngorms 110, 153, 280-3, 285, 352
Cambon, Jean-Michel 275
Cameron (5873m), Caucasus 138
Campbell, Joanna, author review 366-7
Canisaya (5706m), Bolivia 337
Carbon Monoxide poisoning, art 195-202
Carleton, George 297
Carn Dearg 281, 282
Carnegie, Neil 285
Cartwright, Chris 149
Casaldi, Gerardo 317
Casarotto, Renato 272
Caspersen, Robert 165
Caucasus, art 99-112; 266
Cave, Andy, 41, his art 158-162; 344, 428,
biog 434
Cave, Paddy 282
Central Alaska Range 330
Central Pillar of Frêney 149; in art 247-57, 272
Centre de Recherches sur les Ecosystèmes
d'Altitude 215
Cerro Acay (5716m) Argentina 317
Cerro Camila (c4932m), Argentina 318
Cerro Manantiales (c5100m) Argentina 321
Cerro Medusa N. E. (6046m) Argentina 318
Cerro Nevado (5988m), Argentina/Chile 318
Cerro Plata (5968m) Argentina 320
Cerro Ponta Ladina (c4859m) Argentina 318
Cerro Torre, in art 88-95
Cerro Vallecitos (5475m) Argentina 321-2

Challeat, Ludovic 183
Challenge of K2 (The) by Richard Sale, review 351
Challenge of Rainier (The) by Dee Molenaar, review 384
Chamonix 55, 109, 147-8, 150, 214-5; in art 247-57
Chandellier, Antoine 247, 257
Changla Himal, Nepal 308, 332, 430
Changwathang (5960m) Nepal 308
Chapman, Robin, author obit 417-8
Charcot, Jean-Baptiste 180
Chaukhi massif, Georgia, in art 99-113
Chávez, Christián 318
Chettri, Deepak Kumar 128
Chibitok, Galina 292
Chichicapac (5614m) Peru 430
China 16, 24, 26; articles 40-51; 54, 132-43; 270, 334
CHINA & TIBET Notes 311-3
Chola Shan I (6168m) Sichuan 133
Chola Shan North 133
Chomo I (6878m) Arunachal Pradesh 305
Chomo II (6710m) 305
Cho Oyu 308, 431
Chorley, Roger, author obit 400
Chorten Garpo (6380m) Tibet 313
Church, Tim 313
Churi, West Sikkim 124, 126, 129
Cima Ovest di Lavaredo 279
Civetta 279
Clarke, Ewan 100
Clarke, Jono 327-8
Cleare, John 223, 431
Clearwater, Mulu Caves, Malaysia 337
Climbers' Club Journal 2011, review 384
Climbing Dictionary by Matt Samet, review 382
Cloos, Mt (1200m) 182-90
Clouet, Aymeric 272
Clough, Ian, in art 247-57
Clow, Kate, reviewed 386
Clyma, Julie-Ann 44, 124, 127-28, 303
Cocker, Michael 296
Cohen, Geoff 130, 304
Cohen, Valerie Mendenhall, reviewed 373-4
Coire an Lochain 285
Coire an t-Sneachda 284
Coire na Ciste 280, 282
Cold Wars by Andy Kirkpatrick, review 358
Coles, Becky 287, 336
Collie, Norman 131

Colton, Nick 12, 308, 332, 430
Comi, Michele 278
Contamine Route, Petite Jorasses 147
Conway Peak, NZ 327
Cook, Drew 296
Cook, Frederick 180
Cooper, Julian, author review 377
Cordillera Carabaya 331
Cordillera Carabaya Expedition 430
Cordillera de la Ramada 319
Cordillera Oriental Expedition 430
Cordillera Oriental (Peru) 331
Cordillera Real 315-6
Cordón de los Arrieros 317
Cordón de los Pioneros 319
Cordón del Plata 321
Costa, Stanley 326
Coustick, Dave 100
Cox, David 79
Cradock, Nick 324
Creagan Coire Cha-no 285
Creag an Dubh Loch 283
Creag Meagaidh 280, 284, 285
Crew, Pete 92
Criscitiello, Alison 301
Curran, Jim, reviewed 365-6

D
Daddomain (6380m), Sichuan 141
Dadu He (River) Basin, Sichuan 143
d'Alboy, Pierre 273
Dale, Chris 274
Dallmeyer, Mts 189
Dampier, Mt (3443m), NZ 267
Dam, Satyabrata, in art 16-26; 28, 36, 39
Daneri, Fernando 319
Dare, Ben 274, 279, 308, 324-6, 333
Darran Mountains, NZ 324
Daudet, Lionel 273
Dauru, Garhwal 296
Davidson, Simon 285
Davies, Al, reviewed 390
Davies, Pete 282
Davis, Wade, reviewed 360-2
Dawes, Johnny, reviewed 367-8
Daxue Shan, China 140, 311
Day, Darryl 180, 190
Dean, Steve, author review 355-7
Deavoll, Pat, her art 16-26; 288, 336, 343, biog 434
De las Chullpas (5898m) Argentina 317

Deloncle Bay, Antarctica 188
De los Arrieros (5860m) Argentina 317
De los Grillos (5768m) Argentina 317
Dempster, John, author obit 413-4
Dempster, Kyle, in art 40-51, 291
Densham, Chris 337
Dent du Géant 145
Desert Towers by Steve 'Crusher' Bartlett, review 375
Deshpande, Mangesh 303
Desmaison, René, in art 247-57
Desroy, Graham 5, 308, 333, 429
Detrie, Mathieu 276
Devies, Lucien, in art 247-57
Dhaulagiri 308
Dickinson, Leo 89
Dimitri, Messina 295
Dingjung Ri (6249m), Nepal 310
Dixon, Kevin 337
Djangart, Kyrgyzstan 335
Djuglosz, Jan, reviewed 247
Djupfjord, Norway 164-175
Dmitrienko, Evgeny 290
Dolomites 94, 106, 110, 213, 253, 279, 356, 372
Dome Peak (5650m), Lahaul 298
Dongdong, Yan 311, 313
Dongxung (6095m), Tibet 313
Donini, Jim 291
Donogomba (5960m), Sichuan 141
Doran, Kevin, reviewed 376-7
Douglas, Ed 5, 308, 332, 430
Dowthwaite, Phil 284
Dozhdev, Ivan 290
Drake Passage 179-81, 189
Drayton, Diane 328
Dreybodt, Joerg 337
Drinkwater, Emilie 64
Duda, Klaudiusz 287, 288
Dudas, Paul 272
Dudley, Graham, his article 99-111, biog 435
Dumas, Martial 276
Dunmur, David, reviewed 383
Dunn, Hamish 331, 430
Dych Tau (5198m), Caucasus 266
Dye, Adrian 331

E
Eagle Ski Club 58
Eastern Alaska Range 329
Eastern Crags, FRCC guidebook, review 390
Eastern Karakoram 64

Eavis, Andy 337
Ecstasy, route in art 158-162
Eden Valley & South Lakes Limestone, FRCC guidebook, review 388
Edgar, Mt, Sichuan, in art 40-51
Eggishorn 213
Eiger 275, 278
Eilde Canyon, Glen Coe 285
Ekdant (6100m), Uttarakhand 294
El Muerto, Andes 318
Engadine 209
Engelhörner 158, 160, 162
Eren Habirga & Borohoru mountains 334, 430
Erik Monasterio 270, 314, 315, biog 436
Escalé, Pau 273
Esten, Mike 406
Evans, Charlie 335
Eva's Peak (6119m), Himachal 31-2, 34-6, 39
Everest ii, v-vi, 15, 20, 26, 51, 79, 80, 84, 85-7, 131, 204, 208, 230, 248, 255, 300, 307, 329
Everest & Conquest in the Himalaya by Richard Sale & George Rodway, review 362
Evliya Çelebi Way (The) by Caroline Finkel & Kate Clow, review 386
Exploring Greenland by Jim Gregson, review 376

F
Fairley, John, paintings 1, 75, 97, 145, 193, 221, 245, 269, 339, his article 223-8, biog 435
Farrant, James 328
Far West Nepal Expedition 430
Faur, Freda Du 267
Faux, Ronald, author reviews 352-3, 383
Fava, Gabriel 320
Fazio, Lynn Lacobini De 298
Ferguson, David 188
Ferguson, Rob 299
Ferrari, Casimiro 90
Fersmana III (5210m), Kyrgyzstan 335
Fida Brakk (c5350m), Pakistan 292
Fierro-Carrion, Gustavo 39
Figg, Paul 294
Finkel, Caroline, reviewed 386
Finnigan, Andrew 326
Finsteraarhorn 339
Fiorenza, Luciano 321, 323
Fitzgerald, Dan 331, 430
Fiva by Gordon Stainforth, reviewed 345
Fletcher, Mike 189-90
Fonrouge, Jose Luis 92
Foraker, Mt, Alaska 330

Fordham, Derek, author review 376
Fortune, Steve 324, 327, 333
Fowler, Charlie 138
Fowler, Mick, his art 3-15; 41, 60, 195, 308, 333, 428-9, biog 435
Francou, Bernard 275
Franklin, Rodney, author review 349-51
Frederic, Gentet 295
Fredricksen, Jean-Yves 276
Freedom Climbers by Bernadette McDonald, review 341
Freeman-Attwood, Julian 80, 308, 332, 430
Freshfield, Douglas 103, 118, 240
Fritzer, Charly 285
Full of Myself by Johnny Dawes, review 367
Furlong, Imogen 337

G

Gabl, Karl 60
Gadgil, Rajesh 293, 303
Gallagher, Stuart 190
Gandino, Adrián 317
Gangga massif 134
Gardiner, Rupert 324-5
Garhwal 266, 296, 353, 423
Garibotti, Rolo 91
Garvie, Anthony 324
Gasherbrum I 61, 62, 289
Gasherbrum II, in art 59-62, 289
Gaussot, Philippe 257
Gave Ding (6571m), Nepal 308, 332, 430
Gay, Sébastien 276
Geist, Mt (3268m), Alaska, 330, 430
Genyen (6204m), Sichuan 138
Gervasutti Route, Grandes Jorasses 147
Gestola (4860m), Caucasus 266
Gibisch, Chris 311
Gibson, H B 267
Gietl, Simon 279
Gifford, Terry, author reviews 369-70, 371
Gillman, Peter, author review 362-365
Giri Giri Boys 291
Giuliani, Javier 319
Glacier du Géant 214
Glairon-Rappaz, Patrice 275
Glen Coe 280, 285-6
Gojung (6310m), Nepal, in art 3-15, 308
Golob, Urban 294
Gomba, Antonio 278
González, Gustavo 317
González, Pablo 320

Goodman, Don & Natala 302-3
Goodman, Pat 291
Goodwin, Stephen, his Foreword v-vi, his article 204, 209-218, reviews 345, 354, 370, 375, 380-3, 385-7, 388, author obits 396, 401 & 405, 428, biog 435
Gordon, Alistair, obit of 414-6
Gordon Stainforth reviewed 345
Gorichen (6488m), Arunachal Pradesh 305
Goromity (5609m), Sichuan 142
Göschl, Gerfried 62, 289
Gottlieb, David 309
Gottner, Adolf 120
Goudier Island, Antarctica 181-2
Graham, Dave 387
Graham, W.W. 124, 130, 303
Granberg, Hannes 335
Grand Capucin 272
Grandes Jorasses 147, 275
Gray, Dennis 433
Great Trango Tower (6238m), Pakistan 292
Greaves, Hilary 334
Gregory, Alfred 397, 402
Gregson, Jim, reviewed 376
Griffin, Lindsay, 270-1; 273, 277, 287, 289, 293, review 351-2; 354, 393, 428 biog 435
Grobel, Paulo 308
Gronlund, Toto 296, 428
Grosvenor, Mt (6376m), Sichuan 40, 44-5; 51, 311
Gugliermina 272, 275
Gulmothungos Rocks, Ladakh 300-1
Gunnung Mulu National Park, Sarawak 337
Gupta, Priyadarshi 123
Gurtoo, Anil 295
Gyachung Kang (7952m), Nepal/Tibet 203
Gyalzen Sherpa 121

H

Haast, Mt, NZ 327
Habeler, Peter 131
Hagshu (6515m) E Karakoram 302
Haldane, J.S. 131
Haley, Colin 95
Hall, Pete 337
Hall, Simon 295
Hamilton, Bob 304
Hamilton, Greig 327
Hanafin, Nick 328
Hannigan, Tim, reviewed 354-5
Hans Meyer Peak, Kilimanjaro massif 267

Harding, John, author obit 418-20
Harlin, John 278
Harris, Kate 301
Harrison, Jimmy 324
Harrison, Rev James, obit of 417-8
Harrop, Mike 147
Haspel, Rebecca 301
Hassan Peak, Pakistan 291
Haston, Dougal 85, 92
Hauslabjoch, Ötztal Alps 218
Hawker, Rev William 238
Hawley, Elizabeth 307
Healey, Eileen 431
Hearing Silence, Edward Williams, review 371
Hegde, Vinay 296
Hei Shui Dong (Black Water Cave), China 334
Hengduan Mountains Club (Japan) 134
Henry, Emil, reviewed 346-9
Hepp, Günther 120
Here, There and Everywhere (autobiography) by Jim Curran, review 365
Herford, Siegfried 267
Hersey, Paul 327
Hersey, Shelley 327
Herzog, Maurice 79, 248
Hesleden, Dave 285
Hew, Cath 180, 190
Hicks, Mt, NZ 327
Hidden Peak, Pakistan 289
High Atlas (The), Hamish Brown, review 386
Hill, Florian 315
Himachal, in art 27-39
Himalayan Club 123
Himalayan Journal 28, 39, 114, 117
Hindu Kush 287-8; 336, 354
Hinku valley, Nepal 309, 333
Hiraide, Kazuya 313
Hoare, Rupert, reviewed 349; obit of 418-20
Hocquemiller, Romain 276
Hodgkinson, Terry 242
Holden, John 388
Holloway, Stuart 327
Holmberg, Malin, in art 163-75
Holmes, Steve 309, 334
Hopong region, Myanmar 337
Horobin, Christopher 300
Horodyskyj, Ulyana N, her art 203-8; biog 435
Horst, Michael 307
Hotine glacier, Antarctica 182, 186-7
Houseman, Andy 309, 333

House, Steve 60
Houston, Charlie 79
Howard, Dave 100
Howard, Tony, reviewed 372-3
Huaguruncho Chico (c5300m), Peru 331, 430
Huarancayo Sur (c5200m), Peru 430
Huayna Potojsi (5600m), Bolivia 314-5
Huayna Potosi (6088m), Bolivia 316
Hudowska, Iwonna 334, 428, 430
Hudowski, Tadeusz 334, 428, 430
Hudson, John 296
Hudson, Mark 391
Hughes, Glyn 130, 131, 242, 428
Hunt, John (Lord) 79, 122, 402
Hunter, Mt (4441m), Alaska 331
Hurancayo Sur (c5100m) 331
Hynes, Kevin 123

I
Ibsti Kangri (6340m), Ladakh 302
Illimani, Bolivia 314-5
Imeson, Barry 393
INDIA Notes 293-306
Indian Mountaineering Foundation 64
Íñiguez, Alfredo, jt article 258-265, biog 435
Into The Silence: The Great War, Mallory and the Conquest of Everest, Wade Davis, review 360
Iñurrategi, Alberto 60
Inverleith 188-90
Isaksson, Olov 276
Isherwood, Allan 39
Isherwood, Dick 270, 289, 292, 304, 307, biog 436
Itching To Climb, Barbara James, review 357

J
Jakofcic, Tomaz 279
Jambu Peak (5105m), Himachal Pradesh 299
James, Barbara, reviewed 357-8
Jamieson, Murdo 284
Jangpar glacier, Himachal 29, 30
Jankhopiti (5723m), Bolivia 315-6
Jannin, Louis 248
Jarjinjabo massif, Sichuan 135-6
Jasper, Robert 277
Javakhishvili (3650m), Georgia 111
Jefferies, Craig 325
Jentoft, Harald 266
Jiazi Feng (6540m), Sichuan 44, 311
Jiwa Nala , Kullu 296
Jobo Rinjang (6778m), Nepal 334

Johnson, Chris 329, 430
Joll, Daniel 324, 326
Jones, Robin 332
Jopuno, Sikkim 127-30; 303-4
Joshi, Dhruv 295
Josten, Martin 58
Jost, Matija 294
Jot Mund (5130m), Himachal 299
Jujuy, Argentina 317
Julien, Pierre 247
Jurgalski, Eberhard, reviewed 380
Jurm valley, Wakhan, Afghanistan 288

K
K2 79, 289, 351-2; 354, 366
K7 West 291
Kabru 130-1
Kali Behin, West Sikkim 124, 126
Kaltenbrunner, Gerlinde 289
Kamchatka Peninsula 336
Kamet 266, 294
Kanchi Behin, West Sikkim 124, 126
Kangchenjau (6919m) 267
Kangchenjunga, in art 114-23; 124, 130, 240, 241, 242, 255
Kangto, Arunachal Pradesh 305
Kangto I (7042m) & II (6953m) 306
Kapadia, Geeta 305
Kapadia, Harish 270; 293-306; author obit 421-3; biog 436
Karakoram 36, in arts 59-62 & 63-73, 158, 287, 289, 291, 350, 354
Kawarani I (5992m) and II (5928m), Sichaun 134-5
Kawecki, Slawomir 287-8
Kazbek (5034m), Caucasus, in art 99-109
Kedar Dome 223
Kekus, Nick 147
Kellas, Alexander 118, 131, 266
Kellogg, Chad 309
Kennedy, Hayden 88, 91
Kennedy, Michael 291
Kennedy, Sandra 297
Kennedy, Steve 304
Kentchat Bashi (4171m), Caucasus 266
Kentish, John 58
Kenyon, Ron, reviewed 388
Kerr, Jim 274
Khan, Genghis 99
Khuiten (4374m), Mongolia 54
Khumbu, Nepal 203, 205, 208, 308, 333-4;

396-7, 399, 401
Kilimanjaro 267
King, David 39
Kinsella, David 124
Kirby, Matt 337
Kirkpatrick, Andy, reviewed 358-60; reviewer 372-3
Kishtwar, Himachal, in art 27-39
Kitson, James 287, 336
Klute, Fritz 267
Klyuchevskaya Sopka (4721m), Kamchatka 336
Knott, Paul 270, 330, 428, biog 436
Knowles, Colin 120
Koh-e-Baba-Tangi (6516m), Wakhan, in art 16-26; 288, 336
Koh-e-Mandaras (6331m), Afghanistan 288
Koh-e-Nadir Sah (6814m), Afghanistan 287
Koh-e-Sauze (c5730m), Afghanistan 288, 336
Kojichuwa Chuli (6439m), NW Nepal 6, 12; 308, 334
Kojichuwa valley, NW Nepal 333
Koktang, West Sikkim 130
Koller, Igor 279
Kondoriri, Bolivia 314
Kongga Xueshan massif, Sichuan 139
Kongma (4800m), Ladakh 300
Kopteva, Marina 292
Kornilov, Alexander 299
Korol, Evgeny 299
Korzh, Boris 295
Kothari, Vijay 305
Kowalewski, Ryszard 272
Kozu, Kazuo 299
Kramer, Kirsten 64
Kreiss-Tomkins, Jonathan 318
Kret, Wakhan, Afghanistan 17-19, 26
Kruk, Jason 88, 91
Kumar, Raj 299
Kurz, Marcel 266
Kusum Kanguru (6367m), Nepal 309, 333
Kyajo Ri (6186m), Nepal 309, 333
Kyashar (6769m), Nepal 309 333

L
Labbre, Pierre 272, 276
Lachenal, Louis 79, 248
Lacuna glacier, Alaska 330
Lady of The Lake, Norway, in art 163-75
Lafaille, Jean-Christophe 307
Lahaul 293

Lama, David 93
Lamalamani (c5650m), Sikkim, in art 124-9; 304-5
Lammergeyer Peak, Garhwal 296
Landman, Felix 327
Lan, Li 311
Lapina, Natalia 299
La Rioja, Argentina 319
Lastia de Gardas, Dolomites 279
Lates, Mike, reviewed 391
Latok I, II & III Pakistan 290, 291
Latti, Henry 300
Lawford, Anna 428, 431
Lawrence, Hugh St 337
Lawton, Ian & Liz 337
Leadbeater, Philip 295
Leániz, Juan Manuel 319
Lear, Edward, in art 238-42
Leay glacier, Antarctica 183
Lemaire Channel, Antartica 187, 188
Lemon, Edward 335
Lennox, Gordon 283
Leprince-Rinquet, Dominique 256
Lerjen, Michael 276
Les Dames Anglaises 266
Les Droites 273
Lewis-Jones, Huw, reviewed 385-6
Lhotse 59, 204, 307
Liberman, Edgardo 319
Lindic, Luka 279
Lingsarmo (6995m), Ladakh 301
Little, Graham 299
Lizuka, Hidetaka 299
Lloyd, Hywel 431
Lochnagar 283
Lofoten Islands, Norway, in art 163-75
Lofti, Mijel 320
Lonchinsky, Alex 290
Longo, Jesús, jt article 258-265, biog 436
Lopez, Camilo 298
Lorencic, Boris 294
Lovatt, Jerry 334; author review 346-9; 428, 430
Loveridge, Fleur 337
Lowe, George 291
Lowe, Jeff 291
Lowther, Jim 63, 299
Lunag 310, 334
Lyall, John 285
Lynch, Steve 283
Lyalver (4350m), Caucasus 266

M
Mabboni, Mauro 93
MacIntyre, Richmond 190
Mackenzie, Neil 331
MacLeod, Dave 285
MacNeice, Louis 230
Macpherson, Pete 282, 284
Maczka, Janusz 272
Maestri, Cesare, in art 88-95
Mahajan, Arun 124
Maili Mt (4598m), Caucasus 107
Maique, Rodrigo 320
Makalu 59, 255, 257
Malchin (4051m), Mongolia 56, 58
Mamostong Kangri (7516m), Ladakh 302
Mandaras group, Afghanistan 287
Manirang (6593m), Himachal Pradesh 297
Manning, David 328
Marcheggiani, Massimo 298
Marcic, Nejc 291
Mari (6587m), Ladakh 300
Maria Lloco (5523m), Bolivia 314
Marin, Matías 319
Marmolada 279
Marsh, Tim 282
Martin, Guillermo 317
Maruyama, Reiko 299
Marzorati, Andrea 278
Masania, Kunal 295, 332
Mason, Kenneth 266, 301
Maspes, Luca 278
Matheson, Beattie 26
Mathews, William 242
Matin (2415m), Antarctica, in art 179-90
Matterhorn 36, 214, 275, 276, 346, 349
Mawenzi (5149m), Kilimanjaro 267
Mayer, Bernd 294
Mazeaud, Pierre 256
McCormick, Matt 291
Mccullough, Aengus 331
McDonald, Bernadette, reviewed 341-3
McKinnon, Guy 313, 324, 325
McLellan, Andrew 295
McNaught-Davis, Loreto and Ian 124
Mead, Margaret 83
Measures, Reg 324
Medcalf, David, author obit 425
Meinen, Will 291
Melville, Harry 431
Menthosa (6443m), Himachal 300
Messina, Dimitri 311

Messner, Reinhold 59, 83, 86, 91, 94, 131
Metherell, Oliver 190
Middendorf, John 297
Mihelic, Zdenka 214
Millerioux, Hélias 276
Millichamp, Laura 296
Minya Konka, Sichuan 40, 44, 49, 51; 141-2
Miotti, Giuseppe 278
Mitchell, Ian R, 131; reviewed 352-3
Miyar Nala, Himachal, 27 29-30; 298-9
Mogavero, Stefano 278
Moir, Mt, NZ 324
Molenaar, Dee, reviewed 384
Molina, Diego 321
Monasterio, Erik 270, 314-316, biog 436
Mönch 213, 274, 279
Mongolia 52, 53, 54, 58
Mont Blanc 40; in art 147-57; 215-6; 233, 239-40; art 247-57; 266, 271-2, 349, 352, 357
Monte Disgrazia 278
Monte Rosa 212, 277
Monte Viso 238-9, 242
Moodie, Jonathan 332
Moorehead, Catherine, reviewed 383
Moran, Martin, his article 27-39; 149, 284, author review 377-9; biog 436
Morawski, Piotr 59
Moretti, Bruno 298
Morgan, Ant 324
Moro, Simone, his article 59-62; 289, biog 436
Morro Von Rosen (5450m), Argentina 317
Morteratsch glacier 209-10, 212
Moseley, David 300
Moseley, Dr Gina 337
Mottram, Gareth 335
Motyer, Gary 39
Moulin, Christophe 294
Mountaineering Council of Scotland 190
Mountain Heroes Huw Lewis-Jones, review 385
Mountain Views by Rupert Hoare, review 349
Mount Everest Foundation (MEF) 15, 26, 51
MEF Expedition Reports 329-37
Mount Hayes Expedition 430
Mugu Chuli (6310m), art 3-15; 308, 333
Mukherjee, Anindya, his art 114-123, biog 437
Mullin, Alan 283
Mulu Caves, Malaysia 337
Muni, Divyesh 302
Muratti, Glauco 317
Murder in the Hindu Kush: George Hayward and the Great Game by Tim Hannigan, review 354

Murphy, Danny 325, 326
Muryshev, Andrey 299
Muzkol range, Tajikistan 336

N
Naar, Ronald 307
Nadin, Simon 158
Naimona'nyi (7694m), West Tibet 313
Nairamdal (4192m), Mongolia 55
Nakamura, Tamotsu 41, his art 132-143, biog 437
Nanavati, Jagdish, obit of 421-3
Nanda Ghunti (6390m), Uttarakhand 295
Nanda Khat (6611m), Uttarakhand 295
Nanga Parbat 289, 431
Nant Blanc 273, 275
Naofeng Peak (7422m), West Tibet 313
Narsing, Sikkim 125, 130
NEPAL Notes 307-10
Nevado de Cachi (6380m), Argentina 317
Nevado Excelsior (5773m), Argentina 320
Neve, Dr Ernest 266
Newman, Bernard, review 387; 393, 396, 409; 428 biog 437
NEW ZEALAND Notes 324-8
Ngozumpa glacier, Nepal, in art 203-8
Nicholson, Norman 229
Nideng Gonnga (5690m), China 313
Niederbacher, Simon 279
Niederjochferner, Austria 215, 217
Nisbet, Andy 285
Nishijima, Rentaro 300
Nithal Thaur (6236m), India 294
Nobuyugya (5594m), Sichuan 133
Noel, John 80
Nojin Kangsang (7206m), Tibet 313
Norbu, Tapka 295
Normand, Bruce his art 40-51; 313; biog 437
Northern Corries 285
Norway: A ski and kayak odyssey by James Baxter, review 377
Norwegian Wood (7-/E4 6a), Lofoten 172
Noshaq, Afghanistan 287
Nun, E Karakoram 301
Nunn, Paul 158
Nuptse 204
Nyambo Konka (6114m), Sichuan 141-2
Nyegi Kangsang (6983m), India 304-5
Nyenchen Tanglha Main (7162m), Tibet 313
Nygren Mt (1454m), Antarctica 182-4, 190

O

Obra valley, Garhwal 295-6
Ochsner, Kaspar 158
O'Connor, Adrian 120
Odermatt, Willy 266
Odintsov, Alexander 290
Odriozola, Sandra 318
Oehler, Eduard 267
Ohe, Takao 133
Oieni, Fabrizio 319
Okawa, Kenzo 142
Oki, Masato 300
Oliver, Lt P. R. 298
Oliver, Tim, obit of 424-5
Onida, Marco 62, 210-11, 214
On Top of the World: The New Millennium by Sale, Jurgalski & Rodway, review 380
Ormsby, John, in art 258-65
Orobie Alps 279
Ortega, Hernán 321
Ortsveri glacier, Caucasus 102, 104-6, 109
Orville, Mt (3199m) Alaska 330
Otto, Jon 312
Ötzi the Iceman 216-8
Ötztaler Alps 214, 217

P

Pabellón (5331m), Argentina 319
Paduszek glacier, Argentina 319
Pae, Christine Kyungmee 289
Pakistan 24, 60; art 64-6, 270; 289-92; 300, 336, 344
PAKISTAN Notes 289-92
Palmer, Howard 267
Palmer, John 337
Pamirs 19-20, 287, 336, 354
Pandey, Chetan 295
Pandim (6691m), Sikkim 115, 123
Pangbuk Ri (6716m), Nepal 308-9
Pangi valley, Himachal 299
Papert, Ines 285
Paradise Harbour, Antarctica 187-8
Para, Jérôme 272
Paramonov, Dmitry 311
Parimbelli, Yuri 279
Parker, Al, reviewed 355-7
Parkin, Andy 275, 310
Parsons, Kieran 328
Parvati Parvat, Garhwal 294
Pasang Kikuli 119
Patagonia 90, 91, 94-5; 158

Patton, Henry 336
Pawson, Iona 52-4, 58
Payne, Roger 44; his art 124-131; 267; 303-4; biog 437
Peach, Dan 285
Peacock, John, author obit 425-7
Peak 5712m, Sichuan 143
Pearson, James 278
Peary, Mt, Antarctica 182, 184
Pedeferri, Simone 278
Pelvoux, Mt, 275, 347
Pemba Sherpa 119, 121
Penck, Walther 318
Peng, Zhou 311
Pessi, Patrick 273
Peterkin, Grant 266
Petrocelli, Adrián 317
Peuterey Ridge 266
Pfaff, Anna 298
Pfluger, Yvonne 313
Phari Lapcha East (6017m), Nepal 310
Phillips, Jonathan 295
Phillips, Neil 334
Phurtemba Sherpa 121
Picco Muzio 276
Pic du Midi d'Ossau 266
Pickford, David, his art 163-175; review 390; biog 438
Pico Ansilta 4 (5116m), Argentina 320
Pico Polaco (c6000), Argentina 319
Picos de Europa, in art 258-65
Pico Sur, Bolivia 315
Pic Sans Nom 275, 276
Pietron, Doerte 95
Pik Annika (4685m), Kyrgyzstan 335
Pik Georgina (4631m), Kyrgyzstan 335
Pik Lyell (4864m), Kyrgyzstan 335
Pimu Peak (5480m), Himachal 299
Pinelli, Carlo 336
Piolet d'Or 73, 291, 411, 433
Pirpamer, Alois 216, 218
Piunova, Anna 289
Piussi, Ignacio 247
Pivtsov, Vassily 289
Piz Badile 228; 277, 406, 408, 411
Piz Bernina 75, 209-10, 278
Piz Ciavazes 279
Pk 6294m, Himachal 33
Pointe Forastier 276
Point James (4965m), Lahaul 298
Pollet-Villard, Yves 247

Pollitt, Howard 58
Polujabu (5472m). Sichuan 133
Pontoriero, Pablo 321
Pope, Hugh 266
Popowich, Jon, author review 341-3
Potanina glacier, Mongolia 53, 56
Potard, Nicolas 272
Powell, Matt 300
Prabha Behin, West Sikkim 124-6, 130-1
Prà, Pietro Dal 279
Prelude to Everest by Ian Mitchell & George
Rodway, review 352
Presolana 279
Prezelj, Marko 60
Primerov, Nikolay 276
Prinold, Joe 332
Punta Baretti, in art 147-57
Punta Sertori 228
Purtscheller, Ludwig 267

Q

Qonglai Shan, 142; 311
Querlico, José Luis 319

R

Rabbiters Peak, NZ 328
Rai, Bhakta Kumar 307
Raikes, Elizabeth, her art 238-242; biog 438
Raine, Kathleen 232
Raj, Sagar 128
Raldang (5499m), India 297
Ramsden, Paul, his article 195-202; biog 438
Randall, Val, reviews 357-8, 367-8, 373-4
Ranglana (5554m), India 295-6
Ratcliffe, Graham, reviewed 362
Ratcliffe, Jonny 3, 5, 11, 14-5; 308, 333,
429-30
Ratel, Sébastien 273
Rathong, Sikkim 130
Rätikon 158, 278
Rauch, Robert 315
Rawal, Atul 305
Rawls, John 81
Red Bull 94, 95
Reddomain (6112m), Sichuan 311
Redhead, Mark 336
Red Rope 120
Reid, Stephen reviewed 388, 390
Reitchert, Federico 317
Revest, Robin 275
Reynolds, Sarah 301

Richards, Coryin art 59-62; 289
Richardson, Mark 337
Richardson, Simon 99, 108; his arts 109-13
& 147-57; 270, Scottish Notes 280-6; biog 438
Richey, Mark, in art 63-73
Riesner, Andi 103
Rimpfischhorn 266
Rio Negro, Argentina 323
Ripley, Tom 331, 430
Ritchie, Dave 304
Riuche valley, Sichuan 311
Roberts, Michael, in art 229-37
Robertson, Guy 280, 282-5
Rock and Ice magazine 88, 381
Rodríguez, Mariano 321, 323
Rodway, George 131; reviewed 352-3, 362-5,
380
Romero, Jordan 307
Rongqin, Su 312
*Roof at the Bottom of the World (The): Discov-
ering the Transantarctic Mountains* by Edward
Stump, review 379
Rousseau, Louis 62, 289
Rowe, Mike 333
Rowland, Peter 431
Rowsell, Philip 334, 337
Roxo, Paulo 294
Roy, Sukumar 295
Rubenson, Carl 266
Rudatis, Alessandro 279
Ruiz, Sebastián 320
Ruotsi, Anna 326
Russell, C A (Christopher), his art 266-7;
biog 438
Ruthven, Bill, MEF Notes 329-337; biog 438

S

Sadashivan, Sekar 303
Sadzele, Mt (3307m), Caucasus 104
Sahoo, Pradeep Chandra 302
Saichu valley, Himachal 298-9
Sale, Richard reviewed 351, 362 & 380; 354
Salvaterra, Ermanno 93
Samet, Matt, reviewed 382
San Francisco (6016m), Argentina 318
San Lian (6684m), Sichuan 141-2
Sansom, George 267
Sarkar, Shyamal 295
Saser Kangri II, in art 63-73
Satopanth, 294
Scanu, Marcelo 270, 317-323; biog 438

Scavolini, Santiago 320
Schaeli, Roger 277, 279
Schjelderup, Ferdinand 266
Schmidt, Marty 327
Schön, Peter 103
Scott, Doug 86, author obit 408; 429, 432
Scottish Hill Tracks, review 392
SCOTTISH WINTER Notes 280-6
Scott, Martin 296, 428
Scott, Virgil 332
Seghezzi, Ariel 317
Sejong I and II (5816m), Sichuan 133
Selkirk range, Canada 267
Sentinel Peak (5140m), Himachal 324
Serkhe Khollu (5546m), Bolivia 315
Sfilio, Remy 273
Shackleton, Mt, Antarctica 184
Shadow of The Matterhorn: The Life of Edward Whymper by Ian Smith, review 346
Shaluli Shan 312
Shandro, Bret 324
Shapiro, Jeff 311
Sheehan, Hugh 128
Shelter Stone, Cairngorm 280, 282
Sherpa, Dawa 302
Sherpa, Pemba 300
Sherpa, Thendup 121
Shiels, Bob 301
Shipton, Eric v, 27, 39
Shiva (6142m), Himachal 299
Shiva Shankar (6011m), Himachal 38, 299
Shiva Shankar West (5510m), 298-9
Shivling (6543m), Garhwal 193
Shone, Robbie 337
Shotwell, Dave 324
Shotwell Slabs, NZ 324
Shuang, Li 312
Shushko, Denis 311
Siachen glacier, India, 64-66, 73; 266, 293
Sichuan 40, 51; in art 132-43; 311
Signalkuppe 277
Signorelli, Luca 271
Siguniang (6250m), Sichuan 311
Sikkim, in arts 114-23 & 124-31, 266-7, 303-5
Silver, Neil 285
Simond, Maurice 248
Simon, Helmut and Erika 217, 218
Simpson, Joe, reviewed 369-70
Simpson, Sandy 285
Simvu Twins, Sikkim 115
Sim, Will 280

Singekang (6000m), Himachal 296
Singh, Govind 39
Singh, Mangal 39
Single Cone, NZ 326
Sir Duk (6653m), Tibet 313
Sir Sandford, Mt (3530m), Canada 267
Sittakanay Peak (2415m), BC, Canada 331
Skarland, Mt (3145m), Alaska 430
Skye, 3 SMC guidebooks: *Scrambles, Sea-cliffs & Outcrops, The Cuillin*, reviews 391
Sloan, Chris 39
Small, Iain 281-3, 285
Smeede, Sebastiaan Van der 293
Smith, Ian, reviewed 346-9
Smith, Janet Adam 230-3, 235, 237
Smith, Josh 129
Smith, Mark 334
Smith, Zack 93
Snow Church (4073m), Mongolia 57
Snowdon, Vaughan 328, 330
Sound of Gravity, Joe Simpson, review 369
Souness, Colin 336
Sourzac, Bruno 285
Southgate, Dominic 332
South Tyrol Museum of Archaeology 217
Spears, James 324
Spender, Stephen 230
Spiranelli, Ennio 279
Spirit of Adventure edited by Catherine Moorehead & David Dunmur, review 383
Stacheder, Michi 103
Stainforth, Gordon, reviewed 345-6
Stark, Meg 337
Steck, Ueli 60, 276, 278, 307
Stefani, Diego 299
Steward, Tim 324
Stokes, Pete, author obit 414-6
Stone, Tony 283
Store Strandåtind, Norway 266
Store Trolltind, Norway 345
Straight Up: Himalayan Tales of the Unexpected by Steve Berry, review 370
Strazar, Luka 291
Stump, Edward, reviewed 379-80
Summers, Julie, author review 360-2
Summit magazine 79-80, 84
Sunawar, Babu 307
SuperAlp, in art 209-18
Suppe, Isabel 315
Swenson, Steve 63
Swienton, Paul 304

T

Tabei, Junko 299
Tajikistan 16-7, 19-20, 24, 26, 287, 288, 336
Talling, Pete 337
Taniguchi, Kei 313
Tasker, Joe 393
Tasman, Mt, NZ 327
Tasmanian Summits To Sleep On by Kevin Doran, review 376
Tavn Bogd, Mongolia 52-5, 58
Tees, Alan 296
Tees, Andrew 297
Teixeira, Daniela E.N. 294
Tejada-Flores, Lito 175
Telthop (6120m), Ladakh 300
Tenderini, Mirella, author obit 411-3
Thanglasgo valley, Ladakh 300
Thangsing valley, Sikkim 124
The Brack, Southern Highlands 284
The Faber Book of Modern Verse 236
Thendup Sherpa 119, 120
Thinles, Konchok 300
Thomas, Phill, author obit 424-5
Thomas, Robin 39
Thom, Matt 327
Three Smith Brothers (4800m), Sichuan 138
Thurston, Bill 296
Tibet 5, 13; 135-6; 270, 311-3; 334
Tierra del Fuego 323
Tilman, Bill 86
Timar, Mike 32, 39
Tingchenkhang (6010m), Sikkim 303 305
Tiro Tirso, Picos de Europa, in article 258-65
Tobin, Lt Col H. W. 117
Tofana di Rozes, Dolomites 279
Torre de Llambrión 261
Torre La Yaya, Tierra del Fuego 321, 323
Touboul, Nicolas 294
Tovar, Erika 324, 325, 326
Town, John 270, 311; 334, 428, 430; biog 438
Trapezium Wall (E7 6c 90m), Lofoten 175
Treaty of Saint-Germain 218
Tremellen, Richard 335
Treppte, Rainer 291
Trezzi, Corrado 278
Tribulation Point (5125m), Himachal 296
Tridesh, West Sikkim 125, 129
Trisul (7120m), Kumaun 131, 295
Trisuli (7074m), Garhwal 294
Triumph and Tragedy: The Life of Edward Whymper by Emil Henry, review 346

Troillet, Jean 276
Troll Wall by Tony Howard, review 372
Trommsdorff, Christian 40
Tronador (c3500m), Argentina 322-3
Tshering, Lakpa 307
Tunstall, Duncan, in art 147-57
Turnbull, Dave, in art 3-15; 308, 333, 429
Turner, Andy 284
Turner, Rich 324
Turner, Twid 158
Turú, Emilio González 317
Txikon, Alex 289

U

Urubko, Denis 59, 289
Ushkovsky (3954m), Kamchatka 336
Ushuaia 180

V

Valais 215, 276, 278
Val Bregaglia 228
Val Ferret 147
Valsechini, Fabio 279
Vassallo, Eric 214
Vass, Dave 324
Vasuki Parvat 293
Venables, Stephen, author obit 409-11
Vertical magazine 149
Vidal, Sílvia 297
Villa, Elisa, jt article 258-265; biog 439
Viluyo Jankohuma (5540m), Bolivia 316
Vinton-Boot, Jamie 325, 327-8
Vogler, Romain 272
Vola, Eric, his article 247-257; biog 439

W

Wakatipu, NZ 324
Wakefield, Jonathon 330
Wake, James 331, 430
Wakhan Corridor, in art 16-26, 287-8, 336
Walker, Al 324
Walker, Robin 265
Walter, Mt, NZ 327-8
Walters, Richard 337
Ward, Frank Kingdon 223
Ward, Stewart, obit of 425-7
Warren, Neil 329, 430
Warrick, Ben 328
Welborn, Matt 334
Wells, Colin, author review 391-2

Wenden, Switzerland 158
Western Kokshaal-too, Kyrgyzstan 335
Westmacott, Michael, obit of 401-404
Wharton, Josh 93
Wharton, Nick 388, 390
Whillans, Don 85; in art 247-57
White, Claude 117, 118, 120
Whymper's Scrambles With a Camera by Peter Berg, review 346
Wickens, Phil 177, jt article 179-190; biog 439
Wieczorek, Jerzy 120
Wielicki, Krzysztof 59
Wien, Dr. Karl 120
Wiggins glacier, Antarctica 186
Wild Within (The) by Simon Yates, review 366
Wilford, Mark 63
Wilkinson, Freddie, his art 63-73; biog 439
Wilks, Glenn 330
Williams, Edward, reviewed 371
Williams, Noel 391
Wilson, Gerry and Louise 296
Wilson, Guy 329, 430
Wilson, Ken 405
Wind From a Distant Summit, Pat Deavoll, review 343
Windsor, Jeremy 297
Winkler, Max 266
Wojtaszewski, Richard 334, 430
Wolf, Herbert 294
Woman on The Rocks: The Mountaineering Letters of Ruth Dyar Mendenhall, review 373
Workman, Fanny Bullock 301
Wright, Kenneth 331
Wright, Mark 337
Wroz, Wojciech 272
Wylie, Charles 399
Wynne-Jones, Dave, his article 52-58; in article 179-190; biog 439

X
Xiangqiuqieke (5863m), Sichuan 135-6, 313
Xiannairi (6032m), Sichuan, 139-40
Xiao Gongga (5928), Sichuan 311
Xiaozha (5807m), Sichuan 138
Xiaruduo (5958m), Sichuan 139-40
Xingzheng, Zhao 311

Y
Yangmaiyong (5958m), Sichuan 139-40
Yangmolong (6060m), Sichuan 132, 135, 137-8, 312

Yasinskaya, Anna 292
Yates, John, reviewed 384
Yates, Simon, review 365-6; reviewed 366-7
Yearsley, Simon 285, 286
Young, Geoffrey Winthrop 266
Young-Seok, Park 307

Z
Zaluski, Darek 289
Zanskar, in art 27-39, 297, 332
Zavrsnik, Karel 294
Zemu Gap, Sikkim, in art: 114-123
Zhongdian mountains 334
Zhongli, Li 311
Zimmerman, Graham 330
Zink, Albert 218
Zumayev, Maxut 289

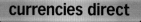

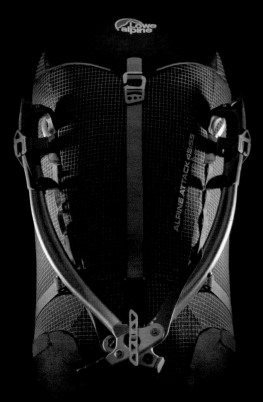

PACK FOR THE MOUNTAIN

Winter climbing in Scotland or thinking about a season in the Alps? Lowe Alpine mountain packs incorporate our award-winning patented **Headlocker** system, which will secure any axes on the market, keeping them stable, streamlined and easily accessible.

The Alpine Attack range offers maximum durability using Dyneema fabric while optimising comfort by incorporating Lowe Alpine's unique Adaptive Fit harness and hip belt system. Weighing in at just 850g* your load is lighter, more comfortable and more stable so you can get on with the job in hand.

For more details contact Lowe Alpine
on 01539 740840, Email: info@lowealpine.co.uk
www.lowealpine.com

**Scan this using
your smartphone to
see how it all works**

Out Door

**INDUSTRY
AWARD 2010**

Alpine Attack 45:55

*Alpine Attack 35-45 stripped weight. Also available in other sizes.

Hardwear Expert Circle.

On a sheer rock face, every detail needs to be just right.
Mammut dealers from all over the world came together
in Ticino, Switzerland, to test the design, ergonomics
and quality of the new Mammut hardwear. The experts
all agreed: exceptional functionality, thanks to a clear
focus on the essentials. To find your new hardwear, visit:

www.mammut.ch

'Our social network'
Philippe, Anna, Leo, Leah & Rob

berghaus®
LIVE FOR ADVENTURE™

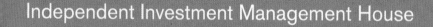

NOTES FOR CONTRIBUTORS

The *Alpine Journal* records all aspects of mountains and mountaineering, including expeditions, adventure, art, literature, geography, history, geology, medicine, ethics and the mountain environment.

Articles Contributions in English are invited. They should be sent to the Hon Editor, Stephen Goodwin, 1 Ivy Cottages, Edenhall, Penrith, Cumbria CA11 8SN (e-mail: sg@stephengoodwin.demon.co.uk). Articles should be sent on a disk with accompanying hard copy or as an e-mail attachment (in Microsoft Word) with hard copy sent separately by post. Length should not exceed 3000 words without prior approval of the editor **and may be edited or shortened at his discretion**. It is regretted that the *Alpine Journal* is unable to offer a fee for articles published, but authors who are not AC members receive a complimentary copy of the issue of the *Journal* in which their article appears. Preferably, articles and book reviews should not have been published in substantially the same form by any other publication.

Maps These should be well researched, accurate, and show the most important place-names mentioned in the text. It is the author's responsibility to get their maps redrawn if necessary. If submitted electronically, maps should be originated as CMYK in a vectorised drawing package (Adobe Illustrator, Freehand or similar), and submitted as pdfs. (Any embedded images should be at 300dpi resolution at A4 size.) Hard copy should be scanned as a Photoshop compatible 300dpi tiff at A4 finished size. This can be arranged through the production editor if required.

Photographs Colour transparencies should be originals (not copies) in 35mm format or larger. Prints (any size) should be numbered (in pencil) on the back and accompanied by a separate list of captions (see below). Pre-scanned images should be CMYK, 300dpi tiffs or Maximum Quality jpegs at A4 final size. Images from digital cameras should be CMYK, 300dpi jpegs or tiffs at the maximum file size (quality) the camera can produce. All images (slides, prints and digital) should have unique names/serial numbers that correspond to a list of captions supplied with your article or as a word processing document or via email.

Captions should include subject matter, photographer's name, title and author of the article to which they refer.

Copyright It is the author's responsibility to obtain copyright clearance for text, photographs, digital images and maps, to pay any fees involved and to ensure that acknowledgements are in the form required by the copyright owner.

Summaries A brief summary, helpful to researchers, may be included with 'expedition' articles.

Biographies Authors are asked to provide a short biography, in about 60 words, listing the most noteworthy items in their climbing career and anything else they wish to mention.

Deadline Copy and photographs should reach the editor by 1 January of the year of publication.